# *Teach Yourself*
# VISUALLY™
## MacBook,® 2nd Edition

**Visual**

by Brad Miser

**WILEY**

Wiley Publishing, Inc.

004·165
MIS

# Teach Yourself VISUALLY™ MacBook® 2nd Edition

Published by
Wiley Publishing, Inc.
10475 Crosspoint Boulevard
Indianapolis, IN 46256

www.wiley.com

Published simultaneously in Canada

ISBN: 978-0-470-56519-3

Manufactured in the United States of America

10 9 8 7 6 5 4 3 2 1

## Trademark Acknowledgments

## Contact Us

For general information on our other products and services please contact our Customer Care Department within the U.S. at 877-762-2974, outside the U.S. at 317-572-3993 or fax 317-572-4002.

For technical support please visit www.wiley.com/techsupport.

Wiley Publishing, Inc.

**Sales**

Contact Wiley
at (877) 762-2974 or
fax (317) 572-4002.

# Praise for Visual Books

"Like a lot of other people, I understand things best when I see them visually. Your books really make learning easy and life more fun."

John T. Frey (Cadillac, MI)

"I have quite a few of your Visual books and have been very pleased with all of them. I love the way the lessons are presented!"

Mary Jane Newman (Yorba Linda, CA)

"I just purchased my third Visual book (my first two are dog-eared now!), and, once again, your product has surpassed my expectations.

Tracey Moore (Memphis, TN)

"I am an avid fan of your Visual books. If I need to learn anything, I just buy one of your books and learn the topic in no time. Wonders! I have even trained my friends to give me Visual books as gifts."

Illona Bergstrom (Aventura, FL)

"Thank you for making it so clear. I appreciate it. I will buy many more Visual books."

J.P. Sangdong (North York, Ontario, Canada)

"I have several books from the Visual series and have always found them to be valuable resources."

Stephen P. Miller (Ballston Spa, NY)

"Thank you for the wonderful books you produce. It wasn't until I was an adult that I discovered how I learn – visually. Nothing compares to Visual books. I love the simple layout. I can just grab a book and use it at my computer, lesson by lesson. And I understand the material! You really know the way I think and learn. Thanks so much!"

Stacey Han (Avondale, AZ)

"I absolutely admire your company's work. Your books are terrific. The format is perfect, especially for visual learners like me. Keep them coming!"

Frederick A. Taylor, Jr. (New Port Richey, FL)

"I have several of your Visual books and they are the best I have ever used."

Stanley Clark (Crawfordville, FL)

"I bought my first Teach Yourself VISUALLY book last month. Wow. Now I want to learn everything in this easy format!"

Tom Vial (New York, NY)

"Thank you, thank you, thank you...for making it so easy for me to break into this high-tech world. I now own four of your books. I recommend them to anyone who is a beginner like myself."

Gay O'Donnell (Calgary, Alberta, Canada)

"I write to extend my thanks and appreciation for your books. They are clear, easy to follow, and straight to the point. Keep up the good work! I bought several of your books and they are just right! No regrets! I will always buy your books because they are the best."

Seward Kollie (Dakar, Senegal)

"Compliments to the chef!! Your books are extraordinary! Or, simply put, extra-ordinary, meaning way above the rest! THANK YOU THANK YOU THANK YOU! I buy them for friends, family, and colleagues."

Christine J. Manfrin (Castle Rock, CO)

"What fantastic teaching books you have produced! Congratulations to you and your staff. You deserve the Nobel Prize in Education in the Software category. Thanks for helping me understand computers."

Bruno Tonon (Melbourne, Australia)

"Over time, I have bought a number of your 'Read Less - Learn More' books. For me, they are THE way to learn anything easily. I learn easiest using your method of teaching."

José A. Mazón (Cuba, NY)

"I am an avid purchaser and reader of the Visual series, and they are the greatest computer books I've seen. The Visual books are perfect for people like myself who enjoy the computer, but want to know how to use it more efficiently. Your books have definitely given me a greater understanding of my computer, and have taught me to use it more effectively. Thank you very much for the hard work, effort, and dedication that you put into this series."

Alex Diaz (Las Vegas, NV)

# Credits

**Sr. Acquisitions Editor**
Stephanie McComb

**Sr. Project Editor**
Sarah Hellert

**Technical Editor**
Dennis R. Cohen

**Copy Editor**
Scott Tullis

**Editorial Director**
Robyn Siesky

**Editorial Manager**
Cricket Krengel

**Business Manager**
Amy Knies

**Sr. Marketing Manager**
Sandy Smith

**Vice President and Executive Group Publisher**
Richard Swadley

**Vice President and Executive Publisher**
Barry Pruett

**Project Coordinator**
Katherine Crocker

**Graphics and Production Specialists**
Andrea Hornberger
Jennifer Mayberry
Heather Pope

**Proofreader**
Melissa Buddendeck

**Indexer**
Potomac Indexing, LLC

**Screen Artists**
Ana Carrillo
Jill A. Proll

**Illustrators**
Ronda David-Burroughs
Cheryl Grubbs
Mark Pinto

# About the Author

**Brad Miser** has written more than 40 books, with his favorite topics being anything related to Macintosh computers. In addition to *Teach Yourself VISUALLY MacBook*, Brad has written *MacBook Pro Portable Genius*, *Teach Yourself VISUALLY MacBook Air*, *iPhoto '09 Portable Genius*, *MobileMe for Small Business Portable Genius*, and *MacBook Portable Genius*. He has also been a co-author, development editor, or technical editor on more than 50 other titles.

In addition to his passion for silicon-based technology, Brad enjoys steel-based technology, riding his motorcycle whenever and wherever possible. A native of California, Brad now lives in Indiana with his wife Amy; their three daughters, Jill, Emily, and Grace; a rabbit named Bun-Bun; and a sometimes-inside cat.

Brad would love to hear about your experiences with this book (the good, the bad, and the ugly). You can write to him at bradmiser@me.com.

# Author's Acknowledgments

While my name is on the cover, it takes many people to build a book like this one. Thanks to Stephanie McComb who made this project possible and allowed me to be involved. Sarah Hellert deserves extra credit for leading me through the details; I'm sure working with me was a challenge at times. Dennis Cohen did a great job of keeping me on my toes to make sure this book contains fewer technical gaffes than it would have without his help. Scott Tullis transformed my stumbling text into something people can read and understand.

On my personal team, I'd like to thank my wife Amy for her tolerance of the author lifestyle, which can be both odd and challenging. My delightful daughters Jill, Emily, and Grace are always a source of joy and inspiration for all that I do, for which I'm ever grateful.

# Table of Contents

## chapter 3 Using the Dock, Esposé, Spaces, and the Dashboard

## chapter 4 Working on the Mac Desktop

## chapter 5 Working with Mac Applications

# Table of Contents

## chapter 6   Personalizing MacBook

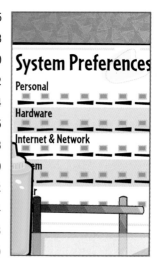

## GETTING CONNECTED

## chapter 7   Connecting to a Network and the Internet

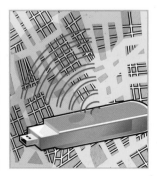

# Table of Contents

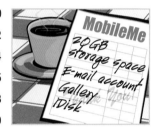

# Table of Contents

chapter **14** Printing on Paper or Electronically

chapter **15** Managing Contacts

# chapter 16  Managing Calendars

# chapter 17  Maintaining and Troubleshooting MacBook

# Table of Contents

## chapter 18  Listening to Music and Watching Video with iTunes

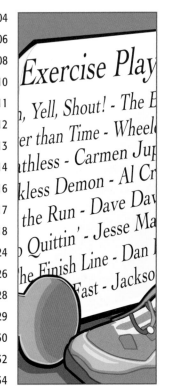

# chapter 19 Creating Photo Books and Other Projects with iPhoto

# chapter 20 Creating Movies with iMovie

# How to use this book

Do you look at the pictures in a book or newspaper before anything else on a page? Would you rather see an image instead of read about how to do something? Search no further. This book is for you. Opening *Teach Yourself VISUALLY MacBook* allows you to read less and learn more about MacBook computers.

## Who Needs This Book

This book is for a reader who has never used a MacBook, and it is also for more computer literate individuals who want to expand their knowledge of the different features that MacBook has to offer. You do not need much experience with MacBook to be able to learn from this book because it begins at the beginning, covering topics such as configuring and using MacBook's keyboard and trackpad. If you already know how to do these tasks, do not worry because they are only the start. As you read through this book, you will know how to get the most out of MacBook, even if you have used it for some time, when you learn about networking, managing the desktop, and other techniques.

## Book Organization

*Teach Yourself VISUALLY MacBook* has 20 chapters.

Chapter 1 gets you started with understanding MacBook's desktop, configuring the trackpad, and other essential tasks.

Chapter 2 helps you learn to look at the world through Mac OS X Finder windows, including changing views, using the sidebar, and making the toolbar work for you.

In Chapter 3, you take command of the desktop using Expose, Spaces, and the Dashboard.

Chapter 4 teaches you how to move around on MacBook's desktop, create and use files and folders, and work with disks and discs.

You explore how to use applications on MacBook in Chapter 5. Topics include installing applications, opening documents, and saving them.

In Chapter 6, you learn how to make MacBook your own by personalizing it. These include setting desktop pictures, creating and managing user accounts, and setting login options.

No MacBook is an island. In Chapter 7, you learn how to connect MacBook to different kinds of networks, the most important of which is the Internet.

One of the great things about MacBook is that you can take it with you. Chapter 8 provides information about moving around with yours.

While MacBook contains all the hardware devices you must have, there are lots more you need, such as external hard drives and mice. In Chapter 9, you learn how to connect MacBook to these devices.

A MobileMe account empowers you to do a lot of great things, including accessing an online disk, creating and publishing your photo galleries, and keeping information in sync. Chapter 10 shows you how.

In Chapter 11, you learn how to use Safari to take advantage of the Web.

Chapter 12 helps you e-mail like a pro (is there really a professional e-mailer?). You learn how to set up e-mail accounts and how to use Mac OS X's excellent Mail application to read, send, and organize e-mail.

If you like to communicate with other people in real time, chatting is a great way to do it. With iChat, you can chat with text, audio, and video. Chapter 13 shows you how.

Computers certainly did not eliminate the need for paper; in Chapter 14, you learn how to print your documents in a number of ways. If you want to save a few trees and distribute documents electronically, you learn that too.

When you communicate with people, you need to manage and use contact information. Chapter 15 explains how using Mac OS X's Address Book.

Chapter 16 enters the picture with iCal. If you are memory challenged like I am (and even if you are not), having a way to manage the times and dates that are important is helpful. You can use iCal to create and manage your own calendars, share those calendars with others, and access calendars people share with you.

In Chapter 17, you focus on tasks that are important to keep MacBook running in top form. You also learn what to do in the unlikely event that MacBook experiences a problem.

Chapter 18 fills you in on the basics of iTunes music and video. You learn how to stock the shelves of your iTunes Library and how to listen and watch the great content you store there.

Digital photos are great, and iPhoto is just the application you need to store, organize, and use your own photos. In Chapter 19, you can see how easy these tasks are.

Most of us would like to go Hollywood from time to time. With iMovie, you can be your own producer by transforming your video into movies with soundtracks, special effects, and more. In Chapter 20, you'll see how powerful this application is.

## Chapter Organization

This book consists of sections, all listed in the book's table of contents. A *section* is a set of steps that show you how to complete a specific computer task.

Each section, usually contained on two facing pages, has an introduction to the task at hand, a set of full-color screen shots and steps that walk you through the task, and a set of tips. This format allows you to quickly look at a topic of interest and learn it instantly.

Chapters group together three or more sections with a common theme. A chapter may also contain pages that give you the background information needed to understand the sections in a chapter.

## What You Need to Use This Book

To use this book, you need a MacBook running Mac OS X (of course, you can read the book even if you do not have a MacBook, but it will not be nearly as much fun). The book's screen shots and steps are for the Snow Leopard version of Mac OS X, which is the operating system the MacBook runs.

## Using the Trackpad

This book uses the following conventions to describe the actions you perform when using the trackpad:

### Point

Slide your finger on the trackpad. The pointer on the screen follows your finger motion on the trackpad. Pointing to something is how you indicate that you want to do something with whatever you point to.

### Click

Press the trackpad once — the entire trackpad is a button. You generally press the trackpad to select something. This is equivalent to a single mouse click and to a left-button click on a two-button mouse.

### Double-click

Press the trackpad twice. Double-clicking something on the computer screen generally opens whatever item you have double-clicked.

### Secondary Click or Control+click (also known as Right-click)

One way to perform a secondary click is to hold the Control key down and press the trackpad; this is the equivalent of pressing the right button on a two-button mouse. When you perform a secondary click on anything on the computer screen, a shortcut menu containing commands specific to the selected item is shown (this is called a contextual menu).

### Click and Drag, and Release the Trackpad

Drag your finger on the trackpad to point to an item on the screen. Press and hold down the trackpad to select that item. While holding down the trackpad, move your finger so the pointer (to which the item will be attached) moves to where you want to place the item and then release the trackpad. You use this method to move an item from one area of the computer to another.

## The Conventions in This Book

A number of typographic and layout styles have been used throughout *Teach Yourself VISUALLY MacBook* to distinguish different types of information.

### Bold

Bold type represents the names of commands and options that you interact with. Bold type also indicates text and numbers that you must type into a dialog box or window.

### Italics

Italic words introduce a new term and are followed by a definition.

### Numbered Steps

You must perform the instructions in numbered steps in order to successfully complete a section and achieve the final results.

### Bulleted Steps

These steps point out various optional features. You do not have to perform these steps; they simply give additional information about a feature.

### Indented Text

Indented text tells you what the program does in response to you following a numbered step. For example, if you click a certain menu command, a dialog box may appear, or a window may open. Indented text may also tell you what the final result is when you follow a set of numbered steps.

### Notes

Notes give additional information. They may describe special conditions that may occur during an operation. They may warn you of a situation that you want to avoid, for example the loss of data. A note may also cross reference a related area of the book. A cross reference may guide you to another chapter or to another section within the current chapter.

### Icons and buttons

Icons and buttons are graphical representations within the text. They show you exactly what you need to click to perform a step.

 You can easily identify the tips in any section by looking for the TIPS icon. Tips offer additional information, including tips, hints, and tricks. You can use the TIPS information to go beyond what you have learned in the steps.

# Discovering MacBook

The MacBook might be the most beloved laptop ever (especially on college campuses!); it combines outstanding capabilities with well-conceived design, creating a computer that is powerful, reliable, and distinctive. Your MacBook is capable and intuitive, and its compact size makes it an ideal traveling companion. In this part, you learn fundamentals to guide you on your journey of discovery toward MacBook mastery.

# Tour MacBook

MacBooks are elegantly designed and are simple and easy to use. But do not let that fool you: They are also very powerful and extremely capable computers that can do just about anything you want them to. Here you can learn about the MacBook's major features from the outside, including its controls, ports, and other areas that you use to control your MacBook and to connect it to other devices.

## MacBook

### Display
The MacBook's display provides a sharp, bright, and colorful view into all that you do.

### iSight camera
Use the built-in iSight camera to video conference, take photos, and more.

### Microphone
Input audio-to-audio conference and record your voice or other sound.

### Keyboard
Along with the standard letter and number keys, you have function keys to control your MacBook.

### Trackpad
Enables you to move the cursor on the screen just by sliding your finger.

### Ports
Connect MacBook to other devices, such as drives, iPods, and so on.

### Sleep indicator light
Pulses when MacBook is asleep, glows solid when MacBook is on but its display is dimmed.

### Disc drive
Use or burn CDs and DVDs.

## MacBook Keyboard

**Brightness**
Press F1 to decrease your screen's brightness or F2 to increase it.

**Exposé**
Press F3 to show thumbnails of all open windows so you can easily move into one of them.

**Dashboard**
Press F4 to open or close the Dashboard.

**Previous/Rewind**
Press F7 to move to the previous item or rewind in iTunes and other applications.

**Play/Pause**
Press F8 to play or pause iTunes and other applications.

**Next/Fast Forward**
Press F9 to move to the next item or fast-forward in iTunes and other applications.

**Volume**
F10 mutes MacBook, F11 turns the volume down, and F12 turns it up.

**Eject**
Press to eject a CD, DVD, iPod, or other mounted device.

**Alternate function key**
Hold down while pressing a function key to perform the alternate task.

**Modifier keys**
Press to invoke keyboard shortcuts.

**Power button**
Press to turn MacBook on; press and hold to force MacBook to turn off.

**Scroll keys**
Press to move around the screen.

continued

MacBook includes the ports you need to connect to other devices, such as networks, external displays, speakers, iPhones, iPods, disk drives, and more. The specific port you use for any task depends on the devices to which you are connecting your MacBook.

**MacBook includes some accessories; you should consider adding a few more to your MacBook toolkit, especially an external disk drive for backups.**

## MacBook Ports

**Power adapter**

Connect MacBook to power.

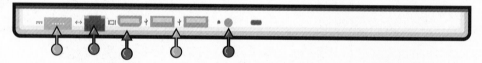

**Ethernet**

Connect MacBook to an Ethernet network.

**Mini DisplayPort**

Use an adapter to connect MacBook to an external display or projector.

**USB**

Connect USB devices, such as iPods, iPhones, and disk drives.

**Analog/digital audio out**

Connect headphones or analog speakers or use a TOSLINK adapter to connect for digital audio, such as with surround sound speakers. (Also can be used for analog sound input.)

## MacBook Companions

### TOSLINK adapter and audio cable

An optional TOSLINK adapter and digital audio cable enable you to connect MacBook to digital audio devices, such as surround sound speakers.

### Remote

Control MacBook from afar, such as when you are listening to music or watching movies.

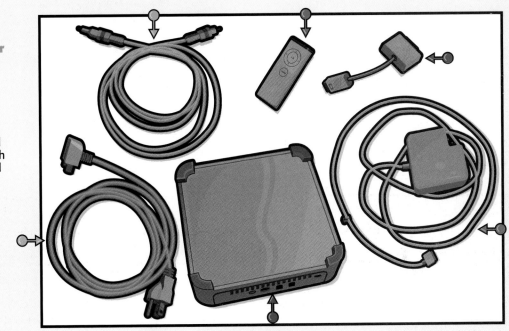

### Mini DisplayPort adapter

An optional Mini DisplayPort adapter enables you to connect MacBook to an external display or projector.

### Power cord

Connects to the power adapter to enable you to be farther away from a power outlet to work from that source or to charge the battery.

### External hard drive

Every MacBook user should have an external hard drive to back up important files and for extra working room.

### Power adapter

Transforms standard outlet power to what MacBook needs to run and charges its battery.

# Start Up and Log In

Starting a MacBook is not much of a challenge. After you turn MacBook on, you might also need to log in to start using it (which is not a challenge either). That is because Mac OS X supports multiple user accounts so that each person who uses MacBook can have her own resources. You created at least one user account when you first turned on MacBook.

**Mac OS X includes an automatic login feature, which bypasses the login process. If this feature is turned on, you do not have to log in to start using MacBook. If it is not turned on, you need to know a user name and password to be able to log into a user account. MacBook prompts you to log in if this is the case.**

Starting a MacBook
• Lift Lid
• Press Power button
• Log In
• Desktop Appears

## Start Up and Log In

### Start Up

1 Open MacBook by lifting its lid.

2 Press the **Power** button.

MacBook turns on and starts the boot process and you see the Apple logo and the processing "spinning" wheel on-screen. When the startup process is complete, you see the Login window if automatic login is turned off, or the Mac OS X desktop if automatic login is turned on.

If the Login window appears, it has either a list of user accounts or empty user name and password fields. Each option requires slightly different steps to log in.

### Log In with the User List

1 Start up MacBook.

The Login window appears, showing a list of user accounts on the MacBook.

2 Slide your finger over the trackpad until the pointer is over the appropriate user account.

3 Click the trackpad.

**Note:** To click the trackpad button, just press down once on the trackpad; the whole trackpad is a button. Later, you learn how to configure different ways to click.

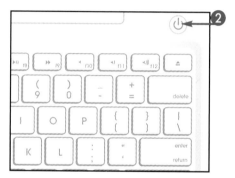

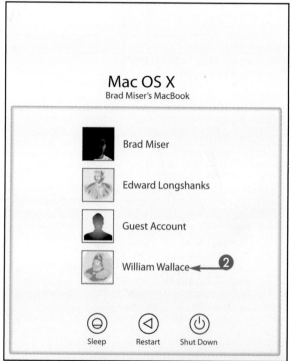

Mac OS X
Brad Miser's MacBook

Brad Miser

Edward Longshanks

Guest Account

William Wallace

Sleep    Restart    Shut Down

The Password field appears.

④ Enter the password for the user account.

⑤ Point to the **Log In** button (🏠)
and click the trackpad, or press
`Return`.

You log into the user account and the
Mac OS X desktop appears.

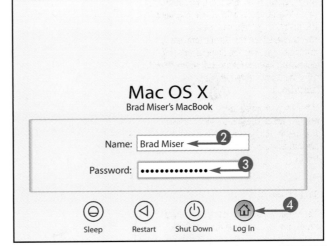

Mac OS X
Brad Miser's MacBook

William Wallace

Password: •••••• ← 4

Back     Forgot Password     Log In ← 5

## Log In with a User Name

① Start up MacBook.

The Login window appears, showing the
Name and Password fields.

② Enter the name of the user account in
the Name field.

③ Enter the password for the account in
the Password field.

④ Point to the **Log In** button (🏠)
and click the trackpad, or press
`Return`.

You log into the user account and the
Mac OS X desktop appears.

Mac OS X
Brad Miser's MacBook

Name: Brad Miser ← 2

Password: •••••••••••• ← 3

Sleep     Restart     Shut Down     Log In ← 4

TIPS

### What if I forget my password?

If you enter a password
incorrectly, the Login screen
shudders when you try to
log in. This lets you know
that the password you
provided does not work. Try
entering it again. If that does not help, click the
**Forgot Password** button (🔒) and a password
hint appears on the screen. If you still cannot log
in, try a different user account.

**WRONG!**

### What kind of user accounts are there?

Mac OS X supports several different
types of user accounts. An Administrator
account enables you to configure
various aspects of the system; the first
user account you created during the
first time you started your MacBook is
an Administrator account. Standard accounts cannot access
very many of the configuration tools and can be limited
even further to specific applications or documents. Guest
accounts also have limited access to the system.

**Accounts**
- Administrator
- Standard
- Guest
- Root

MacBook operates through the Mac operating system, which is currently in version 10.6 Snow Leopard.

**The Mac OS X desktop is the overall window through which you view all that happens on MacBook, such as looking at the contents of folders, working on documents, and surfing the Web.**

## Mac OS X Desktop

### Menu bar

A menu bar usually appears at the top of the screen so that you can access the commands it contains. (This is sometimes hidden in certain situations.)

### Hard drives

MacBook stores its data, including the software it needs to work, on hard drives. It includes one internal drive, but you can also connect external drives.

### SuperDrive

You can read from and write to DVDs or CDs using MacBook's SuperDrive.

### Folders

Containers that you use to organize files and other folders stored on MacBook.

### Files

Documents (such as text, graphics, movies, and songs), applications, or other sources of data.

### Finder windows

You view the contents of drives, folders, and other objects in Finder windows.

### Application and document windows

When you use applications, you use the windows that those applications present for documents, Web pages, games, and so on.

## Finder Menu Bar and Menus

### Apple menu

This menu is always visible so that you can access special commands, such as Shut Down and Log Out.

### Finder menu

This is where you control the Finder application itself, such as to empty the Trash or set preferences.

### File menu

Use commands on this menu to work with files and Finder windows.

### Edit menu

This menu is not as useful in the Finder as it is in other applications, but here you can undo what you have done or copy and paste information.

### View menu

Enables you to determine how you view the desktop; it is especially useful for choosing Finder window views.

### Go menu

Takes you to various places, such as specific folders.

### Window menu

Enables you to work with open Finder windows.

### Help menu

Use when you need help with Mac OS X or the other applications.

### Configurable menus

You can configure the menu bar to include specific menus, such as Displays, Volume, AirPort, Battery, and many more.

### Clock

Here you see the current time and day.

### Spotlight menu

Enables you to search for information on MacBook.

continued

11

The Finder application controls the Mac OS X desktop, and so you see its menu bar whenever you work with this application. When you view the contents of a folder, you do so through a Finder window.

**The Dock and sidebar on the desktop enable you to access items quickly and easily.**

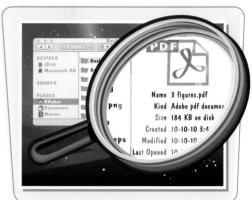

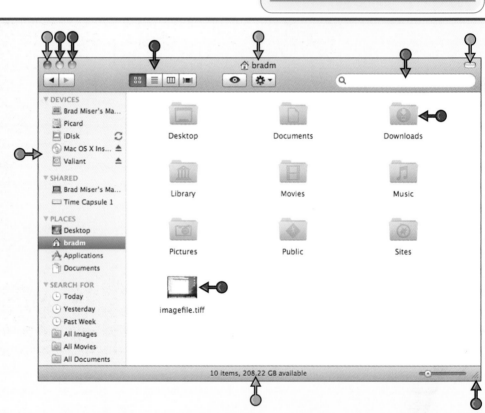

### Finder Windows

**Close button**
Click to close a window.

**Minimize button**
Click to shrink a window and move it onto the Dock.

**Zoom button**
Click to expand a Finder window to the maximum size possible; click it again to return to the previous size.

**Window title**
The name of the location whose contents you see in the window.

**Toolbar**
Contains tools you use to work with files and folders.

**Search bar**
Use this tool to find files, folders, and other information.

**Hide/Show toolbar and sidebar**
Click to show or hide the toolbar and sidebar.

**Sidebar**
Enables you to quickly access devices, folders, and files, as well as searches you have saved.

**Files and folders**
Within a window, the contents of a location are shown; this example shows the Icon view.

**Status information**
Shows information about the current location, such as the amount of free space when you are viewing the MacBook drive.

**Resize handle**
Drag this handle to change the size of a window.

## Dock and Sidebar

### Devices

Contains your iDisk (MobileMe members), the internal drive, a DVD or CD, external hard drives, and other devices that your MacBook can access.

### Shared

Computers and other resources being shared on a network.

### Places

Files and folders that you can open by clicking them.

### Searches

Saved searches that you can run by clicking them.

### Dock

Shows files and folders you can access along with applications currently running.

### Applications

Icons on the left side of the Dock are for applications; open applications have a glowing dot under their icon.

### Files, folders, and minimized windows

Icons on the right side of the Dock are for files, folders, and minimized windows (the default Dock includes the Downloads folder for files you download from the Internet).

### Trash/Eject

Items you delete go here (to get rid of them, empty the Trash); when you select an ejectable device, such as a DVD, this becomes the Eject icon.

# Point and Click, Double-click, or Secondary Click

If you logged into your MacBook using the earlier steps, you already know the basics of using the trackpad. But, because this is such a fundamental skill, it bears repeating here. To tell MacBook what you want to do, point the on-screen pointer (an arrow when you are working on the desktop) to the object that you want to work with by sliding a finger over the trackpad.

**After you tell MacBook what you want to work with, you tell MacBook what you want to do with it. You do this by clicking the trackpad, which is the same as the trackpad itself. (To make this action easy to recognize, it is referred to as clicking the trackpad button even though there is no separate physical button.) The number of times and how you click it determines what happens to what you are pointing at.**

## Point and Click, Double-click, or Secondary Click

## Point and Click

1. Slide your finger on the trackpad until the pointer points at something you want to work with, such as the icon of a file or folder.

2. Press the trackpad once to click the trackpad "button," which is a single click.

   The object is highlighted to indicate that it is now selected.

*Note: Some objects on the desktop have an action associated with a single click. For example, if you click an icon on the sidebar or the Dock, the item opens. If you click a folder in Columns view, you go down another level into the contents of that folder.*

## Double-click

1. Slide your finger on the trackpad until the pointer points at something you want to work with, such as a file's or folder's icon.

2. Press the trackpad twice.

   Whatever you were pointing at opens. For example, if you were pointing to a document, it opens in the associated application. If you pointed to a folder, it opens and you see its contents.

## Point, Click, and Drag

1. Slide your finger on the trackpad until the pointer points at something you want to move, such as a file's or folder's icon.

2. Press the trackpad and hold it.

   The object at which you were pointing becomes attached to the arrow and remains so until you release the trackpad.

③ Hold the trackpad down and drag your finger on the trackpad to move the object.

④ When you get to the object's new position, release the trackpad.

The object is moved or copied to the new location.

**Note:** *If you drag something to a different hard drive, flash drive, or disk volume, it is copied there. If you move it to a different location on the same disk, it is moved instead.*

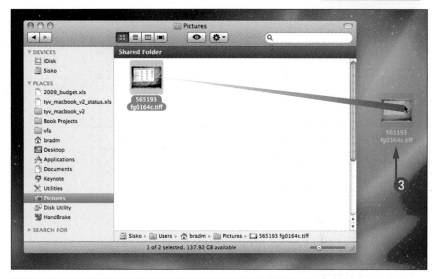

## Secondary Click (Control-click)

① Point to an object on the desktop or even the desktop itself.

② Press and hold Control.

③ Click the trackpad.

A contextual menu appears. It is called a contextual menu because the commands appearing on it depend on what you are pointing to.

④ Choose a command on the resulting menu by pointing to it and clicking the trackpad once.

**Note:** *A secondary click is also known as a right-click. This comes from mice that have two buttons (one on the left for the primary action and one on the right for the secondary action). Over time, any action that caused this secondary click became known as a right-click.*

## TIPS

### Why do things I click stick to the arrow?

You can configure the trackpad so you can drag things without having to hold the trackpad down. When this setting is on and you click something, it gets attached to the pointer. When you move the pointer, the object moves too. You learn how to configure this setting later in this chapter.

### Nothing happens when I double-click things to open them. Why?

Two clicks have to happen within a certain amount of time to be registered as a double-click. You learn how to set the amount of time between clicks to register a double-click later in this chapter.

# Understand Disks, Volumes, Optical Discs, Folders, and Files

As you use MacBook, you work with data. Underlying all this data is the need to store and organize it. The major items that MacBook uses for storing and organizing data are described in this section.

**These items include disks, volumes, discs, folders, and files. These are managed by the Finder, and you access them directly from the desktop or from within applications.**

## Hard Disk

A disk drive, also known as a hard drive, is one type of physical device that MacBook uses to store data. A hard disk contains a magnetic disk accessed through a read/write head to read or store information. MacBook has one internal hard drive that contains the software it needs to work with the operating system (OS), applications you install and documents you create. You can connect external disk drives to MacBook through its USB port to expand the available storage room. Drives come in various storage capacities, such as 500GB or 1TB, and operate at different speeds (faster is better). Disks are represented on MacBook with icons that look different to represent different kinds of drives (internal versus external, for example).

## Volume

A volume is an area of a disk created using software rather than a physical space. A drive can be partitioned into multiple volumes, where each volume acts like a separate disk. A volume performs the same task as a disk, which is to store data. In fact, when you work with a volume, you might not be able to tell the difference. You can also access volumes being shared with you over a network. Some files (called disk images) appear as volumes that you use as if they were a volume on a disk. Volumes are used to organize data in different ways and to represent various resources you work with.

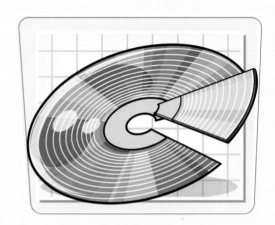

## Optical Discs

CDs and DVDs serve many purposes. Examples abound, including listening to audio CDs, watching DVD movies and TV shows, and installing applications stored on a CD or DVD. You can also put your own data on CD or DVD, such as burning audio CDs with iTunes, creating DVDs with iDVD, and backing up your data on DVD. MacBook has a slot-loading disc drive located on its right side; to use a disc, simply insert it into the slot.

## Folders

Like manila folders in the physical world, folders on MacBook are a means to organize things, such as files and other folders. Mac OS X includes many folders by default. You can create, name, delete, and organize folders in any way you see fit (mostly any way — there are some folders you cannot or should not change). You open a folder in a Finder window to view its contents.

## Files

A file is a container for data. Files can contain many different kinds of data. For example, some files are documents, such as text documents you create with a word processor. Files can also be images, songs, movies, and other kinds of content. Files also make up the operating system that runs MacBook; you typically do not interact with system files directly. Files have names that include filename extensions, such as .jpg and .doc (which can be hidden), and are represented by icons in Finder windows and e-mail attachments.

# Configure the Keyboard

Obviously, using MacBook is a hands-on experience. One of your primary inputs is the keyboard, through which you make commands, add content to documents, send and receive e-mail, and so on. You can configure the keyboard to work the way you want it to.

**You use the Keyboard pane of the System Preferences application to configure your keyboard. For example, you can set keyboard shortcuts for commands so you can activate the command by pressing a combination of keys.**

## Configure the Keyboard

### Configure General Keyboard Settings

1. Open the **Apple** menu (🍎) and choose **System Preferences**.

2. Click the **Keyboard** icon.

3. Click the **Keyboard** tab.

4. Drag the **Key Repeat Rate** slider to the right to increase the number of times a letter or number repeats while you press and hold a key, or to the left to decrease the rate.

5. Drag the **Delay Until Repeat** slider to the right to increase the amount of time you have to press and hold a key for its letter or number to repeat, or to the left to shorten the time.

6. If you do not want to use the built-in functions for the function keys but instead want them to act as normal function keys, check the **Use all F1, F2, etc. keys as standard function keys** check box.

**Note:** If you check this box, you press the Fn key to use the preprogrammed functions of the function keys, such as F2 to brighten the screen.

7. To be able to quickly access the Keyboard and Character Viewers through the Input menu on the menu bar, check the **Show Keyboard & Character Viewer in menu bar** check box.

8. Click the **Modifier Keys** button.

9. In the Modifier Keys sheet, use the pop-up menus to choose the key presses associated with the various modifier keys. For example, you can disable the Caps Lock key by choosing **No Action**.

10. Click **OK**.

Your changes take effect and the sheet closes.

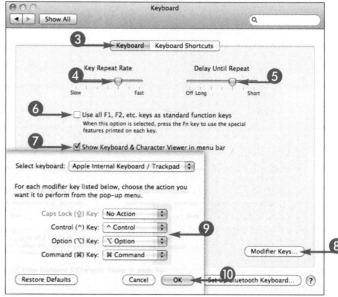

## Configure Keyboard Shortcuts

1 Click the **Keyboard Shortcuts** tab.

You see a list of commands and the associated keyboard shortcuts organized by category, such as Front Row and Keyboard & Text Input.

2 Click the category for the shortcuts you want to view, such as **Keyboard & Text Input**.

3 Uncheck a shortcut's check box to disable it.

That keyboard shortcut is grayed out in the list and no longer has any effect.

4 Change the keys used for any shortcut by clicking the current shortcut, waiting for it to become highlighted, and pressing the new keyboard combination you want to use.

**Note:** If you hover over a keyboard shortcut, a tool tip listing the keys appears. This is helpful because the symbols used in the shortcuts do not appear on the keys, except for the ⌘ key.

5 Add a new keyboard shortcut by clicking ⊞.

6 On the **Application** menu on the New Shortcut sheet, choose the application to which the shortcut applies or choose **All Applications** to have it impact all of them.

**Note:** If the application for which you want to set a shortcut is not listed in the menu, choose **Other**, move to and select the application, and click **Add**.

7 Type the name of the command in the Menu Title field (you must type the name exactly as it appears on the menu, including a trailing ellipsis).

8 Click in the Keyboard Shortcut field and press the key combination you want to use.

9 Click **Add**.

The new shortcut is created and is ready for you to use.

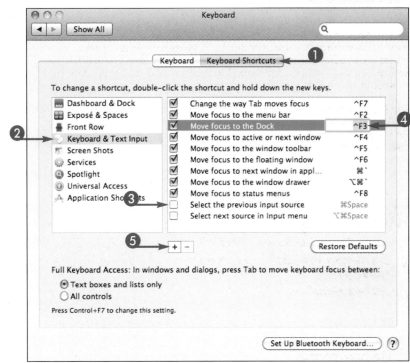

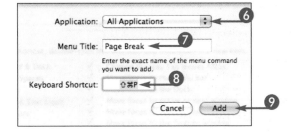

## TIPS

### Where do I see the new keyboard shortcuts I have created?

On the Keyboard Shortcuts tab, select the Application Shortcuts section. Then expand the All Applications section to see all application shortcuts or expand a specific application, such as Microsoft Word, to see the shortcuts created only for that application.

### I messed up my shortcuts. How do I get back to where I started?

On the Keyboard Shortcuts tab, click the **Restore Defaults** button to set all keyboard shortcuts as they were when you first started MacBook. You lose any changes you have made over time, so if you only want to reset a couple of shortcuts, just change those back to what you want them to be.

# Configure the Trackpad

The other primary control MacBook has is its trackpad. At its most basic, you can use the trackpad to move the pointer on the screen by dragging your finger around the trackpad. As you learned earlier, you also click the trackpad to perform various actions, such as to select a command on a menu.

**However, you can do a lot more with the trackpad than just moving the pointer and clicking. You can also configure it so that you can scroll in windows, rotate objects, and much more with various motions with up to four fingers.**

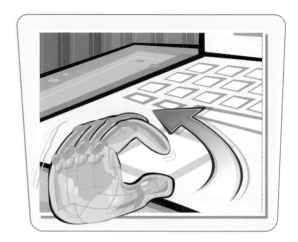

## Configure the Trackpad

① Open the **Apple** menu (![]) and choose **System Preferences**.

② Click the **Trackpad** icon.

③ Drag the **Tracking Speed** slider to the right to cause the pointer to move more for the same amount of finger movement or to the left to cause it to move less for the same finger movement.

④ Drag the **Double-Click Speed** slider to the right to lower the interval between clicks to register a double-click, or to the left to increase the time between clicks to register a double-click.

⑤ Drag the **Scrolling Speed** slider to change how far you scroll on the screen with the same amount of finger motion.

⑥ To learn about a gesture, point to it so it becomes highlight in a light bar.

● A video showing the gesture in action appears in the lower pane of the preview.

● The effect of the gesture appears in the upper pane. The video continues to play until you point to a different gesture.

⑦ Review and enable any of the One Finger and Two Fingers gestures that you think you will use.

*Note: If you enable the Secondary click gesture, choose* **Bottom Right Corner** *or* **Bottom Left Corner** *on the menu to set the location you tap to perform a secondary click.*

⑧ If you enable the Screen Zoom gesture, click the **Options** button.

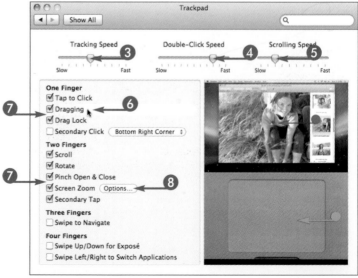

**9** On the **Zoom while holding** pop-up menu, choose the key you want to hold down to zoom.

**10** To keep the screen image moving with the pointer when you are zoomed in, click **Continuously with pointer**.

**11** To move the screen image only when the pointer reaches the edge of the display, click **Only when the pointer reaches an edge**.

**12** To move the screen image so the pointer is always at the center, click **So the pointer is at or near the center of the image**.

**13** To smooth images while zooming, check the **Smooth images** check box.

**14** Click **Done**.

**15** To be able to "flip" through a document by dragging three fingers to the left or right, enable the **Swipe to Navigate** check box.

**16** To activate Exposé by dragging four fingers up or down the trackpad, check the **Swipe Up/Down for Exposé** check box.

*Note: You learn about Exposé in Chapter 3.*

**17** To move between applications by dragging fours fingers to the left or right, check the **Swipe Left/Right to Switch Applications** check box.

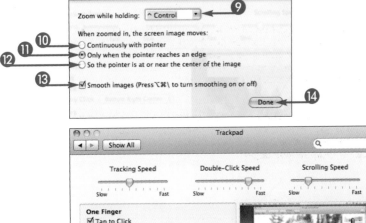

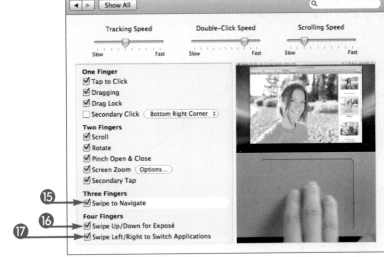

## TIPS

### How can I use a mouse with MacBook?

You can connect any Mac-compatible USB mouse to MacBook. You can also use a Bluetooth mouse with MacBook; see Chapter 9 for the steps to configure and use a Bluetooth mouse. When a mouse is connected, use the Mouse pane of the System Preferences application to configure it.

### How do I drag things with the trackpad?

This one can take some getting used to. Enable dragging by checking the **Dragging** and **Drag Lock** check boxes. Click the object you want to move once so it is selected. Quickly tap your finger on the trackpad two times. The object sticks to the pointer (if it opens instead, tap twice more quickly). Move the pointer to where you want to place the object. Tap the trackpad again to drop the object in that location. (If Drag Lock is disabled, the object drops as soon as you lift your finger.)

# Sleep, Log Out, Restart, or Shut Down

As great as MacBook is, you probably will not use it all the time. When your work with MacBook is complete for the day, there are several ways to stop using MacBook. Most of the time, you either put MacBook to sleep or log out. During sleep, everything you had open remains open, but MacBook goes into low-power mode; you can wake it up to quickly get back to whatever you were doing. When you log out, all open documents and applications close and you return to the Log In screen, but MacBook continues to run.

**When you want to turn MacBook off, you shut down. You need to do this only when you are not going to be using MacBook for extended periods of time. There are also times when you want to restart MacBook, such as when you are troubleshooting a problem.**

## Sleep, Log Out, Restart, or Shut Down

### Sleep or Log Out

**1** Open the **Apple** menu ( ) by pointing to it and clicking once.

**2** Scroll down by dragging on the trackpad until **Sleep** or **Log Out** *Account Name* (where *Account Name* is your user account name) is highlighted.

**3** Click the trackpad.

If you selected **Sleep**, MacBook's display goes dark, its hard drive stops, and the Sleep indicator light pulses.

***Note:*** *You can put MacBook to sleep even faster by simply closing its lid.*

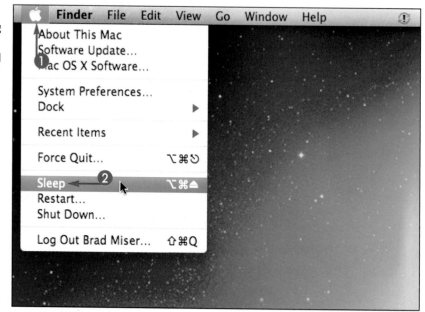

If you selected **Log Out**, the Log Out confirmation dialog appears.

**4** Click **Log Out**.

All applications and documents close, and the Log In screen opens.

***Note:*** *A faster way to log out is to press* ⌘ + Shift + Q .

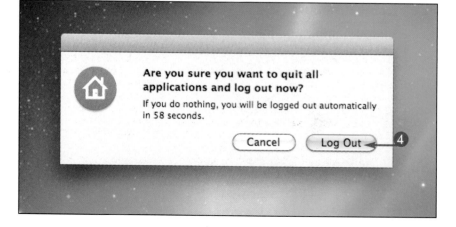

### Restart or Shut Down

1 Open the **Apple** menu (🍎) by pointing to it and clicking.

2 Drag down the trackpad until **Restart** or **Shut Down** is highlighted.

3 Click the trackpad.

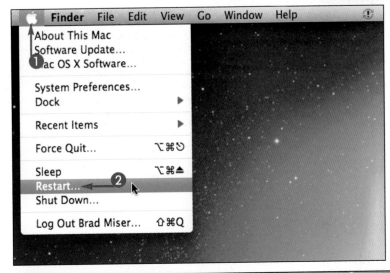

Depending on which option you chose, the appropriate confirmation dialog appears.

4 To restart MacBook, click **Restart**.

MacBook shuts down and then starts up again.

5 To shut down MacBook, click **Shut Down**.

MacBook turns off.

**Note:** *You can also perform the tasks in this section by pushing the* **Power** *button. The dialog that appears contains Restart, Sleep, and Shut Down buttons. Click a button to perform that action.*

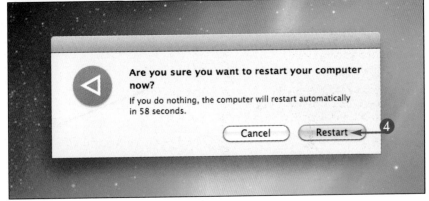

### Should I turn my MacBook off?

In most cases, no. It is usually better to just put it to sleep. When you want to use it again, wake MacBook up and it is ready in just a few seconds. Starting it up again can take several moments. If you will not be using MacBook for an extended period of time and it is not connected to the power adapter, it is better to shut it down so the battery does not get completely drained.

### When should I log out instead of shutting down my MacBook?

If you leave your MacBook in a place where other people can get to it, you probably do not want to leave it running in case someone decides to see what he can do with it. You can shut it down. However, if automatic login is turned on, someone can simply turn MacBook on and start using it. To prevent someone from using MacBook, log out. Everything you had open closes and you return to the Login screen. When you want to use it again, you can quickly log back in. Later, you can learn how to set MacBook so it automatically locks to protect it when you are not actively using it.

# Understand Finder, Application, and Document Windows

Like windows in the physical world, windows on MacBook enable you to view objects on-screen, such as folders, files, and documents.

In Mac OS X, most windows have common elements no matter what application you are using. In some cases, particularly with games and utilities, you might not see document windows when you run an application; instead, you see windows specific to the functions of those applications. It is important to be comfortable with any kind of window you encounter.

## Finder Windows

### Title

Shows the name of the drive, folder, or other location you are currently viewing.

### Toolbar

Contains tools to control windows, move among them, change views, and perform actions.

### Search tool

Enables you to search for files or folders.

### Files and folders

The contents of the folder you are viewing appear within the main part of Finder windows.

### Sidebar

Contains icons for locations; you can click an icon to view its contents in the Finder window or open an application or document.

### Status

Displays status information for what you are viewing, such as available disk space on the current drive.

### Scroll bars

Enable you to move up, down, left, or right within a window to see all of its contents.

### Resize handle

Drag this handle (⬚) to change the size and shape of a window.

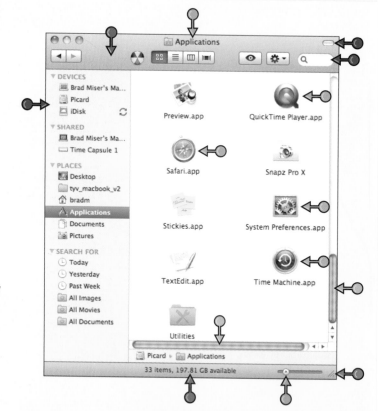

### Hide/Show Sidebar and Toolbar

Click to show or hide the sidebar and toolbar.

### Size slider (Icon view only)

Drag to the left to make icons smaller or to the right to make them larger.

## Application Windows

### Document, application, or other title

The name of the document being shown in the window, or the application's name.

### Window controls

Enable you to close, minimize, or zoom the window.

### Toolbar

Provides buttons for specific actions in the application.

### Content

The main window of the application presents the content you can work with in the application, such as a document or Web site.

## Document Windows

### Document title

The name of the file being shown in the window.

### Scroll bars

Enable you to move up, down, left, or right within a window to see all of its contents.

### Application-specific tools

Most applications provide tools in their windows specific to the application.

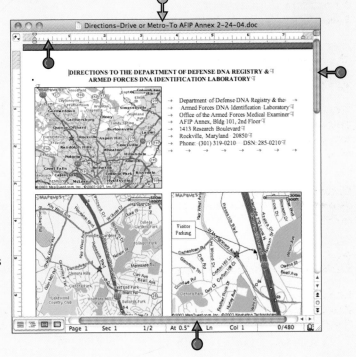

# View Finder Windows in Icon View

Icon view is the view most synonymous with Mac computers. Icons are pleasing to look at and visually indicate the kind of object they represent, such as a file or folder.

**While being pretty, Icon view is not the most useful one, but it does have a few things to offer. This view is pretty because the icons themselves are pleasing to look at, and some icons are miniature works of art. You also have more control over how a window in Icon view looks because you can set the window's background color or use an image as the background.**

## View Finder Windows in Icon View

① Open a Finder window by clicking a folder in the sidebar.

**Note:** You can also click the **Finder** icon (the Mac "happy face") on the Dock or open a folder on the desktop to open a Finder window.

② Click the **Icon View** button ( ⊞ ).

The objects in the window are represented with icons.

③ Click **View** and then click **Show View Options**.

④ To have the folder always open in Icon view, check the **Always open in icon view** check box.

⑤ Drag the **Icon size** slider to increase or decrease the size of icons.

The current icon size, in pixels, is shown above the slider.

⑥ Drag the **Grid spacing** slider to decrease or increase the space between icons.

⑦ Click the **Text size** pop-up menu and choose the size of the text for icon labels.

⑧ To have icon labels appear at the bottom of icons, click **Bottom**, or click **Right** if you want labels to appear on the right side of icons.

⑨ To show additional information about items, check the **Show item info** check box.

⑩ To show a preview of items within the icon, check the **Show icon preview** check box.

**Note:** Not all types of files support the preview function.

⑪ Use the **Arrange by** pop-up menu to choose how items are arranged in the window.

**Note:** Choosing **Snap to Grid** enables auto aligning of the icons in the window.

⑫ Click **White** to make the window's background white.

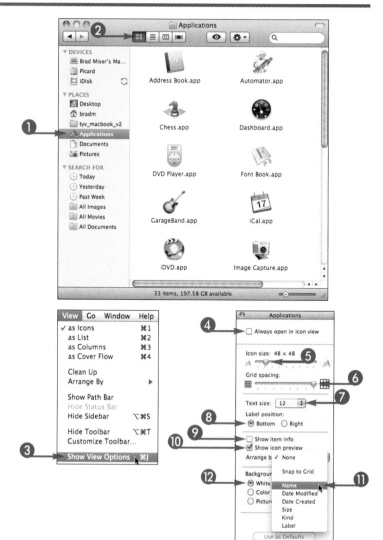

**13** Click **Color** to use a different color for the background.

**14** Click the color button.

● The Color Picker appears.

**15** Use the Color Picker to choose the color you want for the background.

**16** When you have the color you want, click the **Close** button (⊙).

● The Color Picker closes and you move back to the window, which now has the color you selected as its background.

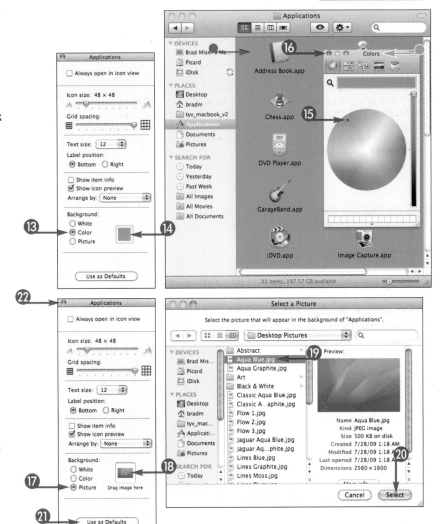

**17** To use an image as the background, click **Picture**.

**18** Click the image well.

**19** Use the Select a Picture dialog to move to and select the file you want for the window's background.

**20** Click **Select**.

The image is applied to the window's background.

**21** To have every window you open in Icon view use the current settings by default, click **Use as Defaults**.

**22** Close the View Options dialog by clicking ⊙.

 **TIPS**

**Where does a file's icon come from?**

Mac OS X automatically creates icons for some documents based on their content, while others get their icons from the associated application. For example, an image file's icon is a thumbnail view of the image, whereas a Word document's icon is a text file with the word "DOC" on it. Application files display the application's icon. This makes it easy to identify a file's type by simply looking at its icon.

**How can I change how icons are arranged in a window?**

Perform a secondary click in the window's background (one way is to press Control-click). The contextual menu appears. Select **Arrange By** and then choose how you want the icons to be arranged. For example, select **Kind** to have icons grouped by their kind, such as all image files together. You can straighten up the icons in a window by selecting **Clean Up** on the contextual menu.

# View Finder Windows in List View

Icon view is pretty, but it does not provide a lot of information about the files and folders you see. And, even if you make the icons small, they take up a lot of room, making it harder to see all the contents of a Finder window.

**List view may not look as nice as Icon view, but it does provide a lot more information. Also, you can easily sort the content in windows so that the items appear in the order you want. And, you can select items stored in different folders at the same time, something you cannot do with any other view.**

## View Finder Windows in List View

① Open a Finder window by clicking a folder in the sidebar.

*Note: You can also click the **Finder** icon (the Mac "happy face") on the Dock or open a folder on the desktop to open a Finder window.*

② Click the **List View** button (▤).

③ Click **View** and then click **Show View Options**.

④ If you want the window to always open in List view, check the **Always open in list view** check box.

⑤ Choose the icon size for the view by clicking the larger or smaller icon button.

⑥ Use the **Text size** pop-up menu to choose the text size for the List view.

⑦ Check the boxes for each column you want to see.

⑧ If you want relative dates to be displayed, such as Yesterday or Today, check the **Use relative dates** check box.

⑨ If you want the sizes of folders to be shown, check the **Calculate all sizes** check box.

*Note: Calculating the size of folders can take a lot of processing power, which may slow MacBook's performance somewhat.*

⑩ If you want to see previews in the icons for each item, check the **Show icon preview** check box.

⑪ If you want other windows in List view to use the current settings by default, click **Use as Defaults**.

⑫ When you are done making changes, click ⊙.

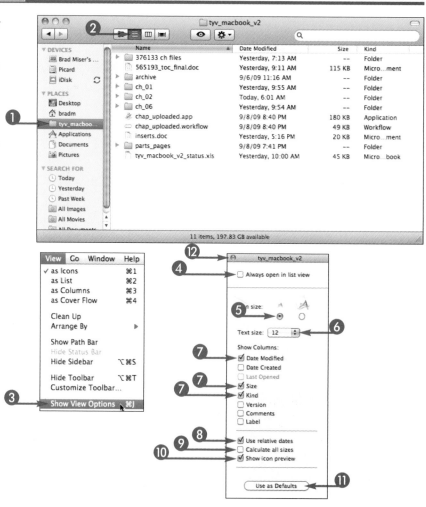

⑬ To change the order in which columns appear in the window, drag a column to the left or to the right.

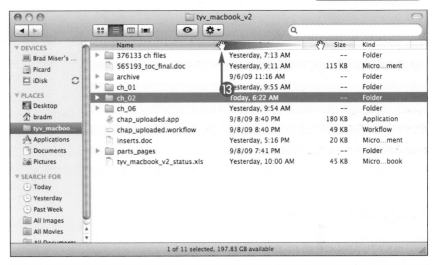

⑭ When the column is in its new position, release the trackpad.

⑮ To change the order in which the items are sorted, click the column heading by which you want to sort the items.

⑯ To reverse the sort order, click the triangle at the far-right edge of the column currently being used to sort the window.

⑰ To open the contents of a folder, click its disclosure triangle (▶ changes to ▼).

● The folder expands so that you can see the folders and files it contains.

⑱ Click ▼ to collapse the folder again.

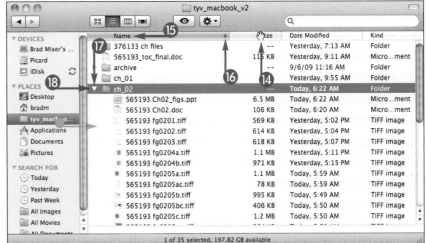

 **TIPS**

**How do I expand all the folders within a window at the same time?**

Press and hold the Option key while you click a folder's disclosure triangle. The folder expands, along with all the folders contained within that folder. Press and hold the Option key and click the folder's disclosure triangle to collapse all the folders in the window again.

**How do I tell where a folder is when I view its window?**

Click **View** and then click **Show Path Bar**. A bar appears at the bottom of the window that shows you the path from the startup disk to the location of the current folder.

# View Finder Windows in Column View

Column view is best for navigating quickly around MacBook. This view allows you to see the contents of folders along with the locations of those folders. You can click any folder's icon to immediately see the contents of that folder in the same window.

**As you learn to use MacBook, you should become comfortable with the Column view so that you can use it to quickly move to any location.**

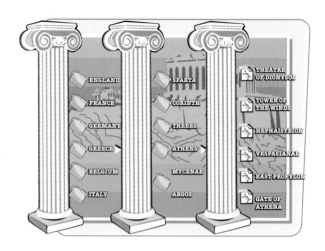

## View Finder Windows in Column View

① Open a Finder window by clicking a folder in the sidebar.

*Note: You can also click the **Finder** icon (the Mac "happy face") on the Dock or open a folder on the desktop to open a Finder window.*

② Click the **Column View** button (⊞).

③ Click **View** and then click **Show View Options**.

④ If you want the window to always open in Column view, check the **Always open in column view** check box.

⑤ Use the **Text size** pop-up menu to choose a text size for the labels shown in Column view.

⑥ If you want to see an icon for each item, check the **Show icons** check box.

⑦ If you want to see a preview of items within their icons, check the **Show icon preview** check box.

*Note: The icons in this view are very small so do not be surprised if you have a hard time recognizing them.*

⑧ If you want to see a preview of a file you select, check the **Show preview column** check box.

⑨ Use the **Arrange by** pop-up menu to determine how items in the window are listed.

⑩ When you are done making changes, click ⊙.

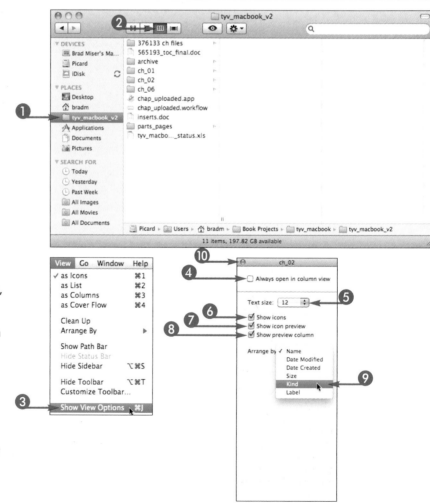

⑪ Select a location in the sidebar to view it.

⑫ Click a folder to see its contents.

As you move through the folder hierarchy, columns shift to the left so that you always see the last column opened toward the right side of the window.

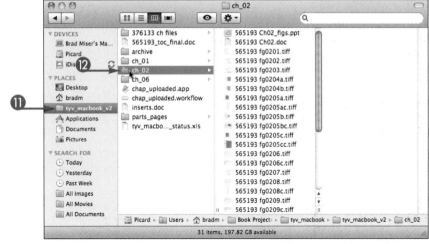

⑬ Click a file.

● You see information about the file in the far-right column, including a preview of the file if that option is enabled. If the file is dynamic, such as audio or video, you can play its content in the preview.

⑭ To change the width of a column, drag its **Resize** handle (⬚) to the left or right.

⑮ To scroll in the current column, drag the scroll bar up or down.

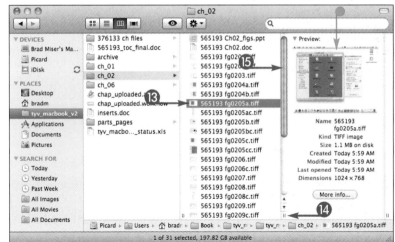

**TIPS**

**How do I resize all the columns at once?**

Press and hold the `Option` key while you drag one column's **Resize** handle (⬚). All the columns are resized at the same time. If you double-click the **Resize** handle, the column expands to be the width of the longest file or folder name shown.

**How do I tell the difference between a folder and a file?**

In Column view, folders always have a right-facing triangle at the right edge of their column to show that when you select this triangle, the folder's contents appear in a new column to the right. Files do not have this arrow.

# View Finder Windows in Cover Flow View

Cover Flow view is a graphical way to quickly scan through contents of a Finder window. In addition to making scrolling through lots of files and folders faster, this view displays thumbnail images of each item you are browsing.

**The easiest way to think about the Cover Flow view is to visualize a stack of CDs that you flip through. A Finder window in Cover Flow view behaves similarly. You can flip through the various folders and files to browse them in the top part of the window. In the bottom part of the window, you see the items in the folder you are browsing in List view.**

## View Finder Windows in Cover Flow View

① Open a Finder window by clicking a folder in the sidebar.

*Note: You can also click the Finder icon (the Mac "happy face") on the Dock or open a folder on the desktop to open a Finder window.*

② Click the **Cover Flow View** button (▥).

● The Cover Flow viewer appears at the top of the window.

● The items in the window appear at the bottom of the window in List view.

③ Click **View** and then click **Show View Options**.

④ If you want the folder to always open in Cover Flow view, check the **Always open in Cover Flow** check box.

⑤ Configure the rest of the settings just as you would for List view (see "View Finder Windows in List View," earlier in this chapter).

⑥ To browse the contents of the folder quickly, drag the scroll bar to the left or right.

● As you drag, a preview of each item flips by in the Cover Flow viewer at the top of the window. The item currently selected is the one directly facing you and is highlighted on the list at the bottom of the window.

⑦ To jump to a specific file or folder, click its icon.

⑧ To make the Cover Flow part of the window larger or smaller, drag its **Resize** handle (▬) up or down.

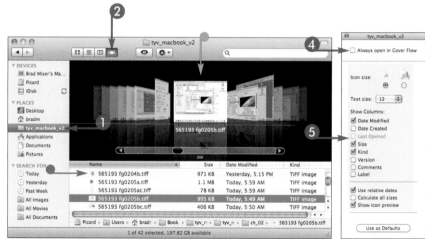

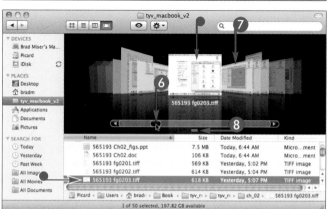

The Finder's sidebar makes it easy to get to specific locations, documents, folders, applications, and searches. It comes with a number of default locations, folders, and searches, but you can add items to or remove them from the sidebar so that it contains the items you use most frequently.

**The sidebar is organized into sections. Devices includes hard drives and other devices (such as iPods) mounted on your MacBook. Shared includes disk drives or computers you are accessing over a network. Places contains folders and files. Search For presents saved searches.**

## Configure the Sidebar

① To remove an item from the sidebar, drag it from the sidebar onto the desktop and release the trackpad.

● The item disappears in a puff of smoke.

***Note:** When you remove something from the sidebar, it is not removed from the computer. The item remains in its current location on MacBook; it is just no longer accessible from the sidebar. You can always add it back again later.*

② To add something to the sidebar, drag its icon from a Finder window or the desktop onto the sidebar.

③ When the item is over the location of the sidebar where you want to place it, release the trackpad.

● The item's icon is added to the sidebar and you can use it just like the default items.

④ To change the order of items in the sidebar, drag them up or down the list.

⑤ To collapse or expand sections of the sidebar, click their disclosure triangles (▶ changes to ▼).

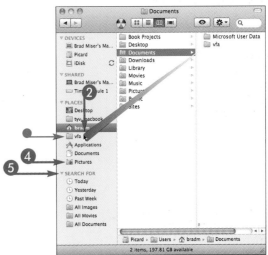

# Use the Action Pop-up Menu and Quick Look

The Action pop-up menu is a powerful element of Finder windows, though you might not think so to look at it. This menu contains a list of contextual commands that you can use.

**The Finder's Quick Look command enables you to view the contents of a file or group of files without actually opening them. This can save time, especially when you are looking for specific files on the desktop.**

Use the Action Pop-up Menu and Quick Look

## Use the Action Pop-up Menu

1 Open a Finder window by clicking a folder on the sidebar.

*Note: You can also click the Finder icon (the Mac "happy face") on the Dock or open a folder on the desktop to open a Finder window.*

2 Click the **Action** pop-up menu (⚙▾).

3 Choose the command you want to use.

*Note: You can also access the commands on the Action pop-up menu by performing a secondary click on an object or the desktop.*

## Use Quick Look

1 Open a Finder window containing files.

2 Select the files you want to view.

*Note: To select multiple files at the same time, press and hold the ⌘ key while you click each file.*

3 Click the **Quick Look** button (👁).

*Note: You also open the Quick Look window by pressing* **Spacebar**.

4 Use the controls in the Quick Look window to view the files.

*Note: The controls you see depend on the kind of files you are viewing. For example, if you selected multiple images, you can click the Play button (▶) to see those images in a slideshow.*

5 To see Quick Look in full screen, click the **Full Screen** button (⛶).

6 When you are done with Quick Look, click its **Close** button (⊗).

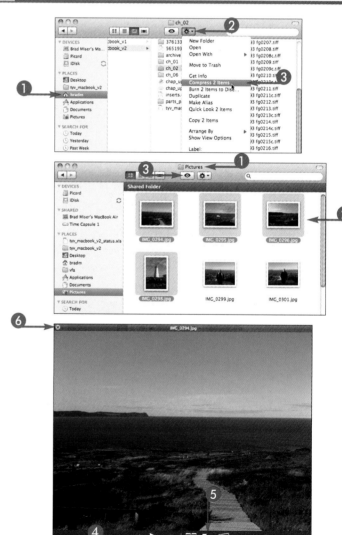

# Configure the Finder Window Toolbar

The toolbar that appears at the top of the Finder window contains buttons that you can use to access commands quickly and easily. For example, the various View buttons appear there along with the Quick Look and Action menu buttons.

**Although the Finder toolbar includes a number of buttons by default, you can configure the toolbar so that it contains the buttons you use most frequently.**

## Configure the Finder Window Toolbar

① Open a Finder window by clicking a folder on the sidebar, clicking the **Finder** icon on the Dock, or opening a folder on the desktop.

② Click **View** and then click **Customize Toolbar**.

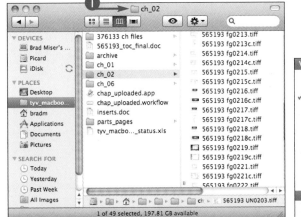

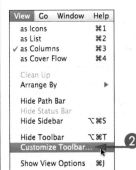

③ To remove a button from the toolbar, drag its icon from the toolbar onto the desktop.

④ To add a button to the toolbar, drag its icon from the sheet and drop it on the toolbar at the location in which you want to place it.

When you release the trackpad, the button is added to the toolbar.

⑤ To change the locations of buttons on the toolbar, drag their icons from the current location to the new one.

⑥ When you are finished customizing the toolbar, click **Done**.

The Customization sheet closes and you see your customized toolbar.

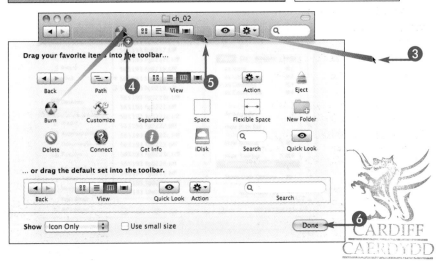

# Explore the Dock, Exposé, Spaces, and the Dashboard

Mac OS X's Dock, Exposé, Spaces, and Dashboard help you use your MacBook's desktop more effectively.

**The Dock is a bar containing many icons you can click to open the related item. Exposé is a feature that helps you manage open windows quickly and efficiently. Spaces allow you to create groups of applications and windows, and switch between them easily. The Dashboard presents mini-applications, called *widgets*, that you can quickly access and use.**

## The Dock

### Application icons

Application icons can be stored on the Dock for easy access; icons for all open applications are also shown.

**Running applications**

Applications that are open are marked with a blue dot in their reflection.

**Dividing line**

File and folder icons can also be placed on the Dock for one-click access.

**Files and folders**

File and folder icons can also be placed on the Dock for one-click access.

**Minimized windows**

When you minimize a window, it shrinks and moves onto the Dock.

**Trash**

This is the holding place for files that you are going to delete from MacBook.

## Exposé

### Thumbnail windows

When you activate Exposé (by pressing F3 on current MacBook models), all open windows are shrunk and organized so that you see them on the desktop; titles appear at the bottom of each window.

### Window in focus

When you point to a window, it is highlighted in blue; click a window to make it active.

## Spaces

### Spaces

When you activate Spaces, the desktop is hidden and the spaces available to you are shown.

### Space

Each space includes a collection of open document and application windows; when you move into a space, you can use the windows it contains.

### Applications

Each space can have many applications included in it.

## Dashboard

### Dashboard

When opened, the Dashboard fills the desktop and presents the active widgets.

### Active widgets

To have widgets appear when you activate the Dashboard, you install them on it. You can use any of the active widgets when you open the Dashboard.

### Available widgets

You can add widgets that are installed on MacBook to the Dashboard by dragging them onto it. You can also download and install more widgets.

# Use and Configure the Dock

The Dock is a very useful part of Mac OS X because it provides quick-and-easy, single-click access to various items, including applications, documents, and folders.

**The Dock includes a number of default icons, and you can add as many icons to your Dock as you want. You can also customize the way the Dock looks and works to suit your preferences.**

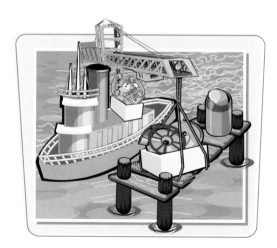

## Use the Dock

1 Point to an icon on the Dock.

The name of the related item appears above the icon.

2 Click the trackpad.

● What happens depends on the icon you click. If the icon is a closed application, for example, the application opens, and you see its initial window.

3 To open a Dock icon's contextual menu, perform a secondary click on it (one way is to press and hold the `Control` key and click).

4 Choose the command you want to use from the menu.

**Note:** As more icons appear on the Dock, they get smaller and the Dock expands so it can contain all its icons.

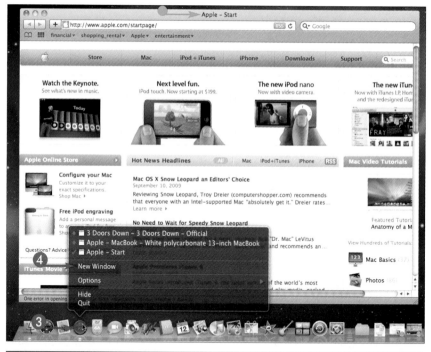

## Configure the Dock

1 Perform a secondary click on the dividing line so that the pointer (↖) becomes a horizontal line with arrows on the top and bottom (⬍).

The Dock menu appears.

2 Choose **Dock Preferences**.

The Dock pane of the System Preferences application appears.

**3** Drag the **Size** slider to the left or right to make the default size of the Dock smaller or larger.

*Note: The default size refers to when only installed icons are shown and no windows have been minimized. As icons are added to the Dock, its size changes accordingly.*

**4** If you want icons to be magnified when you point to them, check the **Magnification** check box and drag the slider for more or less magnification.

**5** To position the Dock on the left, bottom, or right side of the desktop, click **Left**, **Bottom**, or **Right**.

**6** On the **Minimize windows using** pop-up menu, choose **Genie effect** to see windows get whisked onto the Dock when you minimize them; **Scale effect** scales the window down as it moves onto the Dock.

**7** To cause windows that you minimize to move onto the associated application's icon instead of being added next to the Trash icon, check the **Minimize windows into application icon** check box.

*Note: To move into a window that has been minimized onto its application icon, open the icon's menu and choose the window you want to see.*

**8** To have icons bounce while their applications are opening, check the **Animate opening applications** check box.

**9** To automatically hide the Dock when you are not pointing to it, check the **Automatically hide and show the Dock** check box.

*Note: When the Dock is hidden, position the pointer over its location; it pops up so you can use it.*

**10** Press ⌘+Q to close the System Preferences application.

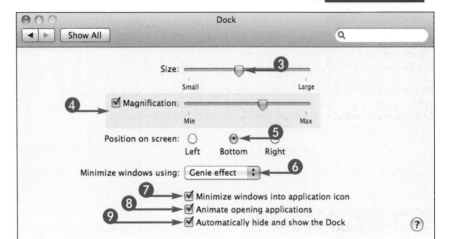

### How can I add icons to or remove them from the Dock?

To add an icon to the Dock, drag it from a Finder window onto the Dock; an application's icon must be placed on the left side of the dividing line, whereas a document or folder's icon goes on the right side. When the icon is at the desired location, release the trackpad button. To remove an icon, drag it up onto the desktop and release the trackpad.

### What happens when I add folder icons to the Dock?

When you click a folder's icon, a fan or grid showing the folder's contents appears. You can click an icon to work with one of the items, such as a document icon, to open it. For example, the Dock contains the Downloads folder, which is the default location for files you download from the Web. When you click this icon, the files you have downloaded appear, either in a fan or a grid (which one appears depends on how many items the folder contains).

# Manage Open Windows with Exposé

Exposé greatly helps with the inevitable screen clutter as you use MacBook and open window after window for documents and applications.

**Exposé has three modes: You can hide all open windows to show the MacBook desktop. You can reduce all open windows to thumbnails so that you can quickly jump into a window you want to use. You can create thumbnails of all the open windows within a specific application for quick access.**

## Manage Open Windows with Exposé

### Hide All Open Windows with Exposé

1 Open as many windows as you want, including those from the Finder and from applications.

2 Press Fn + F11.

**Note:** On current MacBook models, you can also activate Exposé by pressing F3 ; other models may have a different key preprogrammed for Exposé.

● All the windows are moved off the MacBook screen, leaving an uncluttered desktop for you to work on.

**Note:** To return the desktop to its cluttered state, press Fn + F1 again, or click one of the sides of the windows that you see at the edges of the desktop.

### Show Thumbnails of All Open Windows with Exposé

1 Open as many windows as you want, including those from the Finder and from applications.

2 Press F3 or Fn + F9 .

● All windows shrink down so that they fit on the desktop. You see the window's title under its thumbnail.

3 Point to a window.

● The window is highlighted with a blue line.

4 Click a window to move into it.

The window becomes active and moves to the front so that you can use it. The rest of the windows move into the background.

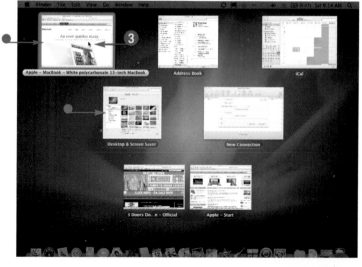

## Show All Open Windows for an Application with Exposé

① Open multiple documents within the same application.

② Press Fn + F10.

**Note:** *You can also click an application's icon and hold the trackpad down for a few seconds.*

All windows for the application shrink down so that they all fit on the desktop; you see the title of each underneath its thumbnail. The application's icon on the Dock is also highlighted.

③ Point to a window.

⦿ The window is highlighted with a blue line.

④ Click a window to move into it.

The window becomes active and moves to the front so that you can use it.

## Configure Exposé

① Open the **System Preferences** application.

② Click the **Exposé & Spaces** icon.

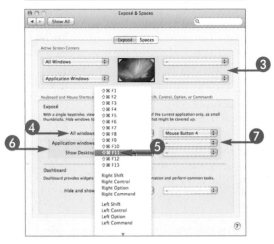

③ To cause an Exposé action to occur when you point to a corner of the desktop, use the pop-up menus located next to each corner of the desktop thumbnail.

For example, select **All Windows** on the upper-left menu to perform the same action as F3 / Fn + F9 when you point to the upper-left corner of the screen.

④ To change the keyboard shortcut for using Exposé with all open windows, open the **All windows** pop-up menu.

⑤ Choose the function keys you want to use for this Exposé command.

**Note:** *To select a key combination, hold down the keys you want to use while the menu is open.*

⑥ Use the **Application windows** and **Show Desktop** pop-up menus to configure the keyboard shortcuts for those actions.

**Note:** *Because the function keys are assigned to default actions, you have to press and hold the Fn key while you press the key combination you select.*

⑦ To assign one of the actions to a trackpad-click, use the menus on the right side of the window.

⑧ Press ⌘ + Q to close the System Preferences application.

# Create and Use Desktop Spaces

*Spaces* are collections of applications and documents that you can use to jump between sets of windows easily and quickly. When you use spaces, you do not have to bother locating individual windows, which is not always easy when you have many windows open. You can have as many spaces as you need up to 16.

**For example, if you have several Internet applications that you use at the same time, you can create an Internet space and add your applications to it. To use the Internet, you just open the space, and its open applications are ready to use immediately.**

## Create and Use Desktop Spaces

### Create and Configure Desktop Spaces

① Open the **System Preferences** application.

② Click the **Exposé & Spaces** icon.

③ Click the **Spaces** tab.

④ Check the **Enable Spaces** check box.

  At the top of the pane are thumbnails of the spaces you will be configuring.

⑤ Click the **Add** button (⊞).

  A menu showing applications and the Other command appear.

⑥ If the application you want to add to a space appears on the menu, choose it; if not, choose **Other** and use the resulting sheet to move to and select the application, and then click **Add**.

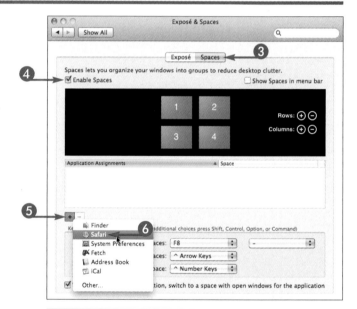

⑦ Repeat Steps **5** and **6** until you have added all the applications you want to include in Spaces.

● On the Spaces pane, you see the applications available for your spaces.

**Note:** *To remove applications from the list, select the applications you want to remove and click the **Remove** button (⊟). The application is removed from the list, but is not affected in any other way.*

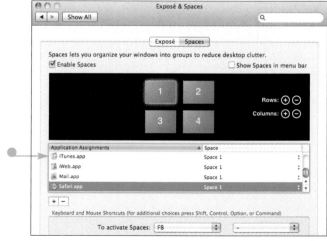

8 To add more spaces in a row, click the **Add** button (◉) next to Rows.

9 To add more spaces in a column, click ◉ next to Columns.

10 Repeat Steps **8** and **9** until you have created all the spaces you want to manage.

**Note:** *To delete spaces, click the **Remove** button (◉) next to Rows or Columns.*

11 Open the **Space** pop-up menu for the first application on the list.

12 Choose the number of the space in which you want to include that application, or choose **Every Space** to include it in all spaces; refer to the thumbnails to see the numbers of your spaces.

After you make a selection, the space number is shown on the menu for the application, and the space's thumbnail at the top of the window is highlighted.

13 Repeat Steps **11** and **12** until you have assigned all the applications to the spaces in which you want them to be available (or to Every Space to have them available at all times).

**Note:** *To see the list sorted by space number, click the Space column heading.*

14 On the **To activate Spaces** menu, choose the keyboard shortcut you want to use to activate Spaces (the default is Fn + F8 ).

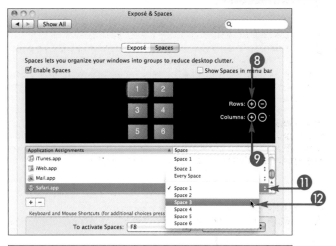

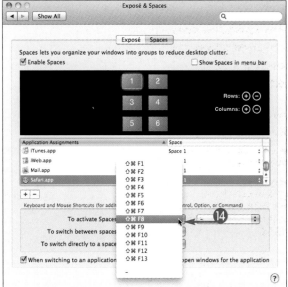

**TIP**

**How many spaces should I use?**
You want to keep the number of spaces you use to a manageable number. If you have too many spaces, it will be cumbersome to work with them; too few and each space may have too many applications in it. Try the default number (four) for starters and adjust over time as you use spaces. Realize that you do not need to add every application you use to a space; just add those that you use most often.

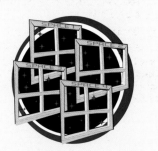

# Create and Use Desktop Spaces *(continued)*

Spaces can take a bit of getting used to because they are not familiar to many Mac users. It might take some trial and error to configure your spaces in a way that you get the most benefit from them. The most common problem is having too many spaces or too many applications in one space.

**Use these steps to configure your spaces initially. Over time, you will discover which spaces work for you and which do not. Keep tweaking your spaces until they are "just right" for the way you work.**

## Create and Use Desktop Spaces *(continued)*

⑮ On the **To switch between spaces** pop-up menu, choose the modifier keys you want to use with the arrow keys to jump to your spaces; the default is `Control` + ➡.

⑯ To set the modifier key you use to jump directly to a space by its number, open the **To switch directly to a space** pop-up menu and choose the modifier key you want to use; the default is `Control` +*spacenumber*, where *spacenumber* is the number of the space you want to move to.

### Use Desktop Spaces

① Open the applications associated with your spaces.

As you open applications, the Spaces bar appears briefly to indicate to which spaces the applications belong.

② To display all your spaces, press the Spaces activation key (the default is `Fn` + `F8`) or click the **Spaces** icon on the Dock.

● The desktop is hidden and the Spaces Manager appears. Here, you see each of the spaces you have configured. Within each space, you see the windows that are open in that space.

③ Click a space to move into it (when you point to a space, it is highlighted in a darker shade of blue).

The applications associated with that space appear.

④ To jump directly to a space, press the keyboard shortcut for switching directly to a space, which by default is `Control` + *spacenumber*, where *spacenumber* is the number of the space you want to move into.

The applications associated with that space appear.

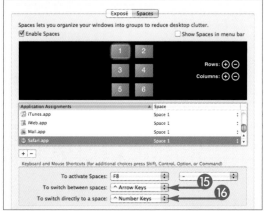

⑤ To move between spaces without using a number, press the keyboard shortcut for switching between spaces, which by default is `Control` + `→`.

● The Spaces Manager palette appears. Each box on the palette represents one of your spaces. The box highlighted in white is the space currently being shown on the desktop.

⑥ While pressing and holding `Control`, press an arrow key to move to the space you want to enter.

● As you press an arrow key, the white box moves to the next space.

⑦ When the space you want to use is highlighted with the white box, release `Control`.

The applications associated with that space appear, and you can work with them.

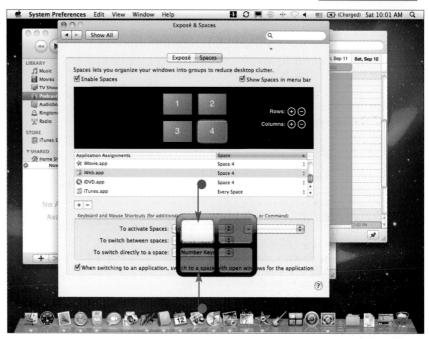

**TIPS**

**How can I access Spaces using a menu?**

On the Spaces pane of the System Preferences application, check the **Show spaces in menu bar** check box. The Spaces menu becomes available on the menu bar; it is indicated by the number of the space you are currently using. Open the menu and choose the space number you want to work with. That space opens.

**What happens when I open an application that is not part of the space I am using?**

If an application is available in only one space, when you open it from any source, such as the Dock or the Finder, you switch into the space with which that application is associated. If the application is not part of a space, it opens in the space you are currently using.

# Use and Configure the Dashboard

The Dashboard offers an easy way to access *widgets*, which are small applications that provide very specific functionality. To use a widget, you activate the Dashboard, which fills the desktop and presents the widgets installed on it. You use the widgets you want; when you are done, close the Dashboard again.

**Mac OS X includes a number of useful widgets by default, such as Weather, Calculator, Address Book, and Flight Tracker. There is even a widget to help you manage your widgets.**

### Open the Dashboard

1 Press `F4` on current MacBook models or click the **Dashboard** icon on the Dock.

● The desktop and open windows move into the background and the Dashboard appears, displaying the widgets already on the Dashboard.

● If a widget is informational, such as a weather widget, you can view the information it provides.

2 If the widget needs input, click the widget to make it active.

Many widgets require configuration in order to provide useful information to you.

3 Point to the widget you want to configure.

The Info button (a lowercase *i*) appears.

4 Click the **Info** button (■).

*Note: Many widgets require an Internet connection.*

The widget moves into configuration mode.

5 Use the widget's configuration tools to change its settings.

6 Click **Done**.

The widget returns to its normal mode and reflects the changes you made.

## Configure the Dashboard

**1** Open the Dashboard.

**2** To change the location of widgets, drag them around the screen.

When you release the trackpad, the widget is saved in its new location and appears in that spot each time you open the Dashboard.

**3** Click the **Add** button (⊕).

The Dashboard moves into configuration mode. A bar showing the available widgets appears at the bottom of the screen, and a Close button is added to each widget currently on the Dashboard.

**4** Browse the available widgets by clicking the scroll arrows (◄ and ►).

**5** To add a widget to the Dashboard, drag it from the bar and place it on the Dashboard.

When you release the trackpad, the widget is installed on the Dashboard and starts to work.

**6** To remove a widget from the Dashboard, click its **Close** button (⊗).

The widget is removed from the Dashboard, but remains installed so you can add it again later if desired.

### TIPS

**How can I change the key combination to open the Dashboard?**

Open the Exposé pane of the System Preferences application and click the **Exposé** tab. On the **Hide and show** pop-up menu, select the key combination you want to use to launch the Dashboard. You can press key combinations while the menu is open to be able to select them. For example, press and hold Option and Control to see those keys added to the options on the menu.

**How else can I activate the Dashboard?**

You can set a hot corner so that when you point to that corner, the Dashboard activates. To do this, open the Exposé pane of the System Preferences application and click the **Exposé** tab. Use the **Active Screen Corner** pop-up menu to choose **Dashboard** for the hot corner you want to set. When you point to that corner, the Dashboard opens.

continued

# Use and Configure the Dashboard (continued)

Although Mac OS X includes a number of widgets, these are by no means all of the widgets available to you. Thousands of other widgets are available on the Internet for you to download, install, and add to your Dashboard to expand the functionality available to you there.

**Downloading and installing widgets is a snap because Mac OS X recognizes widget files and automatically prompts you to install them as soon as they are downloaded to your MacBook.**

Use and Configure the Dashboard (continued)

### Find and Install More Widgets on the Dashboard

1. Open the Dashboard, click the **Add** button (⊕), and then click the **Manage Widgets** button.

● The Manage Widgets widget appears.

2. Click **More Widgets**.

Your Web browser opens and takes you to the Dashboard Widgets page on the Apple Web site.

3. Use the Web page to browse or search for widgets.

**Note:** Details about using Safari to browse the Web are provided in Chapter 11.

4. When you find a widget you want to install, click its **Download** button.

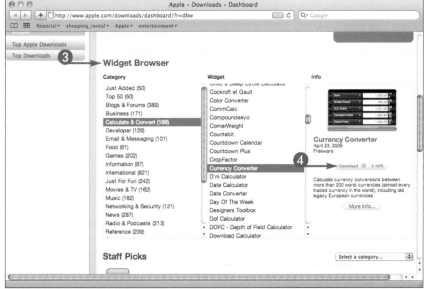

The widget is downloaded to your MacBook. When the process is complete, you are prompted to install the widget.

*Note: If the widget you downloaded does not install automatically, open your Downloads folder to install it.*

**5** Click **Install**.

*Note: To run the widget without installing it, press and hold* `Option` *and* `⌘` *and click the* **Run** *button.*

The Dashboard opens and you see the widget you are installing.

**6** Click **Keep**.

The widget is added to the Dashboard.

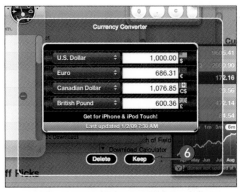

**7** Locate the widget on the screen and configure it.

### What if I want widgets to show information for more than one location or situation?

You can have as many copies of the same widget on your Dashboard as you want. For example, if you want to track the weather in five locations, add five copies of the Weather widget to your Dashboard and configure one for each area you want to track.

### What does the iTunes widget do?

Some applications include a widget that you can use to access that application more quickly and conveniently than opening it directly. The iTunes widget enables you to control content playing in iTunes from the Dashboard. Many other applications have similar widgets that are typically installed with the application; usually you are prompted to install the widget along with the application.

# Move to Locations on the Desktop

The Mac desktop provides many ways to get to specific folders that you want to view. Two of the most useful of these are the sidebar and the Go menu.

**Starting from the sidebar and using the Column view, you can quickly get to any location on the desktop. With the Go menu, you can easily jump to many locations that you commonly visit, along with locations that are typically hidden on the desktop.**

## Move to Locations on the Desktop

### Go Places from the Sidebar with Column View

① Open a new Finder window.

**Note:** *For information about working with Finder windows, see Chapter 2.*

② Click the **Column View** button (▥).

③ On the sidebar, select a starting point such as your Home folder or a disk.

④ Click the first folder whose contents you want to view.

● The contents of that folder appear in the column immediately to the right of the folder you selected.

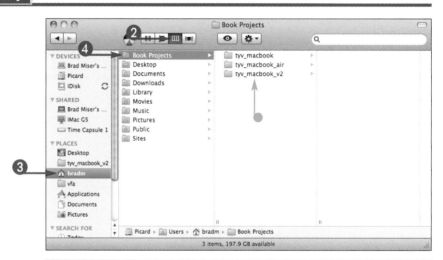

⑤ Click the next folder you want to move into.

● The contents of that folder appear in the column immediately to the right of the folder you selected.

**Note:** *In Column view, folders have a right-facing arrow at the end of the column; files do not.*

⑥ Keep selecting folders until you get to the specific folder or file you are interested in.

**Note:** *You can always select one of the other views (Icon or List) after you have moved into a folder if you prefer to see a window in one of those views.*

## Go Places with the Go Menu

1. With a Finder window active, open the **Go** menu on the Finder menu bar.

2. Select the location you want to move to.

● A Finder window opens, showing the location you selected.

**TIPS**

### How can I go places with the keyboard?

The standard folders on the MacBook desktop all have keyboard combinations that you can press to jump to them. The following list shows the location and keyboard combination (in parentheses):

Computer (Shift + ⌘ + C)

Home folder (Shift + ⌘ + H)

Desktop (Shift + ⌘ + D)

Network folder (Shift + ⌘ + K)

iDisk (Shift + ⌘ + I)

Applications folder (Shift + ⌘ + A)

Utilities folder (Shift + ⌘ + U)

### How do I make it even easier to move to a folder I use all the time?

Drag the folder onto the right end of the Dock and drop it anywhere on the right side of the dividing line. The folder is installed on the Dock, and you can easily get to its contents. Or, drag the folder onto the sidebar so that you can click its icon there to open it in a Finder window.

# Use Recent Menus

As you work on the desktop, you will probably want to move back to items that you have used recently. Of course, you can always move back to a location in the same way you got there originally, such as by using the sidebar or Go menu. However, Mac OS X maintains two recent lists, Recent Folders and Recent Items, that you can use to quickly move back to places you have been recently by selecting them on menus.

## Use Recent Menus

### Return to Previous Folders

1 With a Finder window active, open the **Go** menu on the Finder menu bar.

2 Choose **Recent Folders**.

3 Select the folder you want to open.

The folder you selected opens in a Finder window.

### Return to Previous Applications, Documents, or Servers

1 Open the **Apple** menu (🍎).

2 Choose **Recent Items**.

3 Choose the application, document, or server you want to access.

The item you selected opens.

*Note: To remove all the items from either recent list, you can choose the **Clear Menu** command. The next time you go to an item, it is added to the appropriate menu again.*

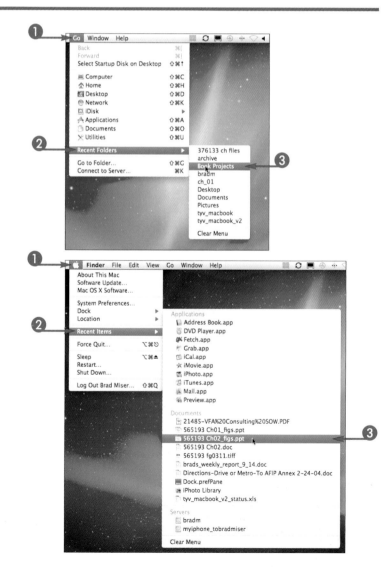

A *smart folder* is smart because instead of manually placing items within it, you define a set of search criteria, and the items that meet those search criteria are placed within the folder automatically.

**For example, you can create a smart folder for a specific project that includes a key phrase that is part of all the file and folder names related to that project. Whenever you create a folder or file whose name includes that phrase, it is included in the project's folder automatically. Each time you open the smart folder, you see all of the files and folders that currently meet its criteria, such as being associated with the project.**

## Create Smart Folders

① With the Finder active, click **File** and then choose **New Smart Folder**, or press Option + ⌘ + N, to open a new smart folder window.

② Enter the text or numbers you want to search for.

● As you enter conditions, files and folders that meet those conditions appear in the window.

③ Choose where the Finder should search.

For example, click **This Mac** to search all areas; click **"currentfolder"** (where *currentfolder* is the folder you were viewing most recently) to search only that folder; or click **Shared** (when you are connected to network resources) to search the network.

④ Click **Contents** to search by the contents of files or **File Name** to search only by name.

**Note:** The Contents option does not work for all types of files, but will successfully search the most common types.

⑤ To make the search more specific, click the **Add** button (⊕).

A new condition appears.

⑥ Choose the attribute you want to search by on the first pop-up menu.

For example, choose **Last modified date** to search for files that have changed within a specific time period, or choose **Kind** to look for a specific type of file.

⑦ On the second pop-up menu, select the operand.

⑧ Configure the rest of the parameters for the condition you created.

⑨ Repeat Steps **5** to **8** to add more conditions to the search until you find all the content you want to include in the folder.

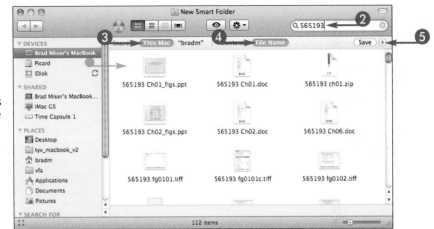

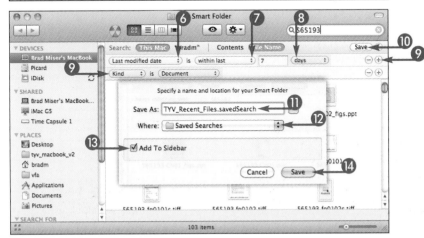

**Note:** To remove a condition, click its **Remove** button (⊖).

⑩ Click **Save**.

⑪ Enter the name of the folder.

⑫ Choose a save location. The default location is your Saved Searches folder, but you can choose another folder.

⑬ Uncheck the **Add To Sidebar** check box if you do not want the folder to appear in the Search For section of the sidebar.

⑭ Click **Save**.

# Rename Files and Folders

You can change the name of files or folders as you need to. Just as when you create them, you can change the names to be just about anything you want, using up to 255 characters.

**When you change the name of files, you should usually avoid changing the filename extension (everything after the period in the name) because this extension is one important way that Mac OS X associates documents with applications. However, you can change the part of the name before the period.**

## Rename Files and Folders

① In a Finder window, select the folder or file whose name you want to change.

② Press **Return**.

● The name becomes highlighted to indicate that you can change it. If you are changing the name of the file, Mac OS X selects only the filename part of the name (the text before the period) so you do not change the filename extension.

**Note:** *If your user account does not have write permissions for a folder or file, you cannot change its name.*

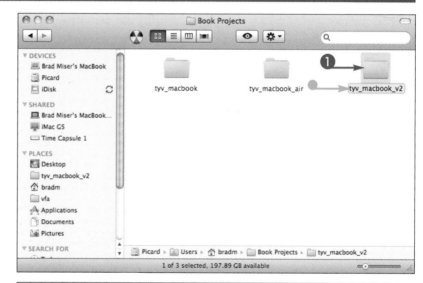

③ Type the new name of the folder or file.

④ Press **Return**.

The new name is saved.

**Note:** *One of the ways Mac OS X associates a file with an application is the filename extension (everything after the period in a filename). When you change the filename extension, you can change the application with which the file is associated. This can make the file unusable or damage it if the new application is not compatible with the file. Mac OS X warns you so that you do not inadvertently change the filename extension.*

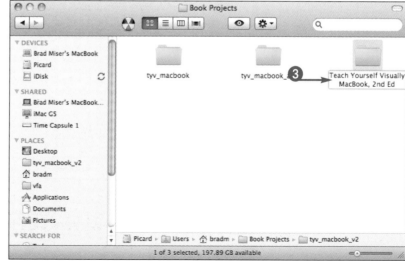

Files and folders take up disk space. You can compress them to reduce the space they consume.

**This is most useful when you move these files over a network, especially when you e-mail files as attachments. Not only do compressed files move more quickly, but you can also include all the relevant files in one compressed file to make them easier for the recipient to work with. (See Chapter 12 to learn how to attach files to e-mail messages.)**

## Compress Files and Folders

### Compress Files and Folders

1 In a Finder window, select the files and folders you want to include in the compressed file.

**Note:** Press and hold ⌘ or Shift to select multiple items.

2 Perform a secondary click on one of the selected files (such as by Control-clicking it) and select **Compress *X* Items**, where *X* is the number of items selected.

The files and folders are compressed, and a file called Archive.zip is created.

3 Change the name of the Archive.zip file using the steps in the previous section.

**Note:** Leave the filename extension as .zip or the file might not expand correctly.

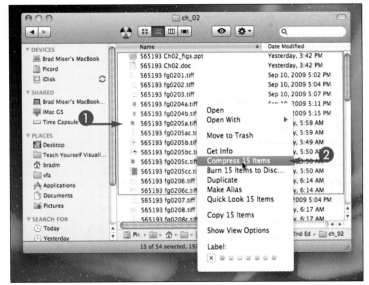

### Expand Compressed Files

1 In a Finder window, double-click a compressed file.

● The Archive Utility launches and expands the file. It stores the uncompressed files in a folder with the same name as the compressed file.

2 Open the expanded folder to work with the files and folders it contains.

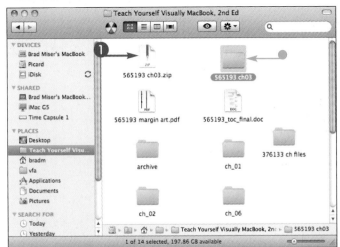

# Find Files, Folders, and Other Information

As you use MacBook, you create a lot of data in various documents, images, movies, and other kinds of files. You also interact with e-mail, Web pages, and other sources of information. Over time, you might not remember where all this information is. Mac OS X includes tools to help you find the information you need.

**You can search for files using the Search tool in Finder windows. You can also use Spotlight on the desktop to search many kinds of information at the same time.**

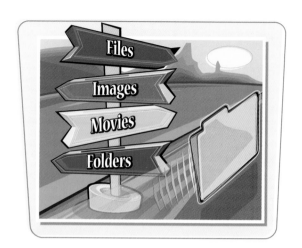

## Find Files, Folders, and Other Information

### Find Files and Folders with Finder

① In a Finder window, type the information you want to search for in the Search bar.

● As you type, the search results appear in the Finder window.

② Choose where the Finder should search.

For example, click **This Mac** to search all areas; click **"currentfolder"** (where *currentfolder* is the folder you were viewing most recently) to search only that folder; or click **Shared** (if connected to a network resource) to search the network.

③ Choose how the Finder should search.

For example, click **Contents** to search by file content or **File Name** to search only by filename.

④ To see where a folder or file is located, select it.

The path to the file or folder is shown at the bottom of the window.

⑤ To make your search more specific, click the **Add** button (🛨).

⑥ Configure the search just like when you create a smart folder (see the section, "Create Smart Folders," earlier in this chapter).

● As you add more conditions, the search results become more specific.

## Find Information with Spotlight

**1** Click the **Spotlight** icon (🔍) located in the upper-right corner of the desktop.

The Spotlight bar appears.

**2** Type the information you want to search for.

● As you type, Spotlight searches MacBook to locate information that relates to the text or numbers you entered.

**3** Continue typing to make your search more specific.

**4** Point to a result to see more information about it.

● Additional information appears.

**5** To open one of the found items, click it.

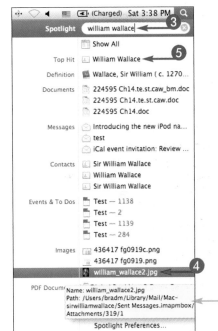

### How can I save a search so I do not have to reconfigure it each time I want to run it?

Perform a search in a Finder window. When the search works the way you want it to, click the **Save** button. Name the search, choose a save location, and click **Save**. You can run the search again by opening it on the desktop or by clicking it on the sidebar. A saved search is also called a smart folder.

### How can I use keyboard shortcuts for Spotlight?

You can start a Spotlight search by pressing ⌘+Spacebar. If you click outside the Spotlight window, it closes, but you can easily open it again by pressing ⌘+Spacebar. If you do not like this keyboard shortcut, open the Keyboard Shortcuts tab of the Keyboard pane of the System Preferences application. Select **Spotlight;** click its keyboard shortcut and press a new key combination.

When you search with Spotlight, you find a variety of content at the same time. This is good because your searches can easily and quickly expose many different kinds of documents that might be of interest to you. However, if you are not specific when you enter a search term, you might be overwhelmed by the results. Use as specific a search term as you can at first, and make it less specific if you do not find what you want. You can also configure the items included in searches and the order in which they appear.

**You can search for help using the Mac OS X Help system or the help systems provided by third-party applications.**

## Find Files, Folders, and Other Information *(continued)*

- The item you clicked on opens and you can work with it.

⑥ To return to the search results, click the **Spotlight** icon again (🔍).

The Spotlight results window appears, and you can view other items in the results or you can change the search criteria.

**Note:** *To clear a Spotlight search, click the **Clear** button ( ).*

### Configure Spotlight

① On the **Spotlight** menu, choose **Spotlight Preferences**.

② Uncheck the check box for any category of items that you do not want to be included in Spotlight searches.

③ Drag categories up or down the list to change the order in which those categories appear in the Spotlight results window.

④ To change the keyboard combination that activates Spotlight, use the **Spotlight menu keyboard shortcut** menu.

⑤ To change the keyboard combination for the Show All command (see the tip at the end of this section) use the **Spotlight window keyboard shortcut** menu.

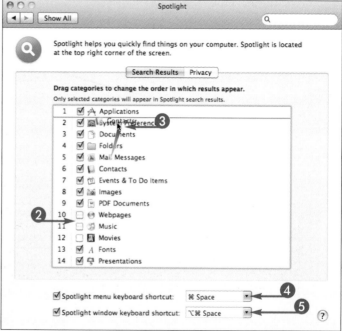

**6** Click the **Privacy** tab.

● On this pane, you see areas that are not searched when you perform Spotlight searches. Although it is called the Privacy pane, you can use it to exclude an area for any reason, such as to limit the kind of results that you see.

**7** Add folders or volumes to the list using the **Add** button (⊞) or by dragging them from the desktop onto the list.

**8** Quit the System Preferences application.

The next time you search with Spotlight, your preferences are used in the search.

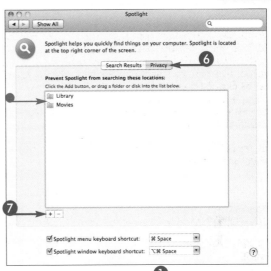

## Find Help

**1** While on the desktop, open the **Help** menu on the Finder menu.

**2** Type the information related to the help you need.

As you type, the Mac Help system is searched.

**3** To see where a menu item is, point to it.

● The menu opens and a large pointer indicates the menu item.

**4** To read a help topic, click it.

● The Help window opens and you see the help topic you selected.

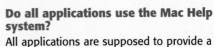
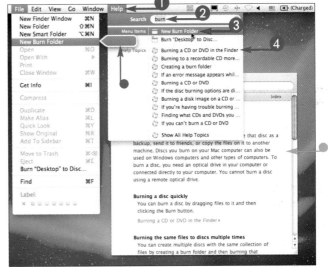

 **TIPS**

**What does the Show All result in the Spotlight results window do?**

When you click **Show All** in the Spotlight results window or press `Option` + `⌘` + `Spacebar`, a Finder window appears, configured with the search information you entered in Spotlight, as if you had started the search from the Finder window rather than from Spotlight. Like other Finder searches, you can add search criteria, save the search, and so on.

**Do all applications use the Mac Help system?**

All applications are supposed to provide a Help menu that you can use to get help. Apple applications use the help system provided by Mac OS X so that you can use the same tools to find help in any of these applications. Some non-Apple applications also use the Mac OS X Help system, but others (such as Microsoft Office) implement their own help systems that work a bit differently. No matter what application you happen to be using, start a search for help from its Help menu.

# Get Information about Files and Folders

As discussed in Chapter 2, you can choose the specific information you see in some of the views, such as the List view. However, what you see in Finder windows is just some of the information about these items.

**To see more detail about any file or folder, you can use the Finder's Get Info command. This command opens the Info window, which provides a lot of detailed information about what you have selected. The information in this window depends on the type of item you selected. For example, you see a different set of information when you select an application file than when you select a document.**

## Get Information about Files and Folders

① In a Finder window, select a file or folder you want to get information about.

② Open the **File** menu and choose **Get Info**, or press ⌘+ⓘ.

③ Click a section's disclosure triangle to see the information it contains (▶ changes to ▼).

**Note:** *In addition to viewing information about a file or folder, you can also use the Info window to make changes to a file or folder. For example, the following steps show you how to change the application used to open a file. You can do other tasks as well, such as change the permissions for an item or enter comments for Spotlight searches.*

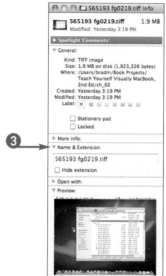

④ Scroll down the window to see all of the sections available for the selected item.

⑤ Expand the **Open with** section.

⑥ On the **Open with** pop-up menu, choose the application in which you want the document to open.

⑦ If you want all documents of the same type to open in that application, click **Change All**.

The next time you open the document (or one of the same type if you clicked **Change All**), the application you selected is used.

⑧ When you are done viewing or changing information, click 🔘 to close the Info window.

*Note: You can leave the Info window open as long as you want, and you can have many Info windows open at the same time, which makes comparing items easy.*

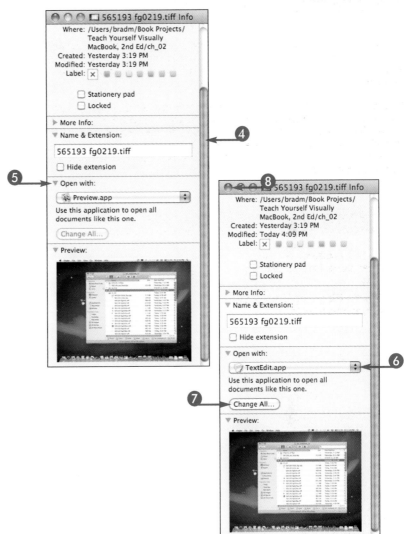

### What are Spotlight Comments?

The Spotlight Comments section appears at the top of the Info window. You can enter text in this field to associate that text with an item. When you search using Spotlight, the information you enter in the Spotlight Comments section is included in the search. For example, you could type a keyword into the Spotlight Comments field for all the files relating to the same project. When you perform a Spotlight search for that keyword, all the files and folders are found based on the keyword you entered.

### What does the Sharing & Permissions section do?

This section shows the security settings for the selected item. You see each person or group who has access to the item along with the permissions each has. You can use the controls in this section to change the access people or groups have to the item. First, click the **Lock** icon (🔒) and enter an administrator user name and password. Second, use the pop-up menus to change privileges and the **Add** or **Remove** buttons (➕ and ➖) to add or remove people and groups in the list.

# Store Files and Folders on CDs or DVDs

All MacBooks include a drive that you can use to burn CDs and DVDs. You might want to burn files and folders from the Finder to CDs or DVDs for many reasons, such as to transfer them to someone else or to safeguard copies of important folders and files for future use.

**You can burn folders and files onto disc in several ways. One of the most useful is by creating a burn folder. You can place and organize folders and files within a burn folder and then burn the folder onto a disc.**

## Store Files and Folders on CDs or DVDs

### Create and Organize a Burn Folder

1. Open a Finder window showing the location in which you want to create a burn folder.

2. Open the **File** menu and choose **New Burn Folder**.

● A new burn folder is created; its name "Burn Folder" is highlighted and ready for you to edit.

3. Type the name of the burn folder and press Return.

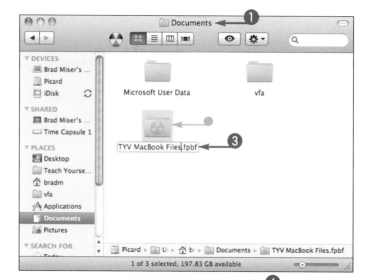

4. Open the burn folder in the Finder window.

● The folder's name and the Burn button indicate it is a burn folder.

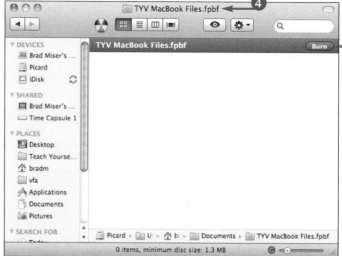

⑤ Open a new Finder window so that you have two windows on the desktop.

⑥ In the second window, move to the first folders or files you want to burn to a disc.

⑦ Drag the folders or files from the second window onto the burn folder's window.

Aliases (which are pointers that tell the Finder where the original file or folder is located) are created in the burn folder for each file or folder that you move there.

⑧ Repeat Steps **6** and **7** until you have moved all the folders and files into the burn folder that you want to put on a disc.

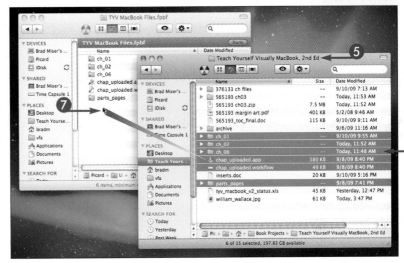

⑨ Organize the files and folders in the burn folder as you want them to be organized on the disc. For example, you can create new folders and place the files and folders into them.

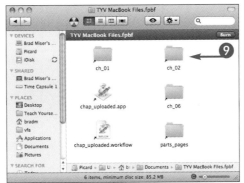

## TIPS

**Can I use erasable disks?**

You can erase and reuse disc media of the type CD-RW, DVD-RW, or DVD+RW.

**How much do discs hold?**

A CD holds about 650MB of data and a DVD holds approximately 4.7GB of data. A DVD-DL disc holds about 8.5GB of data.

Using a burn folder is a great way to store data files onto a disc for backup purposes. If you use a nonerasable disc format, make sure you test the folder you intend to put on disc; if you burn it to a disc and then find a mistake, you have to start over, which wastes both your time and money.

**Organizing your files and folders in a burn folder is the labor-intensive part of the task. The disc burning process can take a while for lots of data, but you do not need to do anything other than start it.**

## Burn a Disc

**①** Open the burn folder you want to place on a disc.

**②** Check the minimum disc size for the folder by looking at the status bar at the bottom of its window.

If the size is less than about 650MB, you can burn the folder onto a CD. If it is larger than that, you need to use a DVD (up to 4.7GB for a single-layer DVD or 8.5GB for a dual-layer DVD) or burn the folder to multiple discs.

**③** Click the **Burn** button.

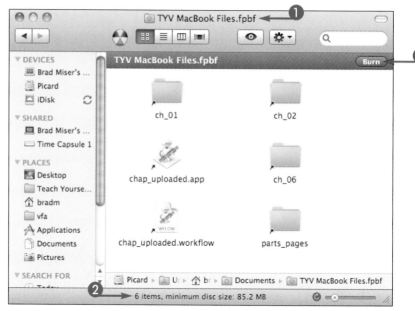

● The insert disc prompt appears. The prompt also tells you how much disc space you need to burn the disc.

**④** Insert a blank CD or DVD.

The burn dialog appears.

⑤ Enter the name of the disc you are burning; by default, its name is the same as the burn folder. You can change it or leave the default.

⑥ On the **Burn Speed** pop-up menu, choose the speed at which you want the disc to be burned. In most cases, leave the setting as **Maximum Possible**.

**Note:** *If the burn process fails, try a slower burn speed.*

⑦ Click **Burn**.

MacBook starts the burn process and you see the Burn progress window. This window remains open until the burn is done. How long the process takes depends on the size of the burn, what else MacBook is doing, and the media you use. You can use MacBook for other tasks while the disc is burning.

When the process is complete, the progress window disappears and the disc is mounted.

⑧ Open a Finder window.

⑨ Select the disc you burned.

You see the contents of the disc, which look exactly like the burn folder. You can use the contents of the disc on MacBook or on any other computer.

⑩ Click 🔼 to eject the disc.

**Note:** *You can make copies of the disc by repeating the burn process. When you are done, you can delete the burn folder. If you save files or folders only in the burn folder, they will be deleted too, so make sure the burn folder contains only alias files or folders or files you do not need to have on MacBook.*

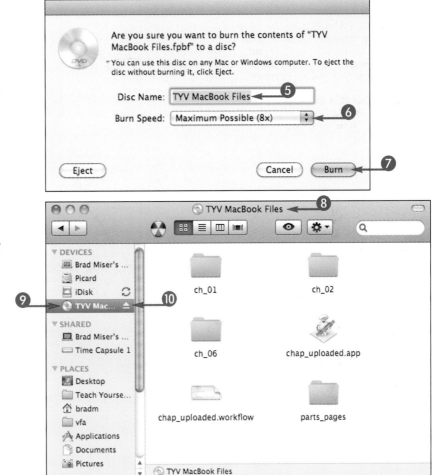

### What other applications can I use to burn CDs or DVDs?

Many applications enable you to burn discs. For example, you can use iTunes to create audio CDs or to back up your iTunes Music Library onto CD or DVD. Using iDVD, you can create DVDs that play in a standard DVD player just like those you might rent or buy. From iPhoto, you can burn photos to disc to archive them or make them easy to share. Each of these applications provides its own burn commands, typically located on the File menu or on the application's toolbar.

### How can I create my own application installation discs?

As you work with MacBook, you use various disk image files, especially when you download applications from the Web (see Chapter 5 for information about using disk images to install applications). You can use the Disk Utility application to burn those disk images onto a CD or DVD; this is especially important when you download applications that you have purchased so that you can reinstall the application if you ever need to. Launch Disk Utility and select the disk image you have downloaded. Choose the **Burn** command and follow the prompts to burn the disk image to a CD or DVD. Should you ever need to install the application again, you can do so from the disc you create.

# Understand Applications

All applications share fundamental concepts that apply to each of them. Understanding these fundamentals will help you use a wide variety of applications on your MacBook.

## Applications

The reason computers work so well is that they are very good at following repetitive instructions that adhere to very specific syntax and logic rules. An *application* is a collection of programming statements, more commonly called *code*, constructed according to a specific programming language. Applications separate you from the detailed code so that you can control what the application does by interacting with menus and graphical elements of the user interface, rather than having to re-create the lines of code each time you want to do something. Applications are created for many purposes, from running MacBook (Mac OS X is a very complex collection of applications) to providing the weather at a glance through a simple Dashboard *widget* (a specific kind of application delivered through the Dashboard).

## Documents

Most applications, but certainly not all of them, work with documents. A document is much more than just a text file; documents can certainly contain text, but they can also be images, e-mails, and songs. Basically, a *document* is the content an application works with. So, for a text processor such as Microsoft Word, a document can include text and graphics. A graphics application, such as Photoshop, uses images as documents. The songs and video stored within iTunes can also be considered documents. If you open or save something with an application, that something can be called a document.

## Windows

Chapter 2 talked about the various kinds of windows you see on your MacBook. As that chapter mentioned, applications provide windows through which you view documents, or controls and functions when an application does not work with documents (such as a game). An application's windows are whatever you see when you open and use that application. Most applications allow you to have many documents open at the same time, with each appearing in a separate window.

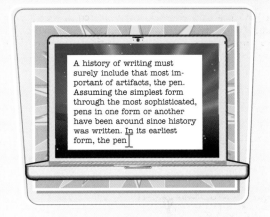

## Standard Menus

Applications contain commands that you use to perform actions. For example, when you want to save changes you have made, you use the Save command. Commands are organized into logical collections on menus. When you open a menu, you can see and choose the commands it contains. Mac OS X applications are supposed to support a set of standard menus that have the same or similar commands; these include the *Application* menu (where *Application* is the name of the application), File, Edit, Window, and Help. These menus also contain sets of standard commands; for example, the application menu always contains the Preferences command. Applications can and usually do have more menus than just the standard menus that are part of Mac OS X design specifications. Some applications, mostly games, do not include standard menus at all.

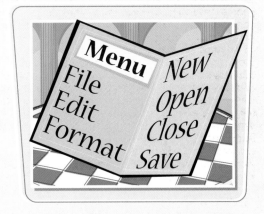

## Application Preferences

Not everyone uses applications in the same way; everyone has her own preferences. Because of this, applications include preferences that enable you to configure various aspects of how the application looks and works. You can use preferences to enable or disable functions, change the appearance of the application's windows, and so on. In effect, these commands enable you to tailor the way they work to your preferences, thus the name for this type of command.

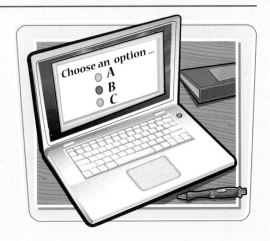

# Install Applications

To be able to use applications, they must be installed. MacBook includes a large number of applications that were installed by Apple, including Safari, Mail, iChat, iTunes, iMovie, iDVD, and many more. You can add more applications by installing them.

**Some applications include an installer program; to install the application, you open the installer and follow the on-screen instructions. Other applications use a drag-and-drop installation method that requires you to drag a folder or file into the Applications folder.**

## Install Applications

### Install Applications with an Installer

① Download the application's installer from the Internet or insert the CD or DVD it came on.

**Note:** In most cases, the installer starts automatically; if so, skip Step **2**.

**Note:** When you download an installer from the Web, by default it is stored in the Downloads folder on the Dock. Go there to access the installer.

② Double-click the application installer's icon to launch it.

The installer starts running.

③ Read the information on the first screen of the installer and click **Continue**.

④ Continue reading the information presented on each screen of the installer and providing the required input, such as clicking **Continue**, to complete the installation process.

Eventually, you move to the Install screen.

⑤ Click **Install**.

You are prompted to authenticate yourself as an administrator.

⑥ Enter your user name (if you are logged in under an administrator account, this is filled in automatically).

⑦ Enter your password.

⑧ Click **OK**.

The installer runs and presents progress information in its window. When the process is done, you see the Complete screen.

⑨ Click **Close** or **Quit**.

The installer quits and the application is ready for you to use.

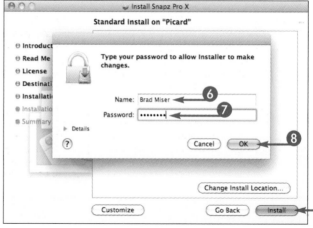

## Install Applications with Drag and Drop

1 Download the application from the Internet or get it from the CD or DVD it came on.

*Note: In most cases, the files are provided as a disk image, which usually mounts on MacBook automatically. If so, skip Step 2.*

2 Double-click the disk image file (its filename ends in .dmg).

The disk image is mounted on MacBook.

3 View the files in the disk image; typically, they are organized into a folder and explain what you need to do.

4 Open the **Go** menu and choose **Applications**.

A new Finder window appears, showing the Applications folder.

5 Drag the application folder from the disk image window onto the Applications window and release the trackpad.

The application is copied to and installed in the Applications folder, ready for you to use.

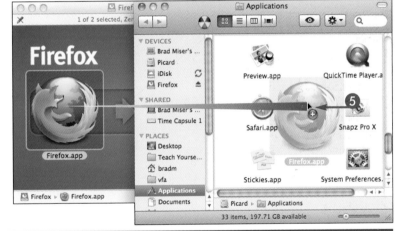

 TIPS

### What is the Customize button in the Install window for?

Most installer applications include a Customize button that enables you to customize the application's installation, such as to exclude features or resources you do not need. In most cases, you can ignore this and just perform a standard install. However, if your MacBook is very low on disk space, you might want to take a look at the customization options to see if you can skip features or resources you do not need.

### Where should I install an application?

In most cases, you should install it in the Applications folder on the MacBook startup drive. Most installer applications choose this folder by default, and the instructions with drag-and-drop installations tell you to install there. Keeping your applications in the Applications folder makes them easier for everyone who uses MacBook to find, as well as updaters and other programs that need to know the location of applications to run. You can install applications in other locations, but you need to make sure everyone who needs that application has the necessary permissions to get to the location in which you install it, such as within your Home folder.

# Launch and Control Applications

The first step in using an application is to open (also called launch) it. There are many ways to do this, and as you use MacBook, you will no doubt develop your preferred method. You can have multiple applications running at the same time, such as Mail, Safari, iTunes, and so on.

**Once applications are running, you can control them in a number of ways. For example, you open applications by opening documents they are associated with; you can move between the open applications to jump from one to the other.**

## Launch and Control Applications

### Open Applications from the Dock

① Click an application's icon on the Dock.

**Note:** *The first time you open an application you have downloaded from the Internet, you see a warning dialog. This is intended to prevent you from unintentionally opening applications that might harm your computer, such as viruses. Click **Allow** to open the application if you are sure it is legitimate.*

The application's icon bounces to show you it is opening, and it is marked with a light-blue dot to show that the application is running.

● When complete, the application's windows appear and it is ready for you to use.

**Note:** *You can also install applications on the sidebar by dragging their icons there. To open the application from the sidebar, click its icon.*

### Open Applications from the Desktop

① Open the **Go** menu and choose **Applications**.

The Applications folder appears in a Finder window.

② Scroll in the window until you see the application you want to open.

③ Double-click the application's icon, or click the icon once to select it, and press ⌘+O.

The application opens and is ready for you to use.

**Note:** *If an application is not installed on the Dock, its icon appears on the right or bottom side of the Dock when it is running. When you quit the application, its icon disappears from the Dock.*

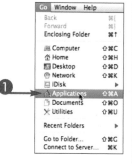

## Open Applications from Documents

① Find a document in a Finder window.

② Double-click the document's icon.

The application that the document is associated with opens, and you see the contents of the document.

*Note: Chapter 6 explains how to have applications open automatically when you log in to your user account.*

## Switch Applications

① Open applications as you need to use them; you do not need to close one application to open another one.

② Press ⌘ + Tab.

The Application Switcher appears. Here you see an icon for each currently running application.

● The application you are currently working with is highlighted in the white box.

③ Click the application you want to move into, or press Tab or Shift + Tab (while pressing and holding ⌘) until the application you want to use is highlighted, and release the trackpad.

The application you selected becomes active, and you can use it.

**TIPS**

**What does it mean when an application does not appear to be doing anything and I see a spinning wheel on the screen?**

Occasionally, an application hangs and stops working, even though its windows remain on the screen. Let some time pass to see if the application starts working again. If it does not, open the **Apple** menu (⬛) and choose **Force Quit**. The Force Quit window appears. Select the application having problems (its name will be in red) and click **Force Quit**. Click **Force Quit** again in the resulting dialog. The application is forced to quit. You lose any unsaved changes in the application's open documents, so only do this as a last resort. Restart MacBook after normally quitting all other applications.

**I have opened a lot of applications and do not want to quit all of them one by one. Is there a faster way?**

Yes. Log out of your user account by pressing Shift + ⌘ + Q and clicking the **Log Out** button. When you log out, all open applications are closed. The next time you log in, no applications are open (unless some are configured to automatically open when you log in).

# Save Documents

As you make changes to a document, you need to save those changes to keep them. This sounds simple, and it is, but many people do not regularly save their work. If an application quits before you save changes, you lose all the work you have done. So, get in the habit of saving documents frequently and often.

**When you save a document for the first time, you use the Save As command. This is important because you name the document and choose the location in which you save it.**

## Save Existing Documents

1. Open a document and work with it using its associated application.

2. Open the **File** menu and choose **Save**, or press ⌘+S.

**Note:** *The first time you save a document, you use the Save As command instead; see the next step section for details.*

The document is saved in its current state, and the new version replaces the previous version you saved.

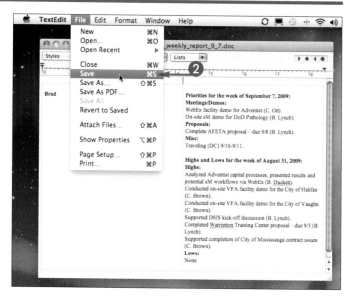

## Save New Documents

1. Open the application with which you want to create a new document.

2. Open the **File** menu and choose **New**. Some applications have the **New Document** command, where *Document* is the kind of document you want the application to create, such as a text document, presentation, or image.

● An empty document appears in a new window.

3. Open the **File** menu and choose **Save As**.

**Note:** *The first time you save a document, you can use the Save or Save As command because they do the same thing. When you want to rename a document or save a new version, you can use the Save As command.*

The Save As dialog appears.

**4** In the Save As field, enter a name for the file; you should leave the filename extension, which is everything after the period, as it is.

**5** Click the **Show Details** button (▾).

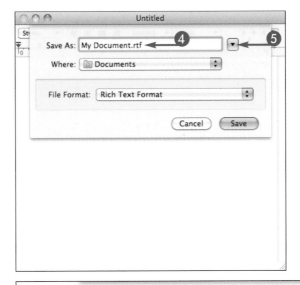

The dialog expands so that you see more details.

**6** Choose the location in which you want to save the file; this works just like a Finder window. For example, you can use the three view buttons above the sidebar to change the view.

*Note: You can choose save locations on the pop-up menu just under the Save As field.*

**7** Use the other controls, such as the **File Format** pop-up menu, to change how the file is created.

**8** Click **Save**.

The document's file is created in the location you set, and you are ready to get to work.

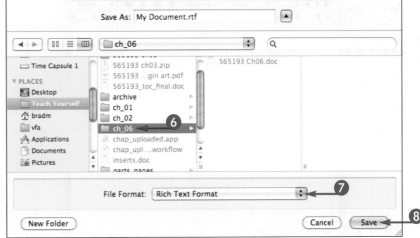

 **TIPS**

### Can my documents be saved automatically?

Many applications, such as Microsoft Word, have preference settings that you can configure to save your documents periodically — for example, every five minutes. Open the application's Preferences dialog and look for the save preferences. Set them to save frequently. The amount of time that passes without saving your document is the amount of time you have to spend redoing what you have already done if something bad happens, such as an application quitting unexpectedly.

### My hard drive crashed. Can I recover my saved document?

It depends on what kind of failure your disk had. In some cases, the documents and other data can be restored. In other cases, you are out of luck. You should always keep important documents backed up so you can recover them if needed. Chapter 17 discusses how to use the Mac OS X Time Machine feature to protect your documents.

# Remove Applications

If you no longer use an application, you can remove it from your MacBook. However, the storage space an application requires is the only downside of leaving it on your MacBook. If you need to free up storage space or you are sure you will never use an application again, you can remove it. Like installing applications, you can remove an application from MacBook in two ways: You can use an uninstaller application or drag-and-drop.

**If your computer has a lot of available space, you can just leave the application installed in case you ever need it again.**

### Remove Applications with an Uninstaller Application

1 If the application included an uninstaller application, locate it; you can usually find these in the application's folder.

2 Double-click the uninstaller.

The uninstaller application launches.

3 Read the information in the window and click **Continue**.

4 Continue following the on-screen instructions.

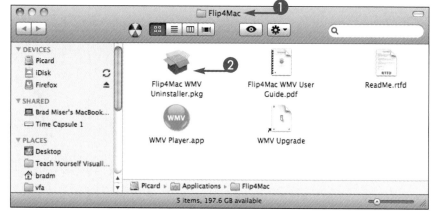

● When the uninstallation is complete, you see the completion screen.

**Note:** *This is sometimes confusing because it says the installation is complete, when it would be more precise to say the uninstallation is complete.*

5 Click **Close** or **Quit**.

The installation was completed successfully.

⊖ Introduction
⊖ Destination Select
⊖ Installation Type
⊖ Installation
⊖ Summary

**The installation was successful.**

The software was installed.

Go Back    Close

## Remove Applications with Drag-and-Drop

1 Click the desktop so you see the Finder menu bar.

2 Open the **Go** menu and choose **Applications**.

The Applications folder appears in a Finder window.

3 Scroll in the window until you see the application you want to remove.

4 Drag the icon to the Trash; when the Trash icon is highlighted, release the trackpad.

5 If prompted to do so, enter your name (if needed) and password, and then click **OK**.

The application is moved into the Trash. The next time you empty the Trash, the application is deleted from your MacBook.

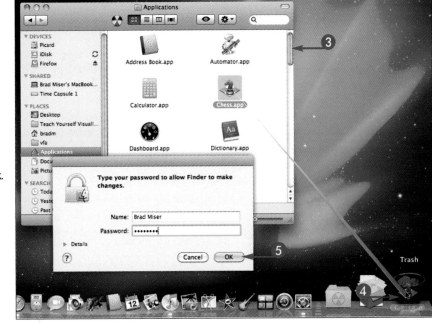

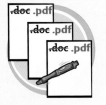

**TIPS**

**I want to keep an application that I do not use on my MacBook, but documents I open still open in that application. What can I do?**

You can stop MacBook from opening an application by changing the association between documents and that application. See the section "Get Information about Files and Folders" in Chapter 4 to learn how to use the Info window to change the application associated with documents.

**If I remove an application and then decide I need it again, what do I do?**

The answer depends on how you obtained the application. If you received it on CD or DVD, you can reinstall it from the original discs (you must also reapply any patches). If you downloaded the application from the Internet, you must have the original files you downloaded to reinstall it; sometimes these continue to be available at the developer's Web site, but sometimes they are not. You should always keep a backup of any software you download from the Internet in case you ever need to reinstall it.

# Set Finder Preferences

The Finder is the application that controls the MacBook desktop, how files and folders are managed, and many other aspects of the way MacBook operates. Like all the other applications you use, Finder has a set of preferences you can configure to change the way it looks and works.

**You change Finder preferences using its Preferences command. The resulting dialog has several tabs that you use to configure specific aspects of how the Finder looks and behaves.**

## Set Finder Preferences

① Open the **Finder** menu and choose **Preferences**.

The Finder Preferences window appears.

*Note: A faster way to open the preferences for most applications, including the Finder, is to press ⌘ + ,.*

② Click the **General** tab.

③ Check the **Hard disks, External disks, CDs, DVDs, and iPods**, or **Connected servers** check boxes if you want any of these to show up as icons on the desktop (they are always available on the sidebar within Finder windows).

④ Use the **New Finder windows open** pop-up menu to choose the default location for new Finder windows; choose your account's user name to always open your Home folder, choose **Documents** to open your Documents folder, choose a volume (such as iDisk) to go there, or choose **Other** and select a start location.

⑤ If you always want folders to open in a new window rather than inside the current one, check the **Always open folders in a new window** check box.

⑥ If you want folders to spring open when you drag icons onto them, check the **Spring-loaded folders and windows** check box, and drag the slider to the left to shorten the time before a folder springs open or to the right to increase the time.

⑦ Click the **Labels** tab.

*Note: You can associate files and folders with labels to help you identify and organize them more easily on the desktop. To do so, perform a secondary click on a file's or folder's icon and select the color of the label you want to apply.*

⑧ Enter a name for each label in the field next to its color.

*Note: When you apply a label to a file or folder, both the color and name are used, but you do not always see both on the desktop.*

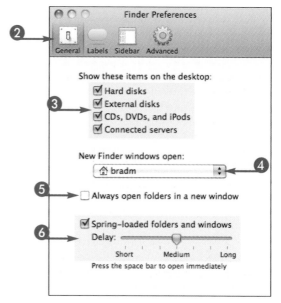

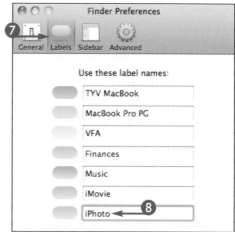

**9** Click the **Sidebar** tab.

**10** Check the box next to each item you want to appear in the sidebar, or uncheck the box next to each item you do not want to appear in the sidebar.

**Note:** When you uncheck an item's check box, it is still available in Finder windows; you just do not see its icon on the sidebar.

**11** Click the **Advanced** tab.

**12** If you always want filename extensions to be shown, check the **Show all filename extensions** check box.

**13** To be warned when you change a filename extension, check the **Show warning before changing an extension** check box.

**Note:** Checking both boxes in Steps **12** and **13** is recommended because being aware of filename extensions is important to understanding the kind of application you use for each file.

**14** If you want to have to confirm emptying the Trash, check the **Show warning before emptying the Trash** check box.

**15** If you want the Trash to be emptied securely, making things you delete harder to recover, check the **Empty Trash securely** check box.

**16** Choose the default search scope on the **When performing a search** pop-up menu; choose **Search This Mac** to search MacBook, **Search the Current Folder** to search the active folder, or **Use the Previous Search Scope** to repeat your last search.

**Note:** You can change the scope of any search regardless of the default scope setting.

**17** Click the **Close** button (⊗).

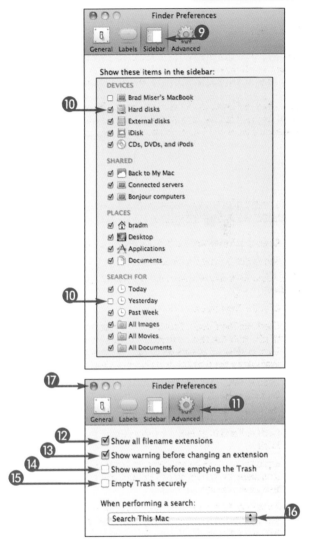

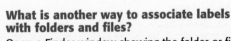

**TIPS**

**Which folders can I use as my start folder for new Finder windows?**

The initial location is your Home folder, but you can choose any folder you want. For example, if you keep all of your active projects in a folder, you might want that folder to open by default instead. On the **New Finder windows open** pop-up menu, choose **Other**. In the resulting dialog, navigate to and select the folder you want to be the default, and then click **Choose**. Each time you open a new Finder window, you move to that folder automatically.

**What is another way to associate labels with folders and files?**

Open a Finder window showing the folder or file you want to label. Press ⌘ + ⓘ. The Info window opens. Expand the General section. Click the label color that you want to apply. The file or folder is marked with that color. You can search for files and folders by their labels; for example, you can create and save a search that automatically finds all folders and files with a specific label. You can also more easily see which files and folders are related because of the label color visible in Finder windows.

# Explore the System Preferences Application

The System Preferences application is used to configure many different aspects of how MacBook looks and works. In fact, most of the personalization you do is through this application.

**System Preferences is one application organized in many different panes, with each pane used to configure a specific aspect of MacBook. You open the pane you want to use to configure a specific area. For example, you use the Dock pane to configure the Dock, and the Network pane to connect MacBook to a network.**

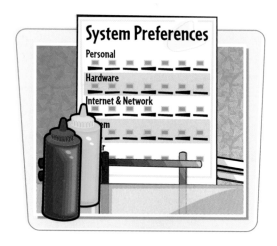

Explore the System Preferences Application

**Open and Use System Preferences**

① Open the **Apple** menu (  ) and choose **System Preferences**.

The System Preferences application opens and you see all of the panes it offers.

② Click an icon.

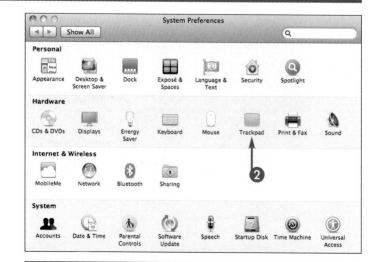

The pane associated with that icon appears.

③ Use the controls on the pane to make changes to the way MacBook works.

④ When you are done with the pane, click **Show All**.

The open pane closes and you see all the icons again.

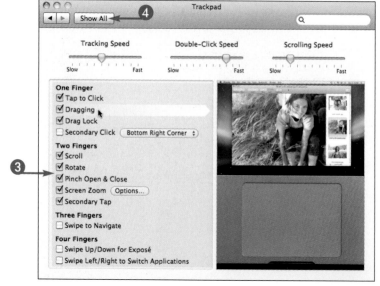

## Show Panes Alphabetically

1 From the **View** menu, choose **Organize Alphabetically**.

● The panes are organized alphabetically instead of by category.

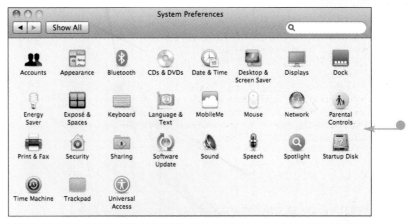

## Search for a Pane

1 To search for a pane, type text in the Search field.

● As you type, panes that meet your search criteria are highlighted.

2 Click the icon you want to use.

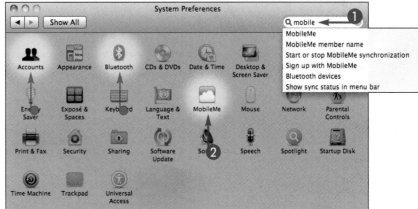

TIPS

**I cannot make some changes in the System Preferences application, but I can make others. Why?**

In order to make changes to various, but not all, settings using the System Preferences application, you must be logged in under an administrator user account or verify that you are an administrator. The easiest way to tell is to look at the Lock icon located in the lower-left corner of a pane. If you do not see the Lock icon, any user can change the pane. If the Lock is "locked," click it to verify that you are an administrator by entering your user name and password. If the Lock is "unlocked," you are verified as an administrator and can make changes.

**Why do I see a section called Other in my System Preferences application?**

Some software you install, especially when it is associated with a hardware device, includes a pane installed on the System Preferences application that you use to configure that software or hardware. All of these additions to the default panes are placed in the Other category.

# Change the Desktop's Appearance

Using the Appearance pane, you can configure the color of buttons, menus, and windows along with the color used when something is highlighted to show that it is selected. You can also configure how scrolling in Finder windows works.

**While not directly related to appearance, you also use the Appearance pane to determine how many items are stored on Recent menus. You can also control how font smoothing works.** *Font smoothing* **makes the edges of large letters and numbers look smoother on the screen – they sometimes can look pixilated or "jaggy."**

June Report

## Change the Desktop's Appearance

### Choose Finder Colors

1 Open the System Preferences application and choose the **Appearance** pane.

2 On the **Appearance** pop-up menu, choose **Blue** to see the default button, menu, and window colors.

*Note: For a more subdued color for these items, choose Graphite.*

3 On the **Highlight color** pop-up menu, choose the color you want to be used to show when a file or folder is selected on the desktop.

4 To create your own highlight color, choose **Other** on the **Highlight color** pop-up menu.

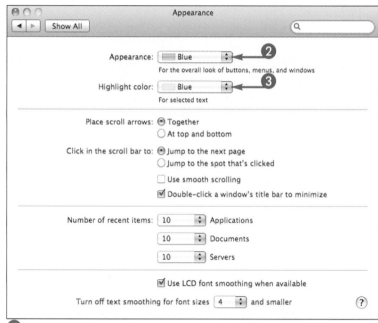

The Color Picker appears.

5 Click the type of color picker you want to use, such as the **Crayon**.

The controls for the color picker you selected fill the window.

6 Use the controls to configure the color you want to use.

7 Click 🔘.

The color you configured is shown on the Highlight Color menu and is used to highlight items on the desktop.

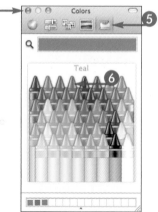

## Configure Scroll Tools

1️⃣ Open the System Preferences application and choose the **Appearance** pane.

2️⃣ Click the **At top and bottom** radio button if you want scroll arrows to be at the corners of windows; click **Together** if you want them placed together in the lower-right corner of windows.

3️⃣ Click **Jump to the next page** if you want to move to the next or previous page when you click above or below the scroll box; click **Jump to the spot that's clicked** if you want to move to a location on the window relative to where you click.

4️⃣ If you want scrolling to be smoother when you use a mouse, check the **Use smooth scrolling** check box.

5️⃣ If you do not want to be able to minimize a window by double-clicking its title bar, uncheck the **Double-click a window's title bar to minimize** check box.

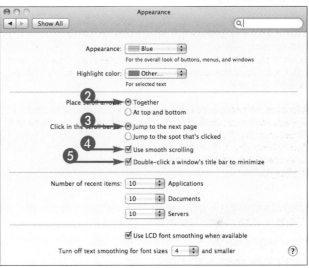

## Set Recent Items and Font Smoothing

1️⃣ Open the System Preferences application and choose the **Appearance** pane.

2️⃣ On the **Number of recent items** pop-up menus, choose the number of items you want to be shown on each of the Recent menus.

*Note: Most applications also have a Recent list; the System Preferences application setting impacts only the Apple menu's Recent Items list.*

3️⃣ To apply font smoothing, check the **Use LCD font smoothing when available** check box.

4️⃣ To determine the point size at which font smoothing is turned off, use the **Turn off text smoothing for font sizes** pop-up menu.

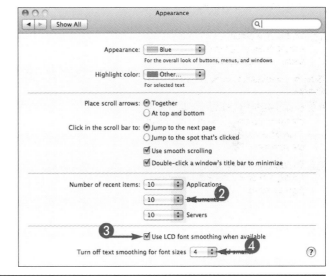

### Which Color Picker is the best?

The Color Picker has different pickers that change the way you choose colors. The easiest to use is the Crayon picker because you simply choose colors by clicking a crayon. The other pickers offer more control and specificity. For example, you can use the Color Wheel picker to select any color in the spectrum by dragging the intensity bar up or down and then clicking in the wheel to choose a specific color. Other pickers offer different tools. To add a custom color to a mode's palette, drag it from the sample box at the top of the window to the palette at the bottom; you can choose your custom color again by clicking it on the palette.

# Set a Desktop Picture

As you use MacBook, you look at the desktop quite often. So why not look at something you want to see? That is where setting the desktop picture comes in; the desktop picture fills the background on the desktop and you see it behind any open windows.

**Although it is called a desktop picture, you are not limited to pictures. You can use just about any kind of graphic file as a desktop picture.**

## Set a Desktop Picture

### Set a Default Image as the Desktop Picture

1 Open the System Preferences application and choose the **Desktop & Screen Saver** pane.

2 Click the **Desktop** tab.

The Desktop picture tools appear.

3 Choose a source of images in the left pane of the window, such as the **Nature** folder in the **Apple Images** collection.

*Note: To see the contents of any collection or folder, click the triangle located to the left of the item's name. To collapse the item, click the triangle again.*

● The images in that source appear in the right pane of the window.

4 Click the image that you want to apply to the desktop.

That image fills the desktop.

5 To have the image changed automatically, check the **Change picture** check box.

6 On the pop-up menu, choose how often you want the picture to change.

7 If you want images to be selected randomly instead of by the order in which they appear in the source, check the **Random order** check box.

A new image from the selected source is applied to the desktop according to the timing you selected.

8 If you want the menu bar to be solid so that you cannot see the background through it, uncheck the **Translucent menu bar** check box.

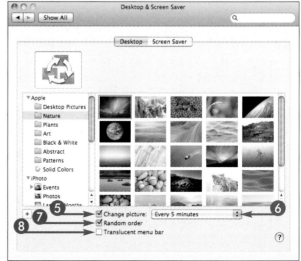

## Set a Photo from Your iPhoto Library as the Desktop Picture

1. Open the System Preferences application and choose the **Desktop & Screen Saver** pane.

2. Click the **Desktop** tab.

3. Scroll down the source list until you see the iPhoto collection; expand it and the sources it contains, such as **Events**.

4. Click the source of photos, such as an event, containing the images you want to use on the desktop.

● The images in the selected source appear in the right pane of the window.

5. Use the pop-up menu at the top of the window to choose how you want photos to be scaled to the screen; this example chooses the **Fit to Screen** option.

6. Click the **Color** button and use the Color Picker to choose the background color shown behind photos when they do not fill the desktop.

7. To have the image changed automatically, check the **Change picture** check box.

8. On the pop-up menu, choose how often you want the picture to change.

9. If you want images to be selected randomly instead of by the order in which they appear in the source, check the **Random order** check box.

● A new image from the iPhoto source is applied to the desktop according to the timing you selected.

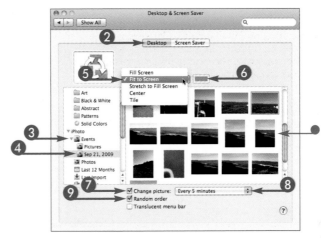

TIPS

### What is the Pictures folder source?

By default, a number of applications store image files in the Pictures folder within your Home folder. If you choose this folder in the source list, you see all the images it contains; you can select images from this source just as you do from one of the other sources.

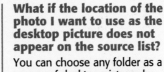

### What if the location of the photo I want to use as the desktop picture does not appear on the source list?

You can choose any folder as a source of desktop pictures by clicking the **Add** button (⊞) located at the bottom of the source list. Use the resulting dialog to navigate to and select the folder containing the images you want. After you click the **Choose** button, that folder appears as a source in the list.

# Choose a
# Screen Saver

With some types of displays, a screen saver prevents possible damage to the screen from having the same image on it for a long period of time; you do not have to worry about this with MacBook's display, but this can be an issue with some external displays. Probably more important, a screen saver entertains you by displaying images that you choose on the screen. The most functional aspect of a screen saver is that you can require a password to be entered to stop the screen saver, which is a good security measure.

**When you are running on battery power, it is better to put MacBook to sleep when you are using it instead of showing the screen saver, which uses more power than sleep. The screen saver is more useful when you are running on the power adapter. For more about sleep, see the section "Save Energy."**

## Choose a Screen Saver

### Choose an Apple Screen Saver

① Open the System Preferences application and choose the **Desktop & Screen Saver** pane.

② Click the **Screen Saver** tab.

③ Click the screen saver you want to use from the list in the Apple section in the left part of the window.

● You see the selected screen saver run in the right pane of the window.

④ Drag the slider to set the amount of idle time that passes before the screen saver activates.

⑤ If you want a screen saver to be selected at random, check the **Use random screen saver** check box.

⑥ If you want the time displayed on the screen saver, click the **Show with clock** check box.

⑦ Click the **Options** button.

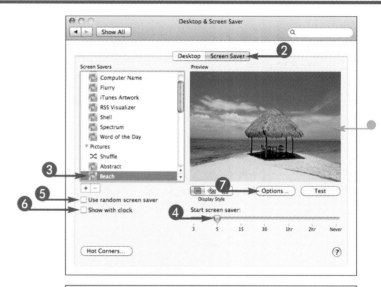

The Options sheet appears.

⑧ Use the tools on the Options sheet to configure the screen saver.

*Note: Each screen saver has its own set of options, and so what you see on the Options sheet depends on the screen saver you select.*

⑨ Click **OK**.

The Options sheet closes.

⑩ Click **Test**.

You see the screen saver in action.

⑪ Press a key or drag on the trackpad to stop the screen saver and go back to the System Preferences application.

## Create Your Own Screen Saver

1 Open the System Preferences application and choose the **Desktop & Screen Saver** pane.

2 Click the **Screen Saver** tab.

3 Scroll down until you see the options in the Pictures section, which include your photos, such as those stored in iPhoto.

4 Click the source of images you want to use in the screen saver, such as an event.

5 If you want the photos to appear as a collage, click the **Collage** button (⊞).

6 If you want the images displayed in a mosaic, click the **Mosaic** button (⊞).

● You see the selected images in the screen saver run in the right pane of the window.

7 Drag the slider to set the amount of idle time that passes before the screen saver activates.

8 If you want the time displayed on the screen saver, click the **Show with clock** check box.

9 Click the **Options** button.

The Options sheet appears.

10 Use the tools on the Options sheet to configure the screen saver.

*Note: Each type of screen saver has its own set of options that appear in the Options menu.*

11 Click **OK**.

12 Click **Test**.

You see the screen saver in action.

13 Press a key or drag on the trackpad to stop the screen saver and go back to the System Preferences application.

## TIPS

**Why do I never see my screen saver?**
The screen saver interacts with the settings on the Energy Saver pane, one of which is the amount of time that passes before the screen darkens to save energy (which also happens to be the best way to save the screen). If that time is less than the screen saver is set for, then you do not see the screen saver before the screen goes dark; you see a warning telling you the screen saver will not activate before the screen goes dark below the time slider on the Screen Saver pane. Reduce the time for the screen saver to be less than the time for the display to be darkened.

**How can I manually activate the screen saver?**
You can set a hot corner so that when you position the mouse pointer in that corner, the screen saver activates. Click the **Hot Corners** button and then choose **Start Screen Saver** on the menu for the corner you want to be hot. When you move the pointer to that corner, the screen saver starts.

# Set and Configure the MacBook Clock

MacBook can help you by keeping track of the time and date. Obviously, you can use MacBook to see what time it is, but time and date are also important because MacBook stamps all the files and folders you use with the time and date they were created and when they were changed. Likewise, e-mails are also time- and date-stamped. The time and date applied to these items are those configured on MacBook.

**There are two basic ways to set MacBook's time and date: automatically using a timeserver, or manually. Having MacBook set its clock automatically is a good idea so that you can be sure the current time and date are as accurate as possible.**

## Set and Configure the MacBook Clock

### Configure MacBook to Set Its Clock Automatically

1 Open the System Preferences application and click the **Date & Time** icon.

2 Click the **Date & Time** tab.

3 Check the **Set date and time automatically** check box.

4 On the pop-up menu, choose the time server you want to use.

If you live in the U.S., choose **Apple Americas/U.S.**

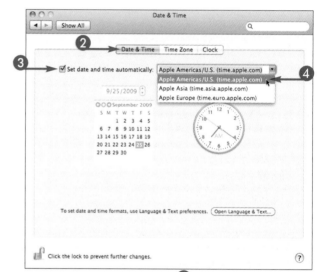

5 Click the **Time Zone** tab.

6 Click the time zone you want to set.

● The time zone you select is indicated by the light band on the map and is next to the Time Zone text.

7 Open the **Closest City** pop-up menu and choose the city closest to your location.

When MacBook is connected to the Internet, it sets the time and date automatically.

**Note:** *If you are connected to an AirPort network, you can check the Set time zone automatically using current location check box to have MacBook set your time zone automatically. This does not always work, but it is easy to try.*

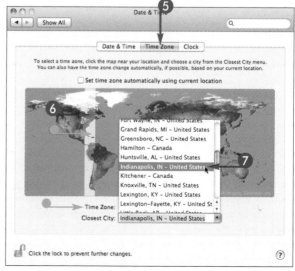

## Configure the MacBook Clock

① Open the System Preferences application and click the **Date & Time** icon.

② Click the **Clock** tab.

③ If you want to see the clock on the menu bar, check the **Show date and time in menu bar** check box.

④ To see the time in the digital format, click **Digital**; to see it in analog format, click **Analog**.

⑤ If you want to see seconds in the time display, check the **Display the time with seconds** check box.

⑥ To flash the colon between the hour and minutes at each second, check the **Flash the time separators** check box.

⑦ To use the 24-hour format, check the **Use a 24-hour clock** check box.

⑧ To show the AM/PM indicator, check the **Show AM/PM** check box.

*Note: This is disabled if you use the 24-hour clock.*

⑨ To show the day of the week, check the **Show the day of the week** check box.

⑩ To include the date, check the **Show date** check box.

⑪ To hear an announcement of the time, check the **Announce the time** check box.

⑫ Use the pop-up menu to choose how often the time should be announced, such as **On the hour**.

⑬ Click **Customize Voice** and use the resulting sheet to select and configure the voice you want MacBook to use to announce the time.

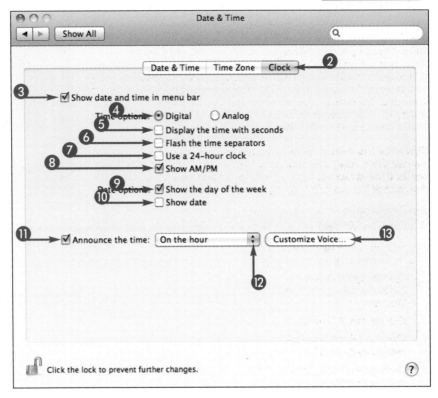

 **TIPS**

### What if I take MacBook to a different time zone?

You can leave MacBook in its previous time zone no matter where you are located. Of course, when you are in a different time zone than the one configured on MacBook, its time will not match the local time. If that bothers you, you can always change the current time zone using the previous steps.

### What if the time and date are not in the right format?

Open the **Language & Text** pane of the System Preferences application. Click the **Formats** tab. Choose the region whose time and date format you want to use, or click the **Customize** button for the format you want to change to customize it.

# Save Energy

When you first think of saving energy, you might think of lowering your electric bill or reducing the need for electricity. However, MacBook uses so little energy that it is unlikely that you can make any difference in either of these areas by changing how MacBook uses energy.

**However, when you are running MacBook on battery power, saving energy is very important because the rate at which MacBook consumes battery power determines how long you can work.**

## Save Energy

1 Open the System Preferences application and choose the **Energy Saver** pane.

2 Click the **Battery** tab.

3 Drag the upper slider to set the idle time after which MacBook goes to sleep.

4 Drag the lower slider to set the amount of inactive time after which the display sleeps.

**Note:** *The display is a major user of power. You should set it to sleep after a couple of minutes of inactivity to conserve battery power.*

5 To have the internal hard drive or external hard drives connected to MacBook go to sleep when they are not being used, check the **Put the hard disk(s) to sleep when possible** check box.

6 If you want the display to dim slightly while running on battery power, check the **Slightly dim the display when using this power source** check box.

7 If you want the screen to be dimmed before it sleeps, check the **Automatically reduce brightness before display goes to sleep** check box.

**Note:** *This gives you some warning before the display goes completely dark.*

8 If you want to see the battery icon (■) in the menu bar, check the **Show battery status in the menu bar** check box.

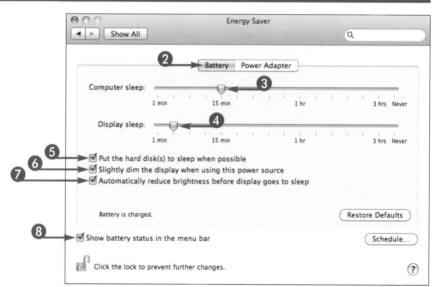

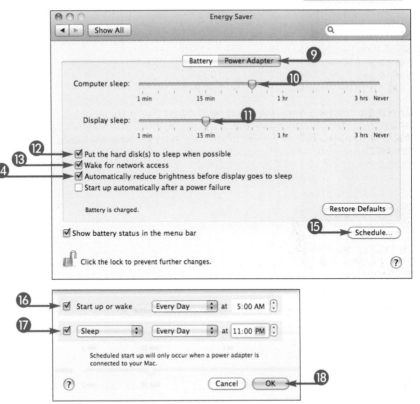

⑨ Click the **Power Adapter** tab.

⑩ Drag the upper slider to set the idle time after which MacBook goes to sleep.

⑪ Drag the lower slider to set the amount of inactive time after which the display sleeps.

**Note:** *When operating on the power adapter, you usually want the idle times set to a longer period of time to avoid interruptions.*

⑫ To have the internal hard drive or external hard drives connected to MacBook go to sleep when they are not being used, check the **Put the hard disk(s) to sleep when possible** check box.

⑬ To enable devices connected to MacBook through the network to be able to wake it up, check the **Wake for network access** check box.

**Note:** *If you do not check this check box, services MacBook provides to other devices are unavailable when it is asleep.*

⑭ If you want the screen to be dimmed before it sleeps, check the **Automatically reduce brightness before display goes to sleep** check box.

**Note:** *The Start up automatically setting is not really needed for a MacBook because it has a battery.*

⑮ Click **Schedule**.

⑯ Use the **Start up or wake** controls to have MacBook automatically start up or wake up at a specific time.

⑰ Use the lower controls to have MacBook automatically sleep, restart, or shut down at a specific time.

⑱ Click **OK**.

⑲ To return MacBook to what Apple considers optimum power settings, click **Restore Defaults**.

 **TIPS**

**Do I need to tell MacBook which power settings to use?**

MacBook detects whether it is running on battery power or is connected to the power adapter and uses the energy saver settings for that power source automatically.

**In addition to configuring the Energy Saver, how can I make my battery last longer?**

The most important way is to put MacBook to sleep whenever you are not using it; you can close its lid or choose **Sleep** on the **Apple** menu (🍎). Because the display is a major power drain, lower its brightness by pressing [F1] until the screen is as dim as possible while you can still see it comfortably. Turn off transmitting or receiving functions that you are not using (such as AirPort or Bluetooth).

# Configure the MacBook Display

MacBook's display is what you look at while you use it, and so it is important to know how to configure the screen so it matches your viewing preferences. You can configure the display's resolution, brightness, and color profile.

**Although the physical size of MacBook's display is fixed, the amount of information that it can show (its resolution) is not. That is because each pixel (short for *picture element*) that makes up the display's images can be larger or smaller. When pixels are larger, what is on the screen is shown on a larger, zoomed-in scale. When pixels are smaller, more content is shown on the screen, but on a smaller, zoomed-out scale.**

## Configure the MacBook Display

### Configure the MacBook Screen on the Displays Pane

1. Open the System Preferences application and click the **Displays** icon.

2. Click the **Display** tab.

3. Click a resolution.

● MacBook's screen updates to use that resolution. The current resolution is highlighted on the list.

*Note: Notice how much less screen space the Displays pane takes on this figure. This is because the display is set to a higher resolution.*

4. Experiment with resolution settings until you choose the highest resolution that is still comfortable for you to see.

**5** Drag the **Brightness** slider to the right to make the screen brighter, or to the left to make it dimmer.

*Note:* *If you are running on battery power, you can keep the screen dimmer to lower the amount of power you use, which extends the time you can work.*

**6** To add a Displays menu to the menu bar, check the **Show displays in menu bar** check box.

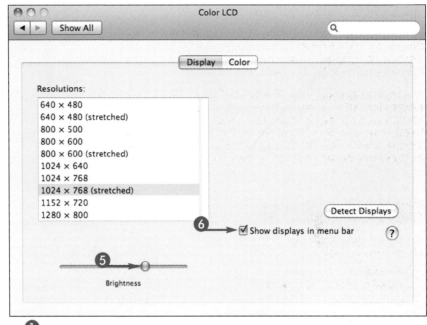

### Configure the MacBook Screen on the Displays Menu

**1** Open the **Displays** menu (▣).

**2** To change the resolution, select the resolution you want to use on the list of recent resolutions.

**3** To set the number of recent resolutions on the menu, choose *number* under **Number of Recent Items**, where *number* is the number of resolutions you want to see on the menu.

**4** Choose **Displays Preferences** to open the Displays pane of the System Preferences application.

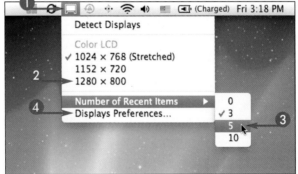

TIPS

### How else can I set screen brightness?

MacBook includes two keys that you can use to change the screen's brightness. Press F1 to lower the brightness or F2 to increase it. These do the same thing as the Brightness slider on the Displays pane. Each time you press one of the keys, an indicator appears on the screen to show you the relative brightness level you have set.

### What do the other controls on the Display tab do?

The Detect Displays button (and command on the Displays menu) is used when you connect MacBook to an external display or projector (see Chapter 9). The Color tab is used to configure a color profile for the display. You will not likely need to do this unless you are doing very precise color printing work, in which case you can configure a screen profile to match your printer output.

# Control MacBook Sound

From sound effects to music and movies, sound is an important part of the MacBook experience. Additionally, you may want to use sound input for audio and video chats, recording narration for movies, and so on.

**The Sound pane of the System Preferences application is your primary stop for managing audio settings on your MacBook.**

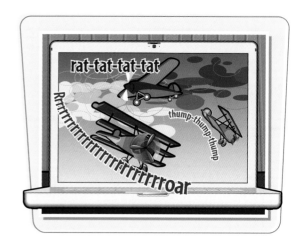

## Control MacBook Sound

### Configure Sound Effects

1. Open the System Preferences application and click the **Sound** icon.
2. Click the **Sound Effects** tab.
3. Click a sound on the alert sound list.

   The sound plays.
4. Drag the **Alert volume** slider to make the alert sound louder or quieter.
5. To hear sound effects for system actions, such as when you empty the Trash, check the **Play user interface sound effects** check box.
6. If you want audio feedback when you change the volume level, check the **Play feedback when volume is changed** check box.
7. If you want to hear Front Row's sound effects, check the **Play Front Row sound effects** check box.

**Note:** When you activate Front Row with its sound effects enabled, you hear sounds for various actions, such as selecting a choice from the on-screen menu.

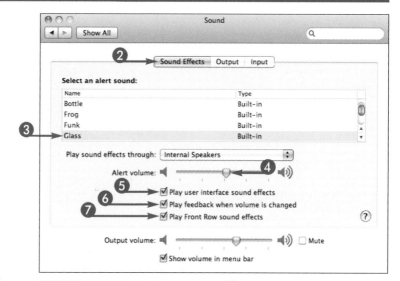

### Configure Sound Out

1. Open the System Preferences application and click the **Sound** icon.
2. Click the **Output** tab.
3. Select the output device over which you want MacBook to play sound.

**Note:** If you do not have any external speakers connected to MacBook, you have only one choice: Internal Speakers. See Chapter 9 for information about connecting MacBook to speakers.

4. Drag the **Balance** slider to set the balance between the left and right speakers.

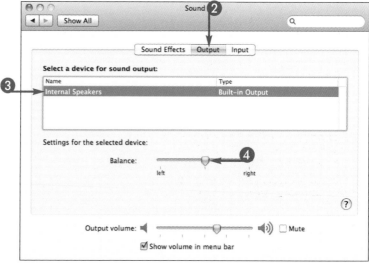

## Control System Volume

1 Open the System Preferences application and click the **Sound** icon.

2 Drag the **Output volume** slider to the right to increase the volume or to the left to decrease it.

3 To mute all sounds, check the **Mute** check box.

4 To configure the Volume menu on the menu bar, check the **Show volume in menu bar** check box.

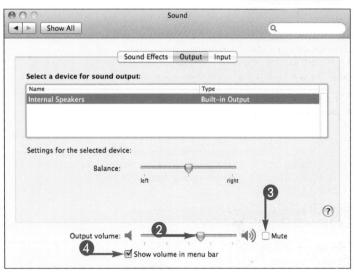

5 To set the volume using the menu, open it and drag the slider up to increase volume or down to decrease it.

## Configure Sound Input

1 Open the System Preferences application and click the **Sound** icon.

2 Click the **Input** tab.

3 Select the input device you want to use; for MacBook's internal microphone, choose **Internal microphone**.

4 Play the sound you want to input; if you are recording yourself or preparing for an audio chat, begin speaking.

● As MacBook receives input, the relative volume of the input is shown on the Input level gauge.

5 Drag the **Input volume** slider to the left to reduce the level of input sound or to the right to increase it.

6 Keep trying levels until the gauge looks about right; in most cases, the slider should be about three-fourths of the length of the bar.

7 If the area you are in is noisy, check the **Use ambient noise reduction** check box.

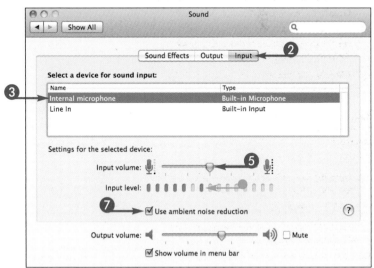

# Create and Configure User Accounts

Mac OS X is a multi-user system. What this means is that you can create user accounts for each person who uses MacBook. Each person who uses it then has a unique desktop, folders, files, and preferences so that MacBook is tailored specifically to her.

**A Standard user account can access all the MacBook's resources, but it cannot perform administrator tasks, such as installing applications; you should use the Standard type for most users. An Administrator account allows access to the administration tasks, many of which are discussed in this chapter. (Other account types are explained in the tips at the end of this section.)**

---

## Create and Configure User Accounts

### Create a User Account

**①** Open the System Preferences application and click the **Accounts** icon.

● The Accounts pane appears. In the accounts list on the left side of the window, you see the accounts that currently exist.

**Note:** *To be able to make changes, you need to click the Lock icon (🔒) at the bottom of the pane, enter an administrator user name and password, and click OK. The Lock icon becomes unlocked, indicating you can make changes.*

**②** Click the **Add** button (➕).

The New Account sheet appears.

**③** Choose the type of account on the **New Account** pop-up menu.

**Note:** *See the tip on the next page to learn about account types.*

**④** Enter a name for the account in the Full Name field. This can be just about anything you want, but it is usually the person's name.

Mac OS X creates a shortened account name based on what you enter.

**⑤** Edit the account name as needed.

**Note:** *The account name is important because it appears in a number of places, such as the URL to that user's Web site on MacBook.*

**⑥** If you manually create a password for the user, do so and then skip to Step **11**. Otherwise, go to Step **7**.

**⑦** Alternatively, if you want help create a password, click the **Key** icon (🔑).

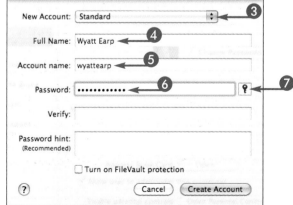

The Password Assistant appears.

**8** Choose a password type from the **Type** pop-up menu.

● Mac OS X generates a password for you. If there are tips related to the type you selected, you see them in the Tips box.

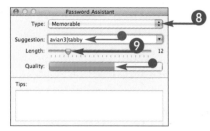

**9** Drag the **Length** slider to the right to increase, or to the left to decrease, the length of the password.

● As you make changes, the Quality gauge shows you how secure the password is. Green indicates a secure password, yellow is less secure, and red is not secure.

**10** When you are happy with the password, click back in the New Account sheet while leaving the Password Assistant window open.

**11** Re-enter the password in the Verify field.

*Note: If you did not keep the Password Assistant open, you need to remember the password you configured to be able to type it in.*

**12** If you want users to be able to access a hint when they cannot remember their password, type the hint in the Password Hint field.

**13** If you want the user's data to be protected with FileVault, check the **Turn on FileVault protection** check box.

*Note: See "Protect MacBook's Data with FileVault" in Chapter 8 for more information on FileVault.*

**14** Click **Create Account**.

● The user account is created and appears on the list of accounts.

**15** To associate an image with the user account, click the image well.

**TIPS**

### Why can I not make changes on the Accounts pane?

You have to be authenticated as an administrator to be able to create or change other user accounts. You can tell if you are verified by the Lock icon located in the lower left corner of the pane. If the Lock is closed, you cannot make changes to other accounts on the Accounts pane. To authenticate yourself, click the Lock icon, enter an administrator user name and password, and click **OK**. The Lock icon opens and you can make changes.

### What types of user accounts are available?

There are six types of user accounts. An Administrator user account has access to all Mac OS X tools and can perform just about any action. A Standard user account can only make changes related to that account. A Managed with Parental Controls account enables you to limit the access a user has to various kinds of content. A Sharing Only account can be used only to access shared files. A Group account is used for configuring access permissions to files and folders. A Root account has unlimited access to all functions and is used primarily during troubleshooting.

continued

# Create and Configure
# User Accounts *(continued)*

As you create new user accounts, be careful about the kind of account you provide to other people. In most cases, you will want to give other people a Standard or Managed with Parental Controls user account so that those people have limited access to MacBook's administrative functions.

**You should have at least two user accounts. One should be an Administrator account (which is the type created when you first started up MacBook) that you use regularly. The other should be an Administrator account that you create but do not use so that it remains in the default state. You use this second account during troubleshooting.**

## Create and Configure User Accounts *(continued)*

16 To use one of the default images, choose an icon from the pop-up menu and skip to Step **23**.

17 Alternatively, choose **Edit Picture**.

The Edit Picture sheet appears.

18 Drag an image file from the desktop onto the image well.

*Note: You can select an image from any location by clicking the **Choose** button, moving to the image you want to use, and clicking **Open**.*

● To use a photo as a user account's icon, click the **Camera** icon (⌗) and place the subject in front of MacBook's iSight camera.

After about three seconds, the image is captured.

19 Drag the **Size** slider to the right to zoom in on the image of the user's icon, or to the left to zoom out.

20 Drag the image within the selection box until the part of the image you want to use is enclosed in the box.

21 Click **Set**.

The image is associated with the user account.

22 If the user has a MobileMe account, enter the member name in the MobileMe User Name field.

23 If you want the user to be able to administer MacBook, check the **Allow user to administer this computer** check box.

24 Give the user name and password you created to the person whom you want to be able to use MacBook.

**Configure Login Items for a User Account**

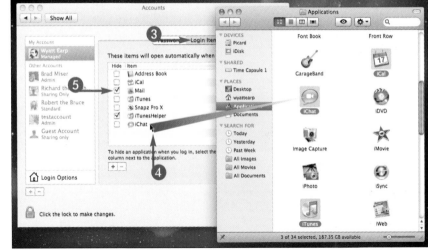

1 Log in under the user's account (you have to be logged into an account to set Login Items for it).

2 Open the System Preferences application and click the **Accounts** icon to open the Accounts pane.

3 Click the **Login Items** tab.

4 Drag the items that should open automatically from the desktop onto the pane; you can drag applications, documents, or folders onto the list.

5 Check the **Hide** check box for any items you want to be hidden by default.

6 Log out of the user's account.

The next time the user logs in, the items you configured open automatically.

 **TIPS**

**Do I have to configure a password for a user account?**

A user account does not have to have a password. If you leave the Password and Verify fields empty, you see a warning that not providing a password is not secure. If you are sure that is not a problem for you, clear the warning prompt and complete the user creation. The user is able to log in to the MacBook without entering a password, which can mean that anyone who has access to the MacBook can use it.

**What if a user forgets his or her password?**

Open the Accounts pane, select the user's account on the list, and click **Reset Password**. Use the resulting sheet to configure a new password just as you do when you create an account. The user is then able to log in with the new password.

# Protect Users with Parental Controls

The phrase *parental controls* is a bit misleading. Although these can certainly be used to protect children from interactions on the Internet that might not be good for them, you can use the same tools to tailor any user's access to MacBook and the Internet.

**You can also use Parental Controls to limit access to applications and system functions.**

## Protect Users with Parental Controls

① Open the System Preferences application and click the **Parental Controls** icon.

② Select the user account for which you want to configure Parental Controls.

*Note: Parental Controls can only be applied to Standard or Managed with Parental Controls user accounts.*

③ Click **Enable Parental Controls**.

The Parental Controls tabs appear.

④ Click the **System** tab.

⑤ To limit the access of the user to specific applications, check the **Only allow selected applications** check box.

⑥ Uncheck the check box for the groups or individual applications you do not want the user to be able to use.

⑦ Use the check boxes at the bottom of the pane to allow or prevent access to system actions.

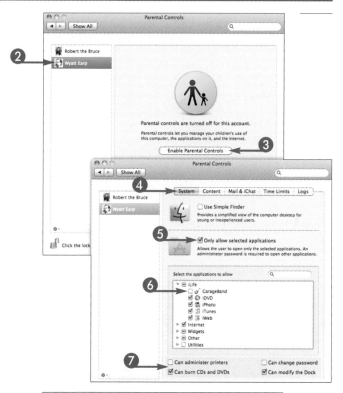

⑧ Click the **Content** tab.

⑨ To prevent profanity from appearing in the Mac OS X dictionary, check the **Hide profanity in Dictionary** check box.

⑩ To attempt to prevent access to adult Web sites automatically, click **Try to limit access to adult websites automatically**.

*Note: Click the Customize button to open the Customize sheet on which you can allow or prevent specific Web sites.*

⑪ To limit access to only specific Web sites, click **Allow access to only these websites**, click the **Add** button (➕), and enter the URLs of the Web sites you want to allow (all other sites are blocked).

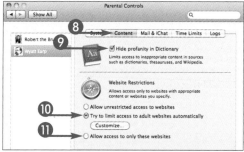

⑫ Click the **Mail & iChat** tab.

⑬ To limit e-mail, check the **Limit Mail** check box.

⑭ To limit chats, check the **Limit iChat** check box.

*Note: The e-mail and chat controls work only with Mail and iChat.*

⑮ Click **Add** (⊞).

The Parental Controls sheet appears.

⑯ Configure the Parental Controls sheet for the person with whom you want to allow e-mail or chat interaction.

⑰ Click **Add**.

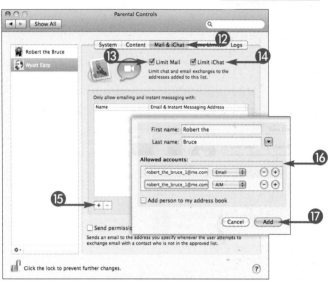

● The person is added to the allowed list.

⑱ Repeat Steps **14** to **16** for each person with whom you want to allow interaction.

⑲ If you want to receive an e-mail requiring you to grant permission when someone not on the list is involved in an e-mail exchange with the user, check the **Send permission requests to** check box and enter your e-mail address.

TIPS

### What is the Time Limits tab for?

You can use the Time Limits tab to limit the amount of time the user can use MacBook. You can configure time on weekdays and weekends. You can also configure "bedtimes" during which the user is unable to access MacBook.

### What is the Logs tab for?

On the Logs tab, you can view the user's activities, such as Web sites visited, Web sites blocked, and applications used.

# Set Login Options

There are a number of ways you can configure the login process for MacBook. In the Login window, you can present a list of users so that to log in, a user clicks his user name and enters a password. Or, you can present an empty user name and password field and the user has to complete both to log in. There are also a number of other ways to configure the Login window by showing or hiding specific buttons. You can also disable or enable Automatic Login.

**Fast user switching is another option, which allows multiple people to be logged into MacBook at the same time. Each user can quickly move back into his account because it is left open instead of each user logging out before another logs in.**

## Set Login Options

### Configure Automatic Login

1️⃣ Open the System Preferences application and click the **Accounts** icon.

2️⃣ Click **Login Options**.

The Login Options pane appears.

3️⃣ On the **Automatic login** pop-up menu, choose the name of the user who you want to be automatically logged in; to disable Automatic Login, choose Off and skip the rest of these steps.

*Note: Automatic Login makes your MacBook less secure because anyone who can access your MacBook can use it. If you use your MacBook where you cannot control it, disable Automatic Login.*

4️⃣ Enter the user's password.

5️⃣ Click **OK**.

Each time MacBook starts or restarts, the user you selected is logged in automatically.

### Configure the Login Window

1️⃣ Open the System Preferences application and click the **Accounts** icon.

2️⃣ Click **Login Options**.

3️⃣ To show a list of users in the Login window, click **List of users**; to show empty Name and Password fields, click **Name and password** instead.

4️⃣ If you want to be able to restart MacBook, put it to sleep, or shut it down from the Login window, check the **Show the Restart, Sleep, and Shut Down buttons** check box.

5️⃣ If you want to be able to choose the language layout from the Login window, check the **Show input menu in login window** check box.

6️⃣ To show a hint when a user forgets his password, check the **Show password hints** check box.

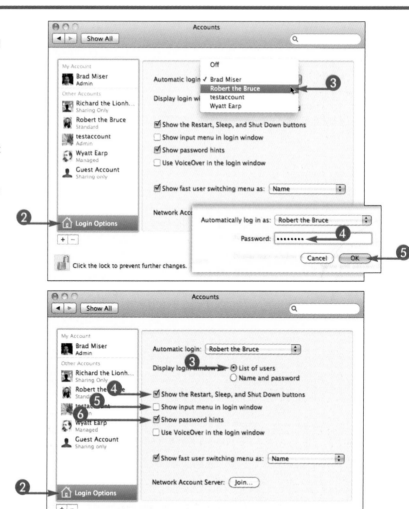

**7** To have MacBook read the text in the Login window, check the **Use VoiceOver in the login window** check box.

## Configure and Use Fast User Switching

**1** Open the System Preferences application and click the **Accounts** icon.

**2** Click **Login Options**.

**3** Check the **Show fast user switching menu as** check box.

**4** Open the pop-up menu; then choose **Name** to see the current user's user name at the top of the Fast User Switching menu, **Short name** to see the user's short name, or **Icon** to see a silhouette.

The Fast User Switching menu appears on the menu bar.

**5** Open the **Fast User Switching** menu.

● All the user accounts on MacBook are shown. The users who are currently logged in are marked with a check mark.

**6** Choose the user to switch to.

**7** Enter the user's password.

**8** Click **Log In** ().

The user is logged in and her desktop appears. The previous user remains logged in; select that user's account on the menu to move back to it.

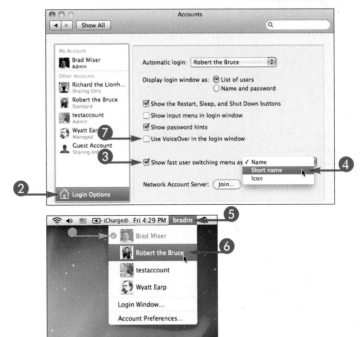

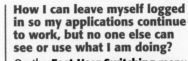

## TIPS

### What happens to running applications when another user logs in using fast user switching?

Because a user does not log out when another one logs in using fast user switching, the applications and processes running under a user account continue to run in the background even while another user is using MacBook. As soon as the previous user logs back in, the results of the activity that was ongoing are seen, such as new e-mails, Web pages, and so on.

### How I can leave myself logged in so my applications continue to work, but no one else can see or use what I am doing?

On the **Fast User Switching** menu, choose **Login Window**. The Login window appears, but you remain logged in (you see a check mark next to your user name). All applications and processes continue to run in the background. To start using MacBook again, choose your user account, enter your password, and click **Login**. You go back to where you left off.

# PART

# Getting Connected

While a stand-alone MacBook is useful, it is not as useful as one connected to a local network and the Internet. Because MacBook is made for traveling, you need to know how to keep connected while you are on the move without risking the computer or its data. There are also devices you will want to connect to MacBook, such as an external hard drive. In this part, you learn how to get and keep MacBook connected.

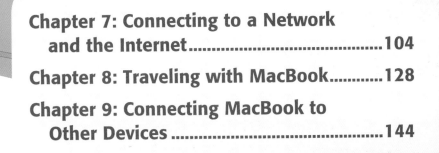

# Understand Networking Concepts

The topic of networking is the most technical in this book. MacBook and Mac OS X manage most of the details for you, but a number of concepts are helpful to understand as you create your own network.

## Network

Simply put, a *network* is two or more computers or other devices connected together using cables or wireless connections. The purpose of a network is to enable the devices on it to communicate with each other. This is done using various *protocols* (which can be thought of as languages) to provide different services. For example, the Transmission Control Protocol/Internet Protocol (TCP/IP) is the basic "language" that devices speak over the Internet. There are other protocols for a variety of services, such as file sharing and printing, but the data for all of these services are communicated over a network. Networks can be large or small, simple or complicated, but they all have the same basic purpose.

## Internet

The Internet is the largest network possible because it literally spans the globe, and millions upon millions of devices and people are connected to it. The Internet makes communication and information available way beyond anything that was possible before it came to be. Many services are available over the Internet, such as e-mail, searching the Web, chats, and file transfers. Connecting MacBook to the Internet is just about as important as being able to charge its battery.

## Local Network

A *local network*, also known as a local area network or *LAN*, is a network that covers a defined physical space. LANs can be quite large, such as in a business or school, or fairly small, such as in a home. A LAN connects its devices together so they can communicate with one another and also connect to outside networks — most importantly, to the Internet. This chapter focuses on helping you create a small LAN, such as what many people use in their homes. The principles of larger LANs are the same, but the details can get much more complicated.

## Wi-Fi Network

*Wi-Fi* is a general term for a set of wireless communication standards and technologies defined in the Institute of Electrical and Electronics Engineers (IEEE) 802.11 specifications. Like Ethernet networks, Wi-Fi enables devices to communicate, but uses radio transmissions instead of physical wires to connect devices. This offers ease of configuration and makes it possible to move around while remaining on a network, which is especially useful for MacBook. The downsides of Wi-Fi are that configuration is more difficult and Wi-Fi networks are not as secure as Ethernet networks. Wi-Fi networks are not as fast as Ethernet networks, either. However, the flexibility they provide more than makes up for the only slightly more difficult configuration.

## Ethernet

*Ethernet* is both a physical means of connecting devices together — for example, an Ethernet cable — and the protocol used to communicate over the physical connection. Ethernet can support various communication speeds, and all of them are quite fast. MacBook has an Ethernet port that you can use to connect it to other devices. In addition to their speed, Ethernet connections offer other benefits, including simplicity and security. The primary downside to Ethernet is the need for a physical connection between the devices, which can involve a lot of cables.

## AirPort

Apple uses the term *AirPort* for its implementation of Wi-Fi. Like other Macs, every MacBook supports AirPort. Apple also offers AirPort base stations that you can use to create your own Wi-Fi networks. Fortunately, AirPort technologies are based on the Wi-Fi standards. As a result, MacBook can access any Wi-Fi network, and other kinds of devices that support Wi-Fi can connect to AirPort networks.

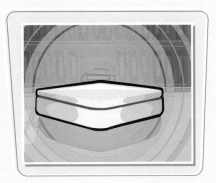

continued

# Understand Networking Concepts *(continued)*

### Hub/Router/Access Point

All networks need a device that controls the flow of information among the various computers, printers, and other resources on the network. These devices are called hubs, switches, routers, or access points. There are many kinds of these devices, and they all offer different features and benefits. They can support Ethernet, Wi-Fi, or both kinds of networks. Because AirPort Extreme Base Stations offer a lot of nice features and support is built into Mac OS X, they are the focus of this chapter. However, MacBook can be used with other kinds of routers as well. Some of the key features of hubs are the ability to share an Internet connection among many devices and to shield those devices from Internet attacks.

### Internet Service Provider

The Internet must be accessed through specific entry points. To do this, you need the services of an Internet Service Provider (ISP). The ISP provides the means that you use to connect your network to the Internet using various connection technologies, such as cable, Digital Subscriber Line (DSL), or even satellite.

### Internet Account

To access the Internet, you need an Internet account with an ISP. The cost and technical details (such as connection speed, server space, and so on) of accounts vary, depending on the specific ISP you use. Typically, ISPs require you to have only one Internet account for your network, but you are responsible for everything connected to the modem (the device that communicates from your LAN to the ISP) on "your side," whereas the ISP is responsible for ensuring that the signal to the modem is working. Depending on the type of Internet access you use, you might need a user name and password to connect to your account, or it might be based on your physical location (such as with a cable connection).

## IP Address

An Internet Protocol (IP) address is the way devices on the Internet are identified. Put another way, to be able to connect to and use the Internet, a device must have an IP address. IP addresses include a set of four numbers with periods between each number, as in 169.455.12.3. In most networks, you do not need to worry about the details of IP addresses because the hub/router uses Dynamic Host Control Protocol (DHCP) to automatically assign addresses to devices as they are needed. You just need to be able to recognize whether or not a device has a valid IP address, which is usually pretty clear because when you do not have one, you cannot connect to the Internet.

## Internet Services and Applications

The reason to connect devices to the Internet is to be able to access the services that are delivered over it. To access these services, you use Internet applications. Obvious examples are Mail for e-mail, and Safari for Web browsing. Many kinds of services are available on the Internet, and many different applications use each of those services, but you will likely end up using just a few of them. Because Mac OS X includes powerful and easy-to-use Internet applications, they are a good place to start.

## Internet Dangers

Although the Internet offers amazing capabilities, they do not come without risk. Unfortunately, just like in the physical world, on the Internet there are many people who want to hurt other people. The dangers of Internet life include the annoying, such as pornography and spam, and the truly dangerous, such as viruses, hacking, or identity theft. Fortunately, with some basic precautions and common sense, you can protect yourself from most Internet dangers relatively easily.

## Local Network Services

Similar to the Internet, you can take advantage of services that you can provide over your local network. These include file and printer sharing, local Web sites, and chatting. Configuring and using local network services are pretty straightforward because these services are built into Mac OS X.

# Obtain an Internet Account

In order to connect your network or MacBook to the Internet, you must have an Internet account. Different kinds of Internet accounts allow you to connect in different ways. The most common high-speed technologies for homes are cable and DSL. Satellite connections are also available. Before you decide on an Internet account, you should know the options available in your location.

**If your location has cable TV service, contact the provider to see if Internet access is available and what the cost is. Then locate providers of Internet access through DSL. Choose the type of account and provider that makes the most sense to you.**

## Obtain an Internet Account

### Determine What Types of Internet Accounts Are Available

1. If cable service is available to you, contact the cable provider to get information about Internet access, including monthly cost, speed options, and installation or startup costs.

2. If you have access to a computer connected to the Web, go to dsl.theispguide.com.

3. Use the tools to search for DSL access in your location.

*Note: When you contact a potential provider, ask if Macintosh is supported. Although you do not really need formal support because Macs work with standard technologies, Mac technical support can be a factor when you are choosing a provider.*

4. Contact DSL providers that serve your area to get details about their service, including monthly cost, installation costs or startup fees, and length of contract.

*Note: Make sure you have potential providers check your actual phone number to ensure that DSL is available. DSL availability in your area does not guarantee service at your specific location.*

*Note: If cable or DSL are available to you, skip to Step 1 in the next section. Satellite is the best option only when cable or DSL are not available.*

5. If cable or DSL is not available, access the Web and move to www.dbsinstall.com.

6. Follow the links on the DSL provider's Web site to search for satellite providers of Internet access.

## Choose, Obtain, and Install an Internet Account

**1** Compare your options.

If you have only one option for a broadband connection, the choice is made for you and you can skip to Step **3**.

**2** If you have a choice between cable and DSL, consider which is best for you based on cost, the provider's reputation for service, and other factors.

Cable offers the fastest optimal performance, but also tends to be more expensive than DSL. Actual performance of cable can vary based on the amount of data flowing to other locations on the same trunk of the cable system you are on. The only technical requirement is that you need a cable outlet near the location of the hub you install for your local network.

● DSL offers steadier performance than cable and tends to be less expensive, but is typically slower. You sometimes have more than one DSL provider from which to choose (unlike cable, which is a localized monopoly). DSL is delivered through a standard phone line, and you probably have phone jacks in more locations, making the installation of a network slightly easier.

**3** Contact the provider you want to use to obtain an account and schedule installation.

The provider activates your account, and if you choose to have the provider install the modem, they schedule an appointment with you. Some providers allow a self-install kit to be used. Using a kit is typically straightforward, but it is more work for you and may introduce problems that you need to solve.

**Note:** *If the provider installs your modem, ask the technician not to install any software on MacBook. You do not need any special software to connect to the Internet, and the applications many providers install are really just ways to get you to visit their home pages more frequently.*

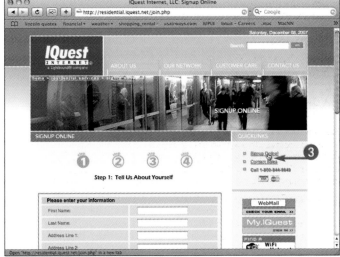

## TIPS

**What about dial-up Internet accounts?**

Internet accounts that you access over a standard phone line and dial-up modem are available just about everywhere, though you need to add a USB modem to be able to use one with MacBook. Dial-up is very slow and unreliable, and you must connect each time you want Internet access. The speed is so slow that using the Internet requires extreme patience. Broadband connections are available in many areas, which is why they are the focus of this chapter.

**If I need an Internet account to connect, why can I use Wi-Fi at public places without an account?**

No matter how you connect to the Internet, you are using an Internet account of some sort. In public places, the organization that controls that place can make a wireless network available to you. Through that network, you can access the organization's Internet account. In some cases, you can do this for free. In others, you need to purchase access from the organization providing the network.

# Set Up a Local Network

After you have a working Internet connection, you are ready to build a local network. You can include a lot of devices on the network, including both wired and wireless devices. The heart of any network is the hub/router you use.

**The best hub choice for most Mac users is an AirPort Extreme Base Station or a Time Capsule, because support for administering the AirPort networks they provide is built into Mac OS X. Also, these base stations shield your network from Internet attacks. The rest of this chapter assumes the use of one of these devices. The steps to install other kinds of hubs are similar. These steps also assume that you have a working Internet connection and modem.**

## Set Up a Local Network

### Install an AirPort Extreme Base Station/ Time Capsule

1. Connect the output cable of the modem to the modem (WAN) port on the base station.

2. Connect power to the base station.

*Note: The only difference between a Time Capsule and an AirPort Extreme Base Station is the inclusion of a hard drive. For the purposes of this chapter, these devices are referred to as a base station.*

3. Start up MacBook.

As long as you have not disabled AirPort, MacBook can communicate with the base station wirelessly. You can also connect the MacBook directly to one of the Ethernet ports on the base station using an Ethernet cable.

### Configure an AirPort Extreme Base Station/Time Capsule

1. In the Finder, open the **Go** menu and choose **Applications**.

The Applications folder opens.

2. Scroll down to the Utilities folder icon.

3. Double-click the **Utilities** folder icon.

*Note: You can jump directly to the Utilities folder by opening the Go menu and choosing Utilities.*

● The Utilities folder opens.

4. Double-click the **AirPort Utility** application.

The application opens and you see a sheet informing you about updates to the AirPort software.

*Note: The specific screens and options you see in AirPort Utility depend on the type of base station you are configuring and its current status (for example, if it has been configured previously). Although the details for your configuration might be different, you follow the same general process as the application leads you through it.*

5. Click **OK**.

*Note: If you see an additional warning prompt, click OK to clear it.*

The sheet closes and you see the application window with the base stations connected to MacBook displayed on the intro screen.

*Note: The first time you connect to a new base station, you can click the **Continue** button on the first screen to be guided through the configuration process. These steps show you a manual configuration process, which you should know about because that is how you should make changes to the configuration when they are needed.*

**6** Select the base station you want to configure.

**7** Click **Manual Setup**.

*Note: If you are configuring a base station that has already been configured previously, you may be prompted to type its administrative password between Steps **7** and **8**. Enter the password and click **OK** to continue.*

*Note: If you have never configured the base station previously, you may be prompted to create a name for the base station along with an administrative password. The name identifies the base station whereas the administrative password is required to be able to change the configuration. Use a different password than you use for the Wi-Fi network.*

**8** Click the **Internet** tab.

**9** Click the **Internet Connection** sub-tab.

*Note: These steps assume an Ethernet connection to a provider that uses DHCP, which is the most common configuration. Check the documentation for your Internet account to ensure you make the appropriate selections.*

**10** Choose **Ethernet** on the **Connect Using** pop-up menu.

**11** Choose **Using DHCP** on the **Configure IPv4** pop-up menu.

**12** Click the **NAT** tab.

**13** Check the **Enable NAT Port Mapping Protocol** check box.

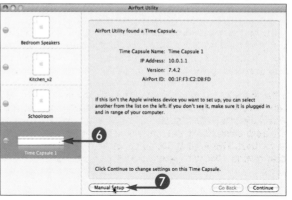

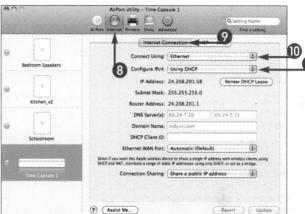

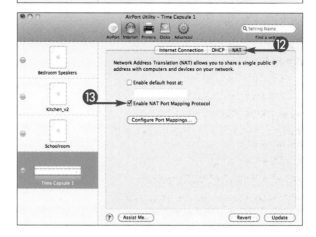

continued

# Set Up a Local Network *(continued)*

There are two ways to configure a base station using the AirPort Utility application. One is to use the manual method as described in these sections. This provides you more control over the options and also makes configuration faster because you can jump immediately to the areas you want to configure. Some options, such as additional security configurations, are available only in Manual mode.

**Being able to work through a manual configuration equips you to better manage your network. Fortunately, the required configuration for the most common situation, which is an Internet connection through a cable or DSL modem using DHCP, is relatively simple. You need to use only a few of the options to configure a base station for this case. The rest of the tools are for more complicated configurations, such as those for a business or other large organization.**

## Set Up a Local Network *(continued)*

⑭ Click the **AirPort** tab.

⑮ Click the **Wireless** sub-tab.

⑯ Use the **Wireless Mode** pop-up menu to choose **Create a wireless network**.

⑰ Enter the wireless network's name in the Wireless Network Name field.

⑱ Use the **Radio Mode** pop-up menu to determine the wireless standards supported on the network.

**Note:** *The more standards you allow, such as 802.11n (802.11b/g compatible), the more types of devices are able to connect to the network.*

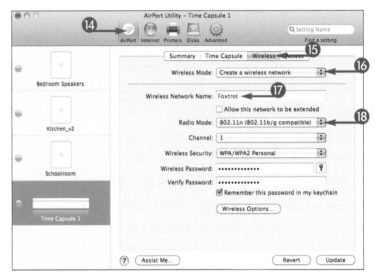

⑲ Use the **Wireless Security** pop-up menu to choose **WPA/WPA2 Personal**.

⑳ Enter the network password in the Wireless Password and Verify Password fields.

**Note:** *This is the password that people have to enter to be able to connect to the secured network.*

㉑ Check the **Remember this password in my keychain** check box.

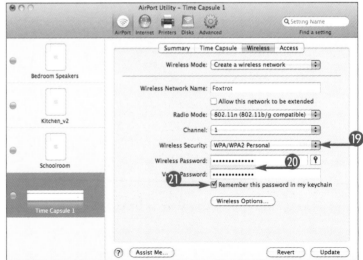

**22** Click the **Time Capsule** tab.

*Note: If you are configuring an AirPort Extreme Base Station, the tab and fields are labeled with the related terms. This example shows the screens for a Time Capsule.*

**23** Enter the base station name in the Time Capsule Name field.

**24** Enter the administration password in the Time Capsule Password and Verify Password fields.

**25** Check the **Remember this password in my keychain** check box.

**26** Check the **Set time automatically** check box, choose the appropriate server on the pop-up menu, and choose your time zone on the **Time Zone** pop-up menu.

**27** Click **Update**.

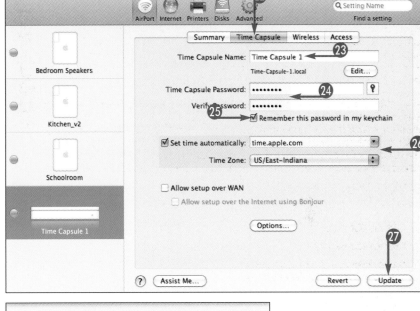

A warning sheet appears.

**28** Click **Continue**.

The base station is configured and restarts. Once that process is complete, the wireless network is ready for use.

**29** Press ⌘+Q.

The AirPort Utility application quits.

**30** If you are connecting the base station to a wired network or to wired devices, connect them using Ethernet cables plugged into the LAN ports on the base station.

This device and its network services will be temporarily unavailable. Are you sure you want to continue?

☐ Do not show this warning again    Cancel    Continue

 **TIPS**

### What is the difference between an Extreme Base Station and an Express Base Station?

The most significant difference is that you cannot have a wired network connected to an Express Base Station because it has only one Ethernet port, which is connected to the modem. Typically, you should use an Extreme Base Station (or Time Capsule) for the primary hub on the network; you can add Express Base Stations to expand the range of the network as needed.

### How do I expand the range of my network?

If an Extreme Base Station or Time Capsule does not provide sufficient coverage of the area in which you use MacBook, you can chain base stations together. Use the AirPort Utility to connect to an Express Base Station and configure it to expand the existing network. You can do this by selecting the Express Base station and using the Wireless tab to add it to the existing network.

# Protect MacBook from Internet Attacks

One of the great things about the Internet is that it connects you to an unlimited number of people and organizations. However, all that connectedness opens you up to various kinds of Internet attacks. The worst of these are attempts to steal your identity and to hack into your computers to steal the information they contain, or to use them to launch attacks on other computers. You also need to be mindful of the threat from viruses.

**Fortunately, although the dangers of these attacks are very real, you can protect yourself with relatively simple techniques. An AirPort Extreme Base Station or Time Capsule protects you from most attacks automatically. If you ever connect MacBook directly to the modem, such as for troubleshooting, make sure you configure its firewall before doing so.**

## Protect MacBook from Internet Attacks

### Check a Base Station to Ensure It Is Protecting MacBook

**1** Open the AirPort Utility application.

***Note:*** *See the section "Set Up a Local Network" for details.*

**2** Select the base station.

**3** Click **Manual Setup**.

The AirPort Utility moves into Manual mode. In this mode, you can make changes to the base station directly, and you can access all possible settings for it.

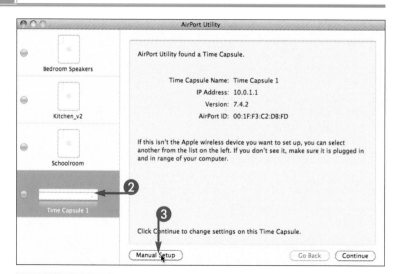

**4** Click the **Internet** tab.

**5** Click the **NAT** sub-tab.

**6** Ensure the **Enable NAT Port Mapping Protocol** check box is checked; if it is, quit the AirPort utility and skip the next step.

**7** If the check box is not checked, check it and click **Update**.

***Note:*** *When NAT is active, the only IP address exposed to the Internet is the base station's. This shields the devices connected to the Internet through the base station from Internet attacks because devices outside your base station cannot identify the devices on the network; they see only the base station, which cannot be hacked like a computer can.*

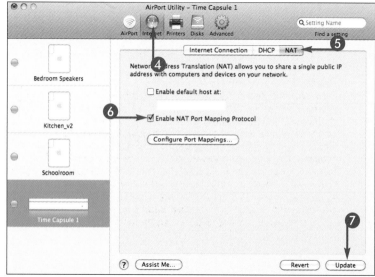

## Use the Mac OS X Firewall to Protect MacBook

1. Open the System Preferences application and click the **Security** icon.

● The Security pane opens.

2. Click the **Firewall** tab.

3. Click **Start**.

**Note:** *Performing more advanced configuration of the firewall is explained in Chapter 8.*

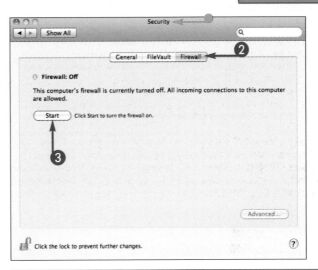

## Protect MacBook from Viruses

1. Purchase and install an antivirus application.

2. Configure the antivirus application so that it updates its virus definitions and scans MacBook automatically (see the instructions for the particular application you use).

 TIPS

### Do I really need antivirus software?

That depends. Mac OS X is less vulnerable to virus attacks than Windows PCs are. To be as safe from viruses as possible, it is a good idea to install and use antivirus software. However, being smart about how you deal with the Internet can be almost as effective. Never open attachments to e-mail messages unless you are very sure of where they came from, especially if they are Office documents or applications. Download software only from reputable Web sites. In general, be cautious about moving any files onto MacBook unless you are very sure of the reliability of the source. Exercising common-sense steps like these offers a good amount of virus protection, but not as much as an antivirus application.

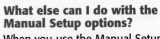

### What else can I do with the Manual Setup options?

When you use the Manual Setup options in the AirPort Utility application, you can configure various features of a base station. For example, you can configure a printer connected to the base station and change other, more advanced configuration settings, which can be useful for troubleshooting.

# Connect to the Internet with AirPort

The whole point of having a MacBook is that you can move around with it. By connecting to an AirPort wireless network, you can connect to the Internet and a local network from any location covered by that network.

**This section assumes your network uses an AirPort Extreme Base Station. If not, the steps you use to connect to a wireless network might be slightly different.**

**1** Open the System Preferences application.

**2** Click the **Network** icon.

● The Network pane appears. In the pane on the left side of the window, you see all the ways you can connect to a network that are currently configured on MacBook. When you select a connection to configure it, tools for that type of connection appear in the right part of the window.

**3** Click **AirPort**.

**4** Click **Turn AirPort On** if it is not on already.

AirPort services start.

*Note: You might see a window that shows the available networks as soon as you turn AirPort on. Select the network you want to join and click Join, or click Cancel to follow the rest of these steps.*

**5** On the **Network Name** pop-up menu, choose the network you want to join.

**6** If prompted to do so, type the network's password.

**7** Check the **Remember this network** check box.

**8** Click **OK**.

MacBook connects to the AirPort network, and you return to the System Preferences application window. The status of the network becomes Connected.

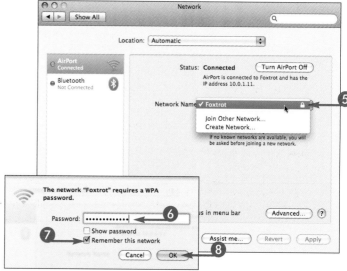

⑨ Check the **Show AirPort status in menu bar** check box.

⑩ Click **Apply**.

⑪ Quit the System Preferences application.

⑫ Open Safari and go to a Web page.

The Web page opens, showing that MacBook is connected to the network and the Internet through AirPort.

If the Web page does not open, troubleshoot the problem.

*Note: See the section "Troubleshoot an Internet Connection," later in this chapter, for information on how to troubleshoot connection problems.*

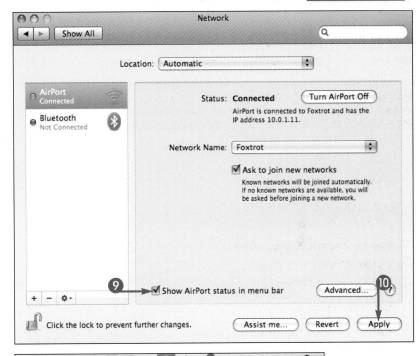

**Use the AirPort Menu**

① Open the **AirPort** menu (📶).

● You can determine the signal strength of the network by the number of waves at the top of the menu.

More waves mean a stronger and faster connection; one or two waves may result in slow or intermittent performance.

② Choose another network you want to join by selecting it on the menu.

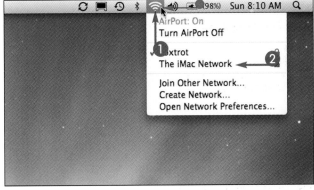

 **TIPS**

**How can I connect directly to another Mac using AirPort?**

Open the **AirPort** menu on the Finder menu bar and choose **Create Network**. Name the network, give it a password, and click **OK**. Other Mac users can connect to your network using the same steps you use to connect to a network provided by an AirPort Base Station.

**I see only one or two waves and MacBook seems to lose its connection. What can I do?**

The most likely cause is that MacBook is too far away from the base station. The most common solutions are to move MacBook closer to the base station so that the signal is stronger or use Wireless Distribution System (WDS) to add another base station to the network to expand its coverage.

# Connect to the Internet with Ethernet

Because MacBook has Ethernet support built in, you can connect MacBook to the Internet by connecting it to a wired network over which an Internet connection is being shared.

**There are two steps. You can connect MacBook to the network and then configure it to access the Internet over the network. This section assumes you are using an AirPort Extreme Base Station or Time Capsule. If you have a different network configuration, the details might be slightly different.**

## Connect to the Internet with Ethernet

① Connect an Ethernet cable to one of the available ports on the Extreme Base Station or Time Capsule.

② Connect the other end to the Ethernet port on MacBook.

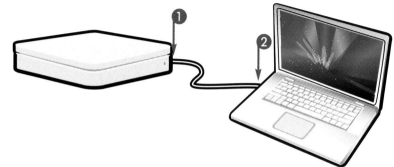

**Configure MacBook to Access the Internet Over an Ethernet Network**

① Open the System Preferences application.

② Click the **Network** icon.

● The Network pane appears.

③ Select Ethernet in the left part of the pane.

● The status should be Connected. If it is not, the cable is not connected correctly or the base station is not working.

④ On the **Configure IPv4** menu, choose **Using DHCP**.

⑤ Click **Apply**.

MacBook gets an IP address from the base station and should be able to access its Internet connection.

⑥ Quit the System Preferences application.

7 Open Safari by clicking its icon on the Dock.

8 If Safari does not load a Web page automatically, type a URL in the address bar and press Return.

Safari goes to the Web site if MacBook is successfully connected to the network via Ethernet. If not, troubleshoot the problem.

**Note:** *See the section "Troubleshoot an Internet Connection," later in this chapter, for information on troubleshooting connection problems.*

**Note:** *For detailed information about using Safari, see Chapter 11.*

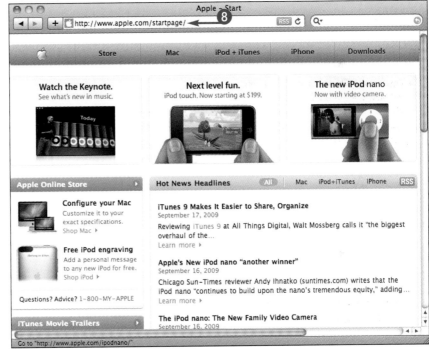

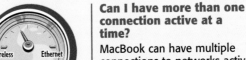

### Why use Ethernet when wireless is available?

Wireless connections are great for MacBook because you are not tethered to one spot. However, the best wireless connection is not as fast as an Ethernet connection. So if you are "parked" in a location where an Ethernet connection is available, you get better performance if you use it instead of the wireless network. Additionally, an Ethernet connection is more secure because a device has to be physically connected to the network to use it.

### Can I have more than one connection active at a time?

MacBook can have multiple connections to networks active at the same time. You can use the steps in this section to configure MacBook for Ethernet access and the steps in the previous section to configure MacBook for wireless access. MacBook chooses the connection to use at any point in time based on how you configure it and the connections available.

# Share Files on a Local Network

Just like services you access over the Internet, you can provide services over a local network. These include sharing files, printers, an Internet connection, Web sites, and iTunes. Any computers that connect to the network, whether they use Ethernet or AirPort, can access any of the services you make available.

**File sharing is one of the most useful local network services because you can easily share resources with multiple computers. You can configure MacBook to share files with others, and you can access files being shared with you.**

## Share Files on a Local Network

### Share Files with Others

① Open the System Preferences application.

② Click the **Sharing** icon.

● The Sharing pane appears. In the list in the left part of the window, you see the services you can provide over a local network. When you select a service, the tools you use to configure it appear in the right part of the window.

③ Type a name for MacBook in the Computer Name field.

This is the name others on the network choose to access MacBook.

④ Check the **File Sharing** check box.

File sharing starts.

By default, the Public folder within your Home folder is shared on the network.

⑤ To share specific folders, click the **Add** button ([+]).

⑥ Select the folder you want to share.

⑦ Click **Add**.

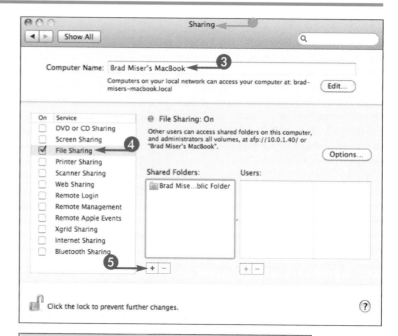

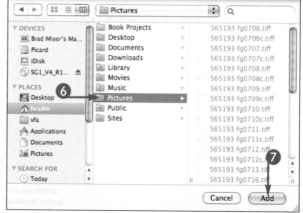

● The folder appears on the Shared Folders list.

⑧ To allow everyone with whom you share files to access the folder, click **Everyone** in the Users list and choose the permission level from the pop-up menu that appears.

**Note:** See the tip on this page for an explanation of permission levels.

⑨ To configure more users, click **Add** (➕) at the bottom of the Users list.

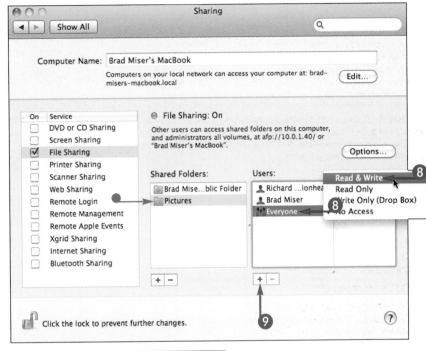

The Select Users sheet appears.

⑩ Choose the users for whom you want to configure access on the list.

**Note:** If the user with whom you want to share files is not on the list, click **New Person** and create a user name and password for that person.

⑪ Click **Select**.

The users appear in the Users list.

⑫ Repeat Step **8** to configure the user's access to the shared folder.

⑬ Repeat Steps **5** to **12** to share other folders and configure users to access your shared files.

 TIPS

**What are the permissions I can assign to folders that I share?**

If you select **No Access**, no one else on the network will be able to use an item. Select **Write Only (Drop Box)** to enable people to place items within the shared folder, but not to be able to view or change its contents. When you select **Read Only**, the people with whom you share a folder can view, but not change, its contents. When you select **Read & Write**, people who can access the shared folder can view and change its contents.

**When should I use Write Only (Drop Box) access?**

This is useful when you need input from other people, but you do not want those people to be able to see each other's input. Suppose you are teaching a class and want your students to place assignments on your computer. You can create a Submission folder and share it with Write Only (Drop Box) access. Your students can then place files in the folder, but they cannot see files that other people have placed there.

When you connect to a local network, MacBook automatically identifies resources on the network that are sharing files. It collects all these resources in the Sharing section of the sidebar so that you can access them easily.

**When you connect to a sharing resource, what you can do with the content of that resource is determined by the permissions that you have been granted for it. For example, if you have Read & Write access, you can use a shared folder just like one you created. If you have Read Only access, you can see its contents, but you cannot change those contents.**

**Access Files Being Shared with You**

1 Move to the desktop and open a Finder window.

● In the Shared section of the sidebar, you see all of the computers sharing files on the network.

2 Select the computer whose files you want to access.

● MacBook connects to that computer as a Guest, and you see the resources to which guest accounts (the permissions assigned to Everyone) have access.

*Note: By default, the Public folder in each user's Home folder is available to everyone on the network.*

3 Click **Connect As**.

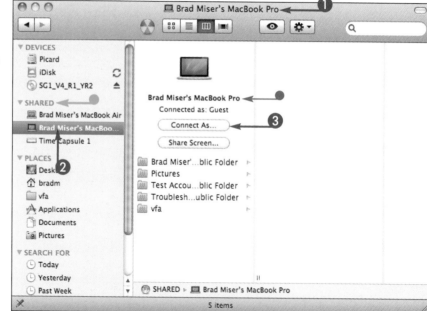

4 To connect as a guest, click **Guest** and skip to Step **9**.

5 To connect as a registered user, click **Registered User**.

6 Type the user name of the account under which you want to connect.

7 Type the password for the user name you typed in Step **6**.

8 Check the **Remember this password in my keychain** check box.

9 Click **Connect**.

MacBook connects to the resource under the user account you entered.

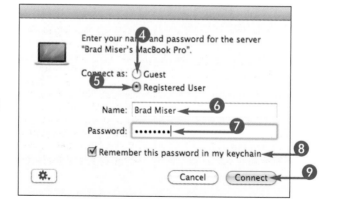

- The Finder window that appears shows the resources available to you based on the kind of access the user account you use has.

- The user account under which you are logged in is shown at the top of the window.

⑩ Open a shared resource.

- At the top of the window, you see the Sharing icon to indicate that the resource you are using is stored on a different computer on the network (⬛ changes to ⬛).

⑪ Open folders on the shared resource.

⑫ Double-click files to open them.

⑬ To copy a file or folder from the shared resource onto MacBook, drag it from the shared resource folder onto a folder stored on MacBook.

**TIPS**

### When are the files that I share available to others?

In order for people to access files you are sharing, MacBook must be awake and connected to the network. If it is configured to go to sleep automatically, people lose access to shared files when MacBook sleeps. Likewise, if MacBook is no longer connected to the network, its files are not available.

*Shhhhhh...*
*Do Not Disturb*

### How can I share files with Windows computers?

Open the Sharing pane of the System Preferences application and turn File Sharing on by clicking its check box. Click **Options**. In the resulting sheet, select the **Share files and folders using SMB** check box. Select the check box next to each user with whom you want to share files and type the password for that user's account. The user can access the files by typing **smb://ipaddress**, where *ipaddress* is the current IP address for MacBook; this address is shown on the Sharing pane. You can also access files being shared by Windows computers.

# Share Screens on a Local Network

With screen sharing, you can control another Mac on your local network just as if you were sitting in front of it. For example, you can log into a different Mac on your network and run an application like you would if that application were installed on your MacBook. This is also useful for helping other users on your network because you can "take over" the other computer to solve problems.

**Like file sharing, you must configure screen sharing permissions on each computer to determine who can access this feature.**

## Configure Screen Sharing on MacBook

**1** Open the Sharing pane of the System Preferences application.

**2** Select the **Screen Sharing** service.

● The controls for screen sharing appear.

**3** Click **Computer Settings**.

The Computer Settings sheet appears.

**4** Check the **Anyone may request permission to control screen** check box if you want to allow anyone who can access your MacBook to request to share your screen.

**5** Check the **VNC viewers may control screen with password** check box and enter a password if you want people using Virtual Network Computing connections to be able to control your MacBook.

*Note: For a local network, you do not really need to allow this, and so most users should leave this option unchecked.*

**6** Click **OK**.

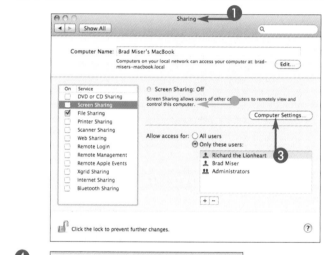

**7** In the Allow access for section, click **All users** to allow anyone who can access your MacBook over the network to share your screen, or **Only these users** to create a list of user accounts that can share your screen.

*Note: To create a user list, click ⊞. The User Account sheet appears. Select the user accounts with which you want to share your screen and click **Select**. You return to the Sharing pane and the user accounts you selected are shown on the user list.*

**8** Check the **On** check box for Screen Sharing.

● Screen sharing services start and your MacBook becomes available to users on your local network.

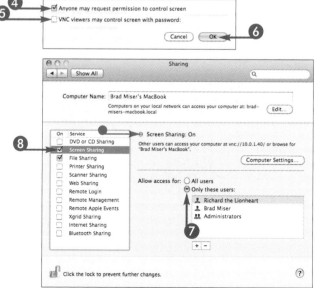

## Share Another Computer's Screen

1. Open a Finder window.

2. In the Shared section of the sidebar, select the Mac whose screen you want to share.

3. Log in under a user account that has permission to share the Mac's screen.

4. Click **Share Screen**.

   If you are connected under a user account with screen sharing permissions, the Screen Sharing application starts and you can control the other computer.

   If you have to request permission, the other Mac's user has to grant permission for you to share; when he does, the Screen Sharing application opens.

● Within the Screen Sharing application's window, which has the other computer's name as its title, you see the other computer's desktop. When you move your pointer within the window, the pointer is resized according to the resolution of the other computer.

5. Within the Screen Sharing window, you can control the shared Mac.

   You can use any application or command on the sharing computer as you would if you were sitting in front of it.

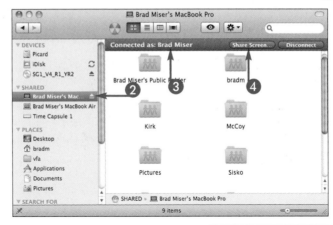

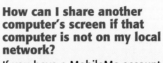

## TIPS

### What happens when someone wants to share my screen?

If you allow anyone to request to share your screen, when someone wants to share your MacBook, you see a permission dialog on your screen. To allow your screen to be shared, click **Share Screen**. The person sharing your screen can then control MacBook.

### How can I share another computer's screen if that computer is not on my local network?

If you have a MobileMe account, you can also share screens across the Internet. To do this, first set screen sharing permissions. On the MobileMe pane of the System Preferences application, register your MobileMe user name and password on each computer among which you want to share screens, and then use the Back To My Mac tab to enable it. You can access any shared services over the Internet like you can on a local network. You can also use iChat to share screens (see Chapter 13 for details).

# Troubleshoot an Internet Connection

You can troubleshoot your Internet connection if you have problems with it. Fortunately, you probably will not need to do this very often. Networks are typically pretty reliable, and once configured correctly, you can usually just keep using them. However, as in the real world, things in the virtual world do not always go according to plan.

## Troubleshoot an Internet Connection

### Diagnose the Problem

● An error message appears.

**Note:** *When you cannot access any Web pages, Safari displays the Network Diagnostics button. Click it to start the Diagnostics application.*

① Determine if the problem is a network issue or if it is related just to one computer by trying the same action on a different computer on the same network.

If the problem occurs, it is a network problem; see the next subsection. If the problem does not occur, it is specific to MacBook. Skip to the subsection "Troubleshoot a MacBook Problem."

### Troubleshoot a Network Problem

① Check the status lights on the modem to make sure the modem is working.

If the modem appears to be working, go to Step **2**. If not, go to Step **7**.

② Check the status of the AirPort Extreme Base Station or Time Capsule.

If the status lights indicate the base station is working, go to Step **3**. If not, go to Step **8**.

③ Disconnect power from the base station and from the modem and wait about 20 seconds.

④ Connect power to the base station and then to the modem.

⑤ Try the task that you had a problem with.

If it is successful, you are done; if not, continue with the next steps.

⑥ If the modem's power light is on but the connection light is not, contact the ISP to make sure service is available. It probably is not, in which case you need to wait until service is restored.

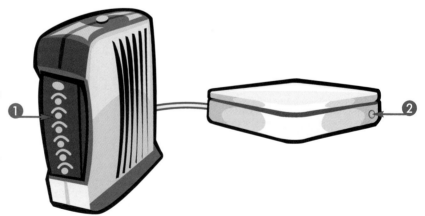

⑦ When you are sure that your Internet service has been restored, remove power from the base station, wait 20 seconds, and connect it again.

⑧ Try the task that you had a problem with.

The problem should be solved.

## Troubleshoot a MacBook Problem

**1** Open the Network pane of the System Preferences application.

**2** Check the status of the various connections.

If the status is Not Connected for a connection, you need to reconfigure that connection using steps shown in the section "Connect to the Internet with AirPort" or "Connect to the Internet with Ethernet" earlier in this chapter.

**3** If the status is Connected, click the **Apple** menu (🍎), and then click **Restart**.

**4** Click **Restart** at the prompt.

**5** After MacBook restarts, try the activity again.

Restarting is always good when you have a problem; it is easy to do and solves a lot of different issues.

TIPS

### When can the Network Diagnostics application help?

Sometimes the Network Diagnostics application can be very helpful because it moves through each phase of troubleshooting to guide you along the way. When the application finds a problem, it identifies it and provides some hints about how to solve it. However, using the steps outlined in this section is usually faster because they include most of what the application tells you to do.

### None of these steps helped. Now what can I do?

Although the steps in this section help with many problems, they certainly do not solve all of them. When they do not work, you have a couple of options. First, find a computer that can connect to the Internet and go to www.apple.com/support. Search for the specific problem you are having and use the results you find to solve it. Second, disconnect everything from your network and connect a computer directly to the modem (ensuring the firewall is on first). If the connection works, you know the problem is related to the network; add devices one by one, starting with the base station, until you find the source of the problem. If the connection does not work, you need help from your ISP.

# Connect to the Internet with Wi-Fi

When you are on the move, there is no reason to be disconnected from the Internet. In most public places, businesses, hotels, restaurants, and other locations, Internet access is readily available through a wireless (Wi-Fi) network connection.

**Connecting to the Internet using Wi-Fi is a two-step process. First, you establish the connection between MacBook and the network. Second, you register MacBook to access the Internet over the network. The second step is required most of the time, especially when you are charged a fee to access the Internet.**

## Connect to the Internet with Wi-Fi

### Connect to a Wi-Fi Network

*Note: When MacBook turns on or wakes up, it scans the area for available wireless networks. If it does not find one of your preferred networks (one that you have used before, such as the one in your home), it presents a list of available networks to you.*

① Select the wireless network you want to join.

② If you will be returning to the location and want to access the network again, check the **Remember this network** check box.

③ Click **Join**.

*Note: If the lock icon appears along the right side of the window for a network, it is secured and you will need a password to be able to join it.*

④ If the network is secured, enter the network password and click **OK** at the prompt. (Most public networks are not secure, in which case you skip this step.)

MacBook joins the network.

⑤ Open the **AirPort** menu (📶).

⑥ Verify that you have connected to the network and that the signal strength is good.

The signal strength is indicated by the number of waves at the top of the menu. You should have at least three waves for best performance.

If you are connected to the network, a check mark appears next to its name.

You are ready to access the Internet over the wireless network.

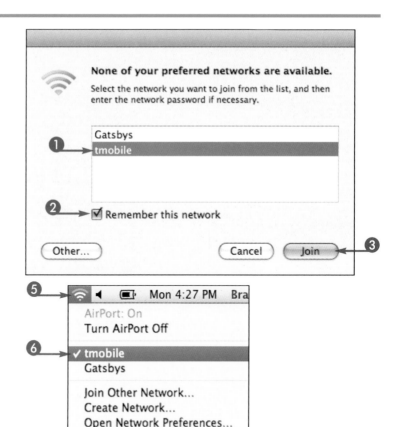

## Obtain and Log Into an Internet Account

**1** Open Safari and try to go to any Web page.

If the page appears, you do not need an account to use the Wi-Fi network to connect to the Internet, and you can skip the rest of these steps. You should be able to use the Internet as you can when you are connected to your local wireless network.

In most situations, you have to have an account with the network's provider to be able to access the Internet, or at the least, you need to agree to terms and conditions to be able to use it. In this case, you move to the provider's Web page that you use to create and log into an Internet account or agree to terms and conditions.

**2** Click the connection link.

*Note: This link goes by different names, such as Create an Account or Access the Internet.*

**3** If you do not currently have an account with the provider, skip to Step **6**.

**4** If you already have an account with the network's provider, type your user name and password.

**5** Click the **Go** or **Login** button.

You should see a message confirming that you have Internet access; if so, you can skip the rest of these steps.

*Note: When you connect from a hotel, you usually see a page that enables you to charge the Internet access to your room. If there is no fee to use the connection, you typically just have to agree to the terms and conditions and sometimes provide an e-mail address.*

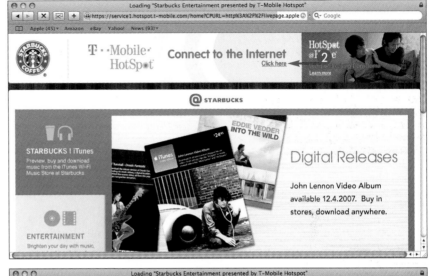

### What does Wi-Fi stand for?

The term *Wi-Fi* stands for wireless fidelity. It applies to a set of standard protocols and technology used to ensure that wireless devices and the software they use are compatible. The technical specifications fall under the Institute of Electrical and Electronics Engineers (IEEE) 802.11 series. The MacBook wireless capabilities are Wi-Fi or 802.11 compatible so that you can connect to any network or device that uses these standards (almost every wireless network and device does).

### What if there is only an Ethernet connection available?

Some places, such as hotel rooms or meeting rooms, have only an Ethernet connection available. In that situation, you have three options: connect wirelessly through an AirPort Express Base Station connected to the Ethernet network, connect using an Ethernet cable, or connect wirelessly with a broadband wireless card. You can find more information on the first and third methods later in this chapter.

In most cases, an Internet account that you purchase is associated with a time period, such as an hour, day, or month. When the period expires, you have to renew your account. If you travel to multiple places where the same provider offers service, consider purchasing a monthly account because those are less expensive than hourly or daily accounts. Some providers offer many hotspots in different locations, so having a monthly account can be a convenient way to obtain Internet access as you travel.

**Also, some accounts enable you to access networks from different providers, which have agreed to "share users." When you sign up for an account, check to see what other providers allow you to access the Internet with your account, especially if you are considering a monthly account.**

## Connect to the Internet with Wi-Fi *(continued)*

⑥ To obtain an account, click the link to sign up.

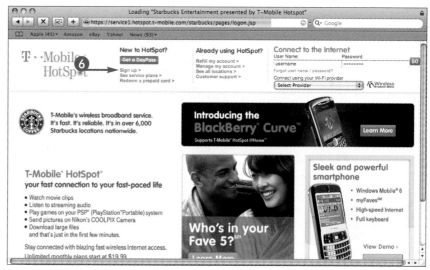

⑦ Follow the on-screen instructions to create an account.

During the creation process, you select a user name and password for your account.

**Note:** *You can usually choose from a variety of accounts, such as daily, monthly, and so on. Each has specific costs and lengths of commitment. Usually, the longer the account is configured, the less expensive it is per hour of use.*

chapter 8

**8** Type the user name and password you created.

**9** Click the **Go** or **Login** button.

- You should see a page confirming that you are connected.

  You can now use your Internet applications, such as Safari, Firefox, Mail, or iChat.

 **TIPS**

### Should I use a wireless network if it is not secured?

If you do not need a password to connect to a network, it is not secure. Any wireless device can connect to the network and might be able to intercept data being communicated across that network. In general, you should avoid such networks when you can (most networks in public places are not secure, and so you cannot always avoid them). When you do use an unsecured network, make sure you configure the MacBook firewall and other security tools to limit access to your computer over that network. Be especially careful about sending sensitive information that is not protected (especially avoid using a Web site whose address does not start with "https" when you have to provide information to use the site).

### What if I cannot see a wireless network?

There are two possibilities. One is that no networks are available, in which case you need to find another option (for example, a broadband wireless card). The other possibility is that the available networks are not broadcasting their identity. If that is the case, you need to know the network name and password before you can join it; when you have this information, choose the **Join Other Network** option on the **AirPort** menu and enter the information for the network.

# Connect to the Internet with an AirPort Express Base Station

An AirPort Express Base Station is a small, portable wireless base station that you can use to easily create your own wireless networks while you are away from your home or office. For example, if you happen to stay in a hotel that only has wired Internet access in its rooms, you can use an AirPort Express Base Station to quickly create a wireless network for MacBook.

**There are two steps to setting up a temporary wireless network with an AirPort Express Base Station. First, you connect the base station to the wired network. Second, you configure the base station to provide a wireless network.**

## Connect to the Internet with an AirPort Express Base Station

### Connect the Base Station to the Network

**1** Using an Ethernet cable, connect the wired network to the Ethernet port on the base station.

**2** Plug the base station into a power outlet.

● The base station starts up and you see its status light start to flash amber. You are ready to configure the base station to provide an Internet connection.

*Note: The rest of these steps assume that the wired network provides an Internet connection using Dynamic Host Configuration Protocol (DHCP), which is almost always the case in public places (such as hotels).*

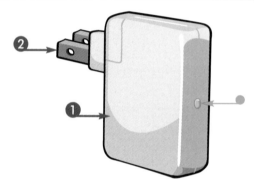

### Configure and Access a Wireless Network

**3** On the **AirPort** menu, choose the network that the AirPort Express Base Station provides.

*Note: If it has been configured before, the base station retains the last network name it provided. If not, the network name starts with "Apple." You must choose the base station's network to connect to it wirelessly to be able to configure it.*

**4** Open the AirPort Utility application (located in the Utilities folder within the Applications folder).

**5** Select the AirPort Express Base Station.

**6** Click **Continue**.

**7** If you are prompted to type the base station's password, do so and click **OK**.

*Note: A base station has a name and password for configuration; these are different than the wireless network's name and password. If the base station is protected with a password, you have to enter it before you can configure the base station.*

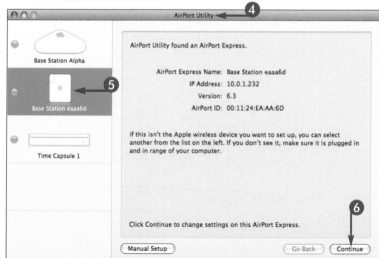

8 Type a name for the base station (different than the network's name).

9 Type the base station's password in the AirPort Express Password and Verify Password fields.

10 Click **Continue**.

The first page of the Network Setup screen appears.

11 Select the **I don't have a wireless network and I want to create one** radio button.

12 Click **Continue**.

13 Type a name for the wireless network you are creating.

14 Select the **WPA/WPA2 Personal** radio button.

15 Type a network password in both Wireless Password fields.

16 Click **Continue**.

The Internet Setup screen appears.

17 Select the **I use a DSL or cable modem with a static IP address or DHCP** radio button.

18 Click **Continue**.

19 On the **Configure IPv4** pop-up menu, choose **Using DHCP**.

20 Click **Continue**.

21 Click **Update**.

22 Click **Continue**.

The base station is updated and restarts. When that process is complete, the status light becomes solid green and you can connect to the Internet through the wireless network.

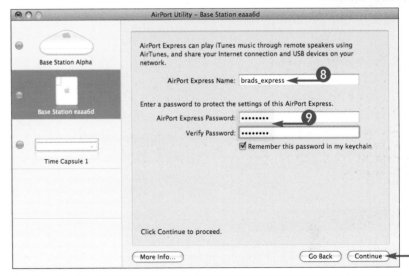

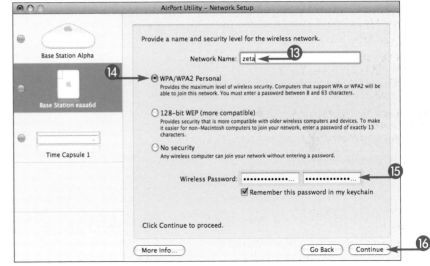

### Do I have to reconfigure the base station when I take it to a new location?

An AirPort Express Base Station uses a profile that saves its configuration. A base station remembers the configuration of the last location in the current profile. As long as each network you connect it to provides access through DHCP, you can simply connect the base station to the new network and it will provide the same wireless network.

### How do I create and use profiles?

In the AirPort Utility, select the base station and click **Manual Setup**. On the **Base Station** menu, select **Manage Profiles**. To create a new profile, click **Add** (＋). You can maintain up to five profiles. To use a profile, click its radio button and then click **Update**.

# Connect to the Internet with a Broadband Wireless Modem

If you travel a lot, you should consider a broadband wireless modem, with which you can connect to the Internet at reasonable speeds anywhere within the network's coverage area. National networks provide broad coverage areas, and so you can usually get a connection wherever you are. This can also save money because you use one account and all your access is included in one monthly fee. Most of the large cell phone companies offer this capability.

**You do not have to find and sign onto networks in various locations; this makes a broadband wireless modem easy to use because you perform the same steps every time you want to connect.**

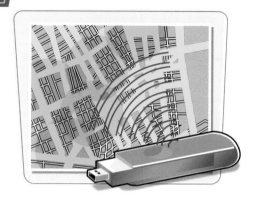

## Connect to the Internet with a Broadband Wireless Modem

### Obtain a Broadband Wireless Modem

1 Explore the major cell phone company Web sites to determine which ones offer a modem you can use; obtaining a broadband wireless modem is a lot like buying a cell phone.

2 Make sure the modem you consider connects using USB.

3 Check the specifications or features to ensure the modem and accompanying software are Mac OS X compatible and to determine the connection speed under ideal conditions.

4 Determine the cost of the modem (many are free when you sign up for an account) and monthly service (typically around $50 per month).

*Note:* Many wireless broadband accounts have a maximum amount of data that can be transferred under the account's monthly fee. If you exceed this amount, the "overage" charges can be quite expensive. If you use the Internet only for e-mail and Web browsing, you will probably be okay. If you download large files or watch streaming video, you can easily exceed the limits on many accounts. Usually, there is no warning when you have exceeded the limits, so you need to carefully monitor your account's status.

5 Check the contract terms; many providers require two-year agreements.

6 Check the coverage area for the provider to make sure it includes the areas you are mostly likely to be in.

You want to be sure you frequent the highest-speed areas of the network.

7 After you have compared your options, choose and purchase the modem and account that makes the most sense to you.

*Note:* Another important consideration is if you travel outside of the country where the provider is located. Roaming charges for a broadband connection can be extreme, so be sure you check out how much roaming costs before you use a wireless broadband card in a different country.

## Install and Configure a Broadband Wireless Modem

① Install the software for the broadband wireless modem using the modem's installer application.

*Note: If you can, download the software from the provider's Web site to be sure you are using the current version rather than installing it from the disc included with the modem.*

② Restart MacBook.

③ Connect the modem to the USB port on MacBook.

④ Launch the modem's setup application.

⑤ Go through the steps of the setup application until you have finished installing the modem's software and configuring MacBook to use the modem.

## Use a Broadband Wireless Modem to Connect to the Internet

① Launch the broadband wireless modem's connection application.

② Select the connection you want to use.

③ Click **Connect**.

The modem connects to the wireless network and provides you with an Internet connection.

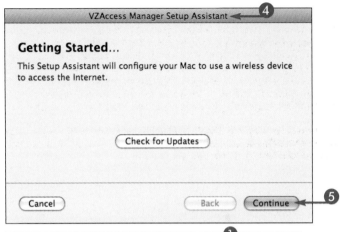

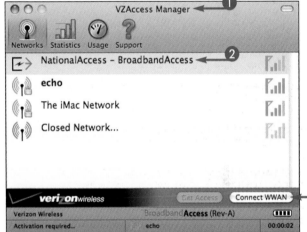

### Why am I unable to connect even though I am in my plan's coverage area?

Like cell phones, broadband wireless modems require a signal from a satellite or tower. If you are in a location where such signals are blocked, such as basements or deep in the interior of some buildings, the modem might not be able to receive a signal and you have to find an alternate way to connect. Signal strength can also impact the speed of the connection even if you are able to connect.

### Why not use a wireless modem all the time?

If a broadband wireless modem provides sufficient connection speeds in the locations you use MacBook the most, you can use it as your primary Internet connection (and so you do not need another account with a cable or DSL provider). However, most accounts have limits on the amount of data that can be transferred per month at the account's monthly cost. If that amount is sufficient for your Internet use, you can use the wireless card for all your Internet activity. If not, you will need another option because overage charges are usually quite expensive (often enough to cover the cost of another type of account). And, even though performance is usually pretty fast, a broadband wireless card is still significantly slower than a cable or DSL connection.

# Manage MacBook's Power

MacBook needs power to operate, just like any other electronic device. Because it has an internal battery, you do not need to be connected to an outlet for MacBook to run (which is what makes it a mobile computer). One of the most important tasks as you travel with MacBook is to manage its power so that you do not run out of power at an inconvenient time.

**You can do a number of things to manage power on your MacBook. First, you can configure MacBook to use as little power as possible. Second, you can monitor the MacBook power status. Third, you can build a MacBook power toolkit.**

## Configure MacBook to Minimize Power Use

① Use the Energy Saver pane of the System Preferences application to configure MacBook so that it uses a minimum amount of power while running on the battery.

**Note:** *See the section "Save Energy" in Chapter 6 for the details.*

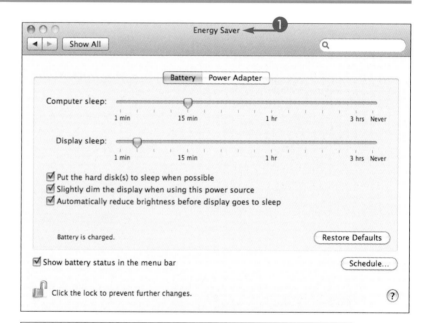

## Monitor the Battery Power

① Look at the battery icon (🔋) in the menu bar.

As battery power is used, the filled part of the icon shrinks to give you a relative idea of how much battery power remains.

**2** To access more-detailed information, open the Battery menu by clicking the battery icon (■).

● The amount of operating time (as time or as a percentage) you have left is shown at the top of the menu.

**3** Click **Show**.

**4** Choose how you want battery information to appear. For example, to display an estimate of the time remaining, select **Time**.

The attribute you select appears next to the battery icon on the menu bar so you can monitor your remaining battery time according to your preference.

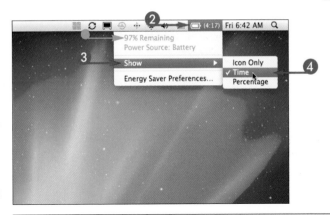

**Build a MacBook Power Toolkit**

**1** When you travel with MacBook, bring its power adapter with you so that you are able to recharge when you can; when possible, work with the power adapter connected to keep your battery fully charged so that you have maximum working time when running on battery power.

**2** If you frequently travel on long plane flights, purchase an Apple MagSafe Airline Adapter. This enables you to connect MacBook to the power outlets provided in some airplanes.

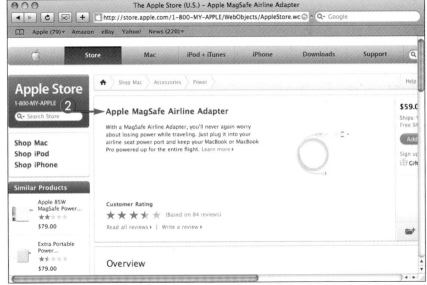

**TIPS**

**What are some other tips to extend my working time on the road?**

Put MacBook to sleep when you are not using it (such as by closing its lid). When it is sleeping, MacBook uses very little power. If you have an iPod, use it to listen to music or watch video instead of iTunes on MacBook. iTunes uses significant amounts of power because it requires a lot of disk activity. In general, the more disk activity required to run an application, the faster MacBook runs out of power, so be aware of the applications you use; keep only those applications that you are actively using open to prevent unnecessary activity. Also, turn off AirPort and Bluetooth to save the power they consume. Making your screen dimmer helps too.

**How can I determine if my seat on an airplane will have power available?**

Many airline Web sites enable you to check the specific kind of plane you will be flying on for flights you have booked or are considering. Often, you can get detailed specifications about the plane you will be on, including whether power ports are available for your seat. Power ports tend to be available on newer, larger planes flying longer routes. Ports are also more likely to be provided for first- or business-class seats. Regional or very old planes seldom have power ports available.

# Protect MacBook's Data with FileVault

When you use MacBook while traveling, you incur a higher risk of someone either accessing your MacBook or stealing it. In either situation, data stored on your MacBook can be compromised. This can lead to the loss of sensitive information, identity theft, or other harmful outcomes.

**The Mac OS X FileVault feature encrypts your data so that it cannot be used without a password. Even if someone does get into your MacBook, he cannot access its data without the password, rendering the information stored on your computer unusable.**

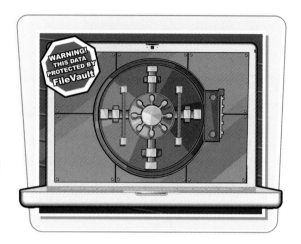

## Protect MacBook's Data with FileVault

① Open the System Preferences application.

② Click the **Security** icon.

③ Click the **FileVault** tab.

④ Click **Set Master Password**.

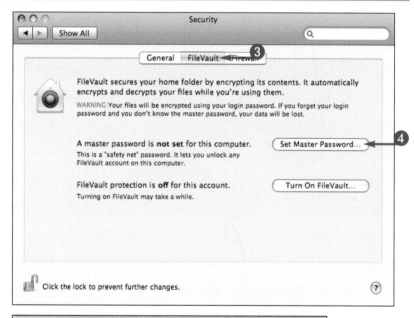

The Master Password sheet appears. You use this to create a master password that can be used to reset other users' passwords or to access their data in case they forget their passwords.

⑤ Type a master password in the Master Password and Verify fields.

⑥ Type a password hint in the Hint field.

⑦ Click **OK**.

The sheet closes, the password is set, and you move back to the FileVault tab. The Set Master Password button becomes the Change button to show you that a master password is set.

⑧ Click **Turn On FileVault**.

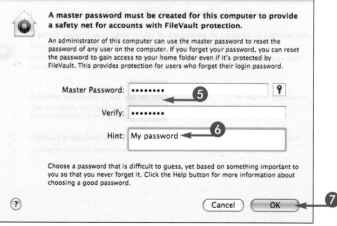

The password sheet appears.

**9** Type the password needed to access the current user's data (this is your user account's password if you are logged in under your user account).

**10** Click **OK**.

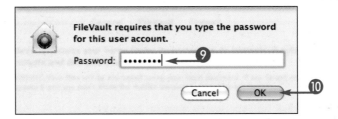

You move back to the FileVault tab.

*Note: If you activate FileVault, disable automatic login or someone can access your data just by starting MacBook.*

**11** If you want data to be deleted securely (overwritten so it cannot be recovered from the Trash), check the **Use secure erase** check box.

**12** If you want MacBook to be even more secure, check the **Use secure virtual memory** check box to encrypt data stored in virtual memory.

**13** Click **Turn On FileVault**.

MacBook logs you out of the current account and encrypts all the data stored in your Home folder. When the process is complete (expect it to take a long time if you have a lot of data), you can log back in.

*Note: When you are logged into your user account, your data is available. Make sure you log out whenever you are not using MacBook if there is any risk of it being accessed by someone you do not know or trust. Only when you are logged out is your data encrypted with FileVault.*

 **TIPS**

### When I log in and FileVault is on, I do not notice any difference. Is it working?
FileVault protects access to your data from outside your user account. For example, if someone tries to access your hard disk as if it were an external hard drive, the data is encrypted and cannot be used. When you are logged in under your user account and FileVault is on, you will probably not notice any difference. Look at the icon on your Home folder; if it is the Secure icon, FileVault is on.

### What happens if I forget my password?
Your FileVault password is the same as your user account's password, so if you forget that, you cannot log into your account and will have to reset it using the Mac OS X install disc. If another user forgets her password, you can use the master password you created to access the user's information because you can use this password to access all the data on MacBook.

# Protect MacBook with System Security

If other people use your MacBook, or there is some chance they will, consider adding some extra security to prevent unwanted access to the data stored on the computer.

**For example, you can require that a password be entered to wake MacBook up or to stop the screen saver. This is good if you sometimes leave MacBook running when someone else can possibly access it. Without your password, other users cannot access your information even if they can physically access MacBook.**

1. Open the System Preferences application.
2. Click the **Security** icon.
3. Click the **General** tab.
4. Check **Require password** if you want a password to be required to start using MacBook after it goes to sleep or the screen saver activates, and choose the amount of time that passes before the password is required on the pop-up menu.
5. If you want to prevent automatic login, check the **Disable automatic login** check box.

*Note: If you use MacBook in unsecured situations, such as in airports or other public locations, you should disable automatic login. If it is enabled, someone can access your data by restarting the computer (by pressing and holding the Power key until MacBook shuts off and then pressing it again) to log into your account.*

6. If you want to require a password to change any settings through System Preferences, check the **Require a password to unlock each System Preferences pane** check box.
7. To automatically log out after a specific period of inactivity, check the **Log out after** check box and enter the amount of idle time until you are logged out.
8. To make the data stored in virtual memory more secure, check **Use secure virtual memory**.
9. To prevent the location of MacBook from being identified through location services, check **Disable Location Services**.
10. To prevent control of MacBook with remote control devices, check the **Disable remote control infrared receiver** check box.

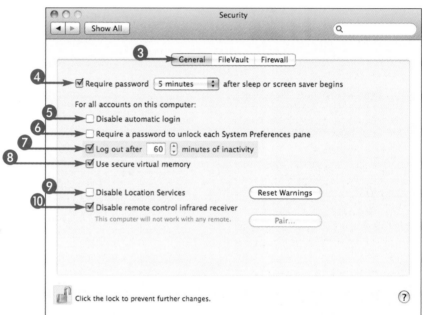

# Protect MacBook with Its Firewall

When you are using a known network to access the Internet, it should be equipped with its own firewall or Network Address Translation (NAT) protection to prevent computers you do not control from being able to see or access MacBook. However, if you are not sure about how much protection a network provides, such as when you are connecting to a network in a public place, you should use the Mac OS X firewall to block attempts to access MacBook from the Internet.

**You might have to tweak the firewall a bit to be as secure as possible while still allowing you to do what you want.**

## Protect MacBook with Its Firewall

① Open the System Preferences application.

② Click the **Security** icon.

③ Click the **Firewall** tab.

④ To prevent most incoming connections while allowing Mac OS X to automatically allow connections for some applications, click **Start**.

⑤ Try your normal tasks.

  If they work as expected, you can skip the rest of these steps. If not, configure the firewall to allow specific tasks.

⑥ Click **Advanced**.

⑦ To add applications through which you want to allow incoming connections, click **Add** (➕).

**Note:** To prevent any network access to MacBook, check the **Block all incoming connections** check box.

⑧ Use the resulting sheet to select the applications or services you want to allow and click **Add** (➕).

  Services and applications that are allowed to have incoming connections are shown on the list.

⑨ To prevent MacBook from being detected on a network by services you did not request, such as through Bonjour, check the **Enable stealth mode** check box.

⑩ Click **OK**.

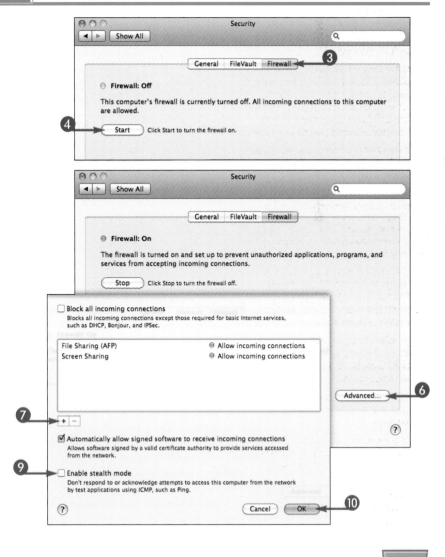

# Synchronize Files with Other Computers

If you use MacBook and another computer, such as an iMac, you should keep documents you work on synchronized on each computer so that changes you make on MacBook are reflected on the iMac, and vice versa.

**You can make sure you have the most current version of documents in both locations in a couple of ways. If you have MobileMe, you can use your iDisk as the synchronizing mechanism; this is good because the process is mostly automatic. You can also use a smart folder to identify files that have changed recently so that you can synchronize them manually.**

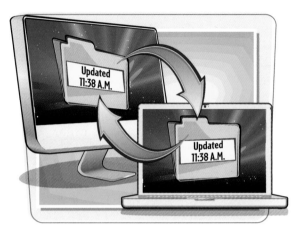

### Synchronize Files Using an iDisk

1. Open the MobileMe pane of the System Preferences application.

2. Click the **iDisk** tab.

3. Click **Start**.

   MacBook creates a copy of your iDisk on its hard drive.

4. Choose **Automatically** on the pop-up menu.

5. Check **Always keep the most recent version of a file**.

   MacBook synchronizes the version of files on the local iDisk (on your hard drive) with the one stored on the Internet.

6. Save documents that you want to keep in synch on a folder on the iDisk.

7. Perform Steps **1** to **5** to configure your iDisk on each computer that you want to keep in synch.

   Each computer you configure accesses the same iDisk. When there are two versions of the same file, the most recent version is kept on all the synced computers. This ensures you always have the current version of a file on each machine.

**Note:** *If you might want to keep multiple versions of a document, name each version you want to keep differently. If you do not, the versions on each computer are overwritten with the most recent version of the file.*

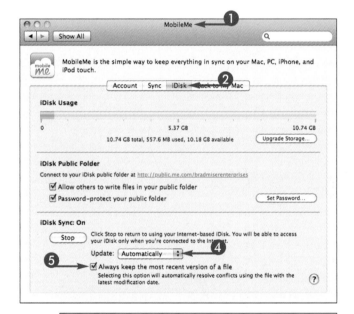

## Synchronize Files Using a Smart Folder

1 Create a smart folder on MacBook that uses criteria by which you want to identify files you have changed while traveling with MacBook.

*Note: See Chapter 4 for the details of creating a smart folder.*

2 When you return from a trip, use the smart folder to find all the documents you have changed recently.

3 Copy the changed files from MacBook to the computer on which you want to synchronize them.

*Note: Configure file sharing to make it easy to copy files between computers (see Chapter 7).*

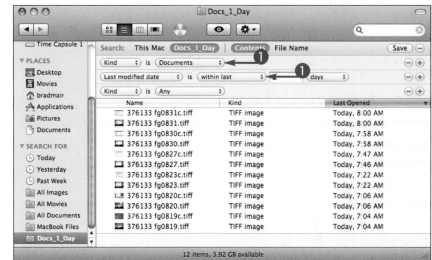

**TIPS**

### What about synchronization applications?

There are third-party applications that keep files stored in multiple locations in synch. You designate a source folder and a target folder, and then you determine the direction of the

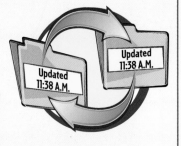

synchronization, such as from the target to the source or in both directions. Based on your settings, the application automatically performs the required synchronization. One example is ChronoSynch, available at www.econtechnologies.com.

### What do I need to do about backing up files that I change while traveling?

If you configure your iDisk to synchronize automatically and store the files on which you work on your iDisk, your files are automatically backed up as soon as you connect to the

Internet. Chapter 17 discusses Time Machine, which enables you to back up information on MacBook. As soon as you return to where your backup hard drive is located, connect the hard drive to MacBook; the backup process launches immediately so that any changes you made while traveling are protected in the current backup.

# Expand Storage Space with an External Hard Drive

Your MacBook includes a hard drive on which you store the operating system, applications, and your own files and folders. Over time, you might run low on available disk space, especially if you do large video or DVD projects. More importantly, you should back up your files using Time Machine, which requires a drive outside your Mac, such as an external hard drive. You can connect MacBook to an external hard drive to expand the working storage space available to you or to use Time Machine.

**There are two basic steps to preparing an external hard drive to work with MacBook. First, you make the connection between the computer and the hard drive. Second, you use the Disk Utility application to format and partition the hard drive.**

## Expand Storage Space with an External Hard Drive

### Connect and Power an External Hard Drive

1 Connect the hard drive to a power source and turn it on.

2 Use a USB cable to connect the hard drive to the MacBook's USB port.

*Note: Most hard drives include the cable you need to connect to MacBook. However, some do not. Check the package information to make sure the cable is included. If it is not, you have to buy a cable separately.*

The hard drive is ready to format and partition.

### Format and Partition an External Hard Drive

1 Open the Applications folder, open the Utilities folder, and then double-click the **Disk Utility** application.

- When Disk Utility opens, you see all available disks in the left pane.
- ② Select the external hard disk.
- ③ Click the **Partition** tab.
- You see the number of partitions in which the disk is currently organized; a new disk has one partition.

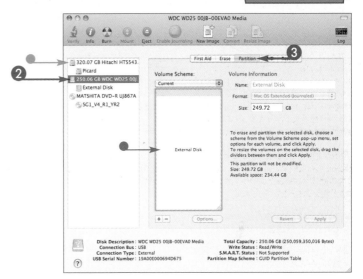

- ④ On the **Volume Scheme** pop-up menu, choose the number of partitions you want to create on the disk.
- The space on the disk is grouped into the number of partitions you selected. Each partition is named "Untitled *X,*" where *X* is a sequential number.

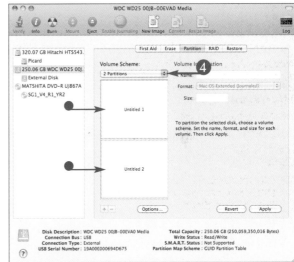

**TIPS**

### What kind of external hard drive works with MacBook?

MacBook can work with any external hard drive that supports USB 2.0, and you want to get the largest drive you can afford. For backing up data, the hard drive should be at least twice as large as the disk in MacBook; for example, if your MacBook has a 500GB hard drive, the external hard drive should be at least 1TB. You can also use Mac- or Windows-compatible hard drives. If a hard drive is formatted for Windows, you should reformat and partition it before using it (any software that comes with it probably will not run on MacBook using Mac OS X, but you could run it under Windows running on MacBook).

### Should I care about how fast a disk spins?

A hard drive uses a spinning magnetic disk on which data is written and from which it is read. The faster a drive spins, the faster MacBook can read data from and write data to the disk. However, unless you are doing very disk-intensive work that you store on the drive, such as very large graphics or video files, you are not likely to notice any difference in performance based on disk speed. For tasks like backing up, the speed of a disk is even less important. In almost all cases, size and cost are much more important considerations.

continued

Although being able to access more storage space is useful for current projects and documents, it is even more important for backing up the information you have stored on MacBook.

**With an external hard drive, you can use the Mac OS X Time Machine feature to back up your important data. Should something happen to this data on MacBook or to the MacBook itself, you can easily recover the data from the external drive so that you do not lose important information or your investment in iTunes content or applications. For more information about Time Machine, see Chapter 17.**

## Expand Storage Space with an External Hard Drive *(continued)*

**5** Select the top partition.

● Its information is shown in the Volume Information section.

**6** Type a name for the partition in the Name field.

**7** On the **Format** pop-up menu, choose **Mac OS Extended (Journaled)**.

**8** Enter the size of the first partition in the Size field and press Return.

*Note: You can also change the size of partitions by dragging the resize handle located in the horizontal bar between the partitions in the Volume Scheme box.*

The partition is named and sized.

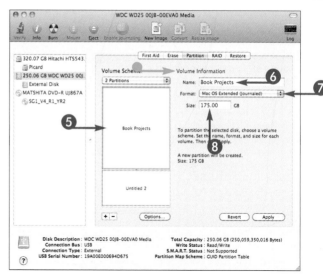

**9** Select the next partition.

**10** Repeat Steps **6** to **8** to name, format, and size the partition.

**11** Repeat Steps **9** and **10** until you have configured each partition.

*Note: The total size of the partitions equals the usable size of the hard disk.*

**12** Click **Apply**.

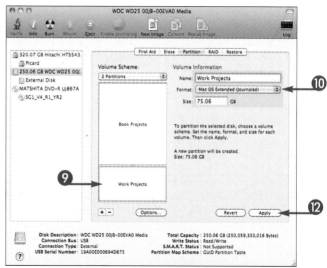

The partition warning appears.

*Note: When you partition a disk, all the data it contains is erased, so make sure you do not need its data before continuing.*

**13** Click **Partition**.

Disk Utility partitions the drive according to your settings.

**14** If the Time Machine dialog appears, click **Cancel**.

*Note: See Chapter 17 for information about configuring Time Machine.*

**15** Quit Disk Utility.

**16** Open a Finder window.

● You see the partitions on the external drive, and they are ready to be used just like the MacBook internal hard drive.

*Note: Before disconnecting a hard drive from MacBook, click the **Eject** button (⏏) next to its icon in the sidebar or press the ⏏ key and wait for the disk icon to disappear from the sidebar. Disconnecting a drive without ejecting it first can damage its data.*

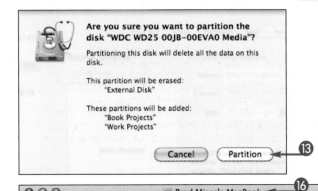

---

**TIPS**

### Why can I not partition a new hard drive?

Some Windows hard drives come in a format incompatible with the Mac operating system, and when you try to partition them, the process fails while displaying an error message that is not all that helpful. Before you click the **Apply** button on the **Partition** tab of the Disk Utility application in Step **12**, click the **Options** button. On the resulting sheet, click **GUID Partition Table** and then click **OK**. The sheet closes. Continue with the rest of the steps as described. This reformats the drive so that it is compatible with MacBook.

### What is a partition and how many should I create on my external hard disk?

Partitions are logical volumes on a hard disk, which means that they behave as if each partition is its own hard disk, even though they are actually on the same physical disk. You can create partitions for various purposes, such as to organize data. In most cases, you should limit the partitions on one disk to one or two so that you do not end up with a lot of partitions that are too small to be usable.

# Connect and Use an External Display

You can never have too much screen space to work with. In addition to making your document windows larger so that you can see more of their contents, more screen space helps you work efficiently because you can have more windows open so you can use them at the same time.

**To add screen space to MacBook, you can connect an external display.**

### Connect the Required Adapter to the External Display

1 Purchase the Mini DisplayPort adapter appropriate for the display you are using.

*Note: You can obtain a Mini DisplayPort adapter for DVI or VGA displays. Modern displays use the DVI.*

2 Plug the small end of the adapter into the Mini DisplayPort on your MacBook.

3 Connect the other end of the adapter to the cable connected to the VGA or DVI input port on the display.

4 Connect the display to a power source, and power it up.

### Configure the External Display

1 Open the System Preferences application and click the **Displays** icon.

● Displays pane opens on the MacBook display and on the external display.

2 Click the **Arrangement** tab on the Displays pane on the MacBook screen.

● You see an icon representation of each display.

3 Drag the external display's icon to match the physical location of the display compared to MacBook (on its left or right side).

4 If you want the external display to be the primary display, drag the menu bar from the MacBook display's icon onto the external display's icon.

5 If you want the displays to show the same information, check the **Mirror Displays** check box and skip the rest of these steps.

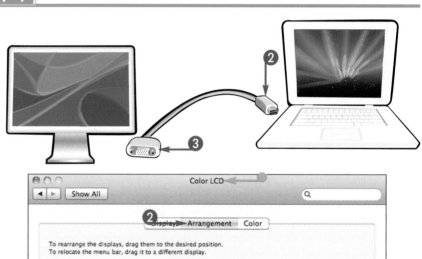

⑥ Select the **Displays** pane from the System Preferences on the external display.

⑦ Click the **Display** tab.

⑧ Choose the resolution for the external display by selecting it on the list of available resolutions.

⑨ If the **Refresh rate** pop-up menu appears, choose the highest rate available.

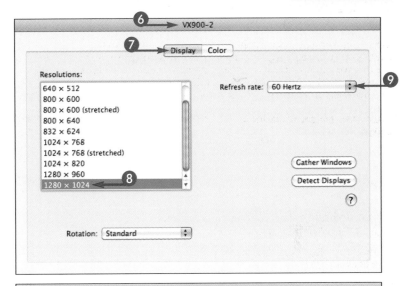

⑩ Click the **Color** tab.

⑪ Select the color profile for the display you are using.

⑫ Quit the System Preferences application.

You now can use the external display. When video mirroring is off, the two displays act as a single, large desktop area. When video mirroring is on, you see the same information on both screens.

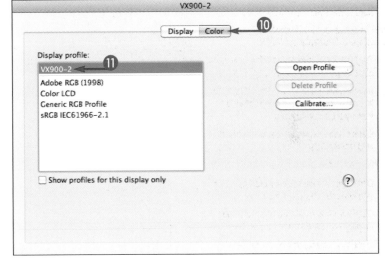

### What kind of external display should I get for MacBook?

MacBook supports many different displays and resolutions. The two most important considerations are size and cost. Larger displays are better because they give you more working space. They also tend to be more expensive, although that depends on the specific brand you choose. Be wary of very inexpensive displays because they tend to have poor image quality. In most cases, if you choose a display from a reputable manufacturer or reseller, such as Apple (the Apple displays are extremely high quality, but are also on the expensive end of the scale) or ViewSonic, any display you get will work well for you.

### Can I use a projector with MacBook?

Yes. You connect and use a projector in the same way as an external display. When you use a projector, you typically want to turn display mirroring on (by checking the **Mirror Displays** check box in the Arrangement tab) so that the audience sees the same information that appears on the MacBook screen.

# Connect and Use a Bluetooth Mouse

You might find that the MacBook trackpad works really well for you and that you never want to use anything else; or, you might prefer a mouse when you are working with MacBook in one place. It is mostly a matter of personal preference.

**If you do want to use a mouse, a Bluetooth mouse is a good option because it has no wires to interfere with you moving the mouse.**

① Insert batteries into the mouse and turn it on.

② Place the mouse in discovery mode.

**Note:** *See the documentation for the specific mouse you use to see how this is done.*

③ Open the System Preferences application and click the **Bluetooth** icon.

● The Bluetooth pane appears.

If you have configured Bluetooth previously, you see the devices that you have connected to in the left pane of the window.

● If you have not configured Bluetooth previously, you see an empty pane with the Set Up New Device button in its center.

④ Check the **On** check box to turn Bluetooth on.

⑤ Check the **Discoverable** check box so that other Bluetooth devices can find MacBook.

⑥ Check the **Show Bluetooth status in the menu bar** check box to enable the Bluetooth menu so that you can control Bluetooth from the desktop.

⑦ Click the **Add** button (⊞), or the **Set Up New Device** button.

The Bluetooth Setup Assistant appears. It looks for any devices it can discover and presents them on the list.

⑧ Click the device you want to set up.

⑨ Click **Continue**.

MacBook attempts to connect to the device. If successful, you see the Conclusion screen.

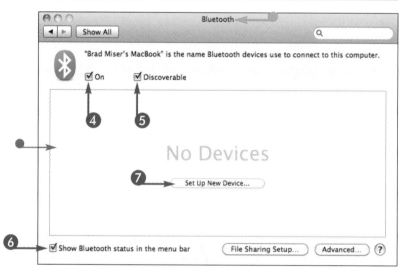

10 Click **Quit**.

You go back to the Bluetooth pane where you see the mouse you configured.

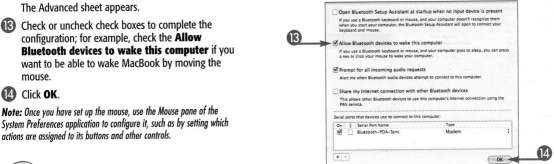

11 Select the Bluetooth mouse.

● You see information about the mouse you configured.

12 Click **Advanced**.

The Advanced sheet appears.

13 Check or uncheck check boxes to complete the configuration; for example, check the **Allow Bluetooth devices to wake this computer** if you want to be able to wake MacBook by moving the mouse.

14 Click **OK**.

*Note: Once you have set up the mouse, use the Mouse pane of the System Preferences application to configure it, such as by setting which actions are assigned to its buttons and other controls.*

 TIPS

**What about other kinds of mice?**

You can use many kinds of mice with MacBook. To use a wired mouse, simply plug its USB cable into a USB port. To use a non-Bluetooth wireless mouse, connect its receiver to a USB port. Regardless of how you connect a mouse to MacBook, you can use the Mouse pane of the System Preferences application to configure it.

**What is the best kind of Bluetooth mouse?**

Choosing a mouse is a personal decision in that one person's favorite mouse might be unusable to someone else. The most important consideration when choosing a mouse is the comfort of the mouse in your hand. If possible, you should try using a mouse before buying it. Next, consider the number of controls, buttons, and other features a mouse offers. At the least, a mouse should have two buttons and a scroll wheel. Some devices have more controls; for example, the Apple Magic Mouse replicates the gesture features of the MacBook trackpad by allowing you to make gestures on the top of the mouse.

# Connect and Use External Speakers

MacBook has speakers, but their sound quality is somewhat less than spectacular. With iTunes, DVD Player, and all the other great applications for which sound is an important element, you should consider using external speakers when you use MacBook in one location.

**You can use a variety of speakers with MacBook as long as they are powered (also called computer) speakers. Some speaker sets have two speakers (left and right), whereas others have three (left, right, and subwoofer). For the ultimate in sound, consider a digital 5.1 sound system.**

## Connect and Use External Speakers

① Connect the speaker input to the Audio line out port, which is marked with the headphones icon.

② Make the connections between the speakers, such as between the left and right speaker and the subwoofer.

③ Power up the speakers.

④ Open the System Preferences application and click the **Sound** icon.

● The Sound pane appears.

⑤ Click the **Output** tab.

⑥ Select the speakers you want to use for sound output.

This option appears as Headphones even when you attach a set of speakers.

*Note: You can also connect any pair of analog headphones to the MacBook audio port, which is a great way to enjoy good sound quality on the move.*

⑦ If controls for the speakers appear, use them to improve the sound.

For example, you might be able to set a balance level and system volume level.

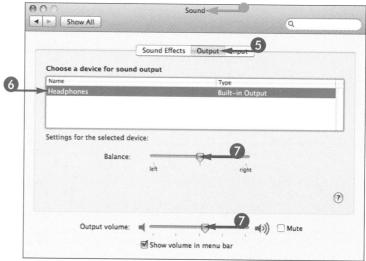

⑧ Play sound with an application such as iTunes.

*Note: For more information about iTunes, see Chapter 18.*

⑨ Use the application's controls to set the specific volume level.

⑩ Adjust the volume level and other settings using the speaker system's controls.

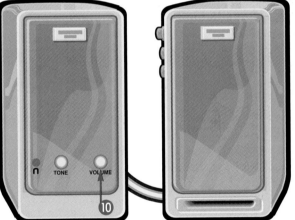

**TIPS**

### Does MacBook support digital audio?

Yes. To use a digital speaker system with MacBook, you need a TOSLINK adapter that connects to the digital audio cable and plugs into the Line out port on MacBook (which supports both analog and digital audio). When you connect the other end to the speaker system, you can enjoy the benefits of digital, such as surround sound coming from multiple speakers.

### What kind of speakers should I get?

The speakers you should get depend on how important sound quality is to you, how much money you want to spend, whether you want digital or analog, and whether you want the speakers to be portable. A nice three-speaker analog set can deliver reasonable sound quality for a modest price. If you want to have better sound when you move around with MacBook, consider purchasing a portable speaker system. Many of these are available for iPods. As long as they have an auxiliary input, you can connect MacBook to them.

# Connect To and Use a USB Hub

Many devices use USB to connect to a computer. Examples of these include external hard drives, mice, iPhones, iPods, digital cameras, and printers. MacBook has two USB ports, and so you are able to connect only two devices to it at a time, which can be inconvenient.

**For situations in which you want to connect more than three USB devices to MacBook at the same time, you can use an external USB hub. You connect the hub to MacBook and then connect USB devices to the ports on the hub. MacBook can access these devices just as if they are connected to its USB port.**

## Connect To and Use a USB Hub

### Obtain an External USB HUB

1. Visit your favorite retailer.

2. Look for a USB 2 hub with the number of ports matching or exceeding the number of devices you want to have connected at the same time.

*Note: You should also consider whether the hub gets its power from MacBook or requires an external power source. An external power source is a nuisance because you have to carry it with you, but a self-powered hub uses power from MacBook, which shortens life when operating on battery power.*

3. Purchase a hub.

### Install a USB Hub

1. Connect the input port on the hub to the MacBook USB port.

2. Connect the hub to a power source, if required.

3. Connect USB devices to the hub.

   The devices are ready to use.

# Connect To and Use Ethernet Devices

MacBook is designed to be wireless when it comes to connecting to many devices — most importantly, local networks and the Internet. However, Ethernet, which is a wired technology, does offer some benefits over wireless connections. Ethernet is faster, and so achieves the best network performance. Ethernet is also more secure than wireless because you have to be physically connected to a network to access it.

**To connect to a network or devices (such as a printer) with Ethernet, you can use MacBook's Ethernet port. Use an Ethernet cable to connect the port to an AirPort Base Station or other Ethernet device.**

## Connect To and Use Ethernet Devices

**1** Connect an Ethernet cable to the MacBook Ethernet port.

**2** Connect the other end of the cable to an Ethernet device, such as an AirPort Extreme Base Station.

**3** Configure the Ethernet connection using the appropriate pane of the System Preferences or other application.

For example, you can use the Network pane to configure an Ethernet network connection.

# Synchronize MacBook with an iPhone

In addition to its amazing cell phone features, the iPhone offers iPod functionality along with calendars, contacts, e-mail, and Web browsing.

**Some of the information you use on iPhone can come from MacBook. For example, if you use iCal to manage your calendar, you can synchronize your calendar on iPhone so that changes you make in iCal are reflected on the iPhone, and vice versa. You can also synchronize your e-mail accounts, contacts from Address Book, and even your Safari bookmarks.**

## Synchronize MacBook with an iPhone

① Connect your iPhone to your MacBook using its USB cable.

The iPhone is mounted on your MacBook, iTunes opens, and you see the iPhone in the Devices section of the iTunes Source list.

*Note: If you have taken photos on the iPhone, iPhoto opens as soon as you connect the iPhone to MacBook so you can import its photos.*

② Select your iPhone.

③ Click the **Info** tab.

④ Check the **Sync Address Book contacts** check box.

⑤ To synchronize all contacts, click the **All contacts** radio button, or to synchronize just specific groups, click the **Selected groups** radio button and check the check box for each group you want to synchronize.

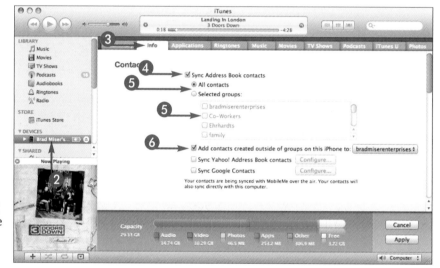

⑥ To add contacts that you create on your iPhone to a specific group in Address Book, click the **Add contacts created outside of groups on this iPhone to** check box and choose the group on the pop-up menu.

⑦ In the Calendars section, check the **Sync iCal calendars** check box.

⑧ If you want to synchronize all of your calendars, click the **All calendars** radio button, or if you want to synchronize only specific calendars, click the **Selected calendars** radio button and check the check box for each calendar you want to synchronize.

⑨ To exclude older events from the synchronization, check the **Do not sync events older than** check box and enter the number of days in the field.

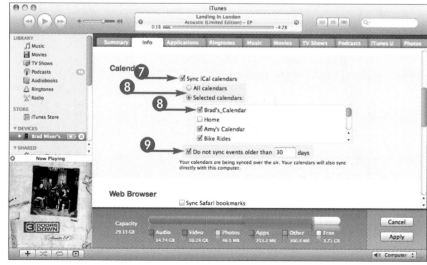

⑩ To synchronize your Web bookmarks, check the **Sync Safari bookmarks** check box.

*Note: For information about bookmarks, see Chapter 11.*

⑪ To move your e-mail accounts to your iPhone, check the **Sync selected Mail accounts** check box.

*Note: For information about e-mail, see Chapter 12.*

⑫ Check the check box for each account you want to synchronize.

⑬ Scroll down to the Advanced section.

⑭ Check the check boxes for the information you want to be replaced on your iPhone when you synchronize.

⑮ Click **Apply**.

Each time you synchronize, including when you click Apply, the information you configured is moved between your MacBook and iPhone.

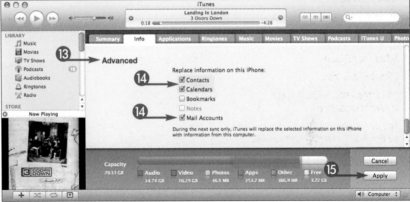

## TIPS

**Can I synchronize MacBook with other kinds of cell phones?**

If your cell phone supports Bluetooth, you can synchronize its information with MacBook wirelessly. In most cases, you can at least synchronize contacts. With other devices, you might be able to move calendar and other information from MacBook to the cell phone, and vice versa; it depends on the specific phone that you use. Some devices require a third-party application to fully synchronize.

**What is a better way to sync?**

Connecting an iPhone to MacBook using a USB cable is easy enough, but why bother? If you have a MobileMe account, you can synchronize your information wirelessly. See Chapter 10 for information about obtaining a MobileMe account. To set up a MobileMe account on an iPhone, go to the Mail, Contacts, Calendars screen, tap **Add Account**, and follow the on-screen instructions to set up the MobileMe account and configure its sync options.

# Enjoying the Internet

MacBook is ideal for taking advantage of all the Internet has to offer. With MobileMe, the Internet becomes an extension of MacBook's desktop, including online disk space and storing information so you can access it using many different devices. Safari is Mac OS X's excellent Web browser. Using Mail, you can send, receive, and organize e-mail. To keep in touch with people near and far, use iChat for text, audio, and even video chats.

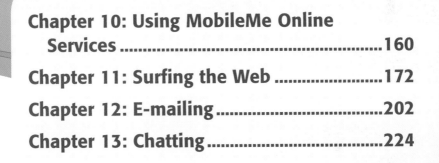

# Explore MobileMe

A MobileMe account gives you access to a number of useful services and online applications that you can use as much as you want. Because your MobileMe account is integrated with MacBook, you can consider MobileMe to be an extension of your MacBook desktop on the Internet.

## MobileMe Account

To use MobileMe, you must have a MobileMe account. You can obtain an account from the MacBook desktop or by using a Web browser. A MobileMe account includes, by default, 20GB of storage space on Apple servers, an e-mail account, space for online galleries of your photos, and more. You can also purchase a family account that provides up to four additional user accounts under a single, master MobileMe account (for distinct e-mail addresses and iDisks). At the time of this writing, the cost of an individual MobileMe account is $99 per year, whereas the cost of a family account is $149 per year when purchased directly from Apple (you can usually pay less at amazon.com). You can also upgrade accounts by adding disk space.

## iDisk

One of the best features of MobileMe is iDisk, which is a virtual disk on Apple servers on which you can store files. Your account includes 20GB of disk space, which is allocated to both your iDisk and your e-mail storage. You can use your iDisk just like the MacBook's internal drive, and it is also where you store other files for online use, such as photos and movies in your Gallery, Web site files, and so on. You can access your iDisk directly from the MacBook desktop, from the iDisk application on the MobileMe Web site, from any other computer you use, including Windows computers, and from an iPhone or iPod touch.

## MobileMe E-mail

Another great feature of MobileMe is that you get an e-mail account, with an e-mail address that is *yourmembername@me.com*, where *yourmembername* is the member name of your MobileMe account. You can send and receive e-mail from your MobileMe account just like you do with other e-mail accounts that you may have, using an e-mail application such as Mail, using an iPhone or iPod touch, or directly from the Mail application on your MobileMe Web site. You can also create e-mail aliases that enable you to use multiple addresses at the same time.

## Gallery

Using the Gallery, you can easily display photos on the Web. You can upload photos to your Gallery from your desktop, or you can publish to your Gallery directly from iPhoto. You can organize your online galleries in different photo albums; once an album is on your gallery, people can use the album's link to view its photos within a Web browser. You can also enable people to download photos from or upload them to your Gallery.

## Synchronization

If you have more than one Mac, such as a MacBook and an iMac, or an iPhone or iPod touch, you probably want to be able to access some of the same information from all your devices, such as your e-mail, calendars, and contacts. Using MobileMe, you can synchronize Macs, Windows PCs, iPhones, and iPod touches so that changes you make to information on one device are copied to the others automatically or on your command. This makes it easy to ensure that you have access to information you need from any computer you happen to be using as well as from an iPhone or iPod touch.

# Obtain and Configure a MobileMe Account

Because MobileMe is integrated into Mac OS X, you can obtain a MobileMe account right from the MacBook desktop. When you do, you are directed to the Apple Web site, where you provide the information required to create your account.

**After you have created your account, you configure MacBook (and your other computers and iPhone) to access MobileMe, and all its services are ready for you to use.**

① Click the **Apple** menu () and then select **System Preferences**.

② Click the **MobileMe** icon.

③ Click **Learn More**.

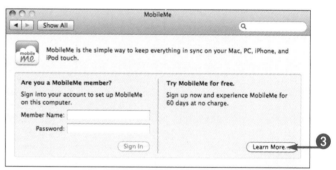

Safari opens and loads the MobileMe Web site.

④ Click **Free Trial**.

The first page of a two-step form appears.

⑤ Fill out the information on this page.

**Note:** *Be thoughtful about what you choose as your member name; in addition to using this to log in to MobileMe, it becomes part of your e-mail address. You cannot change this name after you have created an account.*

⑥ Click **Continue**.

⑦ In a similar way, complete the second page of the form.

The Welcome to MobileMe screen appears, and provides information that you need to use your MobileMe account.

⑧ Go back to the MobileMe pane of the System Preferences application by clicking the **System Preferences** icon on the Dock.

⑨ Type your member name.

⑩ Type your password.

⑪ Click **Sign In**.

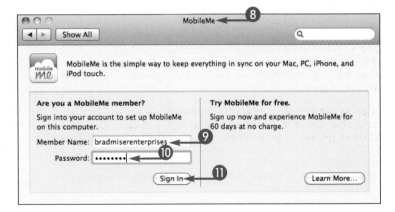

● Your account information is configured on MacBook, and the MobileMe pane updates to show that you have configured MobileMe. You can now access MobileMe services from the desktop or from the MobileMe Web site.

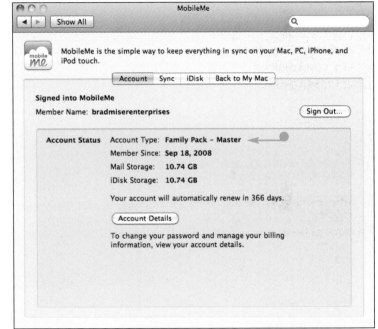

---

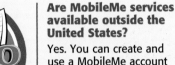

### What happens when my trial period expires?

You can use your MobileMe account for 60 days at no cost to you. If you do not cancel the account prior to the end of the trial period, your account is converted into a full account and is available to you for one year (you have the option to renew the account on a yearly basis). You only need to take action to cancel the account if you do not want it past the trial period.

### Are MobileMe services available outside the United States?

Yes. You can create and use a MobileMe account from many different countries. The rates charged for a MobileMe account vary from country to country, but the MobileMe services that you can access are similar.

# Use an iDisk

An iDisk is a volume of disk space on the Apple servers that you can access through your MobileMe membership. iDisk is built into Mac OS X so that after you configure MacBook for MobileMe, it appears on your desktop just like other hard drives that you use. You can also access your iDisk using the iDisk application on the MobileMe Web site.

**By default, an iDisk has a number of folders on it, such as Public, My Documents, and Sites. Some folders, such as Public, are used to store files that you want other people to be able to access. You can use these folders or create your own and then store documents and other files in them.**

Use an iDisk

### Configure iDisk

1. Open the MobileMe pane of the System Preferences application and click the **iDisk** tab.

● The iDisk Usage gauge shows how much of your iDisk space you are currently using.

2. If you want other people to be able to store files in your iDisk's Public folder, select the **Allow others to write files in your public folder** radio button.

3. To put a password on your Public folder, check the **Password-protect your public folder** check box; if you do not want to protect your Public folder with a password, skip to Step **7**.

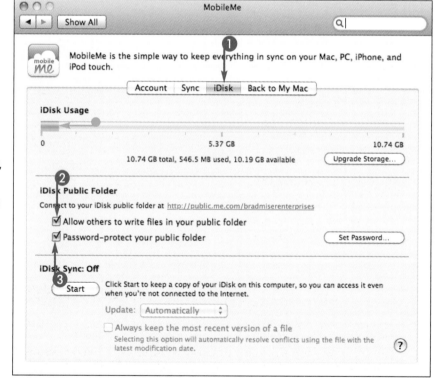

4. Type the password for the folder in the Password field.

*Note: You cannot use your MobileMe password to protect your Public folder.*

5. Confirm the password by typing it again in the Confirm field.

6. Click **OK**.

   The sheet closes and your password is set.

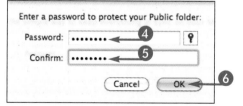

**7** If you want to keep a copy of your iDisk on MacBook so that you can access it even when you are not connected to the Internet, click **Start**. If you only want to access your iDisk over the Internet, skip to Step **11**.

**8** To update your copy of iDisk automatically, choose **Automatically** on the pop-up menu.

**9** If you want to manually update iDisk, choose **Manually** on the pop-up menu.

**10** To ensure you always keep the most recent version of files, check the **Always keep the most recent version of a file** check box.

**11** Press ⌘+Q to quit the System Preferences application.

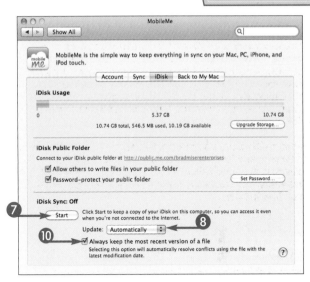

**Use iDisk**

**1** Open a Finder window and click the **iDisk** icon.

***Note:** You can also go to your iDisk by choosing **Go**, clicking **iDisk**, and then clicking **MyiDisk**.*

The contents of your iDisk appear.

If you chose to keep a copy of iDisk on MacBook, all of its data is copied to MacBook.

● The status of the sync process is shown at the bottom of the window.

**2** To sync the contents of your iDisk, click the **Sync** button (⟳) next to the iDisk icon to synchronize the two versions of iDisk.

### How do I access my iDisk from a Windows PC?

To access your iDisk from a Windows computer, open the MobileMe Preferences control panel (you must have installed the latest version of iTunes for this to be available) and sign into your MobileMe account on the PC. Open a desktop window. From the **Tools** menu, choose **Map Network Drive**. Choose the drive letter for your iDisk. In the Folder box, type **http://idisk.me.com/***membername*, where *membername* is your MobileMe user name. Click the different user name link. Enter your MobileMe user name and password and click **OK**. Click **Finish**. You can access the iDisk by using the drive letter you assigned to it.

### Can I use iDisk to back up my files?

You can use your iDisk to store any files, including backups. Even better, you can download Apple's Backup application from the Software folder on your iDisk and use it to automatically back up files to folders on your iDisk. Backing up to iDisk is useful because the files are stored independent of your computer, and even your location, for maximum protection. Because they are stored online, you can access your backups from any computer that can access your iDisk.

# Use MobileMe Webmail

You can access your MobileMe e-mail in an e-mail application, such as Mail. You can learn how in Chapter 12.

**You can also access MobileMe e-mail from any computer through the Web. This makes MobileMe e-mail very convenient because as long as you are using a computer with Internet access, your MobileMe e-mail is not far away.**

Use MobileMe Webmail

① Open a Web browser and go to www.me.com.

The MobileMe Login page appears.

② Type your MobileMe member name if needed.

③ Type your password.

④ Check the **Keep me logged in for two weeks** check box if you want to remain logged into your account.

⑤ Click **Log In**.

You move to the MobileMe Web site.

⑥ Click the **Mail** icon (📧).

The MobileMe Mail Web application appears.

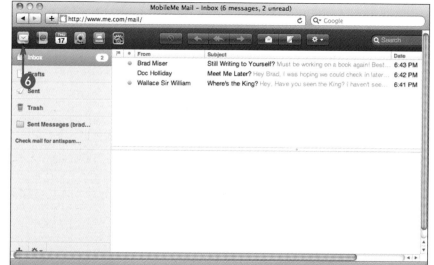

**7** Click an e-mail to read it.

● The message appears in the lower pane of the window.

**8** To reply to a message, click the **Reply** button () and type your reply.

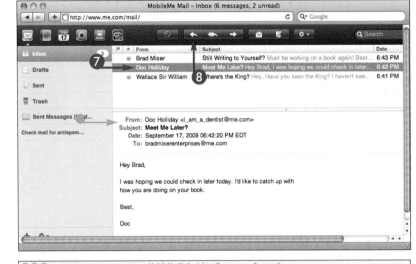

**9** To create a new message, click the **New Message** icon (■).

● The New Message window appears.

**10** Address the message, type the subject, and type the message. (If you are replying to a message, some of this information is completed already.)

**11** Click the **Send** button (■).

The e-mail is sent.

**Note:** *Most of the tools available on the MobileMe Mail Web application work just like they do in the Mac OS X Mail application (see Chapter 12 for details).*

### How do I access my MobileMe e-mail in Mail?

Mail is designed to work with MobileMe e-mail accounts. When you configure MacBook to access MobileMe services, your MobileMe e-mail account is available immediately, and you can set it up with just a couple of clicks. See Chapter 12 for more information.

### Do I have to use Mail or the MobileMe Web site to access my MobileMe e-mail?

No, you can access MobileMe e-mail as you can any other e-mail account. When you sign up for MobileMe, information appears for the servers that you need to configure to access MobileMe e-mail. You can use this information to set up your MobileMe e-mail in any e-mail application, such as Entourage on the Mac or Eudora on Windows or Mac.

# Create an Online Photo Gallery

With a MobileMe account and iPhoto, you can quickly and easily publish photos to the Web, where they are viewable in any Web browser. You can also allow people to download photos from your photo Web site to their computers.

**Use iPhoto to create a photo album and then publish it as a gallery. Then, you can visit the gallery from your MobileMe account or via any Web browser.**

### Use iPhoto to Publish a Gallery

**1** In iPhoto, create a photo album.

**Note:** *For help with iPhoto, see Chapter 19.*

**2** Add the photos you want to publish to the album.

**3** With the album selected, click the **MobileMe** button (⬜).

**4** On the **Album Viewable by** pop-up menu, choose **Everyone** to make the gallery available to everyone who visits the site, **Only Me** to limit access to the site to you, or **Edit Names and Passwords** to identify specific people who can access the site.

**Note:** *If you choose Names and Passwords, a sheet appears. Use the sheet to create user names and passwords and then select the galleries those users will be able to access.*

**5** To allow visitors to be able to download photos, check the **Downloading of photos or entire album** check box.

**6** To permit people to upload photos via the Web, check the **Uploading of photos via web browser** check box.

**7** To allow viewers to add photos via e-mail, check the **Adding of photos via email** check box.

**8** To display titles on the gallery, check the **Photo titles** check box.

**9** If you checked the check box in Step **7**, check the **Email address for uploading photos** check box to display the e-mail address on the gallery page.

**10** Click **Publish**.

iPhoto publishes the photo album to the Web.

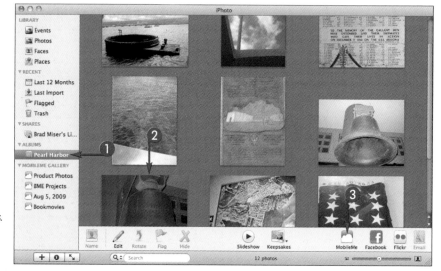

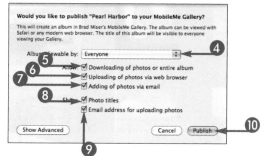

### Visiting a Gallery from Your MobileMe Web Site

1 If you are not already logged in to your MobileMe Web site, log in.

2 Click the **Gallery** button (▣).

The Gallery application opens.

3 Select the album you want to view.

● The images in the album appear.

● The gallery's URL is shown in the upper-right corner of the window.

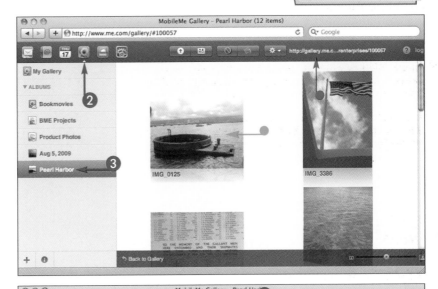

### Visiting a Gallery from a Web Browser

1 Using a Web browser, go to the gallery's URL.

● The gallery appears in the Web browser window.

2 View images in the gallery.

3 Use the controls to change how the photos are displayed, download photos, and so on.

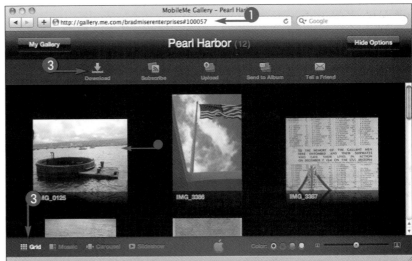

 **TIPS**

#### How do I enable others to view my photos?

Go to the gallery in a Web browser. Click the **Tell a Friend** button (✉). Complete the resulting sheet by typing your e-mail address, the person's e-mail address, a message, and other options. When you send the message, it includes a link the person can click to go to the gallery. If you require a user name and password to view the gallery, make sure you tell recipients that information or they will not be able to view the gallery.

#### How does uploading via e-mail work?

If you allow photos to be uploaded via e-mail, an upload e-mail address is created for the gallery. People can send e-mail messages containing photos to be uploaded to this address. The images they send are automatically added to the gallery, so be careful about whom you provide this address to if you want to control the photos in the gallery.

# Synchronize Information among Multiple Macs

If you have more than one Mac, you can use MobileMe to keep a variety of information synchronized on each Mac. For example, you can make sure you have the same set of contacts in Address Book on each computer or ensure that all your favorite bookmarks are available when you need them.

**To get started, you need to configure each computer to be part of the synchronization process. MacBook then ensures that it is synchronized automatically, or you can perform synchronizations manually.**

① Open the MobileMe pane of the System Preferences application and click the **Sync** tab.

② Check the **Synchronize with MobileMe** check box.

③ On the pop-up menu, select how you want synchronizations to occur.

You can choose **Manually** to synchronize manually; choose a time, such as **Every Hour**, to synchronize at those times; or choose **Automatically** to have synchronizations performed automatically.

④ Check the check box next to each item you want to include in the synchronization.

⑤ Click **Sync Now**.

The information you selected is copied onto MobileMe.

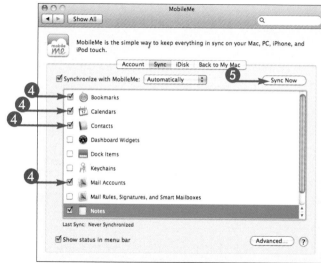

If some of the information already exists, an alert appears.

**6** On the pop-up menu, choose how you want data to be synchronized.

You can choose **Merge Information** if you want the data on MobileMe to be merged with the information on MacBook. Choose **Replace Information on This Computer** to replace the information on MacBook with information stored on MobileMe. Choose **Replace Information on MobileMe** to have the information on MacBook copied to MobileMe to replace the information stored there.

**7** Click **Sync**.

The synchronization process begins.

As changes are made to data, you are alerted about what is going to be done. For example, when data in the two locations seems to be the same, you are prompted to choose the correct version of the information. At the prompt, click **Review Now**.

**8** Select the information you want to keep, and click **Continue**.

**9** Repeat Step **8** until you have reviewed all conflicts, and then click **Done**.

The time and date of the last synchronization appear at the bottom of the Sync pane when the process is complete.

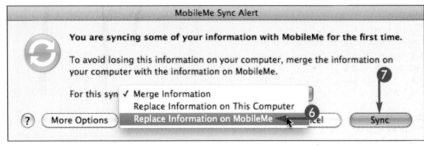

 **TIPS**

**Where is synchronized information stored, and can I access it from the Web?**

All the information you synchronized is stored in your Mobile cloud on the Internet. You can access it from the Web by clicking the appropriate links on the MobileMe Web site. For example, to access your contact information, click the **Address Book** application icon (▣).

**Can I include documents in synchronizations?**

No. MobileMe synchronization works only with specific information. However, if you save documents onto your iDisk and set synchronization to occur automatically, any documents you save are available on each synced computer automatically. You can also manually copy documents to your iDisk and then copy them from the iDisk onto each computer, if you prefer.

# Explore Safari

Safari is an elegant application, meaning that it offers a lot of functionality and is a pleasure to use at the same time. As soon as you open it, Safari is configured for easy use, and you can set various preferences to tailor the way it works for you.

---

## Safari in Browse Mode

### Back
Click ◀ to move back to the previous page.

### Forward
Click ▶ to move forward to the next page.

### Search bar
Enter information here to search for it via Google.

### Add Bookmark
Click ➕ to save the current location as a bookmark.

### Address bar
Shows the current Web address (Uniform Resource Locator, or URL).

### Title
Shows the title of the Web page being shown.

### Refresh or Stop Loading
Refresh (🔄) gets the current version of the page, or stops loading (❌) a page.

### Bookmarks bar
The Bookmarks bar provides quick access to your favorite bookmarks. At the end of the bar, click **More Bookmarks** (»») to show bookmarks that do not fit on the Bookmarks bar.

### Top Sites
Clicking 🔲 provides thumbnails of your favorite Web pages that you can click to visit.

**Brad Miser**

http://www.bradmiser.com/Brad_Misers_Web_Site/Welcome.htm

Loading... ❌    Q▾ Google

Apple   financial▾   Yahoo!   shopping_rental▾   Apple▾   Google Maps   YouTube   entertainment▾   USAirways   Wikipedia   »

Brad Miser          Apple – Start          Netflix: Queue          Netflix: Queue          +

Welcome   Scenic_Photos   Blog   oh-pets

# Brad Miser

iPhoto '09

Teach Yourself VISUALLY
MacBook

Greetings!

Contacting "www.bradmiser.com"

### Tabs
You can open each Web page in its own tab.

### Web page
Provides access to the information and tools on the Web page.

### Status bar
Shows the current status of Safari activity.

**Safari in Bookmarks Mode**

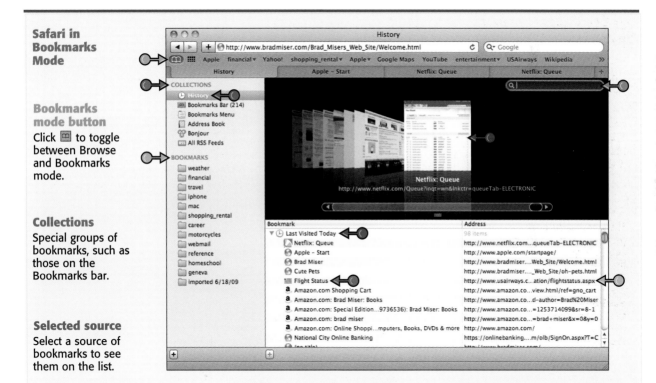

**Bookmarks mode button**

Click to toggle between Browse and Bookmarks mode.

**Collections**

Special groups of bookmarks, such as those on the Bookmarks bar.

**Selected source**

Select a source of bookmarks to see them on the list.

**Bookmarks**

Shows individual bookmarks and folders containing bookmarks.

**List of bookmarks in selected source**

Shows the bookmarks and folders of bookmarks in the selected source.

**Bookmark name**

A descriptive name that you can assign to bookmarks.

**Address**

The URL to which the bookmark points.

**Search tools**

Enables you to search for bookmarks.

**Cover flow browser**

Enables you to "flip" through the Web pages in the selected source to preview and navigate to them.

# Navigate to Web Sites

The most basic task when you use the Web is to move to the Web site you are interested in and then navigate within that site's pages. There are a number of ways to do this, and you will probably use all of them as you explore the Web.

**Moving to a Web site by entering its URL address is the most flexible method, and is the one you can always use. For most sites that you use regularly, you need to type the URL only once. After that, you can move back to it with a bookmark or by using the Safari History menu.**

Navigate to Web Sites

## Navigate to a Web Site by Entering a URL

**1** Launch Safari by clicking its icon on the Dock.

Safari opens and you move to the current home page, an empty page, or your Top Sites page, depending on your preference settings.

**2** Type the address of a Web site.

Although a full Web address begins with either http:// or https://, you do not need to type either of these prefixes because Safari automatically adds them to any address that you type. If the address begins with www, you do not need to type the www part, either. For example, to move to *http://www.apple.com*, you just need to type **apple.com**.

**Note:** *In many cases, you do not need to type .com because Safari assumes addresses include it if you do not type it. If you navigate to a different domain type, such as .org, you do need to type it in the address.*

● As you type in the Address bar, Safari tries to match what you type with a site you have visited previously and shows you the matches on a list under the Address bar.

**3** When the address becomes the one you want or when you finish typing it, press Return.

**Note:** *You can click an address on the menu Safari presents to move to that Web page.*

Safari moves to the address and you see its content.

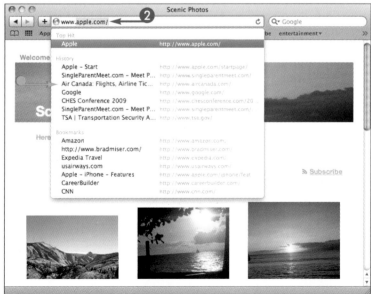

## Navigate to Web Sites with a Bookmark

1 To use a bookmark on the Bookmarks bar, click the bookmark.

● You can also click a folder of bookmarks and select the bookmark you want to move to on the menu.

**Note:** *Folders on the Bookmarks bar have a downward-pointing triangle.*

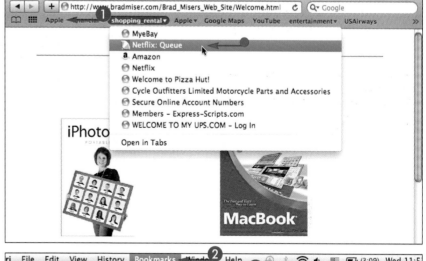

2 To access a bookmark stored on the Bookmarks menu, open the **Bookmarks** menu.

**Note:** *When you select a folder of bookmarks on the menu, its contents appear.*

3 Select the bookmark you want to use.

That Web page opens.

4 To move to any bookmark you have saved using Safari's Bookmarks mode, click **Show All Bookmarks**.

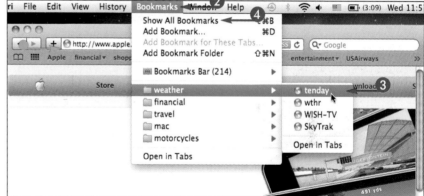

 TIPS

### How can I use bookmarks that I have saved on one computer on all my Macs?

If you use more than one Mac, you are likely to create different bookmarks as you surf the Web on each computer. Re-creating those bookmarks on each Mac can be a nuisance. Fortunately, if you use MobileMe, you do not have to. You can synchronize the bookmarks on each Mac you use so that whether you use MacBook or a different Mac, you always have the same set of bookmarks available to you. See Chapter 10 for detailed information about using MobileMe synchronization.

### How do I know specifically where a bookmark points?

Because you can name a bookmark anything you want, and you usually use an abbreviated name when you add a bookmark to the Bookmarks bar, you might not remember where a bookmark points. To see a bookmark's address, point to the bookmark on the Bookmarks bar without clicking it. After a second or two, the full address for the bookmark appears.

continued

As you move to Web addresses, a new page opens, which is also what happens when you click a link that points to a different address (on the same Web site or elsewhere). As you navigate through pages, you create a "chain" of pages that you can move back and forward through. You can do this because Safari "remembers" each page as you move through it, and each page is temporarily stored on MacBook.

**You can also move to Web pages from outside Safari by clicking hyperlinks in documents, such as e-mail and text documents. When you click a Web link, Mac OS X recognizes it as an address and opens it in your default Web browser.**

## Navigate to Web Sites (continued)

● The Web site is replaced by the Bookmarks window, which means that Safari is in Bookmarks mode.

⑤ Choose a location in which the bookmark you want to visit is saved.

⑥ If the selected source includes folders, click their disclosure triangles to view the bookmarks they contain (▶ changes to ▼).

⑦ Drag the scroll bar to flip through the bookmarks using the browser.

⑧ Single-click a bookmark in the browser or double-click the bookmark that you want to visit in the lower pane.

Whichever method you used to access a bookmark, once you click it, its Web page fills the Safari window.

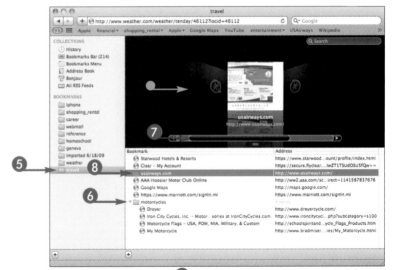

## Navigate to Web Sites Using History

① Open the **History** menu.

In the fourth section of the menu, you see a list of Web pages you have visited most recently.

② If the page you want to return to is on the list, select it.

③ If the site is not on the list, select the folder for the time period in which you visited it.

④ Select the site you want to visit on the resulting menu.

The site you selected opens.

## Navigate to Web Sites Using a Link

**1** Click a link in an e-mail or other document.

Safari opens and moves to the Web site.

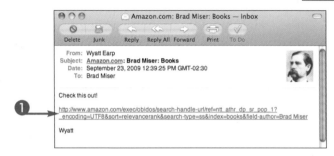

## Move Through Web Pages

**1** Click a link to move to Web pages.

**2** Click the **Back** button (◀) to move to a previous page.

**3** Click the **Forward** button (▶) to move to a later page in the current "chain" of pages you have been browsing.

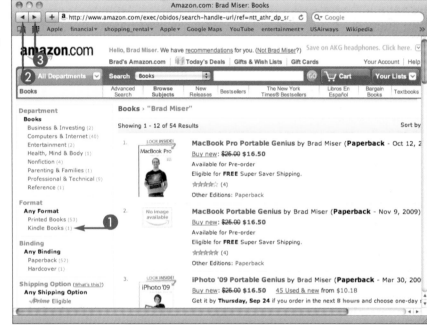

**TIPS**

### What does the http that Safari adds to the front of URLs stand for?

The http prefix stands for Hyper Text Transfer Protocol, and is the basic *protocol*, or language, that Web pages employ. There are other protocols you can access with Safari, such as FTP (File Transfer Protocol), in which case the URL starts with ftp: instead of http:. The vast majority of sites that you will visit with Safari use http, and so Safari assumes that this is the kind of site you want. To move to a different kind of site, you have to add that prefix at the beginning of the URL, such as ftp://.

### What is https?

A lot of Web sites deal with information that needs to be protected, such as bank accounts and credit cards. These sites use Secure Socket Layer (SSL) technology to encrypt and therefore protect the data being sent between the Web page and Safari. These sites use the https protocol (Hyper Text Transfer Protocol Secure). You typically do not have to add https at the beginning of addresses to move to them; when you reach the secure part of the site, https is employed automatically.

One of the most useful things to do on the Web is to search for information, and one of the best search engines is Google. Google searching is built into Safari to make Web searches fast and easy.

**You can perform a Google search by using the Safari built-in Search tool. Of course, you can also move directly to the Google Search page by entering the URL google.com in the Address bar and pressing `Return`, but it is easier and faster to use the Safari Search tool.**

① Type the information you want to search for in the Search bar.

● As you type, Safari presents a list showing you suggested searches and your previous searches; click one of these to perform that search.

② To search on the term you entered, press `Return`.

The search is performed and you see the Google results page.

③ Click a link to visit one of the search results.

That Web page appears.

4 View and use the Web page.

5 Click the **SnapBack** button ().

You return to the search results page.

6 Scroll the page to explore other results.

**Note:** *When you get to the bottom of a search results page, you see how many pages are in the results. Click* **Next** *to move to the next page of results, or click a page's number to jump to it.*

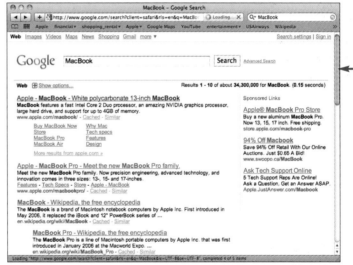

 TIPS

**How can I repeat a previous search?**
Safari remembers the most recent searches you have performed. To repeat a search, click the magnifying glass icon (🔍) in the Search bar and choose the search that you want to repeat on the list that appears.

**Can I use any search page with Safari, or do I have to use Google?**
You can use any search page by moving to its URL. For example, to search with Yahoo!, type **yahoo.com**. The search page appears and you can use its tool to search the Web. When you use the Safari Search bar, you search using Google only.

# Download Files

There are all kinds of great files that you can download from the Web. These include applications that you can run on MacBook (in fact, many applications you obtain are downloaded from the Web), images, PDF documents, and so on.

**After you download a file, how you use it depends on the kind of file it is. Most applications are provided in a disk image file (with the filename extension .dmg), which mounts automatically. Some files, such as PDF documents, are downloaded as they are. Other files are archived so that you need to uncompress them before you use them.**

## Download Files from the Web

1 Move to a file that you want to download.

2 Click the file's download link or button.

● The file begins to download, and the Downloads window appears.

3 Monitor the progress of the download.

*Note: You do not really have to monitor a file download because it downloads in the background. You can continue to do other things as files download.*

When the download is complete, the file is ready for you to use.

## Use Disk Images You Have Downloaded

1 Open a Finder window.

2 Double-click the disk image that you downloaded.

The contents of the disk image are shown just like a hard drive or other volume you select.

3 Run the application installer, or install it with drag-and-drop (see Chapter 5 for details).

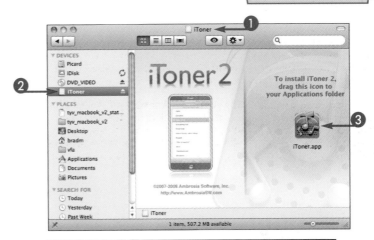

## Use Document Files You Have Downloaded

1 Click the **Downloads** stack on the Dock.

The folder fans out onto the desktop or it appears in a grid if you set that as your preference for the Downloads stack.

*Note: You can also open the Downloads folder in a Finder window. The Downloads folder is located in your Home folder.*

2 Click the downloaded document you want to use.

3 To open the Downloads folder in a Finder window, choose **Open in Finder** or **X More in Finder** (where *X* is a number of items).

It opens using the application with which it is associated.

*Note: When you download a group of files that have been compressed using the ZIP format, they uncompress for you automatically. Instead of a single file, you see a folder with the ZIP file's name. Open that folder to see the files it contains.*

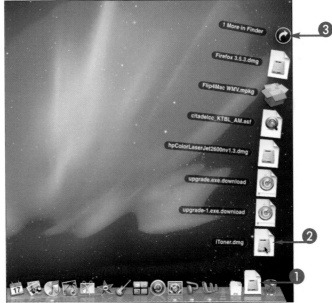

**TIPS**

### What is a SIT file?

These are files compressed with an older scheme first introduced by an application called StuffIt. When Mac OS X was introduced, support for the Windows standard compression (file extension .zip) was built into the OS, and so most files you encounter these days are compressed as ZIP files. However, there are a few older files that might have .sit as their filename extension. If you come across one of these, you need to download and install the free StuffIt Expander application (do a Web search and you will find it) to be able to open SIT files.

### What about FTP?

Some sites use FTP to provide files for you to download. The primary benefit of an FTP site is that files are usually downloaded faster than they are through HTTP. You can access FTP sites in Safari (their URLs start with ftp:// instead of http://), or you can use an FTP application, such as Fetch. Most FTP sites require you to have a user name and password to be able to download files.

Often, you will want to have several Web sites open at the same time. Opening each of these in its own window works, but it can result in screen clutter.

**Tabs in Safari enable you to open as many Web pages at a time as you want, while keeping all those pages in one window so that you do not clutter up your desktop. Moving to a page is as simple as clicking its tab.**

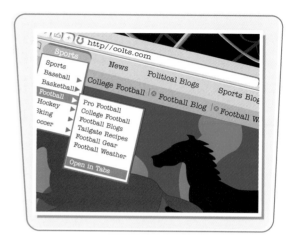

Browse the Web with Tabs

## Configure Safari to Use Tabs

① Press ⌘+,.

The Safari Preferences window opens.

② Click the **Tabs** tab.

③ Check the top check box if you want to be able to press the ⌘ key when you click a link to open a Web page in a new tab.

④ Check the middle check box if you want to move to new tabs and windows when they are created.

⑤ Check the bottom check box if you want to confirm closing a window when it has multiple tabs open.

⑥ Review the keyboard shortcuts shown at the bottom of the window; these reflect the check boxes that you have checked or unchecked.

⑦ Close the Preferences window.

## Open and Use Tabs

① Open a Safari window and move to a Web page.

② Press ⌘+T.

A new tab appears. By default, the Top Sites page appears; you learn more about this later in this chapter.

③ Open a Web page in the new tab using any of the techniques you learned earlier in this chapter.

● The Web page fills the tab.

④ To open a link in a new tab, press and hold ⌘ while you click the link.

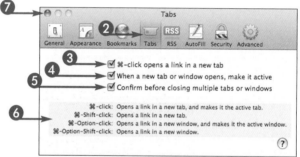

chapter 11

● A new tab opens and displays the destination page of the link. (If you did not enable the make new tabs active preference, you have to click the new tab to make it active.)

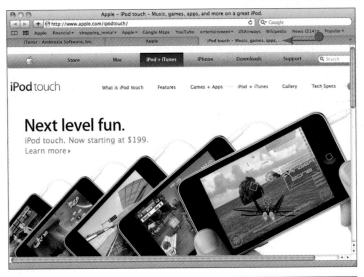

⑤ To move to a tab, click it.

The tab's Web page appears.

⑥ To close a tab, click its **Close** button (⊗), which appears when you point to the left side of a tab.

The tab disappears.

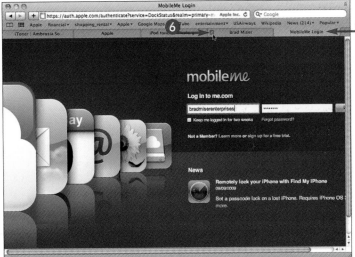

TIPS

**How can I move through open tabs with the keyboard?**
Press ⌘+} to move to the next tab, or press ⌘+{ to move to the previous tab.

**When should I open more windows instead of tabs?**
Tabs are great because you can have many pages open in the same window. However, you can see only one tab at a time. If you open multiple windows instead (press ⌘+N), you can arrange the windows so that you can see multiple windows at the same time. To convert a tab into a window, move to it, click the **Window** menu, and then click **Move Tab to New Window**.

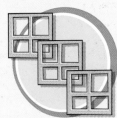

# Set and Organize Bookmarks

By default, Safari includes a number of bookmarks that you can use, but as you explore the Web, there will be a lot of sites that you visit regularly. You can create bookmarks for each of these sites so that it is simple to get back to them.

**Because you are likely to end up with many bookmarks, you need tools to keep them organized. Safari also helps with that.**

### Create Bookmarks

① Move to a Web page that you want to bookmark.

② Press ⌘+D.

You can also open the **Bookmarks** menu and then select **Add Bookmark**, or you can click the **Add Bookmarks** button (⊞).

● The Bookmark sheet appears.

③ Name the bookmark.

④ Open the pop-up menu.

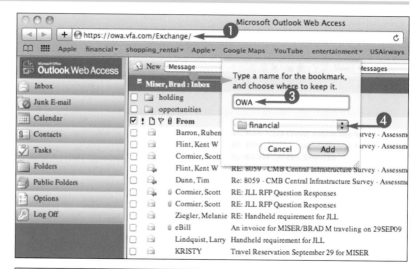

⑤ Choose the location in which you want to store the bookmark.

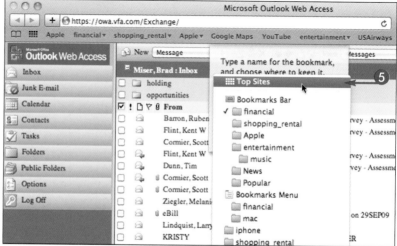

● The location you selected appears in the pop-up menu.

⑥ Click **Add**.

The bookmark is created in the location you selected. You can move back to the site at any time by choosing the new bookmark.

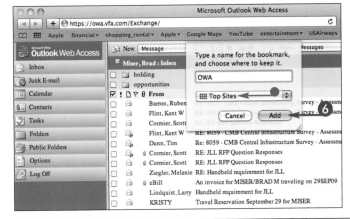

**Organize Bookmarks**

① Press **Option** + **⌘** + **B**, or choose **Show All Bookmarks** from the **Bookmarks** menu.

Safari opens the Bookmarks window.

② To create a new folder for bookmarks, click the **Add** button (⊞).

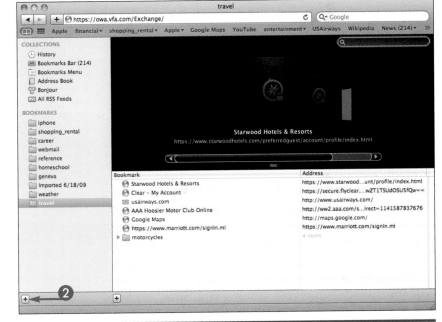
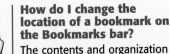

### How do I store bookmarks on the Bookmarks bar?

The Bookmarks bar is a convenient way to access bookmarks because it appears at the top of the Safari window so that you can move to a bookmark just by clicking its button on the bar. To add a bookmark to the bar, choose **Bookmarks Bar** on the pop-up menu on the New Bookmark sheet. Adding the bookmark places it on the left edge of the bar, becoming the first bookmark on the bar.

### How do I change the location of a bookmark on the Bookmarks bar?

The contents and organization of the Bookmarks bar are determined by the contents of the Bookmarks bar collection. To move a bookmark toward the left side of the Bookmarks bar, drag its icon up the list of bookmarks that appears when you select the Bookmarks bar collection. Drag a bookmark down the list to move it to the right on the Bookmarks bar.

continued

185

In addition to making it much easier to move to Web sites, using bookmarks also reduces the chance for errors when you type a URL. Sometimes these errors are merely annoying, and at other times, they can lead you to places on the Web where you would rather not be.

**Over time, you are likely to create many bookmarks. You can use the techniques in this section to keep them organized. Place the bookmarks you use most often on the Bookmarks bar or on the Bookmarks menu so that you can get to them easily. Use folders to create sets of bookmarks related to specific topics or purposes, such as finances or news.**

● A new untitled folder appears. The bookmarks list is empty because no bookmarks are in the folder.

③ Type a name for the folder.

④ Press **Return**.

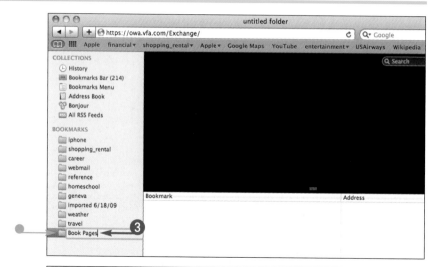

⑤ Select the location containing bookmarks you want to move into the folder.

⑥ Drag a bookmark from its current location onto the folder that you want to contain it; when that folder is highlighted in blue, release the trackpad.

⑦ Repeat Steps **5** and **6** to place more bookmarks in the folder.

8 Select the folder you created.

The bookmarks you placed in it appear on the list.

9 To create a folder within the selected folder, click ⊞.

10 Name the new folder and press **Return**.

11 Drag bookmarks onto the nested folder to place them in it.

12 Drag bookmarks and folders up and down in the folder to change the order in which they appear.

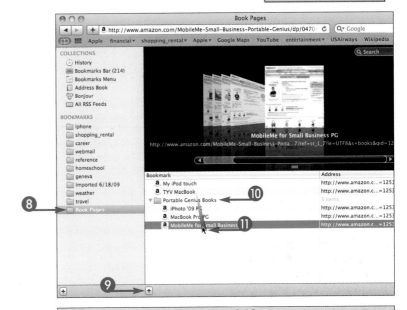

13 To add the bookmarks you use most frequently to the Bookmarks bar or Bookmarks menu, drag them onto the location in which you want them to be available.

14 Organize the contents of the Bookmarks bar or Bookmarks menu just like other locations.

**Note:** *To delete a bookmark or a folder of bookmarks, select what you want to delete and press* **Delete**.

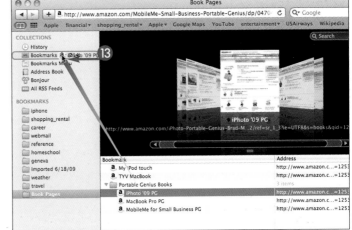

### When should I bookmark a site?

It is best not to think of bookmarks as permanent things. Although some pages that you use over long periods of time you will definitely want to bookmark, others are useful only in the short term. For example, if you are researching a product, you might find several sites that provide useful information.

Bookmark these sites as you go so that you can get back to the ones you need. When you are done, just delete the bookmarks you created to prevent Safari from becoming cluttered with bookmarks you no longer use.

### Can I change the order in which folders are shown in the Bookmarks window?

Yes. To reorder folders in the Bookmarks section of the Source pane, drag them up or down until they are in the order you want.

# Use and Set Top Sites

Safari's Top Sites feature is a window where thumbnails of your favorite Web sites are stored. You can click a thumbnail to move to the Web site; in this respect, the thumbnails on your Top Sites page work just like bookmarks.

**As you move through Web sites, Safari tracks the sites you visit and automatically adds those you visit most to your Top Sites page. Because of this, the contents of your Top Sites page can change over time. You can also manually add pages to your Top Sites page and "pin" them to the page so they are always there. You can also determine how many sites appear on the page.**

## Use Top Sites

1 Click the **Top Sites** button (▦) on the Bookmarks bar.

● Your Top Sites page appears. Each Web page is represented by a thumbnail.

2 Point to a thumbnail you are interested in.

A blue box encloses the thumbnail and the page's name and URL are shown at the bottom of the window.

3 To move to a page, click its thumbnail.

The Web page replaces the Top Sites page.

## Add a Web Page to Your Top Sites

1 Click the **Top Sites** button (▦).

2 Click the **Edit** button.

③ Press ⌘+N to open a new window.

④ Move to the Web page you want to add to your Top Sites.

⑤ Click the icon at the left edge of the Address bar to select the URL and drag it to the location on the Top Sites page where you want it to appear. (As you drag over thumbnails, they shift around to make room for the new one.)

When you release the trackpad, the page's thumbnail is added to your Top Sites.

**Organize Your Top Sites**

① Open your Top Sites page and click the **Edit** button.

② To remove a page, click its **Close** button (⊠).

③ To lock a page on the Top Sites page so it will not be removed as Safari adds new pages, click the **Mark as Permanent** button (⬛).

④ To unlock a page, click the **Unmark as Permanent** button (⬛).

⑤ To change the location of thumbnails, drag them around the window.

⑥ To change the number of thumbnails shown, click **Small**, **Medium**, or **Large**.

⑦ Click **Done** when you are finished making changes.

**TIPS**

**What are other ways to add pages to my Top Sites page?**

You can drag a link from any document, such as an e-mail message, and drop it onto the Top Sites page (it must be in Edit mode) to add it to your Top Sites. You can also open a new document, such as a text document, type a URL, and drag it from the document to your Top Sites page.

**Why are some of the thumbnails on my Top Sites page marked with a star?**

When new content is added to a Web site you have on your Top Sites page, it is marked with a star and a "corner" of the thumbnail is folded down. This helps you know that something has changed on the site.

# Open Several Web Pages at the Same Time

Using tabs, you know you can have many Web pages open at the same time, which is useful. However, opening one tab after another takes longer than it needs to. And who needs that? It would be nice if there were a way to open a lot of pages at the same time.

**Fortunately, Safari allows you to do this. By using bookmarks, folders, and tabs, you can configure any collection of Web pages to open with a single click. First, prepare the folder containing bookmarks for the pages you want to open. Second, open those pages.**

## Open Several Web Pages at the Same Time

### Prepare a One-Click Bookmark Folder

1 Set bookmarks for the pages you want to open.

2 Choose **Show All Bookmarks** under the **Bookmarks** menu.

Safari moves into Bookmarks mode.

3 Create a folder for the group of pages you want to open at the same time.

4 Add the bookmarks you want to open to the folder you created in Step **3**.

5 Drag the bookmarks up or down the list so they are in the order in which you want them to open.

The bookmark at the top of the list becomes the first tab in the Safari window, the next one down is the second tab, and so on.

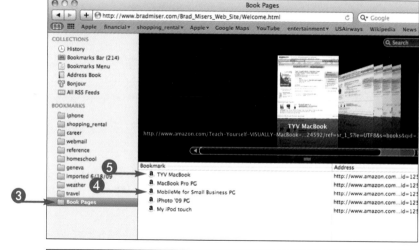

6 Select the **Bookmarks Bar** collection.

7 Drag the folder you created in Step **3** onto the bookmark list in the order in which you want it to appear on the Bookmarks bar (the top of the window represents the left end of the bar).

8 Check the **Auto-Click** check box.

● The folder you created appears on the Bookmarks bar. At the right side of its name on the Bookmarks bar, you see a box, which indicates it is an Auto-Click folder.

## Open a Lot of Pages with a Click

① When you want to open all the bookmarks in the Auto-Click folder, click it on the Bookmarks bar.

● Each bookmark in the folder opens in its own tab.

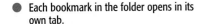

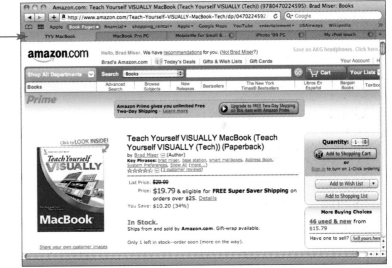

### Can I also put other folders on the Bookmarks bar?

You can place any folder of bookmarks on the Bookmarks bar. When you do, the folder becomes a menu showing the bookmarks it contains (immediately to the right of its name, you see a downward-pointing triangle to indicate this). Click the folder and it opens, showing you the bookmarks it contains. Select a bookmark to open it, or choose **Open in Tabs** to open all the bookmarks, each on its own tab.

### What if I do not want to open all the bookmarks in an Auto-Click folder at the same time?

Click the bookmark's name on the Bookmarks bar and hold down the trackpad. A menu appears, showing you each of the bookmarks in the folder. Choose a bookmark to move to it.

# Watch Movies on the Web

Movies are common on the Web. From trailers for the latest Hollywood productions to instructional videos, commercials, and other video content, there is a lot to watch. You can use Safari to view many of these movies through its embedded QuickTime player.

**1** Move to a site containing a movie you want to watch.

For example, most movie Web sites have previews for you to watch.

**2** Click the size of the movie you want to watch.

Larger movies look better, but require more bandwidth to download.

*Note: If you are using a broadband connection, you can usually choose the largest size.*

● The movie opens, starts to download, and begins to play.

**3** Use the **Volume** menu (🔊) to change the volume.

**4** Click **Pause** (⏸) to pause it.

**5** Drag the playhead to the right to scan forward, or to the left to scan backward.

*Note: The shaded part of the timeline bar indicates how much of the movie has downloaded; you can watch only that part. If the connection slows down for some reason, the movie may stop; just restart it when more of the movie has downloaded.*

# Use AutoFill to Quickly Complete Web Forms

As you use the Web, you will probably need to complete forms, such as when you are registering for an account on a Web site or when you are doing some online shopping. Many of these forms require the same basic set of information, such as your name, address, and telephone number. Using the Safari AutoFill feature, you can complete this basic information with a single click.

**AutoFill can also remember user names and passwords that you use to log into Web sites so that you do not have to retype this information each time you want to access your account on a site.**

## Use AutoFill to Quickly Complete Web Forms

### Configure Autofill Information

1 Press ⌘ + ,.

   The Safari Preferences window opens.

2 Click the **AutoFill** tab.

3 To complete forms using the information on your card in Address Book, check the **Using info from my Address Book card** check box.

**Note:** Your card is automatically populated with the information you entered when you registered your MacBook. You can also edit your card by clicking the **Edit** button when you are viewing your card in Address Book. See Chapter 15 for information about Address Book.

4 To have Safari remember user names and passwords for Web sites you access, check the **User names and passwords** check box.

5 To have Safari remember information for other forms, check the **Other forms** check box.

6 Close the Preferences window.

### Use Autofill Information

1 Move to a Web site that requires your information.

2 Click **Edit** and then click **AutoFill Form** (or press Shift + ⌘ + A).

● Safari completes as much information as it can, based on the form and the contents of your Address Book card. The fields it completes are highlighted in yellow.

3 Manually complete or edit any of the fields that AutoFill did not correctly fill in.

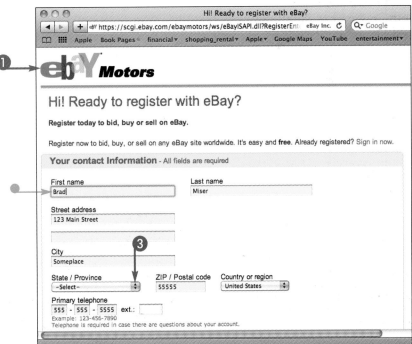

# Create Your Own Web Widget

Chapter 3 explained how to use the Dashboard to access widgets that perform various functions. You can create your own widgets from any Web page and then access the widgets you create on the Dashboard.

**When you create a widget, you capture part of a Web page. Because pages are constructed in different ways, the part of the page you capture may or may not work the way you expect. The only way to know is to try it. Fortunately, creating widgets is easy, and so you will not have wasted much time if it does not work the way you expect.**

## Create Your Own Web Widget

① Move to a Web site containing information that you want to have on a widget.

② Open the **File** menu and choose **Open in Dashboard**.

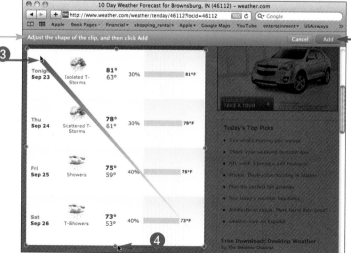

● The widget toolbar appears, and part of the page is selected; the rest of the page is grayed out.

③ Drag over the section of the page that you want to be a widget.

④ Drag the handles on the selection box to fine-tune the selection area.

**Note:** *Safari tries to capture functional blocks on a page. If a section of a page is selected automatically when you click it, you should use that section "as is" for best results.*

⑤ Click **Add**.

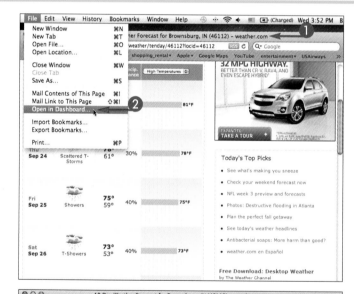

● A widget is created, the Dashboard opens, and you see the new widget.

⑥ Click the **Info** button ().

The widget moves into configure mode.

⑦ Choose a theme for the widget.

⑧ If the widget contains audio, check the **Only play audio in Dashboard** check box if you want that audio to play only when the Dashboard is open.

⑨ To adjust the area captured in the widget, click **Edit** and proceed to Step **10**; otherwise, click **Done** and skip Steps **10** and **11**.

⑩ Resize the widget using its resize handle.

⑪ Click **Done**.

You see the new widget with the theme and size you selected. You can manage widgets that you create (such as by changing locations on the Dashboard) just like the other widgets.

**Note:** See Chapter 3 for more details about widgets.

**Note:** When you click a link on a Web page widget, the page that link points to opens in Safari or another default Web browser.

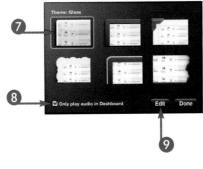

### What happens if the Web page I captured changes?

If the Web page you have captured is reorganized, your widget may also change. When you capture a widget, you capture it based on the area you select on the page. If the content in that area changes, your widget also changes. In that case, you need to re-create or edit the widget based on the new page layout.

### I captured the login section of a Web page, but when I enter my user name and password and then click Login, nothing happens. Why?

Sometimes the underlying code related to a button is not physically in the area of the button that you capture as a widget. When that area is separated from the button on a widget, that button in the widget does not work. You can try capturing other parts of the page or just use AutoFill to make it easier to log in.

# Save or E-mail Web Pages

As you explore the Web, you will probably find Web pages that you want to view again. Because the Web is always changing, there is no guarantee that a page you are viewing now will exist a day from now, or even five minutes from now. If you want to make sure you can view a page in the future, you can save it on MacBook.

**Some pages that you encounter are worth sharing. You can easily send links to Web pages to others, or you can even send the contents of a Web page in an e-mail.**

## Save Web Pages

① Move to a Web page you want to save.

*Note: Any receipts or account information that you see on a Web page are good candidates for saving.*

② Open the **File** menu, and then select **Save As**.

● The Save sheet appears.

③ Enter a name for the Web page.

④ Choose the location in which you want to save it.

⑤ Choose **Web Archive** on the **Format** pop-up menu.

⑥ Click **Save**.

The page is saved in the location you specified. You can view it again later by double-clicking its icon; the page opens in Safari.

*Note: A page that you save is a copy of what it was at the time you viewed it. To see the current version, you need to return to it on the Web.*

## E-mail a Link to a Web Page

① Move to a Web page you want to share.

② Open the **File** menu, and then select **Mail Link to This Page**.

A new e-mail message is created in Mail, and a link to the page is added to the body of the message.

③ Add recipients.

④ Edit the subject, and add comments to the body of the message.

**Note:** Do not change the link that was pasted into the e-mail message or it might not work.

⑤ Click **Send** (📨).

When the recipient receives the message, he can click the link to view the page.

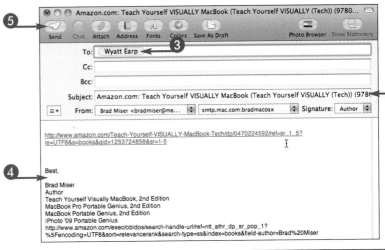

## E-mail the Contents of a Web Page

① Move to a Web page you want to share.

② Choose **File**, and then choose **Mail Contents of This Page**.

A new message is created in Mail, and the content of the page is pasted into the body.

③ Complete the message by adding recipients, editing the subject, and adding comments.

④ Click **Send** (📨).

When the recipient receives the message, she can view the page in it.

**Note:** To be able to view a page in an e-mail, the recipient's e-mail application must be capable of displaying HTML messages.

**How do I tell if I am viewing a page saved on MacBook or one on the Web?**

Look at the URL. If it starts with file://, you are viewing a saved Web page. If it starts with http://, you are viewing a live page on the Web.

**Should I send a link or content?**

When you are viewing a Web site that does not change frequently or that uses direct URLs to the resource you are viewing, sending a link is better because it reduces the size of the e-mail. However, if you want to make sure your recipients see what you intend them to, send the content instead.

# Set Safari Preferences

Safari includes a number of preferences that you can set to change the way it looks and works. You set other Safari preferences similarly to the Tab and AutoFill preferences. (For more information, see the sections "Use AutoFill to Quickly Complete Web Forms" and "Browse the Web with Tabs.")

**You can also move to Web pages from outside Safari by clicking hyperlinks in various documents you work with, such as e-mail and text documents. When you click a Web link, the application you are using recognizes it as an address and opens that address in your default Web browser.**

## Set Safari Preferences

① Press ⌘+,.

The Safari Preferences window opens.

② Click the **General** tab.

③ On the **New windows open with** pop-up menu, choose the page you want to open automatically when you open a new Safari window.

④ On the **New tabs open with** pop-up menu, choose the page you want to open automatically when you open a new Safari tab.

⑤ Type the URL for your home page, or click **Set to Current Page** to make the page you are currently viewing your home page.

**Note:** If you want new tabs or new windows to open with a blank page, choose **Empty Page** on one or both of the **New** pop-up menus.

⑥ Use these settings to specify how Safari handles history items, downloads, and links.

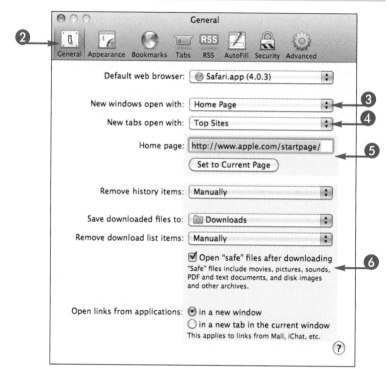

⑦ Click the **Appearance** tab.

⑧ To change the standard font used on Web pages, click the top **Select** button and choose the font you want to use.

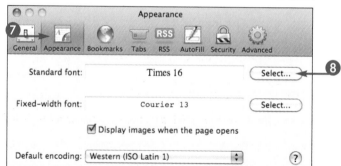

**9** Click the **Bookmarks** tab.

**10** If you want to see your Top Sites pages, links in cards in your Address Book, or sites available via Bonjour as options on the Bookmarks bar, check the **Bookmarks bar** check boxes.

**11** Similarly, check the related **Bookmarks menu** check boxes to include those items on your Bookmarks menu.

**12** To include the Address Book and Bonjour collections in the Bookmarks window, check their respective check boxes.

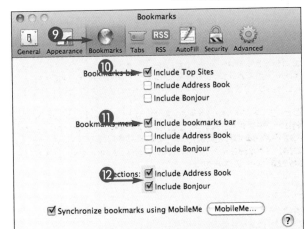

**13** Click the **Security** tab.

**14** Use the **Web content** check boxes to enable plug-ins, Java, and JavaScript or to block pop-ups. If you disable plug-ins or the Java features, many Web sites will not work properly. Some sites will not work with pop-ups blocked, but you should disable the pop-up blocker only when you need to use those specific sites.

**15** In most cases, leave the Only from sites I visit radio button selected; however, if you want to tightly control information that Web sites store on and access from MacBook, click **Never**.

**Note:** If you prevent all cookies from being accepted, some Web sites do not work correctly, and no Web sites "remember" you. Also, you should never choose the **Always** option because it exposes you to security risks from sites you do not visit or do not intend to visit.

**16** Close the Preferences window.

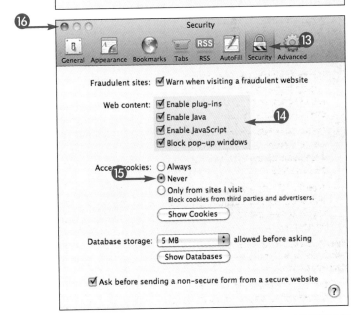

### What are RSS preferences?

RSS (Really Simple Syndication) is a format designed to deliver information in RSS feeds that change frequently, such as news. You can view RSS pages in Safari; these pages are more efficient to view because you can control how much information you see, and you can collect information from different sources on the same page. The RSS preferences enable you to control how Safari works with RSS. For example, you can set Safari to check for updates periodically.

### What are Advanced preferences?

Advanced preferences enable you to set universal access features such as minimum font size and enabling Web page navigation with the Tab key. You can also choose a default style sheet and configure a proxy server if you use one.

Although Safari is the Mac OS X default Web browser, as well as one of the best browsers available for any type of computer, it certainly is not the only one available. Firefox is an alternate Web browser that many Mac users find to be better in some respects (such as speed and compatibility with more Web sites) than Safari.

**Because Firefox is free, there is really no reason not to give it a try to see which you prefer. Of course, you do not really have to have a preference because you can use both browsers if you want to.**

## Explore Firefox

### Download and Install Firefox

1 Launch Safari and type **firefox.com** in the Address bar.

You see the Firefox home page.

2 Click the **Download** link.

Firefox downloads to MacBook. When the application's file has downloaded, you see its license screen.

3 Click **Accept** (assuming you accept the license terms, of course).

● The Firefox disk image is mounted on your desktop, and a Finder window appears showing the Firefox application file.

4 Drag the **Firefox** file to the Applications folder.

The application is installed.

5 Click the **Eject** button (⏏) for the Firefox disk image.

The image is unmounted.

6 Delete the disk image file that you downloaded.

*Note: Step 6 is optional, but it saves some space. You can always download the installer again should you ever need it.*

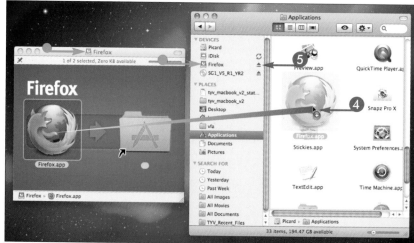

## Browse the Web with Firefox

1. Open the **Applications** folder.

2. Launch Firefox.

3. Click **Open** in the security warning prompt that appears.

● The Import Wizard appears.

4. Leave the Safari radio button selected.

5. Click **Continue**.

6. On the Home Page Selection window, choose **Firefox Start**.

This setting uses a special Firefox page as your home page.

7. Click **Continue**.

After a few seconds, that screen disappears and you move into Firefox. You are prompted to set Firefox as your default browser.

8. Uncheck the **Always perform this check when starting Firefox** check box.

9. If you want to make Firefox your default browser, click **Yes**; if not, click **No**.

10. Review the first run tab and close it when you are done.

**Note:** You only need to perform Steps **3** to **10** the first time you launch Firefox.

● You see your home page in Firefox.

11. Browse the Web.

Although they are different applications, there are enough similarities between Safari and Firefox that you will not have any trouble learning to use Firefox if you know how to use Safari. Because you imported your bookmarks, they are available in Firefox just as they are in Safari.

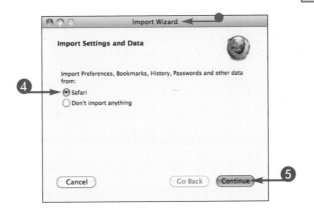

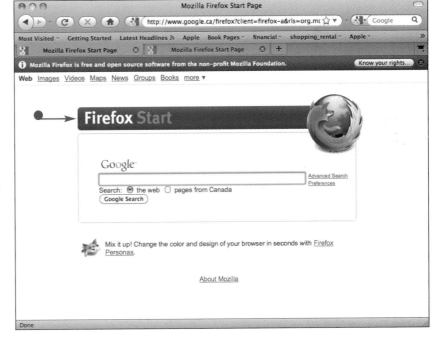

### Can I use both browsers?

Yes, and you can even use them at the same time. If you run into a Web page that does not work properly in one browser, try it in the other. If it works there, add it as a bookmark and use that browser when you want to access that specific page.

### How do I set my default Web browser?

As you work with both browsers, one will probably emerge as your favorite. To make that your default browser, open the **General** tab of the Safari Preferences window and choose your preferred browser on the **Default web browser** pop-up menu. Any Web links you click open in that browser automatically.

# Explore Mail

Mail includes many useful features, and it wraps those features in an interface that makes sense and is easy to use. Mail provides all the capabilities that you want in an e-mail application so that you can work with e-mail efficiently and effectively.

## Mail icon

The Mail Dock icon enables you to launch the Mail application and also shows you how many new messages you have.

## Toolbar
Contains tools you can use to work with e-mail.

## Inbox
Contains mailboxes for each e-mail account.

## Account mailboxes
Contain e-mail for various accounts that you have configured in Mail.

## Account mailbox folders
Organize e-mail in different states, such as Sent or Draft, for each account.

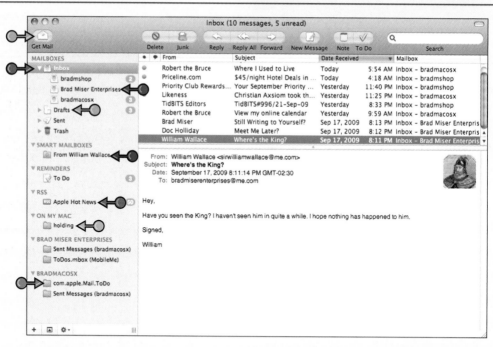

**Smart Mailboxes**
Automatically organize e-mail based on criteria that you define.

**RSS**
Shows RSS feeds that you are managing in Mail.

**Mailboxes**
Folders in which you can store and organize e-mail.

**Online e-mail accounts**
Shows the folders used by your online accounts (such as IMAP accounts).

**Selected source**

The source of e-mails you want to work with, such as those you have received in a specific account.

**Message pane**

Shows the messages in the selected source.

**Read/Unread**

A blue dot indicates a message that you have not read.

**From**

The name of the person who sent the message to you.

**Subject**

The subject of the message.

**Date received**

The date and time you received the message.

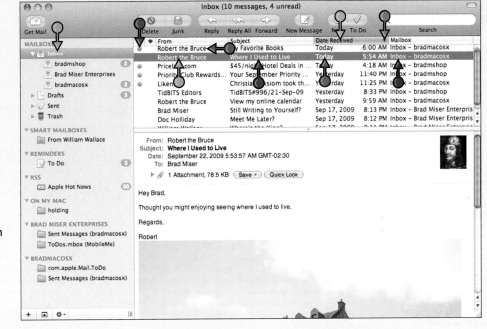

**Sort column**

The column highlighted in blue is the one used to sort the message list.

**Sort direction**

The triangle indicates the direction in which the list is sorted.

**Selected message**

To read a message, you select it; the selected message is highlighted in blue.

**Reading pane**

Displays the selected message.

**Message details**

Who the message is from, the subject of the message, when it was sent, and who the other recipients are.

**Sender's image**

Shows the image associated with the sender in Address Book.

**Body**

The message's text.

**Attachments**

Shows files attached to the message and enables you to save or view them.

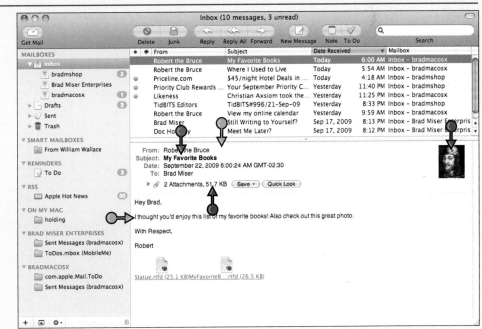

# Set Up E-mail Accounts

Before you can work with e-mail, you must obtain one or more e-mail accounts and configure Mail to access them.

**The details of configuring an e-mail account depend on the type of account it is; for example, configuring a MobileMe account is slightly different from configuring an account you have received from your Internet service provider (ISP). However, in all cases, you enter the configuration details for each type of e-mail account in the appropriate fields in Mail.**

## Set Up E-mail Accounts

1. Launch Mail.
2. Press ⌘ + .

   The Mail Preferences window opens.
3. Click the **Accounts** tab.
4. Click the **Add** button ( + ).

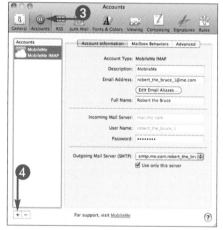

   The Add Account sheet appears.
5. Type the full name for the account.
6. Type the e-mail address for the account.
7. Type the password for the account.
8. If Mail recognizes and can automatically configure the account (such as for MobileMe, GMail, and other popular e-mail services), click **Create**.

   Mail automatically configures the account based on the information you entered, the account is set up, and you return to the Accounts pane.

**Note:** *If the Continue button appears instead of the Create button, Mail does not recognize and cannot automatically configure the account. You are prompted to provide additional information to configure the account, including incoming and outgoing mail server addresses. You should have received this information when you signed up for the account. Provide the required information at each prompt to complete configuration of the account.*

9. Select the new account.
10. Type a description of the account in the Description field. (This is the name that appears on the account's mailbox.)

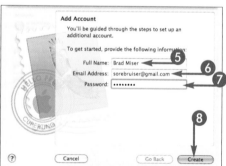

⑪ Click the **Mailbox Behaviors** tab.

⑫ If you want messages you have written but not yet sent to be stored online so you can access them from other computers, check the **Drafts** check box.

⑬ If you want messages you have sent to be stored online, check the **Sent** check box and use the pop-up menu to determine how long your sent messages are kept.

**Note:** If you choose to store messages on the server, those messages count against your total storage space for e-mail. Over time, you may use all or most of your allotted space, which could prevent you from sending or receiving e-mail. Use the **Delete** pop-up menus to configure Mail so that messages stored on the server are deleted periodically.

⑭ If you want messages Mail has identified as spam to be stored online, check the **Junk** check box and use the pop-up menu to determine how long those messages are stored.

⑮ Use the **Trash** check boxes and pop-up menu to determine how Mail deals with messages you delete.

**Note:** The options you see on the Mailbox Behaviors and Advanced tabs depend on the kind of account you are configuring. You may see different options than shown here.

⑯ Click the **Advanced** tab.

⑰ To temporarily disable the account, uncheck the **Enable this account** check box.

⑱ To include the account when Mail checks for e-mail, check the **Include when automatically checking for new messages** check box.

⑲ To store all messages and their attachments on MacBook so that you can access them even when you are not connected to the Internet, choose **All messages and their attachments** on the upper pop-up menu.

⑳ Close the Preferences window and save your changes at the prompt.

● The account's mailbox is added to your Inbox and it is ready to use.

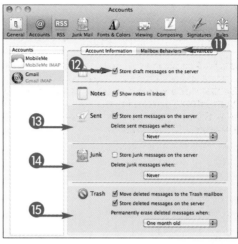
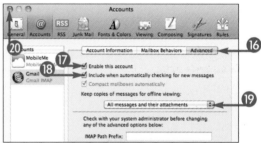

 **TIPS**

**A MobileMe e-mail account was already set up when I launched Mail; how did that happen?**
When you configure a MobileMe account, either during the initial MacBook setup or on the MobileMe pane of the System Preferences application, the MobileMe e-mail account is set up in Mail automatically. See Chapter 10 for more information about MobileMe online services.

**Where can I get free e-mail accounts?**
You can obtain a GMail account at www.google.com. You can also get a free e-mail account at www.yahoo.com. It is a good idea to have at least two e-mail accounts so that you can use one to guard against spam. For more information, see the section "Avoid Spam."

# Read and Reply to E-mail

One of the reasons to use e-mail is, of course, to read it. Mail makes it easy to do that. You can read e-mail in the reading pane, as described in the following steps, or you can double-click a message to open it in its own window.

**You can also easily reply to e-mail that you receive to start or continue an e-mail conversation, also called a *thread*.**

### Read E-mail

1 Select the Inbox.

***Note:*** *You can also select a specific e-mail account to read e-mail that you have received only for that account. If you do not see individual accounts' inboxes, click the triangle next to the Inbox to expand it.*

2 Select the message you want to read.

The message you select appears in the reading pane.

3 Read the message.

***Note:*** *After you have viewed a message in the reading pane, its blue dot disappears so that you know you have read it. The number of new messages is also reduced by one on the Mail icon and next to the source mailbox's icon.*

4 If the message is too long to fit into the current window, press Spacebar to scroll down in the message.

5 To open a message in its own window, double-click it.

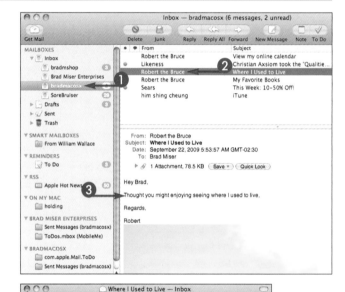

The message appears in a new, separate window.

6 Read the message in its window.

***Note:*** *You can use the buttons in the window to mark the e-mail as junk, or reply to it just as when you read messages from the Mail window.*

7 Close the message when you are done.

## Reply to E-mail

1 Open a message.

2 Click the **Reply** button (icon).

● If more than one person is listed in the From or Cc fields and you want to reply to everyone listed, click the **Reply All** button (icon) instead.

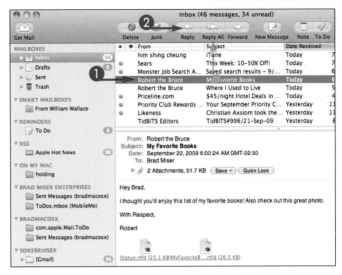

● A new message appears, addressed to the sender of the message (and all recipients if you clicked **Reply All**).

● "Re:" is added to the beginning of the subject to show that the message is a reply.

● The contents of the original message are pasted into the body in blue and marked with a vertical line to show it is quoted text.

3 If you have more than one e-mail account, choose the account through which you want to send the message on the **From** pop-up menu.

4 Type your reply.

5 Click the **Send** button (icon).

The window closes, the e-mail is sent, and you hear the sent mail sound effect.

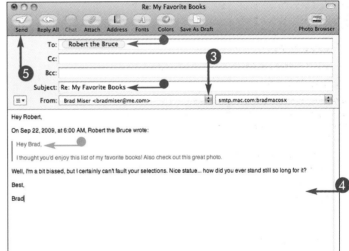

**TIPS**

### How do I delete a message I do not want to keep?

Select the message and click the **Delete** button (icon) on the toolbar. The message is removed from the Message list and placed in the appropriate Trash folder. How long it remains there depends on the Trash settings for that e-mail account. You can recover a message by opening the Trash folder and dragging a deleted message back into an Inbox.

### Can I add more recipients to a reply?

Yes, you can add more addresses to a reply e-mail to include other recipients. In fact, all the tools that are available to you when you create a new e-mail message are also available when you reply to messages. For more information, see the section "Send E-mail."

# Send E-mail

When you want to communicate with someone, you can use the New Mail Message tool to create and send e-mail. You can send a message to as many people as you want.

**People who are the primary recipients should be in the To field. People who are receiving a message for their information only should be in the Cc field. People who should be invisible to other people who receive the message should be included in the Bcc field.**

1 Click the **New Message** button (⬚) on the toolbar.

The New Message window appears.

2 Type the name or e-mail address of the first recipient in the To field.

*Note: As you type, Mail attempts to match a previously used e-mail address or an address in Address Book to what you type. Select an e-mail address to insert it.*

3 Press ➡.

*Note: When it can, Mail replaces an e-mail address with the person's name.*

4 Type another e-mail address.

5 Click in the Cc field or press [Tab] to move there, and type e-mail addresses of people who should receive a copy of the message.

6 Click in the Bcc field or press [Tab] to move there (if it appears), and type e-mail addresses of people who should receive a copy of the message.

7 Type the subject of the message in the Subject field.

8 On the **From** pop-up menu, choose the e-mail address from which you want to send the message.

*Note: In addition to identifying you, the From address determines the address to which replies to your message will be sent.*

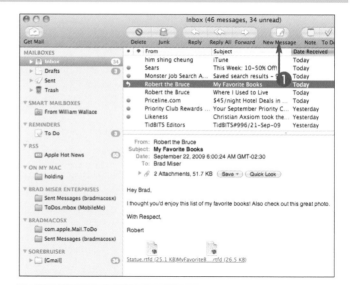

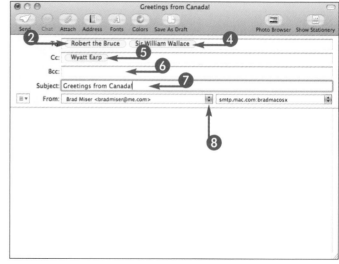

**9** Type the message in the body.

**Note:** *You can use the* **Fonts** *and* **Colors** *buttons (🅰 and 🅒) to format new messages.*

● As you type, Mail checks your spelling. Misspelled words are underlined in red.

**10** To correct a misspelled word, perform a secondary click on it.

**11** Choose the correct spelling on the list.

**Note:** *If the word is spelled correctly and you want to add it to the dictionary so that it is not flagged as a mistake in the future, choose* **Learn Spelling**.

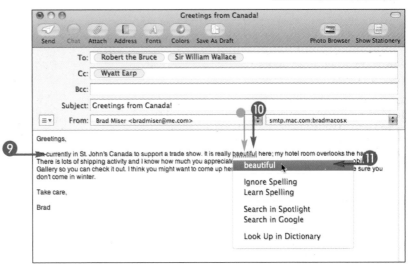

**12** Review your message and make sure it is ready to be sent.

**Note:** *You can save draft versions of messages by clicking the* **Save As Draft** *button (🔲). You can continue working on them later by selecting the Drafts folder and then opening the messages.*

**13** Click **Send** (✉️).

The window closes, the message is sent, and you hear the sent message sound effect.

**Note:** *Once you send a message, you cannot retrieve it, so make sure you are comfortable with it before you click the* **Send** *button.*

### How do I avoid having to type e-mail addresses?

You can store e-mail addresses in Address Book so that you can type an e-mail address by typing a person's name, which is usually much easier to remember. As you type an e-mail address, Mail searches e-mail that you have sent, e-mail that you have received, and cards in Address Book to identify e-mail addresses for you. You can select one of these to easily address a message.

### From where else can I start a new e-mail message?

When you are using a Mac OS X application, such as Address Book, and you see an e-mail address, you can almost always send an e-mail to that address by performing a secondary click on it and choosing **Send Email** on the contextual menu. A new message to that address is created in Mail, and you can then complete and send it. You can send photos using e-mail in iPhoto by choosing the photos you want to send and clicking the **Email** button (🖼️).

# Work with Files Attached to E-mail

In addition to communicating information, e-mail is a great way to send files to other people, and for people to send files to you. Files can be documents, photos, and even applications.

**In Mail, some file attachments, particularly photos, can be displayed within an e-mail message. In all cases, you can save attachments to the MacBook hard drive for your use.**

Work with Files Attached to E-mail

① Select a message containing attachments.

● The Attachments section appears below the To field.

② Click the disclosure triangle to see the attachments to the message.

③ Scroll the message to see the attachments in the body of the message.

● To preview the attachments, click **Quick Look**. The Quick Look viewer appears and you see the contents of the attachments.

***Note:*** *Quick Look works for most, but not all, types of files. If nothing happens when you click the button, the type of file you are trying to preview is not supported.*

● If the attachment can be displayed in the message (most images can be), then you can view it in the body.

④ Click **Save**, and press and hold the trackpad.

⑤ Choose **Save All** to save all of the attachments, or choose a specific attachment to save it.

If you selected **Save All**, the Save sheet appears. If you selected an attachment, it is saved to your Downloads folder and you can skip Steps **6** and **7**.

⑥ Choose the location in which you want to save the attachments.

⑦ Click **Save**.

The attachments are saved in the location you selected, and you can use them just like files you have created.

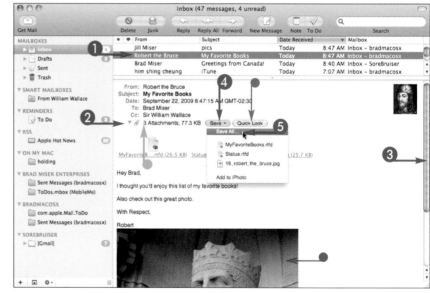

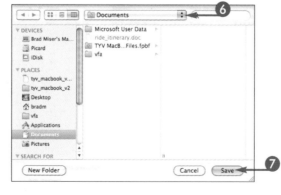

# Attach Files to E-mail

You can attach files to e-mail messages that you send in order to make those files available to other people. You can attach any file to a message and, assuming the recipient has a compatible application, anyone who receives the message can use the files that you attach.

**When you attach files to a message, the size of the e-mail increases by the size of those files and more because of the encoding done to the file to create the attachment. If you attach only one or two small files, you can attach them "as is." However, to attach many or large files, you should compress them and send the compressed file as an attachment instead. See Chapter 4 for more information about file compression.**

## Attach Files to E-mail

① Create a new e-mail message by clicking **New Message** (🖼) in the Mail toolbar.

● A window appears for you to compose your message in.

② Compose the message by addressing it and typing the body.

③ Click **Attach** (📎).

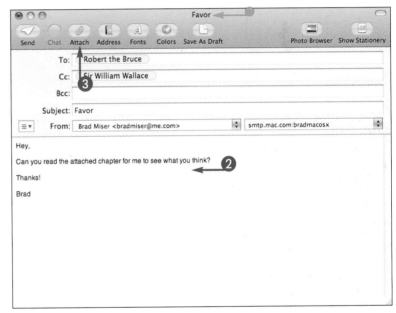

The Attach File sheet appears.

**Note:** *You can also attach files to a message by dragging them from the desktop onto the New Message window.*

④ Move to and select the files you want to attach.

**Note:** *You can select multiple files to attach by pressing and holding ⌘ while you click each file.*

⑤ Click **Choose File**.

The files you selected are attached to the message.

⑥ Send the message.

When the recipients receive the message, they can work with the attachments you included.

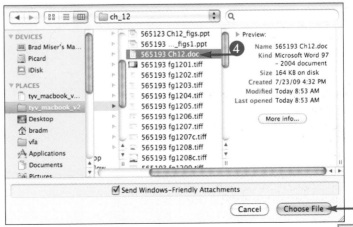

# Organize E-mail

As you use Mail, you are likely to end up with a lot of e-mail messages. Mail provides two great ways to keep your e-mail organized: Mailboxes and Smart Mailboxes. Mailboxes are like folders in the Finder. Smart Mailboxes automatically organize e-mail based on rules that you create.

**However, one of the best ways to keep your e-mail organized is to delete messages that you do not need, which is probably most of those that you receive. The fewer messages you keep, the fewer you have to organize, and the less storage space your e-mail requires.**

## Organize E-mail in Mailboxes

① Click ⊞ in Mail.

② Select **New Mailbox**.

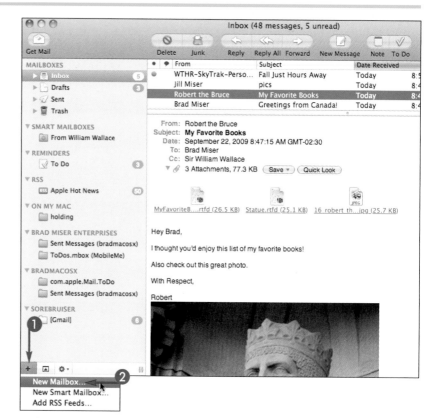

The New Mailbox sheet appears.

③ On the **Location** pop-up menu, choose **On My Mac**.

This setting stores e-mail on MacBook rather than on the mail server.

④ Type a name for the mailbox.

⑤ Click **OK**.

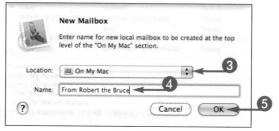

● The mailbox appears in the On My Mac section of the Mailboxes pane.

⑥ Drag messages from the Messages pane onto the mailbox you created.

*Note: You can move multiple messages at the same time by pressing and holding ⌘ while you click each message.*

The message is moved into the mailbox.

*Note: You can create nested mailboxes (a mailbox stored within another mailbox) by dragging one mailbox into another one.*

## Organize E-mail with Smart Mailboxes

① Click ⊞ in Mail.

② Select **New Smart Mailbox**.

The New Smart Mailbox sheet appears.

③ Name the new Smart Mailbox.

④ On the **Contains** pop-up menu, choose **messages**.

⑤ On the **that match** pop-up menu, choose **all**.

You can choose **any** if you want a message to be included if it matches any of the conditions.

⑥ Use the pop-up menus and fields to create a condition for the messages that you want to be included.

⑦ To add another condition, click the **Add** button (⊕).

⑧ Use the pop-up menus and fields to configure the condition.

⑨ Repeat Steps **7** and **8** until you have added all the conditions you want.

*Note: To remove a condition, click its **Remove** button (⊖).*

⑩ Click **OK**.

The mailbox is created and any messages that meet its conditions appear in it automatically.

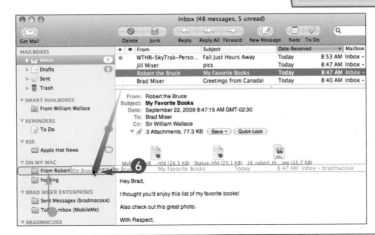

## TIPS

**How do I change how messages are listed on the Messages list?**

Just click the column heading, such as **From**, to sort the list by that column. To change the direction in which messages are listed, click the triangle in the current sort column. You can also drag the right edge of columns to change their width.

**I have received a message saying that I am over my mail storage quota. What do I do?**

Most e-mail accounts have a limit on how much e-mail you can store on the server. When you reach this limit, you can no longer receive or send e-mail with that account. To prevent e-mail server storage overload, store e-mail in mailboxes on MacBook. You should also check account settings to make sure mail is not being stored on the server unintentionally.

As you accumulate messages, you may want to be able to find messages that contain information or attachments you need. You can use the Mail Search tool to quickly find important messages.

**One of the best ways to be able to find e-mail is to keep it organized. A little time spent organizing e-mail earlier prevents some of the effort to find it later. For more information, see the section "Organize E-mail."**

## Search E-mail

① Type the information for which you want to search in the Search bar.

● As you type, Mail presents messages that meet your search in the lower pane.

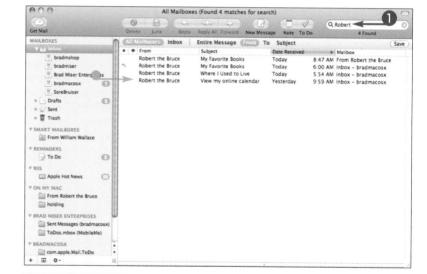

② To read a message, select it.

● The message opens in the reading pane that appears at the bottom of the window.

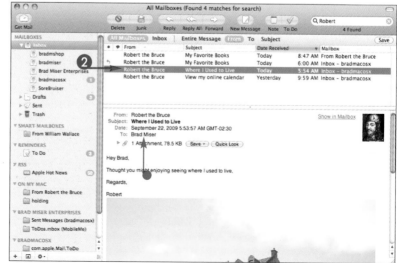

❸ To search in all mailboxes, click **All Mailboxes**, or to search in only the selected mailbox, click the button to the right of the All Mailboxes button, which is labeled with the name of the selected folder or Inbox.

❹ Click the button to indicate what part of the messages you want to search.

For example, to search for messages by recipient, click **To**.

● The results are refined, based on the choices you made.

*Note: When you click **Entire Message**, Mail searches all parts of the messages; the results are sorted by rank, which is how Mail indicates how relevant the messages are to your search term.*

❺ To read a found message, click it.

❻ To save a search as a Smart Mailbox so that you can run it again, click **Save**.

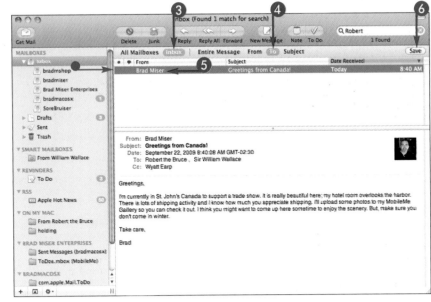

The Smart Mailbox sheet appears.

❼ Configure and save the Smart Mailbox.

*Note: For more information on configuring a Smart Mailbox, see the section "Organize E-mail."*

You can repeat the search at any time by selecting its folder in the Smart Mailboxes section of the Mailboxes pane.

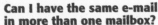
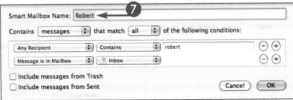

### Do I have to be using Mail to search e-mail?

The Mac OS X Spotlight feature enables you to search for information on MacBook no matter where that information is found, including files, folders, and e-mail. If you are sure the information you need is in an e-mail, search in Mail. If not, use Spotlight instead. To learn how to use Spotlight, see Chapter 4.

### Can I have the same e-mail in more than one mailbox?

An e-mail can exist in only one mailbox in the same location, such as the mailboxes stored on MacBook. (Of course, you can make copies of messages and place the copies in different locations.) Because Smart Mailboxes do not actually contain the messages (a Smart Mailbox makes pointers to the actual e-mail messages), e-mail messages can be included in many Smart Mailboxes at the same time.

# Avoid Spam

One of the perils of receiving e-mail is spam. Spam is annoying at best, with messages that stream into your Inbox with advertising in which you have no interest. At worst, spam contains offensive or dangerous messages that promise all kinds of rewards for just a few simple actions (usually an attempt at identity theft).

**Notice that the title of this section is "Avoid Spam," as opposed to "Eliminate Spam" or "Prevent Spam." Unfortunately, spam is part of receiving e-mail, and the best you can do is to minimize your exposure to it as much as possible.**

## Avoid Spam

① Press ⌘+,.

The Mail Preferences window appears.

② Click the **Junk Mail** tab.

③ Check the **Enable junk mail filtering** check box.

④ Click **Mark as junk mail, but leave it in my Inbox** if you want Mail to highlight junk e-mail, but not do anything else with it.

⑤ Click **Move it to the Junk mailbox** if you want Mail to move spam to the Junk mailbox.

⑥ Click **Perform custom actions (Click Advanced to configure)** if you want to define what Mail does using a mail rule.

If you select this option, use the **Advanced** button and sheet to configure the rules that Mail should apply to junk mail.

**Note:** *For more information about rules, see the section "Create E-mail Rules."*

⑦ Check the check boxes to specify e-mails that are exempt from junk mail filtering.

For example, if the sender of a message is someone in your Address Book, it is unlikely that the message is junk, and so you should check the top check box in this section.

⑧ Close the Preferences window.

As you receive e-mail, Mail takes the action that you selected when you receive e-mail that it identifies as junk.

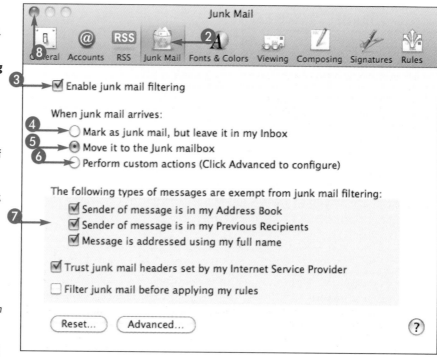

**Note:** *The remaining steps assume that you selected the option wherein Mail moves junk messages to the Junk folder. If you selected a different option, the details will be different.*

9 Click the Junk folder.

● The contents of the Junk filter, which are all the messages that Mail has classified as junk, appear.

10 Select and review each message.

11 If a message is junk, do nothing; the message stays in your Junk folder.

12 If a message is not junk, click **Not Junk**.

The message moves back to your Inbox and is no longer marked as junk.

Over time, Mail learns from your actions and gets better at identifying junk mail.

13 Click **Delete** (🚫) to delete junk messages.

**Note:** *Consider using a sacrificial e-mail address when you participate in activities, such as posting to an online forum, that are likely to get you spammed, while you use your permanent addresses in safe situations. If the sacrificial e-mail address gets spammed, you can just stop using it and obtain another one. Free e-mail accounts and MobileMe e-mail aliases (see Chapter 10) are ideal for sacrificial e-mail addresses.*

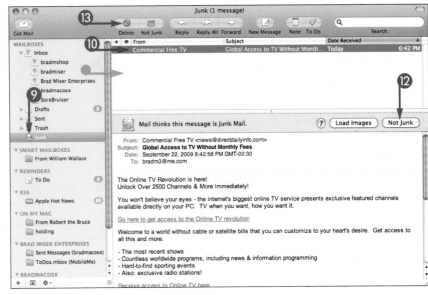

### I have received an important message saying my account is going to be closed unless I update its information. What should I do?

One effective spam technique that criminals use is to model their spam e-mails so that they look just like e-mail from legitimate companies; examples include eBay and online banks. They usually mention that your account is out of date or compromised, and that you need to provide information to correct the situation. These messages are always spam and you should never respond to them. Legitimate companies never ask you to update information through e-mail requests. If you do respond and provide the requested information, your identity will be stolen.

### How can I tell if a message is legitimate or spam?

Just by looking at an e-mail, there is no way to tell whether it is authentic because many criminals make their e-mails look like they are from legitimate organizations. However, most of these e-mails include a link to take you someplace, usually your account so that you can verify some information, which really means that they are trying to steal information from you. Point to these links (**do not click!**), and the URL pops up. You will see that the first part of the URL has nothing to do with the real company, which is a dead giveaway that it is an attempt to steal your identity.

# Create and Use E-mail Signatures

It is good practice to include a signature at the end of your e-mails to make your communication more personal or to provide important information, such as your phone number or Web site address. You can even advertise in your signature.

**You can configure Mail to make adding signatures easier and faster. You can create many different signatures and easily use the most appropriate one for a specific e-mail message that you send. You can also have a signature inserted into new messages automatically.**

## Create Signatures

**1** Press ⌘ + , .

**2** Click the **Signatures** tab.

**3** Click **All Signatures**.

**4** Click ➕.

A new signature is created and its name appears in the center column, ready to be edited.

**5** Type a name for the signature and press `Return`.

When a signature is selected in the center column, its contents appear in the far-right column.

**6** With the signature selected, type the content of the signature in the right column.

Your signature can be any text you want, arranged as you want it to be.

**7** If you use the default font for your messages, check the **Always match my default message font** check box so that the signature uses that font.

**8** If you use standard quoting (where your reply is always above the quoted message), check the **Place signature above quoted text** check box.

**9** Repeat Steps **3** to **6** to create as many signatures as you want.

**Note:** If you want a unique signature for one of your e-mail accounts, select it before creating the signature.

**10** Drag signatures from the center column onto the e-mail accounts with which you want to use them in the left column.

The number of signatures available for each account is shown under the account name.

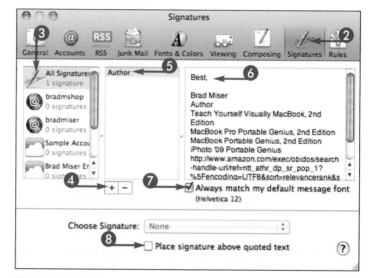

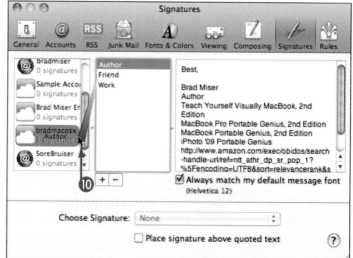

**11** Click an e-mail account.

**12** Choose the default signature for the account on the **Choose Signature** pop-up menu.

Whenever you send an e-mail from the account, the default signature is pasted in automatically.

**13** Close the Preferences window.

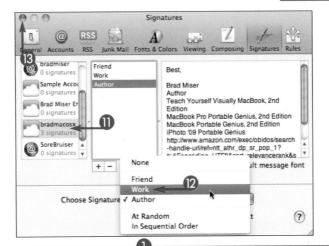

## Use Signatures

**1** Create a new message.

● If you configured a default signature for the e-mail account, it is pasted in the new message.

**2** To change the signature, choose the signature on the **Signature** pop-up menu.

**Note:** If you do not select a default signature for an account, you can choose a signature on the menu to add it to a message. The signatures available on this menu are those that you added to the account on the Signatures tab.

TIPS

**What are the other choices on the Choose Signature pop-up menu on the Signatures tab?**

If you choose **At Random** on the **Choose Signature** pop-up menu, Mail selects a signature randomly each time you create a message. If you choose **In Sequential Order**, Mail selects the first signature on the list for the first message, the next one for the second message, and so on.

**Can I put images or links in my signature?**

Yes. To add an image (for example, a scanned version of your written signature) to a signature, drag the image file from the desktop onto the right pane of the Signatures tab. However, adding an image to your signature greatly

increases the amount of space required to store your messages. You can also add links to a signature by typing the URL in the signature block or by copying and pasting it in.

# Create
# E-mail Rules

If you find yourself doing the same tasks with certain kinds of e-mail, you can probably configure Mail to do those tasks for you automatically by configuring rules, which are automatic actions that Mail performs for you.

**To determine whether you can create a rule, you need to be able to define the conditions under which one or more actions should be taken, and the actions you want to happen every time those conditions are met. In the following steps, you learn how to create a rule to automatically file e-mails from specific people in a folder and to alert you that they have arrived. You can configure other rules similarly.**

① Press ⌘ + ⏸.

② Click the **Rules** tab.

The center pane shows the configured rules. By default, you see a rule for e-mail from Apple.

*Note: For a rule to be active, its check box must be checked. You can disable a rule by unchecking its check box.*

③ Click **Add Rule**.

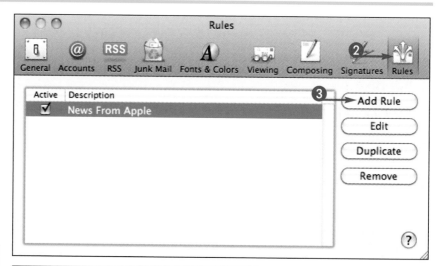

The New Rule sheet appears.

④ Name the rule.

⑤ Choose **any** on the pop-up menu if only one condition has to be true for the rule to apply, or **all** if all of the conditions have to be true for the rule to apply.

⑥ Select the attribute for the first condition on the left pop-up menu.

The default value is **From**.

⑦ Choose the operand for the condition on the center pop-up menu, such as **Contains**.

⑧ Type the condition value in the box.

⑨ Click ⊕.

⑩ Repeat Steps **6** to **8** to configure the new condition.

*Note: To remove a condition, click its **Remove** button (⊖).*

⑪ Repeat Steps **9** and **10** to add and configure more conditions.

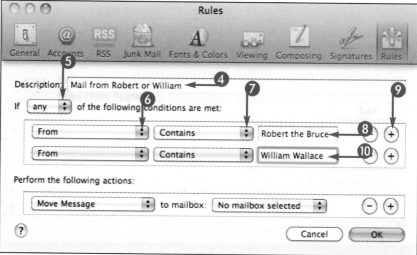

⓬ On the top left **Action** pop-up menu, choose the action you want to happen when the conditions are met.

⓭ On the top right **Action** pop-up menu, choose the result of the action, such as a location or a sound.

⓮ To add another action, click ⊕.

⓯ Repeat Steps **12** and **13** to configure the new action.

⓰ Repeat Steps **14** and **15** to add and configure more actions.

⓱ Click **OK**.

The rule is created and appears on the list of rules on the Rules pane.

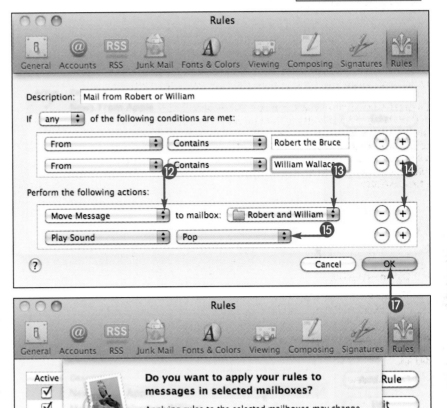

Rules

General  Accounts  RSS  Junk Mail  Fonts & Colors  Viewing  Composing  Signatures  Rules

Description:  Mail from Robert or William

If  [ any ▾ ]  of the following conditions are met:

[ From ▾ ]  [ Contains ▾ ]  [ Robert the Bruce ]  ⊖ ⊕
[ From ▾ ]  [ Contains ▾ ]  [ William Wallace ]  ⊖ ⊕

Perform the following actions:

[ Move Message ▾ ]  to mailbox:  [ Robert and William ▾ ]  ⊖ ⊕
[ Play Sound ▾ ]  [ Pop ▾ ]  ⊖ ⊕

(?)                              ( Cancel )  ( OK )

A confirmation message appears.

⓲ If you want the rule to be applied to the messages currently in your Inbox, click **Apply**; if not, click **Don't Apply**.

The rule is created and appears on the list of rules. When messages are received that meet the rule's conditions, whatever actions it includes are performed automatically.

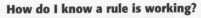

Rules

General  Accounts  RSS  Junk Mail  Fonts & Colors  Viewing  Composing  Signatures  Rules

Active

**Do you want to apply your rules to messages in selected mailboxes?**

Applying rules to the selected mailboxes may change their contents. Active rules will always be applied to new messages.

( Don't Apply )  ( Apply )

(?)

TIPS

**What are some examples of useful actions available for rules?**

Move Message moves e-mail messages to specific locations, such as mailboxes that you have created on MacBook or even the Trash. Forward Message can be useful when you always want to forward messages to another address in specific situations. If you usually reply to a specific person's e-mail, Reply to Message can be useful.

**How do I know a rule is working?**

To test the actions of a specific rule, select a message to which the rule should apply, open the **Message** menu, and then select **Apply Rules**. If the actions you expect happen, then the rule is working. If they do not, then something is wrong with the rule and you need to edit it to fix the problem. You should also select a message to which the rule should not apply and do the same thing. If the actions happen, then the rule is not configured correctly.

# Set Mail Preferences

This chapter has discussed a number of Mail Preferences tools already, but there are several more that you should explore as you use Mail.

**These include the General, Fonts & Colors, Viewing, and Composing preferences. You use the General tab to set general Mail preferences, such as sound effects, where attachments are stored, and what location to include in searches. You use the Viewing and Composing preferences to configure how you view and write e-mail.**

Set Mail Preferences

## Set General Preferences

1 Press ⌘+.

2 Click the **General** tab.

3 On the **Check for new messages** pop-up menu, choose how often you want Mail to check for new messages.

4 On the **New messages sound** pop-up menu, choose the sound you want to hear when you receive new messages.

5 If you do not want to hear sounds for other actions, uncheck the **Play sounds for other mail actions** check box.

6 On the **Dock unread count** pop-up menu, choose the mailboxes for which you want the number of unread messages to be displayed on the Dock icon for Mail.

*Note: You can choose Inbox Only, All Mailboxes, any Smart Mailbox, or None if you want this count to be hidden.*

7 On the **Downloads folder** pop-up menu, choose the folder in which attachments should be stored by default.

8 On the **Remove unedited downloads** pop-up menu, choose what you want Mail to do with attachments that you have not changed when you delete the associated message.

*Note: Usually, you want the attachment to be deleted when you delete the message to avoid cluttering up your hard drive with documents you do not use.*

9 Use the search check boxes to configure specific areas that should be included in searches.

## Set Fonts & Colors Preferences

1 Press ⌘+.

2 Click the **Fonts & Colors** tab.

3 Click the **Select** button next to the type of font you want to format and use the resulting Fonts panel to configure that font.

4 If you want a fixed-width font to be used for plain text messages, check the **Use fixed-width font for plain text messages** check box.

*Note: Using a fixed-width font can be useful because it keeps the text lined up as the sender intended.*

5 Use the **Color quoted text** check box and pop-up menus to determine what colors Mail uses to mark the levels of quotes in your e-mail conversations.

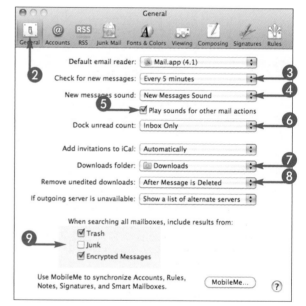

## Set Viewing Preferences

**1** Press ⌘+. .

**2** Click the **Viewing** tab.

**3** For more detail at the top of e-mail messages, such as information about the message path, use this menu to choose the level of information.

**4** If you use iChat, ensure the **Show online buddy status** check box is checked; when it is, you see a green dot next to a buddy's name on e-mail messages when his status is available for chatting.

**5** To add more emphasis to unread messages, check the **Display unread messages with bold font** check box.

**6** If you do not want to display images that are not embedded in messages, uncheck the **Display remote images in HTML messages** check box.

**7** If you prefer to see e-mail addresses and names instead of just names, uncheck the **Use Smart Addresses** check box.

**8** Use the **Message threading** check box and color pop-up menu to set how Mail indicates that messages are part of the same conversation (thread).

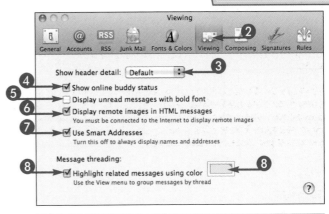

## Set Composing Preferences

**1** Press ⌘+. .

**2** Click the **Composing** tab.

**3** Use this menu to choose the default format for messages.

**4** Use this menu to check spelling in messages you compose.

**5** If you want to see the individuals in a group when you address a message to the group (instead of just the group's name), check the **When sending to a group, show all member addresses** check box.

**6** If you have more than one e-mail address, choose the default account for new messages on this menu.

**7** If you want your replies to use the same format as the original message, check the **Use the same message format as the original message** check box.

**8** If you want to be able to select the text to be quoted when you reply to a message, select the **Include selected text, if any; otherwise include all text** radio button.

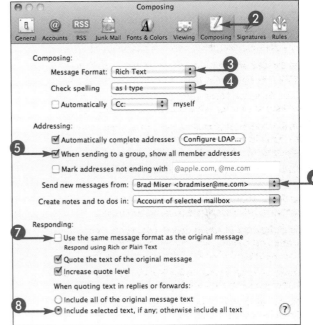

### How else can I use threading?

Threading is a way to identify and group messages on the same topic (that have the same subject line). On the **View** menu, choose **Organize by Thread** to show these messages in groups that you can collapse or expand. This is a useful way to organize your Inbox because it keeps related messages together as conversations. When you select the parent message in a thread, you see a summary of all the messages that thread contains.

### What are the formats used for e-mail in Mail?

Plain Text strips all formatting options from messages so they come through as, well, plain text. Rich Text includes formatting options, such as bold, italics, color, and so on. Plain Text is useful because you always know how the message will appear to the recipient. Using Rich Text allows you to format your messages, but some e-mail applications might not interpret the formats correctly. You can apply formatting to a Rich Text message using the commands on the Format menu.

# Explore iChat

Like the other "i" applications, iChat is both powerful and easy to use. Its interface is simple and elegant, but packs all the features that you need to have great text, audio, and video chats.

After you have done some quick configuration of iChat, you can use it to communicate with people all over the world in any format you choose. It can even help when you have problems because you can use iChat to share the desktop of your MacBook with someone else over the Internet or over a local network, such as a network in your home.

## Text chat window

Text conversations appear in a text chat window.

## Who you are texting with

At the top of the window, you see who you are texting with.

## What the other person is saying to you

On the left side of the window, you see text from the other person involved in the conversation.

## What you have said

On the right side of the window, you see your contributions to the conversation.

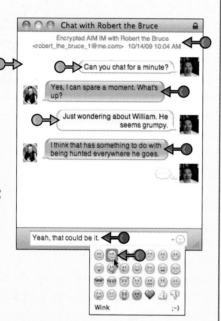

**Text box**

When you want to add to the conversation, enter text in the text box.

**Emoticon menu**

You can add emoticons to a conversation by selecting them on the menu.

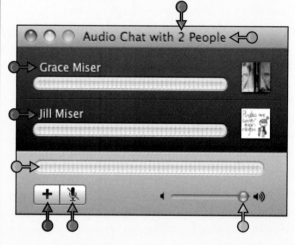

**Audio Chat window**

When you audio chat with people, you see a visual representation of the sounds you hear.

**How many people are involved**

At the top of the window, you see how many people are participating.

**Each person participating**

Participants in the conversation have their own sound bar so that you can see when they speak.

**Your volume level**

The bottom bar represents how loud your speech is.

**Add button**

Click ➕ to add more people to the conversation.

**Mute button**

Click 🔇 to mute your sound.

**Volume slider**

Use this slider to set the volume level of a conversation.

**Video chat window**

Shows each of the people you are video conferencing with.

**Participant windows**

Each participant gets his own window for the chat.

**Your window**

During a video chat, you see yourself as the other participants see you.

**Effects**

You can use the Effects tools to apply a variety of interesting effects to the video.

**Add**

You can add up to three other people in a video conference.

**Mute**

Click 🔇 to block sound from your end.

**Full-screen**

When you click 🔳, the video conference fills the desktop.

**Shared screen**

You can use iChat to view and control another person's computer.

**Your computer**

When you are sharing a desktop, you see a preview of your desktop; click it to move back to your computer.

**Shared applications**

When someone shares a screen with you, you can work with applications and documents on her computer just as if you were seated in front of it.

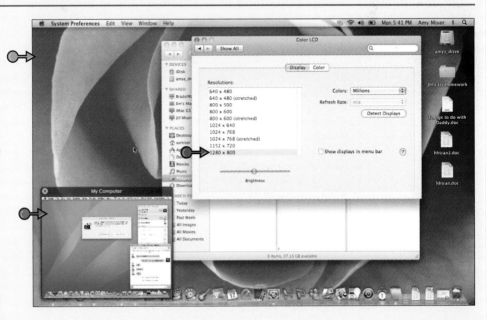

# Configure an iChat Account

Before you start chatting, you need to do some basic configuration of iChat, such as setting up the chat accounts that you are going to use, and setting volume levels for the microphone.

**The first time you start iChat, its Setup Assistant guides you each step of the way. You can also configure iChat using its Preferences.**

## Configure an iChat Account

1 Launch iChat by clicking its icon on the Dock or by double-clicking its icon in the Applications folder.

The first time you launch iChat, the Setup Assistant runs.

2 Read the information in the first screen.

3 Click **Continue**.

*Note: To add an account at any time, open the Preferences dialog, click the **Accounts** tab, and click the **Add** button (⊞) at the bottom of the window. You move to the Account Setup dialog.*

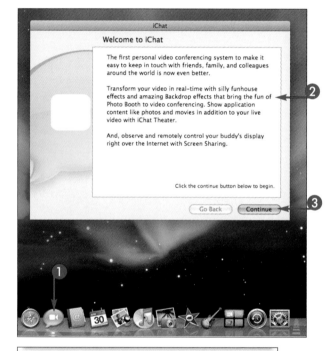

4 From the **Account Type** pop-up menu, choose the type of account you want to use to chat.

*Note: You can use a MobileMe, America Online Instant Messenger (AIM), Jabber, or Google Talk account with iChat. You need a MobileMe account or an AIM account to be able to video chat.*

5 Type a member, screen, or user name for your account.

6 Type the password for your account.

*Note: If you do not have a chat account, click the **Get an iChat Account** button and follow the on-screen instructions.*

7 Click **Done**.

If you use a MobileMe account, you see the Encrypted iChat screen. If you use another type of account, skip the rest of these steps.

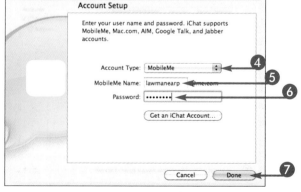

8 If you want your chats with other MobileMe users to be encrypted for better security, check the **Enable iChat encryption** check box.

9 Click **Continue**.

**Encrypted iChat**

iChat can encrypt your text, audio, and video chats with other MobileMe subscribers who have enabled encryption turned on.

To use iChat encryption, you must be a MobileMe member. To find out more about iChat encryption, click Learn More.

☑ Enable iChat encryption

( Learn More... )    ( Go Back )    ( Continue )

10 Click **Done**.

iChat opens, you see your Buddy lists, and you are ready to start chatting.

**iChat Encryption Requested**

Your request for an encryption certificate was sent to MobileMe.

After MobileMe processes your request, iChat encryption will begin for lawmanearp@me.com.

When a chat is encrypted, a lock icon appears in the chat window's title bar:

Chat with steve@me.com

AIM instant messaging with <steve@me.com>

( Go Back )    ( Done )

**TIPS**

**Do I have to use the Assistant to configure iChat?**

No. You can configure all aspects of iChat using its Preferences dialog (press ⌘ + ). For example, you can use the Accounts pane to configure your chat accounts, and the Messages pane to configure the format of text chats.

**What kind of Internet connection do I need to audio and video chat?**

Audio and video chats require broadband Internet connections. As long as you can connect through a Wi-Fi, DSL, cable, or other fast connection, you can chat with audio and video. Prepare to be amazed at the quality of both audio and video chatting.

# Chat with Text

Text chatting is a great way to have almost real-time conversations with other people while not consuming all of your and their attention throughout the conversation. Text messaging is a great way to communicate short messages in the format of a conversation.

**iChat enables you to text message other people (called buddies) easily and quickly.**

## Add a Buddy

1. Launch iChat.

2. Expand the Buddies list and the Offline list.

   If the person with whom you want to chat is not on either list, continue with the following steps.

   **Note:** *A buddy who appears on the Offline list is unavailable for chatting.*

3. At the bottom of the AIM Buddy list, click the **Add** button (⊞).

4. Choose **Add Buddy**.

   The Add Buddy sheet appears. Use the following steps to add someone in your Address Book as a chat buddy (see Chapter 15 for help with Address Book).

5. Click the disclosure triangle (▼ changes to ▲).

   **Note:** *You can also add a buddy by typing her information in the relevant fields instead of choosing someone from your Address Book.*

6. Search for the buddy you want to add.

7. Select the contact with the chat account you want to associate with the buddy.

8. Choose the group in which you want to place the buddy.

9. Click **Add**.

   The person is added to your Buddy list.

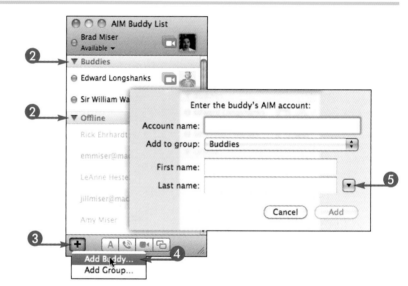

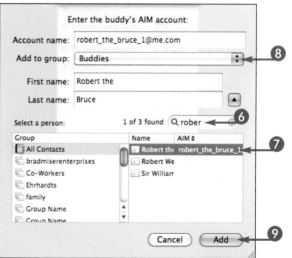

## Start a Text Chat

1. Launch iChat.
2. Select the buddy with whom you want to chat.
3. Click the **Text Chat** button (A).
- A new text chat window appears.
4. Type your message.
5. Press Return.

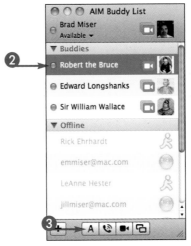
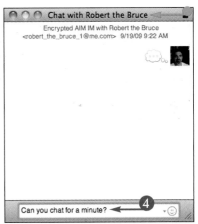

Your message is sent and is added to the message log at the top of the window next to your icon.

- If your chat request is accepted, you see the person's response in the message window next to his icon.

6. Read the reply.
7. Type your response.
8. To add an emoticon to it, choose one on the pop-up menu.
9. Press Return.

Your response is sent and added to the conversation.

**Note:** *Because text chatting is supposed to be fast and simple, you can expect to see misspellings and shorthand in chats.*

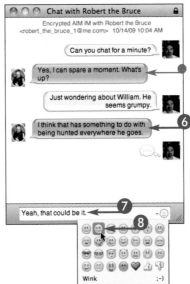

### What happens when someone starts a chat with me?

When someone wants to chat with you, a new message window appears in iChat and you see the message that has been sent to you. Click the message; the window expands to show the response field. To decline the chat, click the **Decline** button. To block all attempts to chat, click the **Block** button. To accept the chat, type your response and click **Accept**. Chat just like when you start a chat session.

### What is the Bonjour list?

You can use iChat and the Mac OS X Bonjour networking function to text, audio, and video chat on your local network. When people on your local network sign in to chat, they appear on your Bonjour list. You can chat with them just like chatting over the Internet, except the conversation never leaves the local network. This is really useful if you have several Macs in the same area because you can communicate with everyone on your network easily.

# Chat with Audio

Text chatting is great, but being able to talk to someone can be even better. Of course, you can always use the phone, but that can be expensive. Using an iChat audio chat, you can have conversations with one or more people at the same time at no cost to you.

**Before you start talking, take a moment to set up your MacBook microphone. Then you can talk whenever you want.**

## Chat with Audio

### Check the Microphone

1. Press ⌘+,.

   The iChat Preferences dialog opens.

2. Click the **Audio/Video** tab.

3. On the **Microphone** pop-up menu, choose **Internal microphone**.

4. Speak normally.

● As you speak, the level indicator just above the pop-up menu measures the relative input volume. When you speak normally, the gauge should register toward the right end of the bar while remaining green (if it becomes red, the input level is too high). If the level needs to be adjusted, perform Steps **6** to **10**.

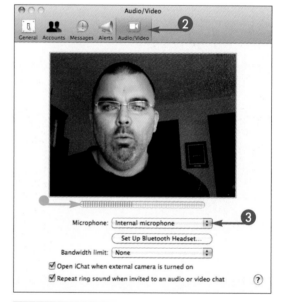

5. Open the System Preferences application and click the **Sound** icon.

6. In the Sound window, click the **Input** tab.

7. Drag the **Input volume** slider to the right to increase the level of sound input, or to the left to decrease it.

8. If you are in a noisy environment, check the **Use ambient noise reduction** check box.

9. Speak normally.

● Use the Input level gauge to measure the level of sound. Like the gauge in iChat, the bars should move toward the right end of the gauge without going all the way to the end.

10. Adjust the input volume until the gauge looks right.

11. Close the iChat Preferences window.

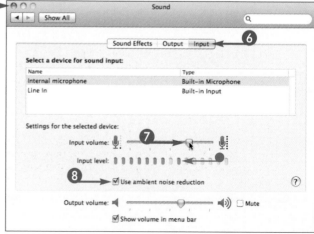

## Audio Chat

**1** On the Buddy or Bonjour list, select the buddy with whom you want to chat.

*Note: If the Audio Chat button does not become active when you select a buddy, the buddy is not capable of audio chatting with you.*

**2** Click the **Audio Chat** button (⟨⟩).

● The Audio Chat window opens and iChat attempts to connect to the buddy you selected. If the person is available and accepts your chat request, you are connected and the audio chat begins.

**3** Speak to the person and listen as you would on a telephone.

**4** To change the volume, drag the slider to the left to decrease the volume level, or to the right to increase it.

**5** To mute your side of the conversation, click the **Mute** button (⟨⟩); click it again to unmute it.

**6** To add another person to the chat, click the **Add** button (⊞) and choose the buddy you want to add.

● Once the second person accepts, all three of you are able to hear each other.

**7** Keep adding people and chatting.

**8** When you are done, close the chat window.

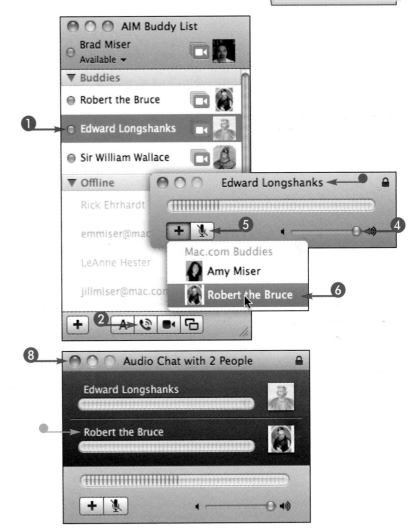

### What if I do not want to chat in any form?

To prevent any chat requests from popping up, you need to quit iChat. If you want to show your status to others, open the **Status** pop-up menu just below your name at the top of the Buddy and Bonjour List windows. Choose the status you want them to see on their Buddy lists. Choose **Offline** if you do not want to chat. To chat again, choose **Available** on the menu. No matter what status you choose, you see windows pop up when someone tries to chat with you. You can just ignore those windows or decline the chats if you do not want to chat.

### Are audio chats basically free phone calls?

Yes. If you already have an account that supports audio and video chats and an Internet connection, there is no additional charge for chatting. In effect, you can make free phone calls and have free video conferences with anyone with whom you can chat, no matter where the person is located in the world.

# Chat with Video

With the rise of iChat, iSight cameras, and broadband Internet connections, video conferencing became simple and easy to do (well, at least it is easy if you use a Mac).

**With MacBook and an Internet connection, you can see people while you talk to them. This is the next best thing to being there in person, and you do not have to go anywhere.**

## Check the Camera

1️⃣ Click the **Camera** icon (▣) next to your name at the top of the Buddy or Bonjour lists.

   The My Built-in iSight window opens.

2️⃣ Move MacBook or yourself until the image is what you want others to see.

*Note: Click the Preferences button to open the Audio/Video pane of the iChat Preferences dialog.*

3️⃣ Resize the window by dragging its resize handle (▨).

4️⃣ When you are satisfied with the view, close the window.

## Video Chat

1️⃣ On the Buddy or Bonjour list, select the buddy with whom you want to chat.

2️⃣ Click the **Video Chat** button (▣).

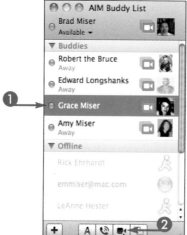

● The video chat window opens. When the person accepts your chat invitation, you can talk to her and see her image in the window.

● The inset preview window shows you what the other person is seeing in his chat window.

③ Drag the preview window so that it is where you want it to be on the screen.

④ To apply special effects to the image, click the **Effects** button.

The Effects pane opens and you can use its tools.

*Note: For more information about effects, see the section "Add Effects and Backgrounds to Video Chats."*

⑤ To mute your end of the conversation, click the **Mute** button (); click it again to unmute it.

⑥ To make the window fill the desktop, click the **Fill Screen** button (📺).

⑦ To add another person to the conversation, click the **Add** button (➕).

● When the person accepts your invitation, a third video window appears and you see the second person.

You can talk to and see the other people, and they can see and talk to each other.

⑧ When you are done, close the window.

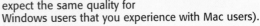

---

**TIPS**

**How many people can I have in a video or audio conference at the same time?**

You can have up to four participants (including yourself) in a single video conference. You can have up to ten people (including yourself) in an audio conference at the same time.

**Is iChat compatible with other kinds of video conference systems?**

To use iChat for video conferences, all participants must be using iChat or the latest version of AOL Instant Messenger for Windows (do not expect the same quality for Windows users that you experience with Mac users).

# Add Effects and Backgrounds to Video Chats

Having a video chat is both an effective way to communicate with other people, and a lot of fun. There are ways to make it even more fun.

**You can apply special effects to the images being shown during a video chat, and you can apply background images or movies to video chats to make them more interesting.**

Add Effects and Backgrounds to Video Chats

1. Start a video chat.
2. Click the **Effects** button.

   The Effects pane appears.
3. Scroll to the left or right in the Video Effects palette to browse the default effects, image backgrounds, and video backgrounds.

4. Click the effect, image, or video that you want to apply.

   Selecting an effect applies it to your image immediately, and you can skip the next two steps.
5. If you selected an image or video background, move out of the camera view at the prompt.
6. When the prompt disappears, move back into the picture.

● To the other participants, it looks as if you are actually in front of the background image or video.

# Present Online with iChat Theater

There are times when you want to share documents with other people while you talk about the documents. The obvious case is a presentation that you want to use to convey information to others, but there are times when you want to "talk" through a document to explain it to someone, such as when you are collaborating with someone on it.

**You can use iChat to present documents to other people over the Internet. When you present a document, the other people see the document, as well as see and hear you through a video chat.**

## Present Online with iChat Theater

① Open the **File** menu and then select **Share a File With iChat Theater**.

The Share with iChat Theater dialog appears.

② Move to and select the document (such as a presentation) that you want to share.

③ Click **Share**.

The document is prepared, and you see a message stating that iChat Theater is ready to begin.

④ Select the buddy with whom you want to share the document.

⑤ Start a video chat.

● When the buddy accepts your invitation, you see the Video Chat window.

● You also see a window showing the document you are sharing.

● In the lower-left corner of the window, you see a preview window showing the buddy with whom you are chatting.

⑥ Move through the document and speak to deliver your message to the audience.

*Note: If you share a presentation created with Apple's Keynote software, you can use the Keynote controls to present the document.*

⑦ When you are done, close the Video Chat window.

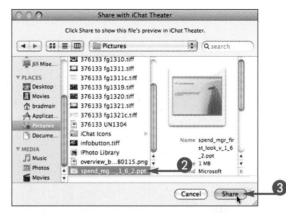

# Share Desktops during Chats

You can share your desktop with other Macs so that the people with whom you are chatting can see and control what happens on your computer. When you share someone else's screen, you can see and control his computer as if you were sitting in front of it. Sharing screens is a great way to collaborate on projects or to share information.

**Screen sharing is especially useful when troubleshooting problems. The person who is having a problem can share his desktop with the person helping so that the helper can see what is happening, which is much easier than trying to describe a problem. The helper can also take control of the computer to actually solve the problem.**

## Share Desktops during Chats

### Share Your Desktop

*Note: Screen Sharing must be enabled on the Sharing pane of the System Preferences application for it to work within iChat. See Chapter 7 to learn how to configure it.*

① On the Buddy or Bonjour list, select the buddy with whom you want to share your desktop.

② Click the **Share Desktop** button (🖵).

③ Click **Share My Screen with buddyname**, where *buddyname* is the name of the buddy you selected.

● When the buddy accepts your invitation, the Sharing status indicator appears (🖵) at the top of the iChat menu on the toolbar.

The buddy with whom you are sharing your screen can now use your MacBook. Do not be surprised when the pointer moves and commands are activated without you doing anything. The buddy also sees what you do on your desktop.

While screens are being shared, you can audio chat. It is a good practice for the person controlling the computer to explain what she is doing as she does it.

④ To end screen sharing, open the **iChat** menu and choose **End Screen Sharing**.

The sharing connection ends and your computer returns to your control.

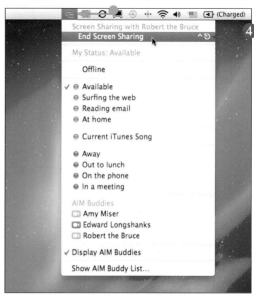

## Share a Desktop Belonging to Someone Else

1 On the Buddy or Bonjour list, select the buddy whose desktop you want to share.

2 Click the **Share Desktop** button (📋).

3 Click **Ask to Share buddyname's Screen**, where buddyname is the name of the buddy you selected.

iChat sends a share request to the buddy. When he responds, you see two windows on your screen.

● One window is the buddy's desktop, which is the larger window by default.

● The other window is a preview of your desktop, which is labeled My Computer.

**Note:** You can move the preview window around the screen if it blocks the part of the shared desktop that you want to see.

4 You can work with the buddy's computer just as if you were sitting in front of it.

5 To move back to your desktop, click in the My Computer window.

The two windows flip-flop so that your desktop is now the larger window.

6 When you are done sharing, click the **Close** button (⊠) on the My Computer window.

**What happens when someone wants to share his screen with me?**

You receive a screen-sharing invitation in iChat. When you click the invitation, you have the following options: Accept to start screen sharing, Decline to prevent it, or Text Reply to send back a text message. If you choose to share the person's screen, you are able to see and control the other person's computer.

**What if I want to share a Mac screen that is on the same local network as my MacBook?**

Open the Sharing pane of the System Preferences application and check the **Screen Sharing** check box to turn it on. Use the Allow Access For tool to configure share permissions for specific user accounts or for all users. On a different Mac on the local network, select the computer whose screen you want to share. Click **Connect** and log in under a user account that has permission to share the screen. Once you are logged in, click **Share Screen**.

# PART

# IV

# Taking Care of Business

Printing is definitely part of taking care of business, and Mac OS X has you covered there, whether you want to print on paper or electronically. Address Book is very useful for organizing and viewing contact information, as well as sending e-mail, visiting Web sites, and printing envelopes. iCal is a calendar program that offers many useful features, such as sharing calendars with other people. And MacBook takes care of business as long as you take care of it, by maintaining it and your data, and troubleshooting problems.

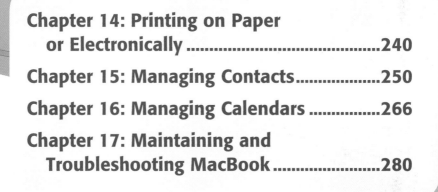

# Understand Printers

Although we live in an electronic world, printing is an important part of using MacBook. You need to understand a number of concepts as you build a printing system for your MacBook and the network it is on.

## Inkjet Printers

Inkjet printers create text and graphics by spraying droplets of ink on paper in various combinations. Inkjet printers produce high-quality output, especially when the output is matched to the right kind of paper. These printers are very inexpensive and many of them offer additional features such as scanning and faxing. Inkjet printers are usually less expensive than laser printers initially, but they consume large amounts of ink, which is relatively expensive. You can expect to pay a significant portion of the purchase price of the printer each time you replace one or more ink cartridges; in some cases, you may pay more for new cartridges than you do for a new printer. Still, for many people, inkjet printers make a lot of sense.

## Laser Printers

Laser printers use a laser, mirrors, and an imaging drum to transfer toner onto paper. Laser printers produce very high-quality output and are fast relative to inkjet printers. Although typically more expensive initially than an inkjet printer, the cost per page of a laser printer can actually be significantly less than that of an inkjet printer. Like inkjet printers, many laser printers print in color. With some careful shopping, you can often get a color laser printer for not much more than an inkjet printer.

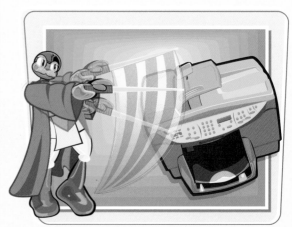

## Printer Connections

No matter what kind of printer you use, MacBook needs to be able to communicate with it to send documents to print. There are three basic ways to connect MacBook to a printer, and each model of printer can support one or all of these types of connections. First, some printers use USB to communicate. Second, networkable printers have an Ethernet port that you can use to connect MacBook directly to the printer, or more likely, to connect the printer to your network. The third, and most convenient, way to connect is wirelessly. Some printers support wireless connections directly; however, you can connect a printer to an AirPort Extreme Base Station, AirPort Express Base Station, or Time Capsule (using an Ethernet port or its USB port) to print to it wirelessly.

## Printer Sharing

If you have more than one computer, you can share the same printer with all the computers over a local network (wired, wireless, or both). The shared printer can be connected directly to a Mac through USB or Ethernet, or it can be connected to an AirPort Base Station or Time Capsule (this is the best option because it does not depend on the Mac running for the printer to be available on the network). See Chapter 7 for information about setting up an AirPort network.

## PDF

Adobe invented the Portable Document Format (PDF) as a means to share and print documents that does not depend on the specific applications or fonts installed on a computer. PDF is the standard format for electronic documents, no matter how they are distributed. This is good news for Mac users because support for PDF documents is built into Mac OS X. You can read any PDF document using the Preview application, but more importantly for this chapter, you can also print any document to the PDF format so that you can easily share it with others through e-mail or over the Web.

# Install and Configure a USB Printer

Connecting a USB printer directly to MacBook is simple, and almost all inkjet printers, as well as some laser printers, support USB connections. After you have connected the printer to MacBook, you need to configure MacBook to use it.

Install and Configure a USB Printer

1. Connect the printer to a power source and turn it on.

2. Connect MacBook to the printer using a USB cable.

3. Open the System Preferences application.

4. Click the **Print & Fax** icon.

● The Print & Fax pane appears.

5. Click the **Add** button (⊞).

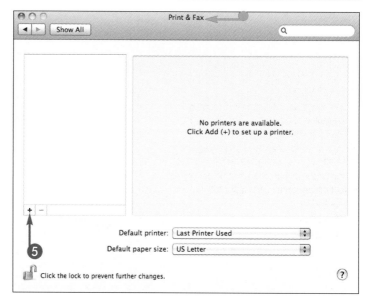

The Add Printer window appears with the Default tab selected.

6. Select the printer with USB shown in the Kind column.

7. If you want to give the printer a different name, edit the name shown in the Name field.

8. Describe the location of the printer in the Location field; in most cases, you should leave the default information.

● If the correct printer is shown on the Print Using pop-up menu, Mac OS X has found a driver for the printer.

9. Click **Add**.

The Add Printer window closes.

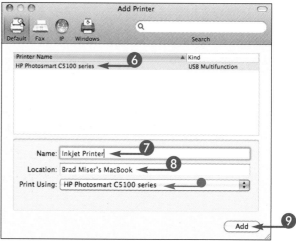

● You return to the System Preferences application and see the printer you added.

⑩ If you want the printer to be MacBook's default, choose it on the **Default printer** pop-up menu.

⑪ Choose the default paper size on the **Default paper size** pop-up menu.

⑫ Quit the System Preferences application.

⑬ Open any document and choose **Print** under the **File** menu.

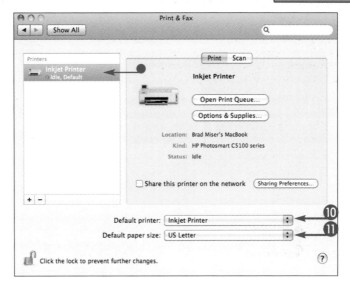

The Print sheet appears.

⑭ Click the disclosure triangle (▼ changes to ▲).

The sheet expands to present additional controls and a preview of the document you are printing.

⑮ Use the pop-up menus, radio buttons, and boxes on the Print sheet to configure the print job (the menus vary, depending on the type of printer you are using).

⑯ Click **Print**.

The document prints.

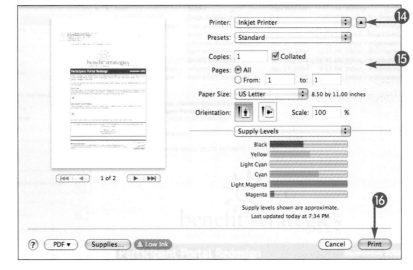

 TIPS

**Can I use any printer with MacBook?**

A compatible printer must support a connection technology that MacBook supports (which is true for almost all printers). More importantly, a printer must have Mac-compatible drivers; most printers do have Mac drivers available, and almost all of these are built into Mac OS X.

**When I try to install a printer, I do not see a driver for it on the list of printer drivers installed with Mac OS X. What do I do now?**

Go to the manufacturer's Web site, look for the Support page, and then look for the Downloads section; there you can search for a Mac driver for the printer. When you find it, you can download and install it. Then, add the printer again; this time, you will be able to select the appropriate driver.

# Install and Configure a Networked Printer

Many printers, especially laser printers, are designed to be connected to a network so that any computer that can connect to the network can use the printer. This is especially useful when a hub provides a wireless network.

**One way to connect a printer to a network is through Ethernet. This provides fast and trouble-free connections. The only downside is that the printer has to be within cable range of a hub, such as an AirPort Extreme Base Station or an Ethernet hub on the network.**

Install and Configure a Networked Printer

1. Connect the printer to a power source and turn it on.

2. Connect the printer to a hub (such as an Airport Extreme Base Station) using an Ethernet cable.

3. Connect MacBook to the same network using AirPort or an Ethernet cable.

4. Open the System Preferences application.

5. Open the **Print & Fax** pane.

6. Click the **Add** button (⊞).

The Add Printer window appears. The printers available on the network are scanned and presented on the list of printers.

7. Select the printer to which you want to connect; the Kind column displays Bonjour, indicating it is a network resource.

8. If you want to give the printer a name, edit the name shown in the Name field.

9. Describe the location of the printer in the Location field.

● If the correct printer is shown on the Print Using pop-up menu, Mac OS X has found a driver for the printer.

10. Click **Add**.

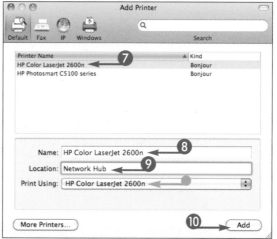

The Printer Selection window closes and you return to the System Preferences application.

● You see the printer you added in the Printers list.

⑪ If you want the printer to be MacBook's default, choose it on the **Default printer** pop-up menu.

⑫ Choose the default paper size on the **Default paper size** pop-up menu.

⑬ Quit the System Preferences application.

⑭ Open any document and choose **Print** under the **File** menu.

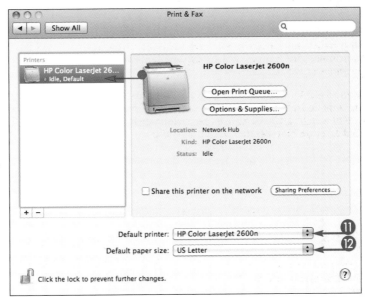

The Print sheet appears.

⑮ Click the disclosure triangle (▼ changes to ▲).

The sheet expands to present additional controls and a preview of the document you are printing.

⑯ Use the pop-up menus on the Print sheet to configure the print job (the menus vary, depending on the type of printer you are using).

⑰ Click **Print**.

The document prints.

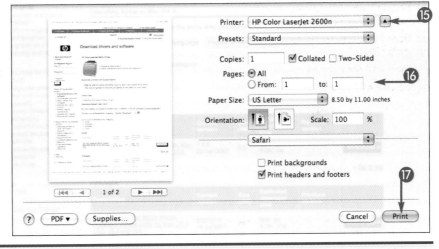

### What is Bonjour?

Bonjour is the Mac OS X network discovery technology. When a device can use Bonjour, it broadcasts its identity on the network. When you connect to that network to search for a device, such as a printer, Bonjour devices are discovered automatically and you do not have to search for them or deal with their network addresses. You simply select the device you want to access and connect to it.

### So, what is the best printer for me?

If you do not print very often or you mostly print photos, an inkjet printer might be your best option, especially if you get one with additional capabilities, such as scanning. However, if you print a lot or print mostly text documents, a laser printer saves you money over the long run. For the ultimate in printing, get a color laser printer, which is not as expensive as it sounds (search on eBay and you can often find reconditioned printers for less than $100).

# Connect to a Printer Wirelessly

If you have created a wireless network using an AirPort Extreme Base Station and have connected a printer to one of its Ethernet ports, you can print to that printer wirelessly without additional configuration (and you can skip the steps in this section). To print to a USB printer wirelessly, you can connect it to the Base Station's USB hub.

**Every computer that prints to a Base Station-connected printer has to have the printer's software driver installed on it before it can use that printer. If the correct driver is not installed on MacBook, download and install it before configuring the Base Station to share a printer.**

### Configure an AirPort Extreme Base Station to Share a USB Printer

1. Connect the printer to the USB port on the AirPort Extreme Base Station.

2. Open the AirPort Utility application, located within the Utilities folder in the Applications folder.

3. Select the Base Station to which the printer is connected.

4. Click **Manual Setup**.

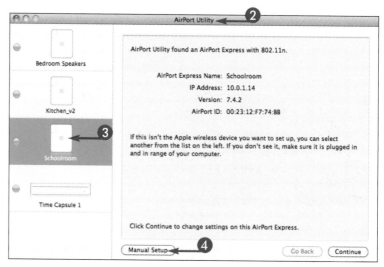

The Manual Configuration window appears.

5. Click the **Printers** tab.

6. Type a name for the printer in the USB Printers field.

7. Click **Update**.

The AirPort Utility updates the Base Station and restarts it.

8. Quit the AirPort Utility.

The printer is accessible wirelessly through AirPort and on a wired network connected to the Base Station.

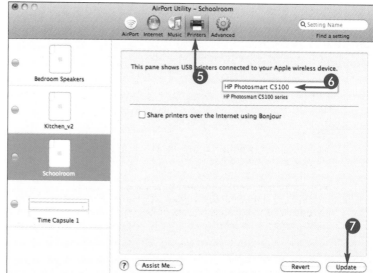

## Connect to a Printer Being Shared by an AirPort Base Station

① Open the **Print & Fax** pane of the System Preferences application.

② Click ⊞.

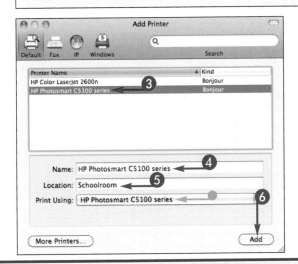

The Add Printer window appears.

③ Select the printer to which you want to connect; the Kind column displays Bonjour, which indicates it is a network resource.

④ If you want to give the printer a name, edit the name shown in the Name field.

⑤ Describe the location of the printer in the Location field.

● If the correct printer is shown on the Print Using pop-up menu, Mac OS X has found a driver for the printer.

⑥ Click **Add**.

The printer is added to the Printers list in System Preferences. You can now print to it.

 **TIPS**

**Can I share a printer connected to a computer over an AirPort network, or do I have to have an AirPort Base Station?**

You can share a printer connected directly to a Mac using USB over an AirPort network as long as that Mac is connected to the AirPort network. This works just like sharing a printer connected to a Base Station except that the Mac always has to be running for the printer to be available.

**Can I print wirelessly to an Ethernet printer by connecting it to a Base Station using an Ethernet cable?**

Yes. If a printer is networkable through Ethernet, just connect it to one of the Base Station's Ethernet ports or to a hub on the network. It is added to the network as a network resource, and you can connect to it using the steps in the section "Install and Configure a Networked Printer," earlier in this chapter. You can print to the printer because an AirPort Extreme Base Station connects the wired and wireless networks together.

# Print to PDF

The Portable Document Format, or PDF, is a great way to distribute documents you create to other people. This is because PDF files appear correctly on any computer equipped with a PDF reader application, regardless of the fonts or other formatting options installed on it, and people cannot easily change PDF documents you create.

**Support for creating PDF documents is built into Mac OS X so that you can create a PDF file of any file you work with.**

① Open the document from which you want to create a PDF file.

② Choose **Print** from the document's **File** menu.

The Print dialog appears.

③ Open the **PDF** pop-up menu.

④ Choose **Save as PDF**.

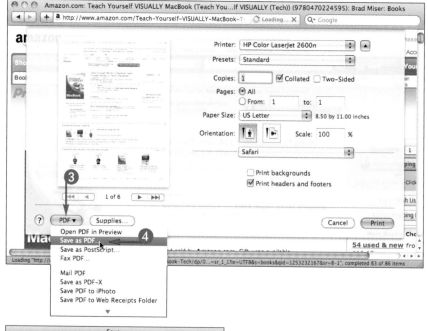

The Save dialog appears.

⑤ Type a name for the PDF file you are creating.

**Note:** The filename extension for PDFs is .pdf. It is added automatically, so you just need to make sure you do not change it.

⑥ Choose the location in which you want to save the PDF file on the **Where** pop-up menu.

⑦ Type a title for the PDF file.

⑧ Type the author name.

⑨ If you want to enter an additional subject, do so in the Subject field.

⑩ Create keywords (used during Spotlight and other searches) in the Keywords field.

⑪ If you want to require passwords for the PDF file to be used, click **Security Options**.

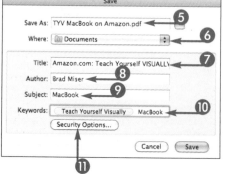

The PDF Security Options dialog appears.

⑫ If you want people to have to enter a password to open the PDF file, check the **Require password to open document** check box and type the password in the Password and Verify fields.

⑬ If you want a password to be required for someone to copy content from the document, check the **Require password to copy text, images and other content** check box and type the password in the Password and Verify fields.

⑭ If you want a password to be required for the document to be printed, check the **Require password to print document** check box and type the password in the Password and Verify fields.

⑮ Click **OK**.

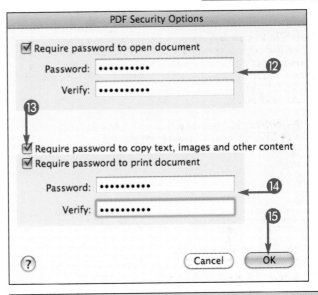

The dialog closes and you return to the Save dialog.

⑯ Click **Save**.

The PDF file is created.

⑰ Open the PDF file.

⑱ If the PDF file is password-protected, type the password at the prompt and press **Return**.

The document appears and is ready to send to other people through e-mail or be posted on the Web.

### What applications can open a PDF document?

By default, PDF documents open in the Mac OS X Preview application, which provides the basic set of tools you need to view and print them. A number of other applications can open PDF files as well, most notably the free Adobe Acrobat Reader application, available at www.adobe.com. Acrobat Reader offers lots of features for viewing and working with PDF documents.

### What if I want to configure or change a PDF document?

One of the benefits of PDF documents is that they are hard to change. If you want to change a PDF or to create more-sophisticated PDFs with features such as tables of contents, hyperlinks, and combinations of PDF documents in different formats, you can use Adobe Acrobat. This is also available on the Adobe Web site at www.adobe.com.

# Explore the Address Book Window

Address Book is both a powerful and easy-to-use contact information manager. You can quickly build your contact information and then use that information in many ways.

**Open Address Book by clicking its Dock icon, which is a book with the @ symbol on its cover, or by double-clicking its icon in the Applications folder.**

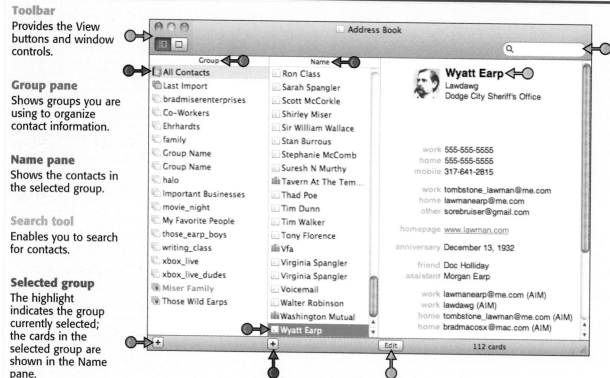

**Toolbar**
Provides the View buttons and window controls.

**Group pane**
Shows groups you are using to organize contact information.

**Name pane**
Shows the contacts in the selected group.

**Search tool**
Enables you to search for contacts.

**Selected group**
The highlight indicates the group currently selected; the cards in the selected group are shown in the Name pane.

**Selected card**
The highlight shows the card selected in the Name pane whose information is displayed in the Card pane.

**Card pane**
Shows the detailed information for the card selected in the Name pane.

**Add group**
Enables you to create groups.

**Add card**
Enables you to add cards.

**Edit**
Use this button to change the information on the card being shown. When the button is blue, you are in Edit mode; when it is black, you are in View mode.

Before you start using Address Book, check out a few important concepts to help you master your contacts quickly and easily.

## Cards

Each contact is represented by a card. Like Rolodex cards of old, Address Book cards contain contact information. Unlike physical cards, Address Book cards are virtual cards, or *vCards*, making them flexible because you can store a variety of information on each card; you can also store different information for various contacts.

## Contact information

Each card in Address Book can hold an unlimited number of physical addresses, phone numbers, e-mail addresses, dates, notes, URL addresses, and so on. Because vCards are flexible, you do not have to include each kind of information for every contact; you include only the information appropriate for each specific contact. Address Book displays only fields that have data in them so that your cards are not cluttered up with a lot of empty fields.

## Groups

Groups are collections of cards. They are useful because you can do something once with a group and the action affects all the cards in that group. For example, you can create a group containing family members whom you regularly e-mail. Then, you can address a message to the one group instead of addressing each person individually.

## Smart Groups

*Smart Groups* are also collections of cards, but unlike regular groups, you do not have to manually add cards to a Smart Group. Instead, you define criteria for the cards you want to be included in the Smart Group, and Address Book automatically adds the appropriate cards for you. For example, suppose you want a group for everyone with the same last name; you can simply create a Smart Group with that criterion, and Address Book adds all the people with that last name to the group automatically.

## Address Book Actions

In addition to using information stored on cards indirectly — for example, looking at a phone number to dial it — you can use some data to perform an action by performing a secondary click on the information and choosing an action. Some of the most useful actions are sending e-mails, visiting Web sites, and looking up an address on a map.

# Add a Contact Manually

Before you can work with contacts, you need to create a card for the contacts you want to manage. There are several ways to capture contact information on cards in Address Book.

**One way is to manually create a card and add contact information to it. This is easy to do and you can choose the specific information you add for a new contact.**

1. Click the **Add Card** button (⊞).

A new, empty card appears in the Card pane.

2. Type the contact's first name in the First field, which is highlighted.

3. Press `Tab`.

4. Type the contact's last name in the Last field.

5. Press `Tab`.

6. Type the contact's company in the Company field.

**Note:** *If the card is for a company, check the* **Company** *check box and type the company name; first and last name information is optional for companies.*

7. Press `Tab`.

8. Click the pop-up menu (⬚) next to the first field (**work**, by default).

9. Select the type of contact information you want to enter.

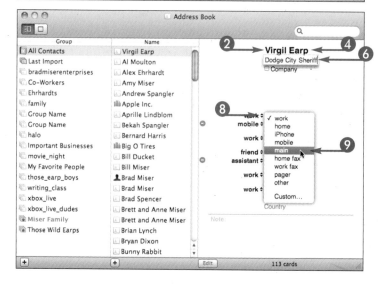

10 Type the selected information in the field, such as a phone number or e-mail address.

**Note:** When you select a data type, Address Book automatically creates a field of the right format, such as for phone numbers when you select **mobile**.

11 Repeat Steps **7** to **10** to enter information into each field to which you want to add information.

12 To remove a field from the card, click the **Delete** button ().

13 To add another field of the same type to a card, click the **Add** button ().

14 To add an image to the card, drag it from the desktop and drop it onto the image well.

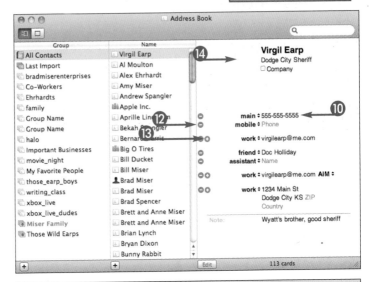

A sheet that enables you to resize the image pops up automatically.

15 Drag the slider to the left to make the image smaller, or to the right to make it larger.

16 Drag the image so that the part you want to appear on the card is contained within the box.

17 Repeat Steps **15** and **16** until the image is sized and placed as you want it.

18 Click **Set**.

The image is saved and the sheet closes.

19 Click **Edit**.

The card is saved and only fields containing information are shown.

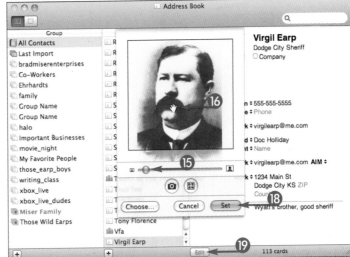
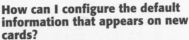

**TIPS**

**What if the information I want to enter is not available on a pop-up menu?**

Open a pop-up menu and choose **Custom**. Type the label for the field you want to add, and click **OK**. You return to the card and the custom label appears on the card. Enter the information for that field. The custom field is added to the card.

**How can I configure the default information that appears on new cards?**

Open the **Address Book** menu and choose **Preferences**. Click **Template**. Remove fields you do not want to appear by default by clicking the **Delete** button (). Add more fields of an existing type by clicking the **Add** button () next to that type. Add fields that do not appear at all by clicking **Add Field** and then choosing the field you want to add to the template. Close the Preferences dialog.

# Work with vCards

Many applications, including Address Book, use vCards to store contact information such as contact managers and e-mail.

**You can add contacts to Address Book using vCards other people send to you; once you have added these cards, you can use them just like those you create in Address Book manually. You can also create a vCard for yourself to send to others so they can easily add your data to their contact information.**

## Work with vCards

### Add Contacts with vCards

**1** Drag the vCard file onto your desktop.

**Note:** *One of the most common ways to receive vCards is through e-mail as attachments. Simply drag the vCard from the e-mail onto your desktop. vCard files have .vcf as their filename extension.*

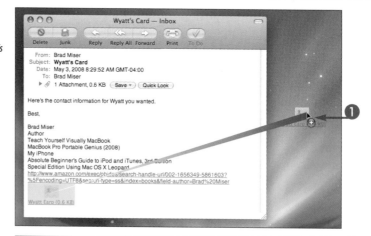

**2** Drag the vCard file from the desktop onto the Name pane of the Address Book window.

A sheet appears, confirming that you are adding a new card.

**3** Click **Add**.

● The vCard is added to Address Book; you can work with it just like cards you create within Address Book.

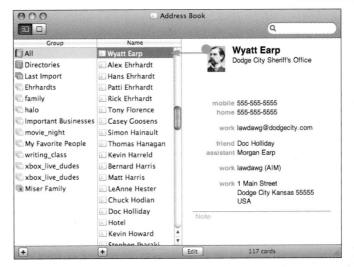

## Create vCards from Address Book Cards

① Search or browse for the cards for which you want to create vCards.

**Note:** To quickly find your card, open the **Card** menu and choose **Go to My Card**. Your card, which is marked with a silhouette icon, appears in the Card pane.

② Drag the card from Address Book onto your desktop.

**Note:** The filename of the vCard is the name of the contact.

The vCard is created, and you can provide it to other people. They can then add its contact information to their contact manager.

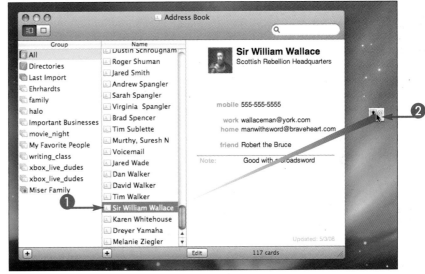

### Can I use a vCard from Microsoft Outlook or some other contact manager?

vCards are a standard file format used by almost all applications that deal with contact information. You should be able to add a vCard to Address Book, regardless of the program used to create that vCard. One caveat is that not all information stored in all applications can be moved into Address Book using vCards, but you almost always get the most important information. You can always add information to the cards you create from a vCard at any time.

### How can I add contact information to Address Book from e-mails when a vCard is not attached?

When you receive an e-mail in Mail, you can add the sender's name and e-mail address to Address Book. Position the pointer over the address shown next to "From," and when the address becomes highlighted, click the trackpad to open the action menu. Choose **Add to Address Book**. A new card is created with as much information as Address Book can extract, usually the first and last name along with an e-mail address. Using Address Book, you can add other information to the card as needed.

# Find Contact Information

The whole point of having contact information is being able to find and use the information you need. Address Book makes it simple to quickly find information you are interested in.

**You can find information by browsing your contacts. Or, you can search for specific contact information.**

## Browse for a Contact

① Select the group that you want to browse; to browse all of your contacts, click **All Contacts**.

● The cards in the selected group appear in the Name pane.

② Use the scroll bar to browse up and down the list of names.

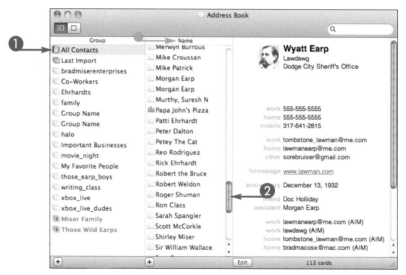

③ Select the name for the contact information you want to view or to use, such as someone to whom you want to send an e-mail.

● The card containing contact information appears in the Card pane.

## Search for a Contact

1 Select the group that you want to search; to search all of your contacts, click **All**.

● All the cards in the selected group appear in the Name pane.

2 Type search text in the Search field.

*Note: Address Book searches all the fields at the same time, and so you do not need to define what you are searching for, such as a name instead of an address.*

As you type, Address Book starts searching all the fields in the cards and reduces those shown in the Name pane so that it contains only those that match your search.

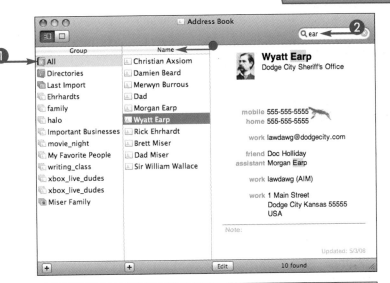

3 Continue typing in the Search field until the card you want appears in the Name pane.

4 Select the card.

● The card's information appears in the Card pane.

● The part of the card that matches your search is highlighted in gray.

5 Clear the Search field by clicking the **Stop Search** button (⊗).

All the cards in the selected group appear again.

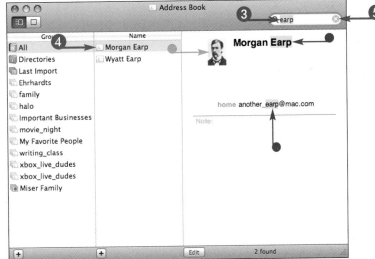

TIPS

**Can I search for contact information by phone number or e-mail address?**

When you search in Address Book, it searches all the fields on all your cards simultaneously. If it finds a match in any of these fields, a card is included in the search results shown in the Name pane. For example, if you enter text, it looks for matches by searching name fields, e-mail addresses, and other fields that include text. Likewise, if you type numbers, Address Book searches phone numbers, addresses, and so on.

**Can I browse or search in multiple groups at the same time?**

You cannot browse the cards in multiple groups at the same time; you can browse only one group at a time by selecting the group you want to browse. You get the best search results if you search only with the All group selected.

# Create an Address Group

A group is useful because it enables you to store many cards within it. Then you can take an action on the group and it affects all the cards included in the group.

**For example, when you want to send an e-mail to everyone in a group, you can do so easily and quickly by sending one message to the group instead of adding each person's e-mail address individually.**

## Create an Address Group

① Click the **Add Group** button (⊞).

● A new group appears in the Group pane with its name ready to be edited.

② Type a name for the group.

③ Press **Return**.

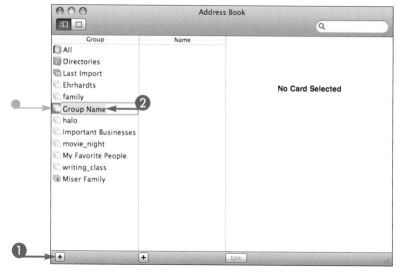

● The group is created and is ready for you to add cards to it.

④ Click **All**.

All the cards in Address Book are shown in the Name pane.

⑤ Browse or search for the first card you want to add to the group.

**Note:** See the previous section, "Find Contact Information," for the steps to browse and search.

⑥ Select a card that you want to add to the group.

● The card appears in the Card pane.

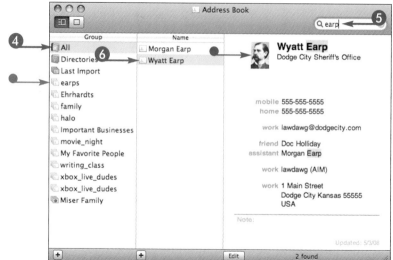

**7** Drag the card from the Name pane and drop it onto the group to which you want to add it.

**Note:** *When you drag a card over a group, a green circle containing a plus sign appears below the card's icon (*◯*). When the group into which you want to place the card is highlighted, release the trackpad.*

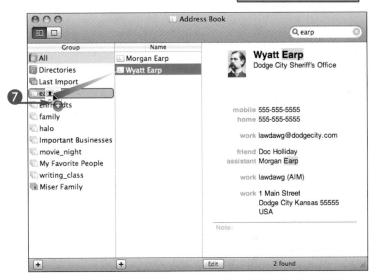

**8** Select the group to which you added cards.

● The cards included in the group are shown in the Name pane.

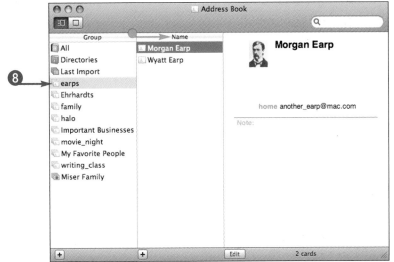

**Can I add more than one card to a group at the same time?**

Yes. To add multiple cards to a group at the same time, press and hold ⌘ while you click each card that you want to add to the group. Then you can drag all of the cards you have selected onto the group at the same time.

**How do I create a Smart Group?**

Open the **File** menu and choose **New Smart Group**. Type the name of the group. Use the pop-up menus and other controls to configure the first criterion, such as "Name includes Smith." Click the **Add** button (⊞) to create more criteria until you have defined all the criteria you want to use. Choose **all** if you require that all the criteria be met, or **any** if you want only one criterion to be required. Click **OK**. The Smart Group is created and all the cards that meet the criteria you defined are added to it automatically.

# Use Address
# Cards and Groups

After you have added all that great contact information, Address Book helps you use your contacts in many ways. Check out the following tricks that Address Book can do for you.

## Address E-mail

1. Find the card for the person you want to e-mail.

2. Click the label for the e-mail address, such as **work** if you want to send an e-mail to the work e-mail address.

   The contextual menu appears.

3. Choose **Send Email**.

   Your default e-mail application opens, and a new message to the address you selected in Step **2** is created.

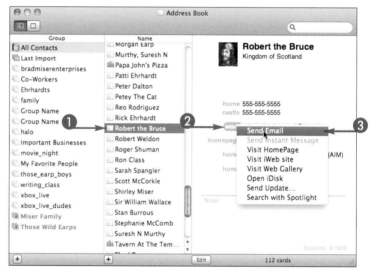

## Visit Web Sites

1. Find a card with a home page or other Web page URL on it.

2. Click the label next to the URL you want to visit.

**Note:** If the URL is in blue, you can click it to go to the related Web site.

3. Choose **Open URL**.

   Your default Web application takes you to the URL you clicked.

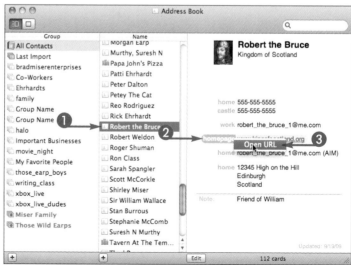

260

## Map a Physical Address

1 Find the card containing the address you want to map.

2 Click the label of the address you want to see on a map.

The contextual menu appears.

3 Choose **Map this Address**.

Your default Web application takes you to a Google map showing the address you clicked.

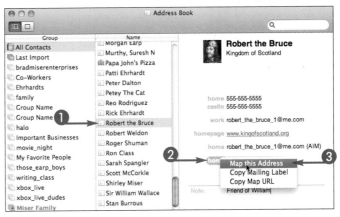

## Print an Envelope or Mailing Label

1 Find the card containing the address for which you want a mailing label.

2 Click the label of the address you want to place on an envelope or label.

The contextual menu appears.

3 Choose **Copy Mailing Label**.

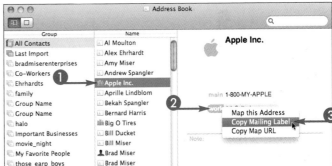

4 Open the application you use to print envelopes or labels.

This example uses a widget called EasyEnvelopes from Ambrosia Software.

5 If the address is not inserted automatically, open the **Edit** menu and then select **Paste**, or press ⌘ + V to insert the address.

Once the address is in the application, use the application's printing feature to print the envelope or label.

TIPS

### How do I know what actions are available for a card or a group?

Each type of information on an address card has a different set of actions available for it. To see what actions are available for specific information on a card, simply click that information's label. To see what actions are available for a card or group, perform a secondary click on the card or group. On the resulting pop-up menus, you see all of the actions available.

### Can I share my Address Book with other people?

You can easily share your Address Book with people who also have a MobileMe account. Open the **Address Book** menu and choose **Preferences**. Click the **Accounts** tab, and then click the **Sharing** sub-tab. Check the **Share your Address Book** check box. Click ➕ and select the other MobileMe users with whom you want to share your Address Book. Click **OK**. If you want those people to be able to change your Address Book, check the **Allow Editing** check box.

# Change or Delete Address Cards or Groups

Over time, you want to be able to update your Address Book by adding new information, changing existing information, or removing information you no longer need. Fortunately, with Address Book, all these tasks are simple.

**You can change information for cards or groups that you want to continue to use. When you decide you do not want a card or group anymore, you can delete it.**

## Change or Delete Address Cards or Groups

### Change Address Cards

**1** Search or browse for the card you want to change.

**2** Click the **Edit** button.

Existing fields become editable and the Delete (◉) and Add (◉) buttons appear.

**3** Click the information you want to change.

**4** Make changes to that information.

*Note: You move between fields on a card by pressing* **Return** *or* **Tab**.

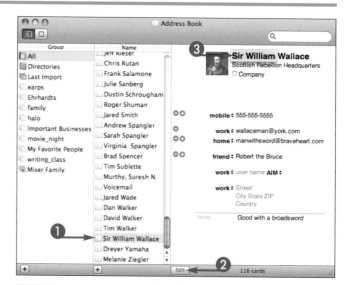

**5** To delete information from the card, click ◉.

The field clears; after you exit Edit mode, that field no longer appears on the card.

**6** To add information to the card, click ◉ next to the type of information you want to add.

**7** Choose a label for the new field on the pop-up menu.

**8** Type information into the new field.

**9** After you have made all the changes to the card, click **Edit**.

The changes you made to the card are saved.

*Note: When the Edit button is blue, you are in Edit mode. When it is black, you are in View mode.*

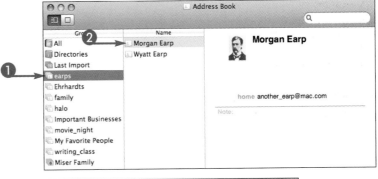

**Sir William Wallace**
Scottish Rebellion Headquarters
☐ Company

mobile ♦ 555-555-5555

work ♦ wallaceman@york.com
home ♦ manwithsword@braveheart.com

friend ♦ Robert the Bruce

work ♦ notalongshanksfan@mac.com
AIM ♦

work ♦ Street
City State ZIP
Country

Note:     Good with a broadsword

Edit     116 cards

## Delete Cards from Address Groups

**1** Select the group you want to change.

**2** Select a card you want to remove from the group.

**3** Press Delete.

A warning sheet appears.

**4** Click **Remove from Group**.

If you started with a manually created group, the card is removed from the group, but remains in Address Book. If you started with a Smart Group, the card is deleted from Address Book, so be careful not to delete a card from a Smart Group that you want to keep.

Do you want to delete "Morgan Earp" or remove the card from the group "earps"?

Cancel     Delete     Remove from Group

**TIPS**

### How do I delete a card I do not need anymore?
Select the card you want to remove and press Delete. Click **Delete** in the confirmation sheet. The card is removed from Address Book.

### How do I delete a group I do not need?
Select the group you want to delete and press Delete. Click **Delete** in the confirmation sheet. The group is removed from Address Book; however, the cards in that group remain in Address Book.

# Print Envelopes and Contact Lists

Address Book enables you print your contact information a number of ways, including mailing labels, envelopes, contact lists, and a Pocket Address Book.

**Printing envelopes takes the tedium out of addressing envelopes and also makes envelopes look better. Contact lists are a good way to carry contact information with you when you do not have your MacBook handy.**

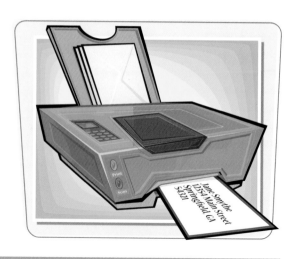

## Print Envelopes

1. Select the cards for which you want to print envelopes.

2. Press ⌘+P.

3. Choose **Envelopes** on the **Style** pop-up menu.

4. On the **Print my address** pop-up menu, choose which of your addresses (those on your card) that you want to be printed as the return address on the envelope.

5. On the **Addresses** pop-up menu, choose the addresses for the contacts to which you want to address the envelopes.

**Note:** To print an envelope for each address for the contacts, choose **All**.

6. Use the **Print in** pop-up menu to determine the order in which the envelopes print.

7. Check the check boxes for additional information you want to include on the envelope, such as Company or Country.

8. Use the Color button to set the color for the envelopes.

9. Click **Print**.

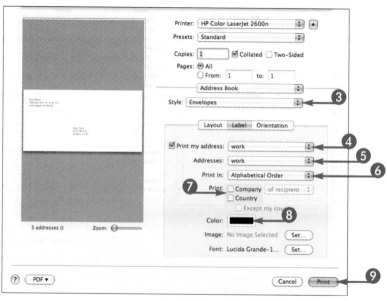

## Print Contact Lists

1 Select the cards you want to include on the list; to include everyone in a group on the list, click the group.

2 Press ⌘ + P.

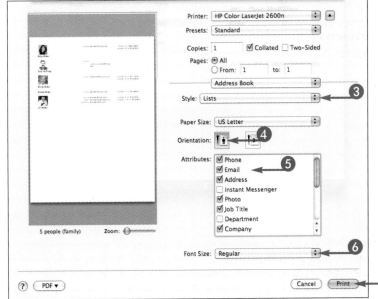

3 Choose **Lists** on the **Style** pop-up menu.

4 Use the Orientation buttons to set the orientation of the list (portrait or landscape).

5 Check the check box for each kind of information you want to include for the contacts on the printed list.

6 Use the **Font Size** pop-up menu to set the size of font used on the list.

7 Click **Print**.

### What is a Pocket Address Book?

A Pocket Address Book is a smaller version of a contact list that is designed to be carried more easily than a list. A Pocket Address Book can be printed in a couple of formats, including Index, which shows contacts by alphabetical order, or Compact, which uses a compressed format.

### How can I print addresses on standard mailing labels, such as those produced by Avery?

On the **Style** pop-up menu, choose **Mailing Labels**. Click the **Layout** sub-tab. On the **Page** pop-up menu, choose the brand of labels you use and then choose the specific type on the related pop-up menu. This creates a format for the addresses that will fit onto the selected label when you print.

iCal is Mac OS X's calendar application. As you can probably guess, you can use it to track calendar events and record To Do items; however, iCal goes beyond these basics.

**One of the best things about iCal is that you can publish your calendars on the Web so that other people can view them, either within their own iCal windows or via a Web browser. By subscribing to other people's calendars, you can see what they are up to, which makes coordinating events among a group of people much easier.**

**Back and Forward buttons**

Click these buttons to move back or forward in the calendar.

**View selection buttons**

Use these buttons to determine whether you view the calendar by day, week, or month.

**Search tool**

Enables you to search events and To Do items.

**To Do items**

Tasks that you need to do or have done.

**Personal calendars**

The calendars you create and manage.

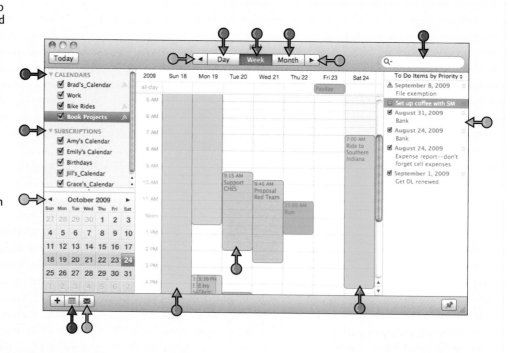

**Subscribed calendars**

Calendars other people or organizations have created to which you have subscribed.

**Mini-Month pane**

A miniature view of the month; the date in focus is shown in a light blue.

**Events**

Colored bars represent events; the color matches the calendar's color on which those events are stored.

**Show/Hide Mini-Month**

Click ▦ to open or close the Mini-Month pane.

**Show/Hide Notifications**

Click ✉ to open or close the Notifications pane.

# Add a Calendar

In iCal, you store events and To Do items on a calendar. You can have as many calendars as you want. For example, you might want one calendar for work information and another for family events.

**Events on a calendar whose check box is checked appear in the iCal window. When you uncheck a calendar's check box, its events are hidden. Each calendar can have its own color so that you can easily see which events and To Do items are associated with it.**

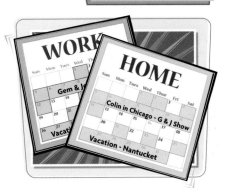

## Add a Calendar

**1** Launch iCal by clicking its icon on the Dock.

The iCal window opens and, if you have not used iCal before, you see two default calendars, labeled Home and Work, on the Calendars list.

**2** Click the **Add** button (➕).

A new calendar appears on the list, and its name is highlighted so that you know it is ready to edit.

**3** Type the name of the calendar and press **Return** to save it.

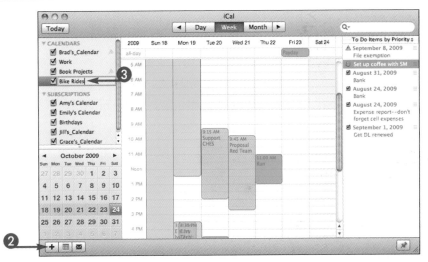

**4** Perform a secondary click on the new calendar.

**5** Choose **Get Info**.

The calendar's Info sheet appears.

**6** Type a description of the calendar in the Description field.

**7** If you want alarms on the calendar to be ignored, check the **Ignore alarms** check box.

**8** Choose the color you want to associate with the calendar on the Color pop-up menu.

**9** Click **OK**.

The sheet closes and the new calendar is ready to use.

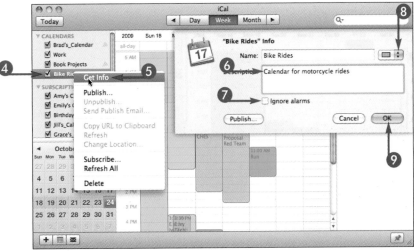

# Add an Event to a Calendar

An event in iCal is some period of time for which you want to plan, such as a meeting, recurring activity, vacation, or other period of time important to you. Events are associated with a specific period of time and a specific calendar within iCal. They can also have lots of other information, including file attachments and Web addresses.

**You can create events on a calendar and then configure them in many ways, such as the time, date, and alarms. If you want other people to attend an event, you can easily invite them to it.**

## Add an Event to a Calendar

① Select the calendar to which you want to add an event.

② Use the Mini-Month tool to move the calendar view so the dates on which the event starts and ends are shown.

**Note:** Click the arrows at the top of the Mini-Month to move the month ahead or behind; then click the specific date you want to see, which becomes shaded in blue.

③ When viewing by week or day, drag over the time period for the event; drag across multiple days if the event extends beyond one day.

④ Release the trackpad.

● The new event is created and its name is highlighted.

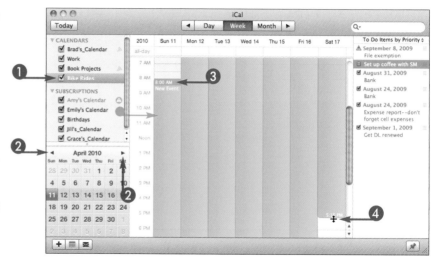

⑤ Type the name of the event.

⑥ Press **Return** to save it.

⑦ Double-click the event.

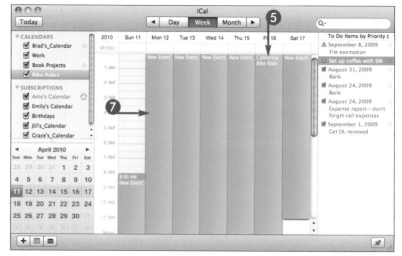

The event's Info window appears. Here you can edit and add to the event's information.

**8** Edit the name, if needed.

**9** Enter a location for the event.

**10** If needed, change the event's dates and times using the date and time tools.

**11** If the event repeats, choose the frequency of the event on the **repeat** pop-up menu, and set the last date on which the event should be scheduled on the **end** pop-up menu.

**12** Use the **show as** pop-up menu to elect how your availability appears to others if they try to schedule you for an event.

**13** To change the calendar with which the event is associated, choose a different calendar on the **calendar** pop-up menu.

**14** To set alarms for the event, choose the kind of alarm on the **alarm** pop-up menu, and then configure it using the controls that appear (these are based on the kind of alarm you select).

**15** To send an invitation to other people, click **invitees** and enter the e-mail addresses for each invitee separated by commas.

*Note: If possible, iCal replaces the e-mail address with the person's name.*

**16** To store a file on the event, click **Add File** and select the file you want to attach.

**17** To include a URL with the event, type it in the url field.

**18** Type notes for the event in the note field.

**19** Click **Send** if you included attendees, or **Done** if you have not.

The event is saved on the calendar, and, if they were added, invitations are sent to other invitees.

*Note: To delete an event, select it and press* `Delete`.

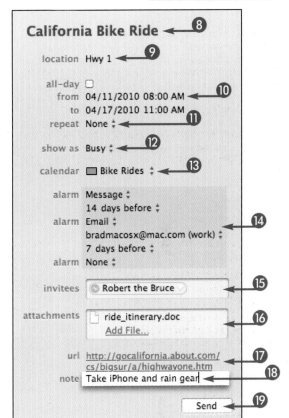

**California Bike Ride** — 8

location Hwy 1 — 9

all-day ☐
from 04/11/2010 08:00 AM — 10
to 04/17/2010 11:00 AM
repeat None — 11
— 12
show as Busy —
calendar ☐ Bike Rides — 13
alarm Message
14 days before
alarm Email — 14
bradmacosx@mac.com (work)
7 days before
alarm None
invitees ⊙ Robert the Bruce — 15
attachments ride_itinerary.doc — 16
Add File...
url http://gocalifornia.about.com/ — 17
cs/bigsur/a/highwayone.htm — 18
note Take iPhone and rain gear —
Send — 19

**TIPS**

**I often forget what the date is. Is there an easy way to see the current date?**

Yes. When running, iCal displays the current month and date in its icon on the Dock.

**When I invite someone to an event, what does that person receive?**

Each invitee receives an e-mail containing information about the event with a calendar item as an attachment. If the invitees also use Mail and iCal or Mail and another compatible calendar application, they can double-click the attachment to add the event to their own calendars in iCal. When you open the event's Info window, you see the status of each invitation, such as a question mark when the invitee has not responded.

You Are Invited

# Add a To Do Item to a Calendar

Whereas events are periods of time for which you want to plan and that you want to manage, To Do items are specific actions that you want to perform. To Do items can contain basic information about a task, such as a description, along with information to associate the action with a date, including the date the action is due.

**Like events, you can add To Do items to iCal, and you can associate them with specific calendars. You can also configure To Do items with alarms, a priority, and related information.**

## Add a To Do Item to a Calendar

### Create a To Do Item

1 Select the calendar with which you want the To Do item to be associated.

2 Perform a secondary click in some empty space on the To Do list.

*Note: If you do not see the To Do list, open the **View** menu, and then select **Show To Do List**.*

3 Choose **New To Do**.

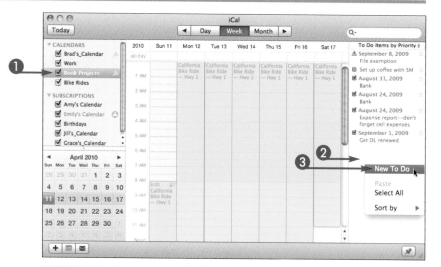

A new untitled To Do item with its title ready to be edited appears on the To Do list.

4 Type the name of the To Do item; in most cases, this is a description of what you need to do.

5 Press Return.

The new name is saved.

6 Double-click the new To Do item.

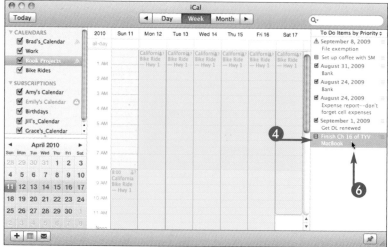

The Info window appears.

**7** Edit the name if needed.

**8** Use the **priority** pop-up menu to assign a priority to the item.

The priority you assign impacts how the item is displayed on the To Do list.

**9** To assign a due date to the item, check the **due date** check box and set the due date.

**10** To set alarms for the item, choose the kind of alarm on the **alarm** pop-up menu and then configure it.

Alarms are reminders to help you remember the task.

**11** To change the calendar with which the item is associated, choose a different calendar on the **calendar** pop-up menu.

**12** To include a URL with the item, type it in the url field.

**13** Type notes for the event in the note field.

**14** Click **Close**.

The item is saved on the To Do list.

### Manage To Do Items

● As events become due, their completion check box changes to an exclamation point.

**1** After you have completed a task, check its check box.

**2** To sort the list of tasks, choose how you want them sorted on the **To Do Items by** pop-up menu at the top of the list.

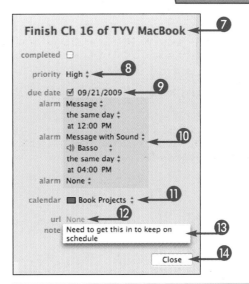

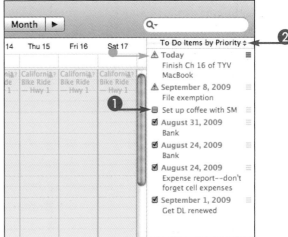

### When I open Mail, I also see To Do items. Are these related to the items in iCal?

Mail and iCal share To Do items. Any To Do items you create in one application show up in the other one. Likewise, if you mark an item as complete in iCal, it also gets marked as complete in Mail. To work with To Do items in Mail, open the **Mailbox** menu, select **Go To**, and then select **To Do**. If you add To Do items in Mail, they appear under a section labeled with your e-mail address.

### How can I set iCal to remove older completed To Do items so that the list is not cluttered with them?

Open the iCal Preferences dialog and click the **Advanced** tab. Check the **Hide To Do items days after they have been completed** check box and enter the number of days that should pass before a completed item is removed from the list. When that number of days passes since an item was marked as completed, it is hidden on the list (but it remains in iCal should you need to refer to it).

# Publish Calendars

iCal's publishing tools make sharing your calendars with other people fast and easy.

**If you have a MobileMe account, you can publish your calendars to the Web. Other people can then view your calendars in a Web browser or subscribe to them so that they can see them in their iCal application. You can also view your published calendars on the Web without iCal, such as from a Windows computer. For more information about subscribing to calendars, see the next section, "Subscribe to Calendars."**

## Publish Calendars

1 Perform a secondary click on the calendar you want to publish.

2 Choose **Publish**.

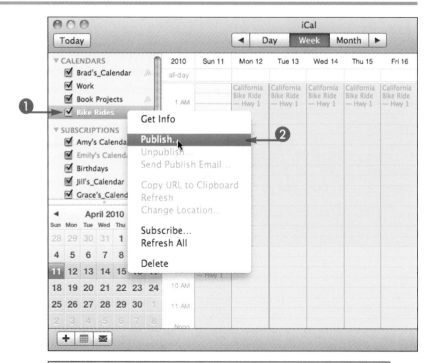

The Publish calendar sheet appears.

3 Type the name of the published version of the calendar in the Publish calendar as field.

4 On the **Publish on** pop-up menu, choose **MobileMe**.

5 If you want changes you make to be published automatically, check the **Publish changes automatically** check box.

6 If you want both titles and notes to be included, check the **Publish titles and notes** check box.

7 If you want to publish the To Do items associated with the calendar, check the **Publish to do items** check box.

8 If you want alarms to be included, check the **Publish alarms** check box.

9 If you want attachments to be available on the published version, check the **Publish attachments** check box.

10 Click **Publish**.

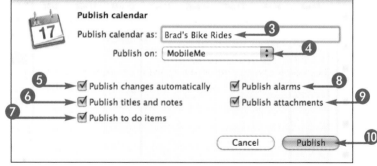

iCal publishes the calendar. When the process is complete, you see the Calendar Published dialog.

⓫ To send the URL and subscription invitation to someone, click **Send Mail**.

An e-mail message with the information about the published calendar is sent so that the recipient can subscribe to the calendar by clicking the link in a message viewed with Mail.

⓬ To see how the calendar appears on the Web, click **Visit Page**.

● Your Web browser opens and you see the Web version of the calendar.

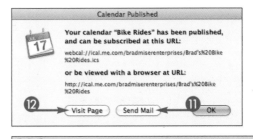

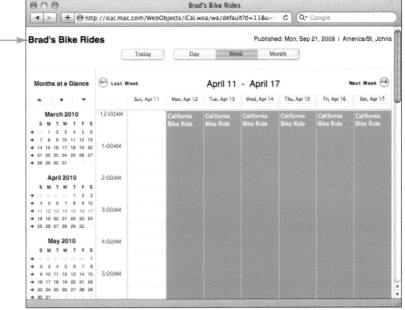

---

**Do I really need a MobileMe account to publish my calendar?**

No. If you do not have a MobileMe account, you can publish your calendars to a WebDAV server. There are several free iCal publishing services available on the Internet; a quick Google search for "publish iCal calendar" will lead you to information about these services. To be able to publish calendars to one of these servers, you need to know the URL for the server and have a user name and password.

**Can people who subscribe to or view my published calendars add or change events or To Do items?**

No. People who subscribe to your calendar in iCal or view it on the Web can only view its events and To Do items.

# Subscribe to Calendars

Other people who use iCal can publish their calendars as easily as you can publish yours. When someone sends his calendar information to you, you can subscribe to the calendar or visit it on the Web.

**When you subscribe to a calendar, it is added as a calendar to iCal, and you can use iCal's tools to view it (you cannot make changes to someone else's calendar). When you visit a calendar on the Web, you view it through a Web browser, such as Safari.**

## Subscribe to a Published Calendar in iCal

1. Open an e-mail containing calendar subscription information.

2. Click the link starting with **webcal://ical.me.com**.

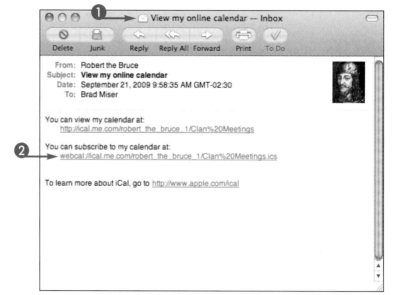

iCal becomes active and the subscribe sheet appears.

3. Review the URL for the calendar to make sure it is one you want to subscribe to.

4. If so, click **Subscribe**.

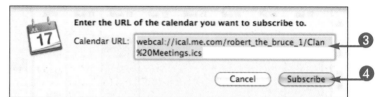

iCal downloads the calendar information, and you see the calendar's Info sheet.

**5** If you want to change the name of the calendar as it appears in your iCal application, edit the name in the Name field.

**6** Use the Color pop-up menu to associate a color with the calendar.

**7** Enter a description of the calendar in the Description field.

**8** If you do not want alarms, attachments, or To Do items removed, uncheck the respective **Remove** check boxes.

**9** On the **Auto-refresh** pop-up menu, choose how often you want the calendar's information updated.

**10** Click **OK**.

● The calendar is added to iCal in the Subscriptions section, and you see its events and other information.

### Visit a Published Calendar on the Web

**1** Open an e-mail containing calendar information.

**2** Click the link starting with **http://ical.me.com**.

Your default Web browser opens the calendar on the Web.

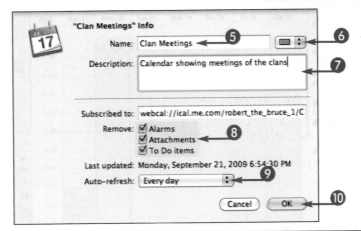

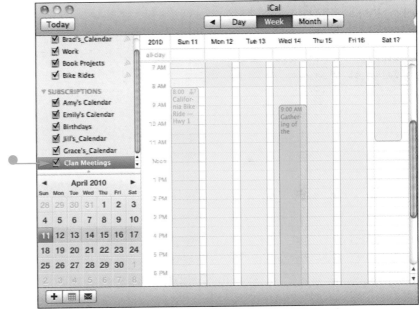

**TIPS**

**Can I add events to a calendar to which I am subscribed?**

No. Calendars published to iCal are read-only, meaning that you can view them, but you cannot change them.

**Do organizations share their calendars?**

Yes. Many organizations, such as professional sports teams, publish calendars to which you can subscribe in iCal. To find them, open the **Calendar** menu and then select **Find Shared Calendars**. You go to the iCal Library Web site, on which you can find and subscribe to many different kinds of calendars.

# Configure iCal Preferences

You can further tailor how iCal works by changing its preferences. For example, on the General tab, you can determine whether weeks are five or seven days long and when days start. You can also configure the start and end time for the "working" part of the day.

**On the Advanced tab, you can determine how To Do items are managed and control alarms for all iCal events and To Do items.**

Configure iCal Preferences

## Configure General iCal Preferences

1. Press ⌘+.

   The iCal Preferences dialog opens.

2. Click the **General** tab.

3. On the **Days per week** pop-up menu, choose **5** if you want weeks to be shown as the five workdays, or **7** if you want to see all seven days.

4. On the **Start week on** pop-up menu, choose the first day of the week.

5. On the **Scroll in week view by** pop-up menu, choose how you want the calendar to scroll in this view, either by **Weeks** or **Days**.

6. Use the **Day starts at** and **Day ends at** pop-up menus to define the times at which "work" days start and end.

   **Note:** *This setting controls the amount of each day that is unshaded on the calendar, indicating when you are "working."*

7. On the **Show** pop-up menu, determine how many hours iCal shows at once.

8. If you want event times to be shown when you are using the Month view, check the **Show event times in month view** check box.

9. If you want the Birthdays calendar in iCal to be shown, check the **Show Birthdays calendar** check box.

10. If you want a default alarm for all events, check the **Add a default alarm to all new events and invitations** check box and enter the default number of minutes before the start time for the alarm to activate in the field.

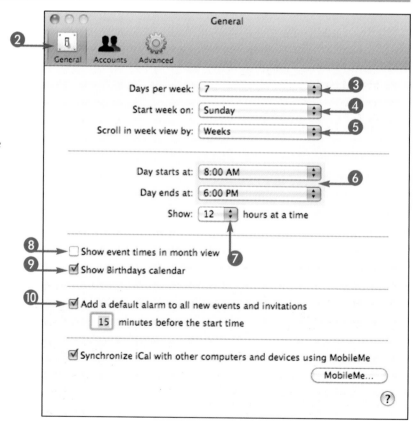

## Configure Advanced iCal Preferences

**1** Press ⌘ + , .

The iCal Preferences dialog opens.

**2** Click the **Advanced** tab.

**3** If you want to be able to manage events in different time zones, check the **Turn on time zone support** check box.

**4** To manage how and when To Do items appear on your calendars, select or deselect this section's check boxes and enter the appropriate number of days in the various fields.

**5** To disable all iCal alarms, check the **Turn off all alarms** check box.

**6** If you want events to open in a separate window when you edit them instead of the "floating" window, check the **Open events in separate windows** check box.

**7** When you change an event, you can choose to be prompted before sending the event to its invitees by checking the **Ask before sending changes to events** check box.

**8** If you want Mail to automatically retrieve event invitations you receive, check the bottom check box.

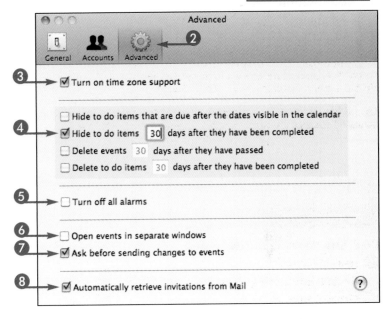

## TIPS

### What is the Birthdays calendar?

One of the attributes you can collect for people in Address Book is **birthday**. If you enable the Birthdays calendar to be displayed, iCal creates events for each birthday captured in Address Book and presents them to you on the Birthdays calendar.

### How does time zone support work?

When you enable time zone support, iCal can help you manage the often confusing situation when you are managing events across multiple time zones. When you create an event, you can associate it with a specific time zone. When viewing your calendars, you can set the current iCal time zone using the Time Zone pop-up menu located in the upper-right corner of the iCal window. When you set this, all events are shifted according to the relationship between their specific time zones and iCal's so that you see all events according to the current time zone. To see an event in a specific time zone (such as when you travel there), choose that time zone on the pop-up menu.

# Print
# Calendars

Although using an electronic calendar is convenient and more powerful than a paper-based calendar, there are times when you might want a paper calendar to carry with you. You can use iCal to print calendars in various formats and with specific options.

**Printed calendars can mimic iCal's Day, Week, or Month view or you can print a calendar list, which is an efficient way to print information for many events.**

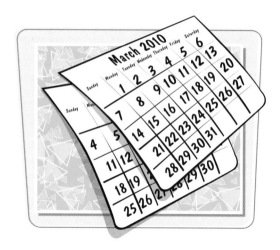

## Print Calendars

### Print Day, Week, or Month View

① Open the **File** menu and choose **Print**.

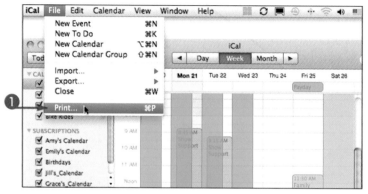

The Print dialog appears.

② On the **View** pop-up menu, choose **Day**, **Week**, or **Month**.

The preview of the calendar shown in the left pane of the dialog changes to reflect your selection.

③ Use the pop-up menus and boxes in the Time range section to determine how much calendar time is represented in the printed version. For example, if you selected the Week format, you can choose the number of weeks that are printed.

*Note: The tools in the Time range selection change depending upon the format of calendar you selected.*

④ Check the check boxes for the calendars you want included on the printed version; uncheck the check boxes for those calendars you do not want to include.

⑤ Use the Options check boxes to configure various options for the printed calendar, such as whether all-day events are shown or if the mini-calendar appears at the top of each page.

⑥ Use the **Text size** pop-up menu to set the relative size of the font used on the printed calendar.

⑦ Click **Continue**.

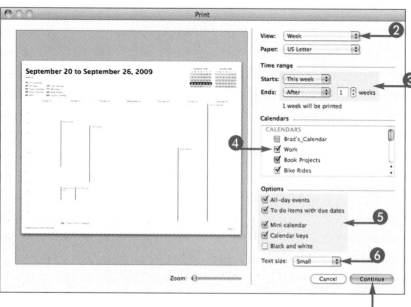

⑧ Use the printer's options to configure the print job; these are specific to the type of printer you are using.

⑨ Click **Print**.

The calendar prints according to your settings.

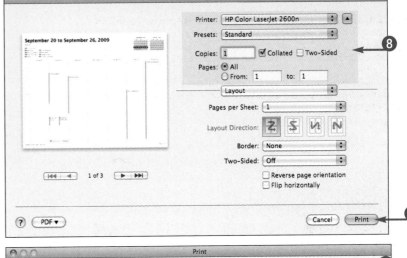

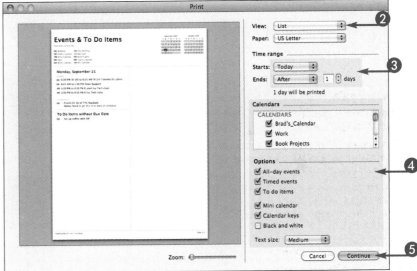

**Print a Calendar List**

① Press ⌘+P.

The Print dialog appears.

② Choose **List** on the **View** pop-up menu.

Calendar events and To Do items are formatted in a list format, which makes them more compact than a calendar view.

③ Use the Time range tools to set the number of days included on the printed list.

④ Use the rest of the controls to set various options for the printed list, such as which calendars are included, whether timed events are included, and so on.

⑤ Click **Continue**.

⑥ Use the Print dialog to configure and print the list.

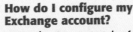

**TIPS**

### Can I access my work's Exchange calendar in iCal?

Yes, under a couple of conditions. One is that your organization must be using Exchange 2007 (Service Pack 1) or later. The second is that your administrator must allow outside access to the Exchange server if you are going to be able to access the Exchange while using your MacBook when you are not inside your organization's firewall.

### How do I configure my Exchange account?

Open the Accounts tab of the iCal Preferences dialog. Click the **Add** button (➕) at the bottom of the dialog. Choose **Exchange 2007** on the **Account type** pop-up menu. Enter your Exchange e-mail address and password, and then click **Create**. Then configure the options on the Account Settings dialog and click **Create** again.

# Keep Apple Software Current

Apple regularly issues updates for its applications to correct problems (hopefully before you experience them). Along with correcting problems, Apple also issues updates to improve its software by adding new features and capabilities.

**Mac OS X includes built-in tools to make it simple to keep your Apple software (Mac OS X plus any Apple applications installed on MacBook) current. Keeping your software up to date is one of the most important things you can do to maintain MacBook and to prevent problems.**

### Update Apple Software Manually

① From the **Apple** menu (🍎), choose **Software Update**.

The Software Update application launches, connects to the Internet, and compares the versions of Apple software installed on MacBook to the current versions.

**Note:** *If the current versions of Apple software are already installed, you see a message stating that no new software was found.*

② Select one of the available updates.

③ Read information about that update to understand what it includes.

④ To install an update, check its check box; to prevent an update from being installed, uncheck its check box.

⑤ Click **Install X Items**, where X is the number of updates you have selected to install.

⑥ Type your administrator user name (if required).

⑦ Type your password.

⑧ Click **OK**.

MacBook downloads and installs the selected updates.

**Note:** *Some updates require you to restart MacBook; click Restart at the prompt and skip the rest of these steps.*

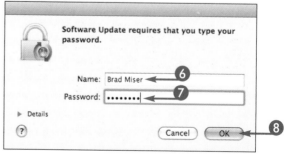

When the process is complete, the Software Update window reappears.

● You see a green check mark () next to each update that was installed successfully.

● Updates you did not install remain on the list; you can install them by checking the **Install** check box and clicking the **Install** button.

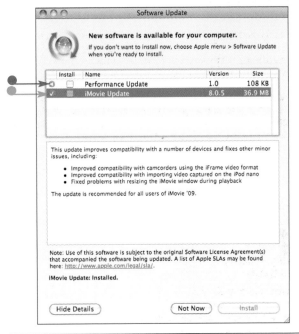

**Update Apple Software Automatically**

① Open the System Preferences application.

② Click the **Software Update** icon.

③ Click the **Scheduled Check** tab.

④ Check the **Check for updates** check box.

⑤ On the **Check for updates** pop-up menu, choose how frequently you want MacBook to check for new software.

For example, choose **Weekly** to check for updates on a weekly basis.

⑥ If you want important updates to be downloaded automatically, check the **Download updates automatically** check box.

**Note:** *If you do not check this check box, you are prompted to download the updates when they are available.*

When the specified amount of time passes, Software Update checks for new software. When it is found, you are prompted to install it.

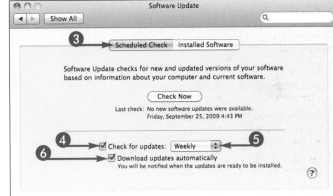

**TIPS**

**Should I install all updates to my software?**

In general, you should install all updates as they become available. In rare situations, an update actually causes more problems than it solves; however, that is unusual, and in such cases the problematic update is immediately followed by one that corrects these problems. You can simplify the update process by configuring MacBook for automatic updates.

**How do I know what updates have been installed?**

Open the Software Update pane of the System Preferences application. Click the **Installed Software** tab. A list of all the updates you have successfully installed appears.

# Maintain and Update Third-Party Applications

The odds are great that you also have third-party software, such as Microsoft Office or Intuit's Quicken. Like Apple, other software companies also issue updates to their software to fix bugs and add features.

**Unfortunately, support for these updates is not built into Mac OS X. Instead, each application provides its own tools to download and install updates. Most of these also support manual and automatic updates. This section shows how to update Microsoft Office applications manually and Snapz Pro X from Ambrosia Software automatically; other third-party applications are updated similarly.**

## Maintain and Update Third-Party Applications

### Manually Update a Third-Party Application

**1** After launching the application, choose **Check for Updates** from the **Help** menu.

The application checks for updates either using built-in tools or through a separate update application.

**2** Download and install the updates using the update application.

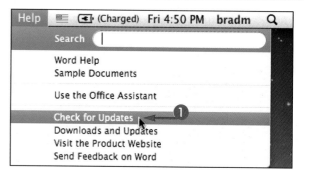

### Maintain and Update Third-Party Applications Automatically

**1** After launching the application, open the application's Preferences tools.

**2** Select the option to check for updates automatically.

**Note:** *This command may use different wording for different applications.*

Each time you launch the application, it checks for newer versions. When one is found, you are prompted to download and install it.

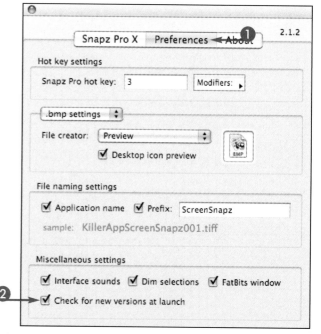

# Profile MacBook

MacBook includes a lot of hardware components and many different kinds of software. Each of these has a specific version and set of capabilities. Most of the time, you do not need to worry about these details. However, there are times when these details can be very important, especially when you are trying to troubleshoot and solve problems.

**Keeping a current profile of MacBook is a good idea so that you have detailed information about it when you need to solve a problem or evaluate your MacBook capabilities (such as if it meets the system requirements for hardware or software you are thinking about adding).**

## Profile MacBook

1. From the **Apple** menu (), choose **About This Mac**.

● The **About This Mac** window appears.

Here, you see information about the version of Mac OS X you are running, the processor in MacBook, and the amount of RAM installed.

*Note: Click the version information to switch to other details, such as the build number.*

2. Click **More Info**.

The System Profiler application appears.

● In the left pane, you see various categories of information about MacBook, such as hardware components.

3. Select an area about which you want detailed information.

● The details appear in the right pane of the window.

4. Continue to select items to get details about them.

● Details for the selected item appear in the lower part of the right pane in the window.

You may want to print the profile and store a hard copy for reference.

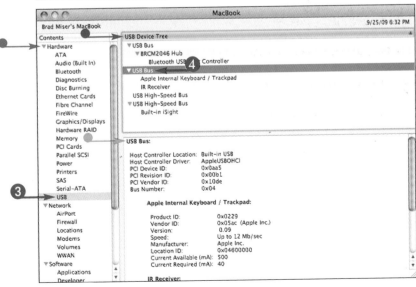

# Monitor MacBook Activity

You cannot always tell what is happening with MacBook just by looking at its screen or observing how applications are performing. It is useful to be able to identify what is happening with MacBook in detail, especially when you are troubleshooting a problem.

With the Activity Monitor application, you can see the status of MacBook in a very detailed way. For example, you can see how much processing power specific applications are using, which can often tell you when an application is having a problem.

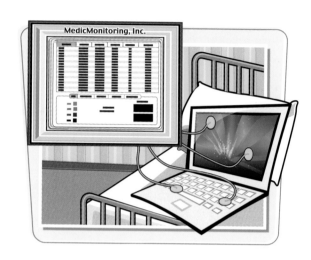

## Monitor MacBook Activity

① Open the Utilities folder within the Applications folder (press ⌘ + Shift + U to jump to that folder).

② Double-click the **Activity Monitor** icon.

The Activity Monitor application opens.

③ Click the **CPU** tab.

● In the upper part of the window, you see a list of all the processes running under your user account.

● At the bottom of the window, you see a graphical representation of the activity of various MacBook processes.

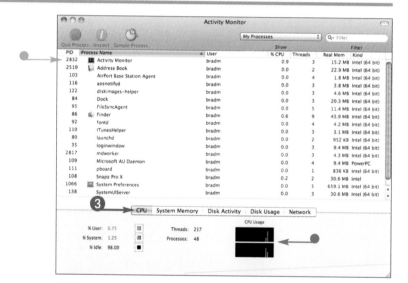

④ Click the **Disk Activity** tab.

● At the bottom of the window, you see how data is being read from and written to the disk.

⑤ Click the % CPU column heading to sort the list of processes by amount of processor activity being used for each process.

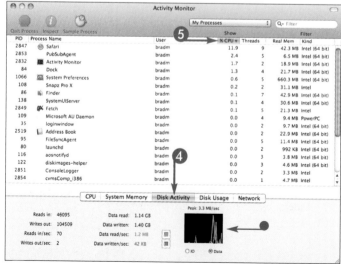

*Note: You can limit the processes shown in the window to be just for applications, which can make the window's information easier to interpret.*

6 On the pop-up menu at the top of the window, choose **Windowed Processes**.

● The list is reduced so that it includes only processes associated with applications.

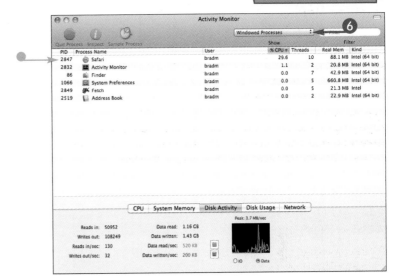

7 Click the **Disk Usage** tab.

8 Select the disk you want information about on the pop-up menu.

● The information at the bottom of the window shows how much of the disk is being used.

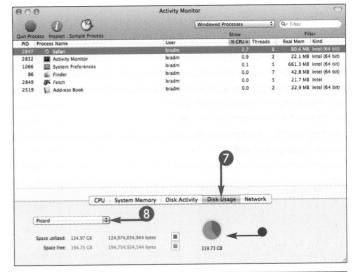

## TIPS

### What do I do if a process is using a lot of the CPU for a long period of time?

This often indicates that an application is *hung*, meaning that its processes are locked up because it is having a problem. Switch to the application and try to quit it. If it does not quit, then it is hung. Go back to Activity Monitor, select the process, and click the **Quit Process** button. Click **Force Quit**; the process is stopped. Forcing an application to quit loses any unsaved data in it, so make sure the application is really hung before doing this (wait several minutes to be sure that it is not busy working on a task). Save your work in other open applications, and then restart MacBook.

### How can I get even more detail about a specific process?

Select a process and click the **Inspect** button. The Inspect window opens and you see several tabs providing information about various aspects of the process such as its memory use, statistics about how it is working, and the files and ports it has open. Sometimes this information is useful when doing detailed troubleshooting. For example, you see the number of recent hangs the process has experienced, which can tell you if the process or application is problematic.

# Maintain the MacBook Hard Drive

If the MacBook drive is not performing optimally, MacBook is not at its best either.

You can do a lot for the MacBook drive by practicing good housekeeping on it to keep as much free space available as possible (see the first tip at the end of this section). If you have an external hard drive, create a second startup disk to use in case something happens to your primary startup disk. You can also use the Mac OS X Disk Utility application to maintain the MacBook drive and to solve some problems if they occur.

## Maintain the MacBook Hard Drive

### Create an Alternate Startup Disk

1 Connect and configure an external hard drive.

*Note: See Chapter 9 for more information.*

2 Insert the Mac OS X installation disc.

● The Mac OS X Install DVD window opens.

3 Double-click the **Install Mac OS X** icon.

The Mac OS X installer application starts.

4 Follow the on-screen instructions to install Mac OS X on the external hard disk.

The installer completes the installation and MacBook restarts using the new startup disk.

5 Complete the configuration of Mac OS X by following the on-screen instructions.

For example, you create a user account on the alternate startup disk just as you did on the MacBook startup disk.

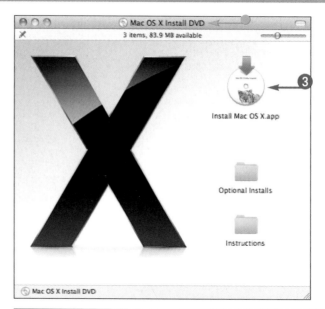

### Choose a Startup Disk

1 Open the System Preferences application.

2 Click the **Startup Disk** icon.

The Startup Disk pane appears. At the top of the pane, you see the available startup disks.

3 Select the startup disk that you want to use.

4 Click **Restart**.

5 Click **Restart** at the prompt.

MacBook starts up from the disk you selected.

*Note: When you start up using the alternate startup disk, perform a Software Update to ensure your alternate startup disk has the most current system software. You should periodically start up from the alternate disk to update its software and to ensure that it is reliable.*

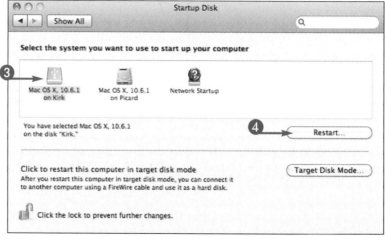

## Maintain or Repair a MacBook Drive Using Disk Utility

**1** Start up from your alternate startup disk.

*Note: You can also choose a startup disk by restarting MacBook and pressing and holding* `Option`*. When the startup disk icons appear, select the disc you want to use and press* `Return`*.*

**2** Open the Disk Utility application located in the Utilities folder within the Applications folder.

**3** Select the disk you want to maintain or repair, such as the MacBook internal disk.

*Note: You cannot repair the current startup disk with Disk Utility, you can only verify it. To repair it, you must start up using a different startup disk and then run Disk Utility to repair the current startup disk.*

**4** Click the **Repair Disk** button.

*Note: If you selected a disk that is the current startup disk, click **Verify Disk** instead of **Repair Disk** because you cannot repair the current startup disk. You will not fix problems, but you will find out if there are any to fix.*

● Disk Utility checks the hard drive for problems and repairs any it finds. The progress appears at the bottom of the window. If it finds and repairs any problems, your disk is back to good operating condition. If it finds, but is unable to repair, problems, you need to use a more-sophisticated disk maintenance application or, in the most extreme case, reinstall Mac OS X or have your MacBook professionally repaired.

*Note: You can also restart using the Mac OS X DVD as the startup disk. When the installation process starts, choose **Disk Utility** from the **Utilities** menu. You can then run Disk Utility to repair the startup disk. However, this uses the old version installed on the DVD, so you are better off creating an alternate startup disk that you can keep current.*

**5** Click **Repair Disk Permissions**.

Disk Utility corrects problems associated with file and folder permissions on the disk. You can monitor the progress of the process in the bottom part of the window.

**6** When complete, restart from the MacBook internal drive.

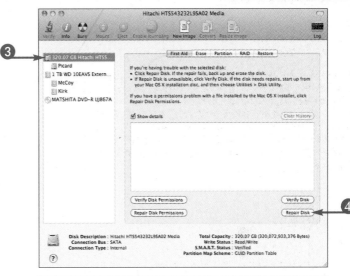

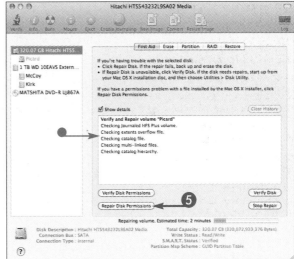

### What are good housekeeping practices for a disk?

When you are done with folders or files, move them off the internal drive. You can do this by deleting them if you are sure you will not need them again, or by archiving them by burning them onto a CD or DVD and then deleting them from the hard drive. You should try to keep your folders and files well organized so that you have a better idea of what you have stored on the disk. You should also make sure that you keep a good backup for all the important files on your internal drive.

### Should I have and use a third-party disk maintenance application?

Disk Utility is a capable disk maintenance application, but it certainly cannot repair all problems that can occur on a disk. If Disk Utility is unable to repair a disk, you can purchase a more-sophisticated disk maintenance application, such as TechTool Pro (micromat.com). These applications usually include a DVD from which you can start up in order to repair your startup disk.

# Back Up with Time Machine and an External Hard Drive

If something really bad happens to MacBook, you can lose all the files it contains. This includes music from the iTunes Store (you have to pay for it again if you want it back) along with other content such as applications you have downloaded. However, what is worse is losing data you create, such as your photos, movies, and documents. Much of this data simply cannot be replaced at any cost.

**The way to minimize the risk of losing important data is to back it up consistently. The Mac OS X Time Machine application is designed to make it easy for you to do this so you can recover important files when you need to. All you need is an external hard drive on which to store your backups.**

Back Up with Time Machine and an External Hard Drive

① With an external hard drive that you will use for backups connected to the MacBook, open the System Preferences application.

*Note: See Chapter 9 for information about connecting MacBook to an external hard disk. You should use a disk with a large storage capacity for this purpose to provide the longest period of protection possible.*

② Click the **Time Machine** icon.

The Time Machine pane opens.

③ Drag the slider to the **On** position.

Time Machine activates.

The Select Drive sheet appears.

*Note: If you have used Time Machine before, click* **Select Disk***.*

④ Select the drive on which you want to store the backed-up information.

⑤ Click **Use for Backup**.

*Note: When you use a hard drive or partition on a hard drive for Time Machine, the hard drive's or partition's icon becomes the Time Machine icon.*

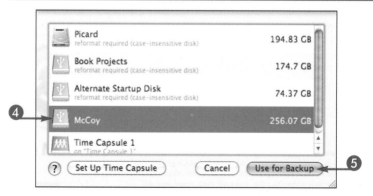

The sheet closes and you return to the
Time Machine pane.

● The drive you selected is shown at the
top of the pane along with status
information about the backup process.

**6** Click **Options**.

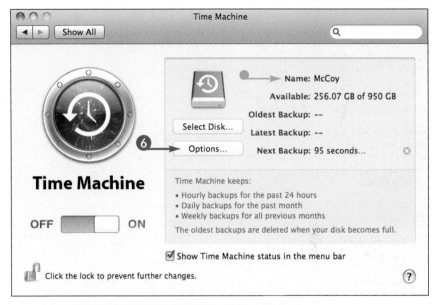

Name: McCoy

Available: 256.07 GB of 950 GB

Oldest Backup: --

Select Disk...

Latest Backup: --

**6** Options...

Next Backup: 95 seconds...

**Time Machine**

Time Machine keeps:

• Hourly backups for the past 24 hours
• Daily backups for the past month
• Weekly backups for all previous months
The oldest backups are deleted when your disk becomes full.

OFF | ON

☑ Show Time Machine status in the menu bar

Click the lock to prevent further changes.

The Do not back up sheet appears,
where you can exclude files from the
backup process. This is useful because
you can exclude files that do not need
to be backed up to make your backups
smaller.

**7** Click the **Add** button (⊞).

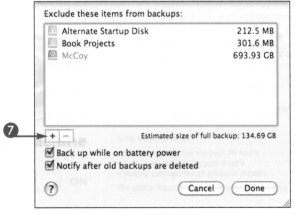

Exclude these items from backups:

Alternate Startup Disk    212.5 MB
Book Projects    301.6 MB
McCoy    693.93 GB

**7**

+ − Estimated size of full backup: 134.69 GB

☑ Back up while on battery power
☑ Notify after old backups are deleted

(?) Cancel Done

**TIPS**

**Why would I exclude files from my backups?**
Backing up files requires disk space, just as storing them does. The more and larger files you back up, the more room each backup consumes on your backup disk, resulting in fewer backups being stored. This lessens the amount of time you can move "back in time" to restore files from the backup. By excluding files, you make your backups smaller, which means you can go further back in time to restore files. You have to trade off the total amount of data you back up versus the number of backups you want to maintain.

**What kind of files should I exclude from backups?**
Files that you have stored on a disc are ideal candidates for exclusion, as are files you did not create or will not need in the future. For example, you should have Mac OS X on a DVD, and so you can exclude the Mac OS X system files from the backups. Should something happen to the Mac OS, you can reinstall it from the DVD (you have to reconfigure and update it, too). Likewise, if you have applications on a disc, you do not need to back up the Applications folder, which can save a lot of space on the backup disk.

continued

289

Many Mac users do not create a backup system, even though it is very easy to do with Time Machine, and after a few minutes of setup time, backing up is automatic. If you do not back up your files, you will eventually lose data. It is not a question of "If," but "When."

**At some point, you will lose files that you either have to pay to get again (iTunes Store content) or cannot re-create at all (your iPhoto collection). With a backup system in place, recovering these files is a simple exercise. Without one, it might be impossible.**

**Back Up with Time Machine and an External Hard Drive** *(continued)*

The select sheet appears.

⑧ Navigate to and select the folders or files you want to exclude from the backup.

⑨ Click **Exclude**.

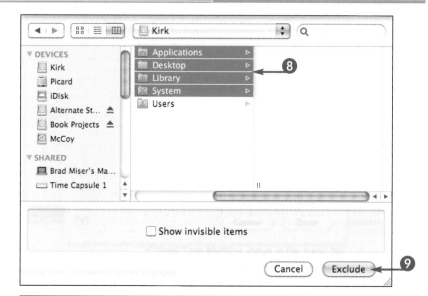

⑩ If you selected system files, click **Exclude System Folder Only** to exclude only files in the System folder, or click **Exclude All System Files** to exclude system files no matter where they are stored.

**Note:** *Exclude All System Files is usually the better option.*

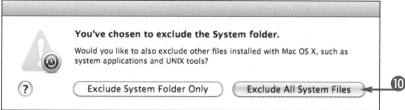

● You return to the Exclude sheet and see the files you have excluded from the backup.

⑪ Click **Done**.

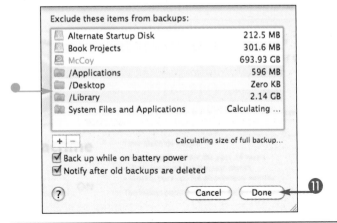

Exclude these items from backups:

| | |
|---|---|
| 🗄 Alternate Startup Disk | 212.5 MB |
| 🗄 Book Projects | 301.6 MB |
| 💾 McCoy | 693.93 GB |
| 📁 /Applications | 596 MB |
| 📁 /Desktop | Zero KB |
| 📁 /Library | 2.14 GB |
| 🗄 System Files and Applications | Calculating ... |

`+` `−`     Calculating size of full backup...

☑ Back up while on battery power
☑ Notify after old backups are deleted

(?)     ( Cancel )  ( Done )  ⑪

You return to the Time Machine pane, and Time Machine starts a countdown to the backup process. When the timer reaches zero, the backup process starts.

● You see status information about your backups in the pane, such as the time and date of the most current backup.

Time Machine automatically backs up your data every hour.

*Note: After you disconnect the external hard drive so you can move MacBook around, the next time you reconnect the external hard drive, the next backup is made. You should connect the backup drive frequently to ensure your backups are current.*

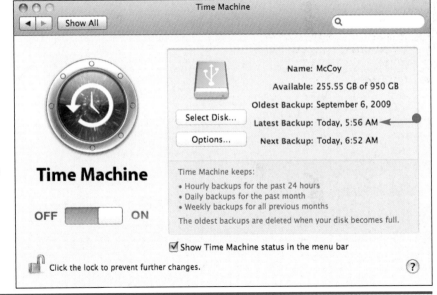

Time Machine

◄ ► | Show All |                 Q

Name: McCoy
Available: 255.55 GB of 950 GB
Oldest Backup: September 6, 2009

( Select Disk... )   Latest Backup: Today, 5:56 AM ◄

( Options... )   Next Backup: Today, 6:52 AM

**Time Machine**

Time Machine keeps:
• Hourly backups for the past 24 hours
• Daily backups for the past month
• Weekly backups for all previous months
The oldest backups are deleted when your disk becomes full.

OFF [ ] ON

☑ Show Time Machine status in the menu bar

🔓 Click the lock to prevent further changes.     (?)

### How long is my data protected?

Time Machine backs up your data for as long as it can until the backup hard drive is full. It stores hourly backups for the past 24 hours. It stores daily backups for the past month. It stores monthly backups until the backup disk is full. To protect yourself as long as possible, use the largest hard drive you can afford, and exclude files that you do not need to back up (such as System files if you have the Mac OS X installation disc) to save space on the backup drive.

### How else should I protect my data?

Hard disks can fail, and no matter how large your backup drive is, it fills up at some point and you will not be able to back up all the files you might need. You should also back up important files in a second way, such as to DVD. You can do this by burning files to a disc from the Finder (see Chapter 4) and from within some applications (such as iTunes, from which you can back up your iTunes Library onto disc). You can also copy files to your online iDisk to store them remotely.

# Back Up Wirelessly with a Time Capsule

The Apple Time Capsule device combines an AirPort Extreme Base Station with a hard drive. This makes wireless backups simple because the Time Capsule provides the wireless network you use so that any computer on the network can also access the Time Capsule's hard drive to back up data.

**To start backing up wirelessly, install a Time Capsule on your network. Then, configure Time Machine on MacBook to back up to it.**

## Back Up Wirelessly with a Time Capsule

### Install and Configure a Time Capsule

**1** Install a Time Capsule on your network.

*Note: See Chapter 7 for details on Time Capsule.*

*Note: If you already use an AirPort Extreme Base Station as the primary hub for your network, consider replacing it with the Time Capsule and use the Wireless Distribution System (WDS) capability to connect the two base stations.*

**2** Open a Finder window.

**3** If necessary, expand the Shared section.

Time Capsule appears as a shared hard drive.

**4** Select the Time Capsule.

**5** Click **Connect As**.

The Connect dialog appears.

**6** Type the Time Capsule's password.

**7** Check the **Remember this password in my keychain** check box.

**8** Click **Connect**.

● The status changes to Connected and you see a folder on the Time Capsule.

You are ready to back up to the Time Capsule.

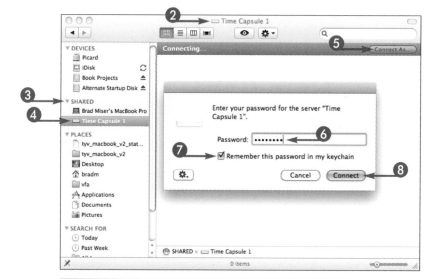

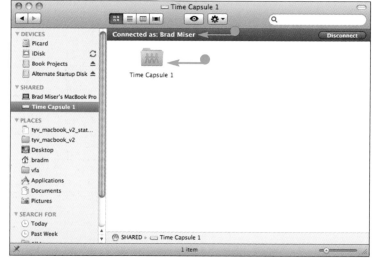

## Back Up to a Time Capsule

*Note: Because backups typically involve a lot of data and even fast wireless networks are relatively slow, the first time you back up requires a long time during which the performance of your network slows. When you configure Time Machine, choose a time during which other network activity is low.*

1 Open the System Preferences application.

2 Click the **Time Machine** icon.

3 Drag the slider to the **On** position.

The Select Drive sheet appears.

4 Select the Time Capsule.

5 Click **Use for Backup**.

6 Type the Time Capsule's password.

7 Click **Connect**.

You return to the Time Machine pane and the Time Capsule is shown as the backup disk.

8 Click **Options**.

The Do not back up sheet appears.

9 Use the Do not back up sheet to exclude files from backups.

*Note: For more details, see Steps 7 to 11 in the section "Back Up with Time Machine and an External Hard Drive."*

10 Click **Done**.

You return to the Time Machine and a countdown to the backup process starts. When the timer reaches zero, the backup process starts.

Time Machine automatically backs up your data every hour.

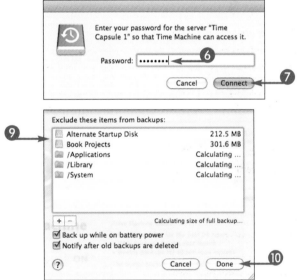

### Can I back up wirelessly to my iDisk?

If you can access the Internet wirelessly, you can always copy files to your iDisk to back them up. This is ideal because the backups are stored on the Apple Web site, which makes them very secure, keeping them isolated from the locations in which you use MacBook. To back up files to your iDisk, simply copy them there. For better results, use a backup application to automate the process. If you are going to back up a lot of data, you probably need to increase the size of your iDisk.

### What other backup applications should I use?

If you have a MobileMe account, you can download and use the Apple Backup application. This application enables you to create more complex backup strategies and also enables you to schedule your backups. You can also use a variety of backup storage locations, including a hard drive, DVD/CD, and your iDisk. To use Backup, open the Software folder on your iDisk and drag the Backup disk image file on to your MacBook, and use it to install the Backup application.

# Restore Files with Time Machine

If you have used Time Machine to keep MacBook backed up, losing data from MacBook is not a big deal. (If you do not have your data backed up, it can be a very, very big deal.) You can use Time Machine to restore files that are included in your backups. You can restore files and folders from the Finder and you can recover individual items from within some applications (such as photos from within iPhoto).

**Even if you have not actually lost files, you should try restoring files regularly to make sure your backup system is working correctly.**

## Restore Files with Time Machine

### Restore Files in the Finder

① Open a Finder window showing the location where the files you want to recover were stored.

② Launch the Time Machine application by clicking its icon (a clock) on the Dock, or by double-clicking its icon in the Applications folder.

The desktop disappears and the Time Machine window fills the entire space.

● The Finder window that you opened in Step 1 appears in the center of the screen. Behind it, you see all the versions of that window that are stored in your backup from the current version as far back in time as the backups go.

● Along the right side of the window, you see the timeline for your backups.

● The Time Machine controls appear at the bottom.

● The time of the frontmost window appears in the center at the bottom.

③ Click the date and time on the timeline when the version of the files you need were available.

The date and time of the backup you select are shown in the center of the Time Machine toolbar.

④ When you reach the files or folders you want to restore, select them.

⑤ Click **Restore**.

The files and folders you selected are returned to their prior locations.

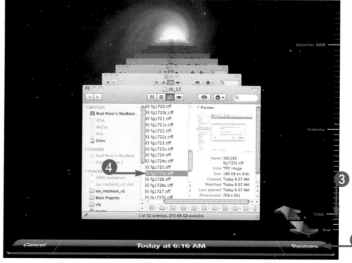

## Restore Files in Applications

**1** Open the application containing the files you want to recover.

**2** Launch the Time Machine application by clicking its icon on the Dock, or by double-clicking its icon in the Applications folder.

The desktop disappears and the Time Machine window fills the entire space.

● Versions of the application window appear in Time Machine, with the most current version being frontmost. Previous versions extend back in time.

**3** Click the date and time on the timeline when the version of the files you need were available.

The date and time of the backup you select are shown in the center of the Time Machine toolbar.

As you go back in time, you see the versions of the application window that are saved in the backup.

**4** When you get to the files you want to restore, select them.

**5** Click **Restore**.

**Note:** *To restore all of the files in the frontmost window, click* ***Restore All***.

The files are returned to the application and you can use them as if they had never been lost.

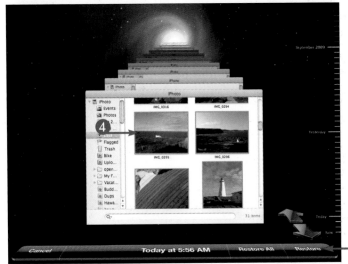

**What other ways can I use to move back in time in Time Machine?**

In addition to using the timeline to move back in time, you can also click the windows behind the frontmost window; each time you click a window, it moves to the front and becomes the active window. You can also click the large backward and forward arrows in the lower-right corner of the Time Machine window to move back or ahead in time, respectively.

**What if an application I use does not support Time Machine? Can I still restore files for it?**

Not all applications support Time Machine; currently only some Apple applications support the ability to back up and restore individual files within an application. Hopefully, more applications will support this technology over time. However, you can always use Time Machine to restore files being managed in an application by including them in the backups you create and then restoring the individual files from the Finder. This is not as easy as using a supported application such as iPhoto or iTunes, but it works well.

# Troubleshoot and Solve MacBook Problems

Once in a while, MacBook is not going to cooperate with you. You might experience applications that hang (they stop doing anything while displaying the spinning color wheel icon) or quit unexpectedly; or, something odd might happen and you cannot quite identify it. In the most extreme case, you might not be able to get MacBook to start up at all.

**The first step in solving any problem is understanding when and how it happens. Part of this is determining if the problem is general or related to a specific user account. Once you have some idea of how and when the problem occurs, you can try to solve it.**

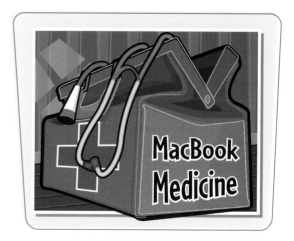

MacBook Medicine

## Troubleshoot and Solve MacBook Problems

### Find the Cause

*Note: Restarting MacBook solves many problems you might experience. Because restarting is easy to do, it should always be one of the first things you try. Except for a minute or two of your time, there is no downside to restarting.*

1. Restart MacBook by choosing **Restart** from the **Apple** menu ().

*Note: If MacBook does not respond to any commands or keys, press and hold the **Power** button until MacBook shuts off. Press the **Power** button again to restart it. This causes all unsaved data to be lost, so let MacBook sit in the "hung" state for a while to make sure you need to restart before you actually do it.*

2. In the prompt, click **Restart**.

   MacBook restarts.

3. Try to replicate the problem by doing the same things you did when it first occurred.

4. If you cannot cause the problem to happen again, assume it was solved by the restart, and you can continue working.

5. If you can cause the problem to happen again, use Activity Monitor to see if any applications or processes appear to be consuming large amounts of resources (such as more than 90 percent of CPU activity). (To learn about Activity Monitor, see "Monitor MacBook Activity," earlier in this chapter.) If they are, you have found a likely source of the problem.

6. Use Activity Monitor to check if the hard drive is too full.

   If the drive is close to being full, it can be a cause of problems. You need to remove files to make more space available on the drive.

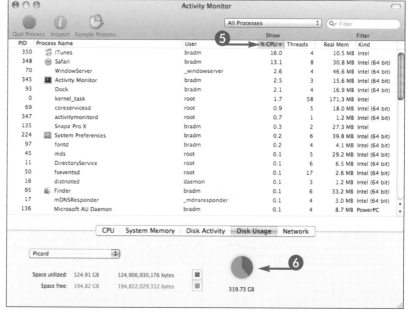

**7** To see if your problem might have to do with newly installed software, generate a MacBook profile. (To learn how, see "Profile MacBook," earlier in this chapter.)

*Note: A MacBook profile includes such information as all the applications you have installed.*

**8** Click the **Applications** category in the Software section.

**9** Sort the window by Last Modified date so the most recent date is at the top of the window.

**10** Look for any applications you installed just before you started having problems.

The detailed information you collected should give you an idea of the cause of the problem.

## Determine If a Problem Is Systemwide or User-Specific

**1** Log into your troubleshooting user account.

*Note: You should create a troubleshooting user account that you use only when you are trying to isolate and solve problems. See Chapter 6 for more details.*

**2** Try to replicate the problem under the new account.

If you can repeat the problem, it is systemic instead of being specific to a user account.

If you cannot repeat the problem, it is likely related to an issue with your user account. In most cases, the issue is related to a preference file that has been corrupted. The next steps explain how to remove preferences files.

### What are the most important things I can do to protect myself from MacBook problems?

Back up your data. You should always have current backups of your data because losing data is the most severe consequence of any MacBook problem you might encounter. Losing data is not just something that might happen to you; it will happen to you at some point. Second to keeping good backups of data is maintaining an alternate startup drive. If something happens to the system software on MacBook, you can restart from the alternate hard drive and get back to work, not to mention having a much better chance of fixing the problem. Third, keep your Mac OS X software installation disc available. If you need to restore your MacBook system software, you need this disc.

When it comes to effective troubleshooting and problem solving, a cool, calm state is your best friend. Unfortunately, problems tend to be very frustrating, especially when you are working under a deadline. Stress and frustration can lead to being unable to take the time and logical approach to problem solving that gets to solutions more quickly. And, an emotional state can lead to rash actions that can make problems worse.

**Sometimes, the most important step in troubleshooting is taking a break. Getting away from a problem for a while can clear your head and make a solution come much more quickly than just continuing to work through it.**

## Troubleshoot and Solve MacBook Problems *(continued)*

③ Navigate to your Home folder.

④ Open the **Library** folder.

⑤ Open the **Preferences** folder.

⑥ Delete the preferences files for the application you are having trouble with.

**Note:** *The application's name is part of the preference's filename.*

⑦ Try to replicate the problem.

If you cannot repeat it, you have likely solved the problem.

### Solve the "Hung Application" Problem

① Identify the hung application.

**Note:** *You can recognize a hung application by the spinning color wheel icon appearing on the screen for a long period of time.*

② Press ⌘ + **Option** + **Esc**.

**Note:** *When you force an application to quit, you lose any unsaved changes in open documents. So, make sure the application is truly hung by letting it sit for a couple of minutes. Sometimes this results in the application working again so you can save your changes and quit the application normally.*

③ In the Force Quit Applications window, select the hung application.

**Note:** *A hung application's name appears in red in the Force Quit window and the text "(Not Responding)" appears next to it. (This is not shown in the figure because there were no hung applications.)*

④ Click **Force Quit**.

**Note:** *If the Finder is hung, when you select it, the button becomes Relaunch, which attempts to restart the Finder.*

⑤ At the prompt, click **Force Quit**.

The application is forced to shut down.

⑥ Restart MacBook.

If the application works normally, the problem is solved. If the application continues to hang, you should update it.

**Note:** *See the sections "Keep Apple Software Current" and "Maintain and Update Third-Party Applications."*

If the update solves the problem, you are done. If not, get help for the problem.

## Solve the "MacBook Will Not Start Up" Problem

① Make sure MacBook is either connected to power or has a full battery.

*Note: If you see a flashing folder icon when you start up MacBook, it cannot find working system software. You have to start up from an alternate disk or from the Mac OS X Installation DVD to repair the Mac OS X software.*

② Connect the alternate startup disk.

*Note: See Steps 1 to 5 in "Create an Alternate Startup Disk" earlier in this chapter.*

③ Press and hold the **Power** button until MacBook shuts off.

④ Press the **Power** button and press and hold `Option`.

After a few moments, the valid startup disks are shown.

⑤ Select the alternate startup disk and press `Return`.

● MacBook starts up from the selected disk.

If MacBook starts up, you know the problem is with the system software installed on the primary startup disk. Reinstall the system software on the primary startup disk.

⑥ Insert the Mac OS X installation disc.

⑦ Launch the Install Mac OS X application.

⑧ Follow the on-screen steps to reinstall or repair the system software on the primary startup disk.

*Note: If you do not have an alternate startup disk, you can start up from the Mac OS X installation disc by inserting it, restarting MacBook, and pressing and holding `C`. MacBook restarts in the Mac OS X Installation application.*

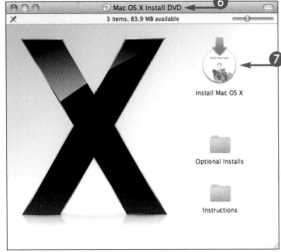

TIPS

**There are a lot more problems possible than just these two specific ones. Why have you listed only these two?**

Many different problems are possible, but you are likely to experience only a few. There is really no way to provide a comprehensive list of problems in a short section like this one. If you can understand how to describe a problem and know where to go for help (see the last section in this chapter), then you will be able to solve most problems you encounter.

**I thought Mac OS X was supposed to be reliable and stable. Why should I have to worry about this?**

Most experts agree that Mac OS X is the most reliable and stable operating system there is, and you are not likely to have very many problems (especially when compared to that "other" operating system). However, a MacBook is a complex system of hardware and software with many permutations depending on the specific applications you install and how you use them. It is inevitable that problems occur once in a while. Fortunately, most are readily solved with the steps in this section.

# Capture a Screenshot

When you experience a problem, capturing a screenshot is a great way to describe and document the problem for yourself. Asking for help is even more useful because you can give the screenshots to the person from whom you are asking help.

**There are two built-in ways to capture a screenshot under Mac OS X. You can use keyboard shortcuts, or for more sophisticated shots, you can use the Grab application.**

## Capture a Screenshot

### Capture a Screenshot with a Keyboard Shortcut

1. Open the window that you want to capture.

2. To capture the entire desktop, press ⌘ + Shift + 3 .

   An image file is created on the desktop.

3. To capture a portion of the screen, press ⌘ + Shift + 4 .

4. If you performed Step 3, drag over the area of the screen you want to capture; release the trackpad when the area you want to capture is highlighted.

   An image file is created on the desktop.

5. Open the image file you created; it is named Screen shot *date* at *time*.png, where *date* and *time* are the date and time when you captured the screen.

   The file opens in Preview.

### Capture a Timed Screenshot with Grab

1. Open the Grab application (within the Utilities folder in the Applications folder).

   When you launch Grab, its menu appears, but it does not have any windows until you take a screenshot.

2. Open the window that you want to capture.

3. Switch back into Grab.

4. On the **Capture** menu, choose **Timed Screen**.

   The Timed Screen Grab dialog appears.

5. Click **Start Timer**.

   You have 10 seconds until the screen is captured; the timer in the dialog counts down.

6. While the countdown is ongoing, get the screen exactly as you want it to be captured.

   When the timer ends, the screenshot is taken and opens in Grab.

7. Save the screenshot.

# Get Help with MacBook Problems

One of the most important troubleshooting skills is to be able to ask for help in the right places and in the right way. Many problems you encounter have been experienced and solved by someone else already.

## Get Help with MacBook Problems

**1** If the problem is related to Apple hardware or software, visit www.apple.com/support.

**2** Search for the issue you are having.

**3** Browse the information on the Search Results page to locate the problem and its solution.

*Note: If you purchased AppleCare, you can use that technical support service. See your documentation for contact information.*

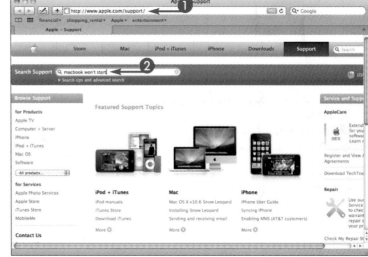

**4** If you do not find what you need, go to www.google.com.

**5** Search for the problem you are experiencing.

**6** Browse the results of the search to find the information you need.

*Note: If you live near an Apple retail store, call or visit Apple's Web site for an appointment at the Genius bar. You can often get excellent technical support for no cost if the problem can be solved in the store.*

# PART

# V

# Having Fun

One of the great things about MacBook is the amazing digital media applications it comes with. Three of the best of these applications are iTunes, iPhoto, and iMovie. iTunes is a very powerful application for digital audio and video, and it is the companion software for iPods and iPhones. iPhoto is an excellent application for storing, organizing, and being creative with your digital photos. iMovie enables you to be your own producer with Hollywood-like effects and editing. These applications make having a MacBook a lot of fun.

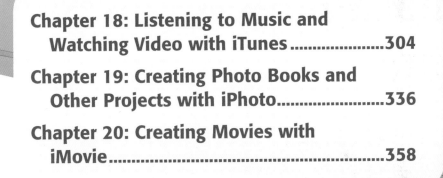

# Explore iTunes

iTunes enables you to organize and enjoy a lot of content on MacBook, an iPod, or an iPhone. With iTunes's integration to the iTunes Store, adding great audio and video to your iTunes Library whenever you want is easy.

**Although incredibly powerful, iTunes is also very well designed so that it is easy to use. In fact, the application is so well designed that a number of its interface elements have been adopted in other applications, including the Mac OS X Finder.**

**Source pane**
Shows all the sources of content available to you.

**Library**
Stores and organizes all the content you manage in iTunes.

**Categories**
The types of content stored in your library.

**Cover Flow view**
Shows content in the selected source as album covers that you can flip through.

**View buttons**
Use these to change views.

**Search tool**
Enables you to search the selected source.

**Artwork/Video viewer**
Shows album art when you select or listen to audio, or video when you play video content.

**Content pane**
Shows detailed information about the content of the selected source.

**Source information**
Shows information about the source you have selected, including how long the content will play and how much disk space it consumes.

## List view

Presents content in the selected source in a list, with the Column Browser shown.

## Column Browser

Enables you to browse the selected source quickly and easily.

## Playback controls

Use these to control audio and video content.

## Information window

Displays information about what you are doing.

## Browse path

Highlighted items show the path to the content you are browsing.

## Grid view

Shows content in the selected source, organized in a grid; in this case, each thumbnail is a season of a TV show.

## Number of episodes

Indicates the number of episodes for each season of each TV show.

## Show/Hide Genius

Click to open or close the Genius bar.

## Start Genius

Starts the iTunes Genius feature.

## Output source

When MacBook can communicate with an Express Base Station or AppleTV, this menu enables you to choose where you want iTunes output to play.

## Show/Hide Artwork/ Video Viewer

Opens or closes the Artwork/ Video Viewer window.

## Create playlist

Enables you to create playlists and smart playlists.

## Repeat

Causes content in the selected source to repeat.

## Shuffle

When active, iTunes randomly chooses content in the selected source to play.

# Understand the iTunes Library

The iTunes Library is where you store all of your audio and video content, including music, podcasts, movies, and TV shows. Before you can enjoy content in iTunes, it has to be available there; you can add content from many sources. Once content is stored in your iTunes Library, you can use iTunes tools to keep that content organized so that it is easily accessible to you, and of course, do all sorts of great things with it.

## Categories

The content in your Library is organized automatically by categories, including Music, Movies, TV Shows, and Podcasts. Within the Library source, you see an icon for each category. When you select a category, the content it includes is shown in the right part of the iTunes window where you browse and search it. When you find the content you want, you can listen to it, view it, create playlists, burn it to disc, and so on.

## Devices

iTunes considers sources of content stored outside of its database to be devices. If you use an iPod or iPhone with iTunes, they appear in the Devices section when connected to MacBook. Devices also include audio CDs and AppleTV. Like other sources, you select a device to work with it. For example, to configure an iPod's content, you select its icon, and its settings tools appear in the right part of the window.

## Tracks

Although it is easy to think of tracks as the songs on a CD, iTunes considers everything that you listen to or watch to be a track. So, each episode in a season of a TV series you download from the iTunes Store is a track, as is each section of an audiobook. Tracks are what you see in each row in the Content pane.

## Tags

A lot of information is associated with the content in the iTunes Library. This includes artist, track name, track number, album, genre, and rating. Each of these data elements is called a tag. Each tag can be shown in a column in the Content pane, and you can view all of the tags for a track in the Info window. Tags are important because they are how you identify and organize content. Fortunately, iTunes automatically tags most of the content you work with, but you can add or change tags yourself when you need to.

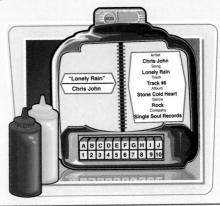

## Playlists

One of the best things about iTunes is that you can create custom collections of content you want to listen to or watch. These collections are called playlists. Playlists can include any combination of content organized in any way. There are two kinds of playlists. You manually place content into a playlist, or when you create a smart playlist, you define criteria for content and iTunes automatically places the appropriate content into it. After you have created a playlist, you can listen to it, burn it to disc, or move it to an iPod or iPhone.

## The iTunes Way

Although iTunes enables you to work with a lot of different kinds of content (such as music, audiobooks, movies, and music videos), it uses a consistent process to work with any kind of content. First, select the source of the content you want to work with; this can be a Library category, device, or playlist. Second, browse or search for content you want within the selected source if it is not ready for you immediately. Third, select the specific track you want to use. Fourth, use iTunes controls to play the content. This process is consistent, no matter what kind of content you want to use, and so once you get used to it, you can quickly enjoy any content you want.

# Browse or Search for iTunes Content

Before you can enjoy audio or video content, you need to find that content so that you can select it. There are two ways to find content: by browsing or by searching.

**Browsing is a good way to find something when you are not quite sure what you want to listen to or watch. Searching is useful when you know exactly what you want, but are not quite sure where it is.**

## Browse or Search for iTunes Content

### Browse for iTunes Content

**Note:** *The iTunes window has several views; this section assumes that you are using the List view.*

1. In the Source pane, select the source of content you want to browse, such as **Music**.

**Note:** *If the Browser does not appear, open the View menu and then choose Show Column Browser. These steps show three columns in the Browser.*

2. Open the **View** menu and choose **Column Browser**.

3. Choose the columns you want to see, such as **Genres**, **Artists**, and **Albums**.

**Note:** *When a column is marked with a check mark, it is shown; when there is no check mark, the column is hidden.*

4. Choose if you want the Browser at the top of the window or on the left side.

5. In the Genres column, select the genre you want to browse.

6. Select the artist whose music you want to browse (only artists with music in the selected genre are shown).

7. Select the album you want to browse; click **All** to see all the artist's albums in the selected genre.

**Note:** *The All option causes a column to display all content for that column.*

● The tracks on that album appear in the Content pane.

8. Select the track you want to hear.

9. Use the playback controls to play the track.

**Note:** *You can double-click a track to play it.*

## Search for iTunes Content

1. In the Source pane, select the source of content you want to search, such as **TV Shows**.

2. Type the text or numbers for which you want to search in the Search tool.

● As you type, only content that meets your search criteria appears in the Content pane and you see what you are searching for at the top of the pane.

3. To make your search more specific, open the **Search** menu.

4. Choose the tag by which you want to limit the search.

5. Select the content you want to listen to or watch.

6. Use the playback controls to play the content.

**How can I make a column wider to see all of its information?**

Point to the line at the right edge of the column. When ▶ changes to ✛, drag to the right to make the column wider or to the left to make it narrower.

**Why does the Column Browser disappear when I select some sources?**

The Column Browser is not all that useful for some sources, such as an Audio CD, because you can usually see all of the content on the source in the Content pane, and most content is from the same genre and, most commonly, artist. When you select such a source, the Column Browser is hidden. You can show it again by choosing **Show Column Browser** on the **View** menu.

# Browse the Library with Cover Flow View

The List view is very functional and efficient, but it is not all that pretty, nor is it that exciting to browse.

**The Cover Flow view makes browsing for music like flipping through a stack of CDs (only easier). You view content by its cover art, and you can flip through the content available to you until you see something that you like.**

## Browse the Library with Cover Flow View

1. Select the source you want to browse, such as **Music**.

2. Click the **Cover Flow View** button (![icon]).

3. To change the size of the Cover Flow pane, drag the **Resize** handle (![icon]) up or down.

4. To move through the content quickly, drag the scroll bar to the left or right.

**Note:** *You can also click album covers to jump to specific collections. If your trackpad is configured for scrolling, you can also scroll across the covers by dragging two fingers to the left or right on the trackpad.*

As you drag, the covers flip quickly.

● The content in the album directly facing you appears on the content list, where you can listen to or watch it.

5. To browse in full-screen mode, click the **Full Screen** button (![icon]).

The Cover Flow pane fills the desktop.

6. Browse the content by using the scroll bar or clicking to the left or right of the artwork facing you.

7. Control the content with the playback controls.

8. To return to the iTunes window, click the **Full Screen** button (![icon]).

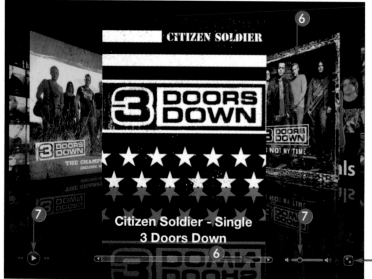

# Browse the Library with Grid View

The Grid view collects the content you are browsing into a grid with thumbnails for the collections you are viewing. What a collection includes depends upon the type of content you are browsing. For example, when you browse the Music source, the thumbnails represent the genres; when you select TV Shows, the thumbnails represent seasons of a show.

**You move into a collection by double-clicking a thumbnail whereupon you see content organized by collections, such as albums.**

## Browse the Library with Grid View

1 Select the source you want to browse, such as **Music**.

2 Click the **Grid View** button (▦).

● In the Content pane, you see the collections for the type of content you selected, such as **Genre** when you select music.

**Note:** If you drag across a genre's thumbnail, you see previews of the albums it contains. You can play all the music in a genre by clicking **Play Selected**.

3 Double-click a genre.

**Note:** If you browse a genre, the album that appears in its thumbnail is at the top of the resulting window.

● The content of the selected genre appears in List view, grouped by album or collection.

4 Browse the genre.

5 Click a column heading to change how the list is sorted.

For example, to sort the groups by album, click the **Album** column, or to sort the groups by artist, click the **Artist** column.

6 Select the content you want to play.

7 Use the playback controls to play it.

# Listen to Audio Content

If you have used any device to listen to audio content, you should be able to quickly listen to audio content in iTunes.

**Of course, whereas most audio players give you just basic controls, iTunes really lets you fine-tune your audio experience by choosing exactly how you want to listen.**

## Listen to Audio Content

1. Browse or search for the audio content you want to hear.

2. Select the first track you want to hear.

3. Click the **Play** button (▶), double-click the track, or press Spacebar.

The audio content begins to play.

● In the Information pane, you see information about what is playing, such as the track name, artist, and a timeline.

● The track currently playing is highlighted and marked with a blue speaker icon (🔊).

The audio continues to play through the tracks in the selected source in the order they are shown in the pane (from top to bottom) until the last track plays or you stop playing (unless you have the repeat function turned on, in which case, the content repeats).

4. Click the **Pause** button (❚❚ changes to ▶) or press Spacebar to pause the audio.

5. Click the **Previous** button (⏮) to jump back to the previous track.

6. Click the **Next** button (⏭) to jump to the next track.

**Note:** You can also jump to the previous or next track by pressing ← or →.

7. Set the volume level by dragging the slider.

# Watch Video Content

iTunes works as well for video content as it does for audio content. You can watch movies, TV shows, music videos, and video podcasts within the iTunes window or in full-screen mode.

**Watching video content works according to the iTunes pattern: Find the content you want to view, select it, and use the iTunes controls to play the content.**

## Watch Video Content

1. Browse or search for the video content you want to watch.

2. Select the first video track you want to see.

3. Click the **Play** button ( ) or press `Spacebar`.

**Note:** By default, iTunes remembers where you were in video content the last time you played it. So, if you stop video playback, when you return to the same content, you pick up right where you left off.

- The video fills the desktop and begins to play.

**Note:** Video content can play full screen (as in this example), within the iTunes window, in a separate window, or within the Artwork/Video Viewer. When it plays by default is determined by the preference settings on the Playback pane of the Preferences dialog.

4. Position the pointer over the video image.

- The video controls appear.

**Note:** To return to the iTunes window, click the **Close** button ( ).

5. Use the controls to play the video.

6. To stop the video and move back into iTunes, click the **Return to iTunes** button ( ).

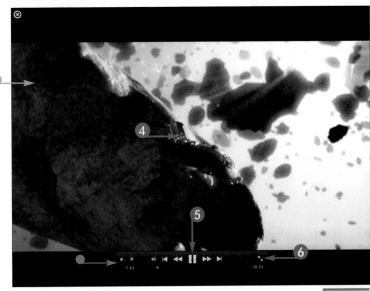

# Add Audio CD Content to the iTunes Library

One of the most useful ways to add content to iTunes is to import music from audio CDs. Once imported, this music becomes part of your iTunes Library and you can listen to it, add it to playlists, and put it on custom CDs you burn.

**First, you need to do a one-time configuration of iTunes to import audio. Then you can import CDs to build up your iTunes Library.**

**Prepare iTunes to Import Audio CDs**

① Open the **iTunes** menu and choose **Preferences**.

② Click the **General** tab.

③ From the **When you insert a CD** pop-up menu, choose **Import CD and Eject**.

④ Check the **Automatically retrieve CD track names from Internet** check box.

⑤ Click **OK**.

*Note: By default, iTunes encodes all audio content using the AAC (Advanced Audio Coding) format. If you want to use a different format, click Import Settings and use the resulting dialog to choose and configure the format you want to use.*

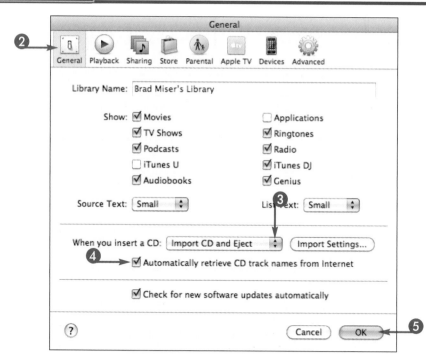

## Import Audio CDs to the iTunes Library

**①** Insert an audio CD.

● iTunes connects to the Internet and identifies the CD you inserted.

The import process starts.

● The song currently being imported is marked with an orange circle (⊘).

● You see information about the import process in the Information pane.

● As songs are imported, they are marked with a green circle and check mark (⊘).

When all the tracks on the disc have been imported, iTunes ejects the disc.

The tracks on the CD are now part of the iTunes Library.

**TIPS**

### How does iTunes recognize an audio CD?

When you insert an audio CD, iTunes connects to the Internet and looks up the CD in an online CD database. When it finds the CD, iTunes adds tags for the album including name, artist, and track titles. It also retrieves album art for any music that is in the iTunes Store. iTunes remembers CDs so that the next time you insert them, the information iTunes looked up is there automatically.

### iTunes supports many different types of formats when importing music. Should I use something other than AAC?

Although iTunes does support a number of audio formats, AAC is the best option for most people because AAC files provide good sound quality in relatively small file sizes. That is a good thing because you can store more content in your iTunes Library and on iPods or iPhones. If you demand the absolute highest audio quality, you can use the Apple Lossless format, which produces significantly larger files with slightly better sound quality.

You have seen how easy adding content you already have on audio CD to the iTunes Library is. Using this process, it is easy to build your iTunes Library from audio CDs that you own. The Apple iTunes Store provides hundreds of thousands of audio CDs, movies, TV shows, audiobooks, podcasts, and other content that you browse, preview, and then purchase. As soon as you buy or rent content from the iTunes Store, it is downloaded to your iTunes Library and is immediately ready for you to use. Because access to the iTunes Store is built into iTunes, shopping for audio and video could not be easier.

**iTunes Store home page**

Links take you directly to specific content as well as to categories.

**Albums**

Album covers and titles are links to those albums.

**Categories**

Click these links to see the home pages for categories of content.

**Top lists**

There are many kinds of lists in the iTunes Store, such as Top Movies and Top Albums.

**Quick Links**

These links take you to tools you use, such as the Power Search tool or Browser.

**Current account**

When you are logged into an iTunes Store account, you see your user name.

**Return to iTunes**

Click to exit the Store.

**Content page**

Displays information about a specific item.

**Buy Album button**

You can buy an album by clicking its **Buy** button.

**Ratings**

Click to see what other people are saying.

**Tracks**

The contents of the current item are shown in the bottom of the window.

**Buy Songs buttons**

You can use a track's Buy button to buy only that track.

**Artist link**

Click the artist to see all content by that artist.

**Preview**

Click to hear a 30-second preview.

# Obtain an iTunes Store Account

To be able to purchase or rent content from the iTunes Store, you need to have an iTunes account and be logged into it (you can browse, search, and preview content without being logged into an account).

**Like other aspects of the iTunes Store, you can get an account from within iTunes.**

## Obtain an iTunes Store Account

① Click **iTunes Store** on the Source list.

iTunes connects to the iTunes Store and you see the home page.

② Click **Sign In**.

The Sign In dialog appears.

③ Click **Create New Account**.

The Welcome to iTunes Store screen appears.

④ Follow the on-screen instructions to create your account.

When you have created your account, you have an Apple ID and password. This enables you to log into your account on the iTunes Store and purchase content from it.

**Note:** *You can use the same Apple ID to make purchases from the online Apple Store.*

# Buy Music, TV, Movies, and More from the iTunes Store

The iTunes Store has a lot of great content that you can easily preview, purchase (some is free), and download to MacBook, where it is added to your iTunes Library automatically. When you are interested in content, you can preview 30 seconds of it to decide if you want it or not. Buying something you want is just a matter of clicking the related Buy button.

## Buy Music, TV, Movies, and More from the iTunes Store

### Log into Your iTunes Store Account

① Select **iTunes Store** on the Source List.

② Click **Sign In**.

③ Enter your Apple ID.

④ Enter your password.

⑤ Click **Sign In**.

Any personalization you have added to your account, such as adding items to your Wish List, becomes available.

### Browse the iTunes Store

① Click the **iTunes Store** link on the Source list.

*Note: If you were previously logged into your account, you remain logged in. If not, log in again.*

② Click the **Browse** link.

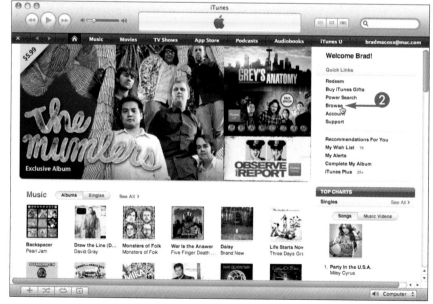

The Store Browser appears.

**3** In the Store Browser, click a content category, such as **Music**.

*Note: This example uses music; different types of content have other categories to browse.*

**4** Select a genre.

**5** Select a subgenre.

**6** Select an artist.

**7** Select an album.

● The contents of the selected album appear in the bottom pane of the window. This pane works just like the Content pane when you browse your iTunes Library.

You are ready to preview and purchase content.

**Search the iTunes Store**

**1** Click the **iTunes Store** link on the Source list.

**2** Type information you want to search for in the Search field.

● As you type, iTunes attempts to match what you are typing and presents the matches on a pop-up menu.

**3** If a match is found, select it on the pop-up menu to perform the search; if not, continue typing until you have entered all the text you want to search for.

● The results of your search appear.

**4** Review the results of the search.

**5** To see the results in a specific category, click the **See All** link for that category.

**6** To get more information for a specific album, click its cover.

continued

# Buy Music, TV, Movies, and More from the iTunes Store *(continued)*

There are many ways to move around the iTunes Store. Just about every object on the screen is linked to more specific information about something, until you get down to the individual items that you purchase, such as songs, movies, or TV shows. Browsing and searching are both useful techniques for finding great content.

## Buy Music, TV, Movies, and More from the iTunes Store *(continued)*

● The album's page appears.

❼ Read other people's feedback on the album.

❽ Read the full text associated with the album.

You are ready to preview and purchase content.

## Preview iTunes Store Content

❶ Select the item you want to preview.

❷ Click the **Play** button ().

A 30-second preview plays. If the content is audio, you hear it. If it includes video, you see the video too.

You can control previews with the same controls you use to play content in your iTunes Library.

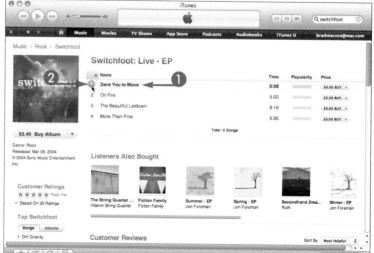

**Buy and Download Content from the iTunes Store**

1. Preview the content you are interested in.

2. Click the **Buy** button for the content you want to purchase.

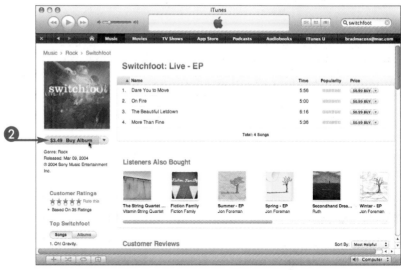

3. Enter your account's password.

4. To have iTunes remember your password for more purchases during this shopping session, check the **Remember password for purchasing** check box.

5. Click **Buy**.

   The content is immediately downloaded to your iTunes Library.

6. Click the **Return to iTunes** button (⊠).

 **TIP**

**Are there any limitations on what I can do with content I purchase from the iTunes Store?**

Audio content you purchase from the iTunes Store is not restricted by any limitations, so you can have and use it on as many computers as you want, burn it to as many discs as you want, add it to multiple iPods and iPhones, and so on. Video content does have some limitations, including the number of computers it can be played on; each computer has to be authorized with your iTunes Store user account to be able to play it. Rented video content can only be played on one device at a time.

You can buy items individually, such as songs or episodes of TV shows. You can also buy collections, including albums or seasons of TV shows. You can even prepurchase some kinds of content. For example, you can purchase a season pass for a current TV show; as new episodes are added to the iTunes Store, they download to your iTunes Library automatically. You can also preorder music; as soon as it is released, it is downloaded to your computer. You can also store items you are interested in on your Wish List, from where you can buy them at a later time.

## Buy Music, TV, Movies, and More from the iTunes Store *(continued)*

⑦ Click **Downloads** on the Source list.

● The items being downloaded are shown. You see the download progress for each item. When an item finishes downloading, it disappears from the list.

*Note: Items that you purchase from the iTunes Store are automatically stored in the Purchased playlist. To see your purchased content, select that source. The items, including audio and video, you have purchased are shown.*

### Add Content to Your Wish List

① View content you want to save in your Wish List.

② Open the menu at the right end of the Buy button and choose **Add to Wish List**.

The item is added to your Wish List.

③ Click your iTunes account and on the pop-up menu, choose **Wish List**.

● Your Wish List opens. You can browse your list, preview items, and purchase them as you can from other pages in the iTunes Store.

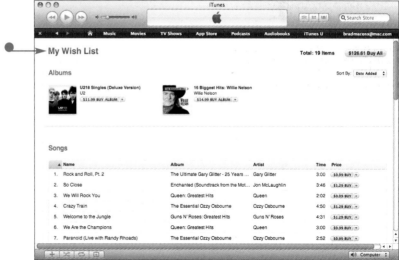

**TIP**

### What about content I purchased previously that was restricted through Digital Rights Management (DRM)?

Previously, there were two kinds of content on the iTunes Store: iTunes Plus and protected. iTunes Plus content had no restrictions. You could use protected content on up to five computers at the same time, and you could burn unique playlists to a disc up to seven times. If you previously purchased protected content from the Store, you can convert that content into unprotected content by clicking the iTunes Plus link in your section on the iTunes Store home page. You have to pay a fee for each item you convert, but this cost is significantly less than the cost of purchasing the content.

# Rent Movies from the iTunes Store

You can rent movies from the iTunes Store. This process is very similar to purchasing movies and other content from the iTunes Store, but there are a couple of differences.

**You can rent movies for less than it costs to buy them. New releases are typically $3.99, whereas older movies are $1.99 or sometimes less. When you rent a movie, you have it for up to 30 days, but you can only watch it for a 24-hour period. Once you start watching a movie, the timer starts and when 24 hours have passed, the movie is deleted from your computer automatically.**

## Rent Movies from the iTunes Store

① Click **iTunes Store** on the Source list.

② Click the **Movies** category.

● The Movies home page appears.

③ Scroll down until you see the Movie Rentals section.

④ Click **See All**.

You can browse all movies available for rental.

⑤ Browse the movies available for rental.

⑥ When you see a movie of interest, click its thumbnail.

You see the movie's home page.

⑦ Preview the movie or view its trailer.

⑧ Click **Rent Movie** or **Rent HD Movie**.

*Note: Some movies are available in standard or HD format. You can rent either version; the HD version is more expensive.*

If you allowed iTunes to remember your password for purchases, the movie begins to download immediately, so make sure you really want to rent it before you click **Rent**. If you did not allow iTunes to remember your information for purchases, you have to enter your password and click **Rent** to complete the process.

The movie downloads to MacBook, and if this is the only rented movie in your iTunes Library, the Rented Movies source is added to the Source List.

⑨ Click **Rented Movies** on the Source list.

The movies you have rented appear.

● On the right side of the window, you see information about when the movie expires.

⑩ Double-click the movie you want to watch.

⑪ If you are sure you want to watch the movie, click **Play**.

The movie plays.

When 24 hours pass from the time you started playing the movie, it is deleted from MacBook automatically, whether you have watched all of it or not.

TIPS

**Explain how the 30-day and 24-hour rental periods work.**

Movies that you rent remain on your computer up to 30 days. However, you rent the movie only for a 24-hour viewing period. Once you start playing the movie, the 24-hour period starts. When 24 hours have passed since you first played the movie, the movie is deleted from your computer whether you have finished watching it or not. (You can watch the movie within the 24-hour period as much as you want.) The movie is also automatically deleted at the end of the 30-day rental period, again whether you have watched it or not.

**Does what I paid for rent count against purchasing the same movie?**

No. In the iTunes Store, renting and buying are totally separate activities. If you rent a movie and later want to buy it, you have to pay the full purchase price.

# Subscribe to Podcasts

*Podcasts* are episodic audio or video programs that you can listen to or watch. Many podcasts are like radio shows, and in fact, many *are* radio shows. Most radio shows offer podcast versions that you can download to MacBook and copy to an iPod. Podcasts go way beyond just radio shows, however. You can find podcasts on many different topics.

**You can subscribe to many different podcasts in the iTunes Store. Once you have subscribed, episodes are downloaded for you automatically so that they are available for you to listen to or watch, which you do in the same way as other content in the Library.**

## Subscribe to Podcasts

1 Click **iTunes Store**.

2 Click **Podcasts**.

3 Search for and click on a podcast of interest to you.

*Note: You can also browse for podcasts.*

The search results appear.

4 Click a podcast to get more information.

The podcast's home page appears.

5 To play an episode, select it and click the **Play** button (▶).

*Note: Because most podcasts are free, the entire episode plays instead of just a preview.*

6 Read about the podcast.

7 To subscribe to a podcast, click its **Subscribe** button.

Available episodes of the podcast are added to your iTunes Library and some of the recent episodes download to your computer.

## Listen to Podcasts

1. Click the **Podcasts** source in the Source list.

● You see all the podcasts to which you have subscribed.

2. Click a podcast's triangle to expand it so you see all the episodes it contains.

3. Select and play an episode of a podcast just like other content.

*Note: Podcasts you have not played are marked with a blue dot (◉).*

4. If an episode you want to listen to has not been downloaded yet, click its **Get** button.

5. Click **Get All** to get all the episodes in a podcast.

## Configure Podcast Settings

1. Click **Podcasts** in the Source list.

2. Click **Settings**.

The Podcasts tab of the iTunes Preferences dialog appears.

*Note: You can configure different settings for a podcast by selecting it and then clicking the **Settings** button. Changes you make impact only the selected podcast.*

3. On the **Check for new episodes** pop-up menu, choose how often iTunes looks for new episodes.

4. On the **When new episodes are available** pop-up menu, choose what you want iTunes to do.

5. On the **Episodes to keep** pop-up menu, choose how you want iTunes to manage your podcasts.

6. Click **OK**.

### What if a podcast I want to subscribe to is not available in the iTunes Store?

For various reasons, mostly having to do with money, some podcasts are not available in the iTunes Store, which is too bad because that is definitely the easiest way to find and subscribe to podcasts. Some Web sites provide a URL to a podcast subscription; copy this, click **Advanced**, click **Subscribe to Podcast**, paste the URL in the dialog, and click **OK**. Others provide podcasts as MP3 files that you can download and add to the iTunes Library; you work with these files just like tracks from a CD.

### A radio show I listen to has a podcast application; what does it do?

When shows offer podcasts as MP3 files for which you have to pay a fee to access, they often provide an application that downloads the files automatically. After you install and configure such an application, the show's MP3 files are downloaded to the location you specify. Add them to the iTunes Library by dragging them there or by clicking **File** and then clicking **Add to Library**.

# Copy iTunes Content from Other Computers onto MacBook

If you have another computer with iTunes content on it that is on the same network as MacBook, you can use the Home Sharing feature to copy content you have purchased from the iTunes Store and any other iTunes content onto MacBook to build up your iTunes Library. This is a fast and simple way to fill your iTunes Library with a lot of audio and video that you can enjoy while you are on the move.

**There are two steps to this process. The first is to configure Home Sharing on the computer from which you will copy content. Then access the sharing computer and import its content into the MacBook iTunes Library.**

## Copy iTunes Content from Other Computers onto MacBook

### Configure Home Sharing

① In iTunes on the computer sharing content with MacBook, open the **Advanced** menu and choose **Turn On Home Sharing**.

The Home Sharing setup screen appears.

② Enter your iTunes Account name.

③ Enter your iTunes account password.

④ Click **Create Home Share**.

Home Sharing starts and you see its information window.

⑤ Click **Done**.

**Note:** You can set up shares on multiple computers at the same time.

### Import New Content to the iTunes Library

① Expand the shared source by clicking its triangle.

② Select the type of content you want to add.

③ Use the browser to find specific content you want to add to your library.

④ Select the content you want to add.

**Note:** To set up content to be imported automatically, click the **Settings** button, check the check box for each type of content you want to have copied automatically, and click **OK**.

⑤ Click **Import**.

The content you selected is copied into the iTunes Library.

**Note:** If you enable Home Sharing on MacBook, other computers can share its iTunes content.

# Create a Genius Playlist

The iTunes Genius is a feature that tries to select music for you based on a specific song; it places that similar music into a genius playlist that you can listen to, put on an iPod or iPhone, or burn to a disc. How the genius picks songs based on other songs is a bit of a mystery, but you may be amazed at how well this feature works.

**You can create as many genius playlists as you want. All you need to do is to turn the genius on, select a song, and tell the genius to get to work.**

## Create a Genius Playlist

### Start the Genius

① On the **Store** menu, select **Turn On Genius**.

● The Genius source appears on the Source list and you see what it can do for you.

② Click **Turn On Genius**.

③ At the prompt, enter your iTunes account password and follow the on-screen instructions to complete the genius configuration.

*Note: Genius transmits information about your Library to the iTunes Store. This process can take a while, but you can use iTunes while it works in the background.*

### Create a Playlist

① Select the song that you want the genius to base the playlist on.

② Click the **Genius** button (📋).

● The genius builds the playlist and you see its contents.

③ Click ▶ to play the playlist.

*Note: To save the playlist permanently, click **Save Playlist**. To have the genius update its contents, click **Refresh**.*

# Create a Standard Playlist

Playlists enable you to create your own custom content collections (such as music, audiobooks, and video) that you can then play, burn to disc, or move to an iPod or iPhone. You can create as many playlists as you want, and they are completely customizable; you can include as many tracks as you want in the order you want them. You can even include the same track in a playlist multiple times for those tracks you just have to hear over and over again.

**A standard playlist is one in which you manually place and organize songs.**

## Create a Standard Playlist

① Click the **Create Playlist** button (⊞).

A new playlist is created, and its name is ready to be edited.

② Name the new playlist and press Return.

The playlist is renamed and moves to a location on the Source list based on its title (playlists are sorted alphabetically).

③ Double-click the playlist.

● The playlist opens in a separate window, making adding songs to it much easier.

④ Position and size the playlist window so you can see it and the iTunes window at the same time.

⑤ Click the iTunes window.

**6** Select the category of content you want to add.

**7** Browse or search for content you want to add to the playlist.

**8** Drag tracks from the Content pane onto the playlist's window.

The tracks are added to the playlist.

**9** Repeat Steps **6** to **8** until you have added all the tracks you want to be included in the playlist.

**10** Click the playlist's window.

● Its contents appear in the Content pane.

**11** Drag tracks up and down the playlist until they are in the order in which you want them to play.

As with other sources, when you play in order, tracks play from the top of the window to the bottom.

**12** Close the playlist's window.

**TIPS**

**Can I sort the contents of a playlist?**
You can sort a playlist that you create by clicking the column heading by which you want to sort the playlist just like any other source. However, when you sort a playlist you have organized manually so that the tracks play in a specific order, that order is lost. You have to manually place the tracks back in the order you want if sorting by one of the column headings does not create the order you want.

**How can I create a playlist for an album I just downloaded from the iTunes Store?**
Select all the tracks on the album. Click **File**, and then choose **New Playlist from Selection**. A new playlist is created, containing all the tracks you selected. If they are all from the same album, the name of the playlist is the name of the album.

# Create a Smart Playlist

Standard playlists are great because you can easily create custom content collections, but you need to do some work to create and fill them. Why not let iTunes do the work for you? That is where a smart playlist comes in.

**Instead of placing content into a playlist manually, you define the criteria for content and iTunes grabs the appropriate content from the Library and places it into the smart playlist for you automatically.**

## Create a Smart Playlist

① Open the **File** menu and choose **New Smart Playlist**.

The Smart Playlist dialog appears.

② Select the first tag on which you want the smart playlist to be based in the Tag menu.

For example, to include genre in the condition, select **Genre**.

③ Select the operand you want to use from the Operand menu, such as **is**, **is not**, or **contains**.

④ Type the condition you want to match in the Condition field.

Your condition can include text or numbers.

***Note:*** *As you type, iTunes attempts to match data in the Library to what you are typing. If a match is found, you can stop typing.*

⑤ To add another condition to the smart playlist, click the **Add Condition** button (⊕).

A new, empty condition appears.

⑥ Select a second tag.

⑦ Select an operand.

⑧ Type a condition you want to match in the Condition field.

⑨ Repeat Steps **5** to **8** until you have added all the conditions you want to include.

⑩ Select **all** on the pop-up menu at the top of the dialog if all the conditions must be met for a track to be included in the smart playlist, or select **any** if only one of them must be met.

***Note:*** *If you click the ellipsis button (⌐⌐), you can create nested condition statements so you can build very complex criteria.*

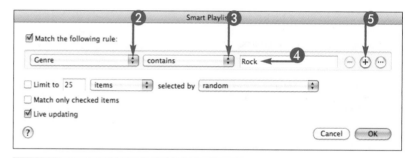

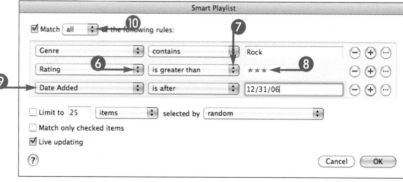

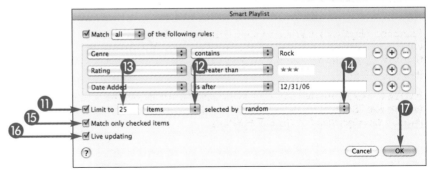

⑪ If you want to limit the size of the playlist, check the **Limit to** check box; if not, skip to Step **15**.

⑫ Select the parameter by which you want to limit the playlist in the first menu, such as **items**.

⑬ Type an appropriate amount for the limit you specified in the Limit to field, such as the number of hours.

⑭ Select how you want iTunes to choose the songs it includes based on the limit in the **selected by** menu.

⑮ To include only tracks whose check box in the Content pane is checked, check the **Match only checked items** check box.

**Note:** You can uncheck the check box next to tracks you want to skip when listening or other situations, such as building a smart playlist.

⑯ If you want iTunes to update its contents over time, check the **Live updating** check box.

⑰ Click **OK**.

The smart playlist is added to the Source list, the tracks that meet the playlist's conditions are added to it, and its name is ready for you to edit.

⑱ Type the playlist's name and press Return.

The playlist is complete.

 **TIPS**

### How do I change the contents of a smart playlist?

If a smart playlist has live updating enabled, the contents of the playlist change over time as new content is added, content is removed, or content changes so it meets or no longer meets the playlist's criteria. If you want to change the contents of a smart playlist, you have to change the criteria for the list. To do so, perform a secondary click on it and choose **Edit Smart Playlist**. Use the resulting Smart Playlist dialog to make changes to the conditions, which changes the playlist's content.

### Can I drag the contents of a smart playlist onto another playlist to move it there?

The smart playlist does not actually contain the content you see or even pointers to that content, and so you cannot move tracks from a smart playlist to another playlist. Likewise, you cannot delete tracks from a smart playlist; you must change the list's criteria so the content no longer meets them, or delete the content from the Library (only do this if you are sure you do not want it anymore).

# Move iTunes Content onto an iPhone or iPod touch

If you are fortunate enough to have an iPhone or iPod, you can enjoy your iTunes content while you are out and about. You can move any of your iTunes content onto one of these devices, including music, podcasts, movies, TV shows, and so on.

**You determine which content is moved onto the device by configuring the synchronization options. Once configured, the synchronization process moves content from MacBook onto the iPhone; when you add content on the iPhone, such as purchasing music using the iPhone iTunes application, that content also moves onto the MacBook.**

## Move iTunes Content onto an iPhone or iPod touch

**Note:** Each type of device has different configuration options. The following steps show the details for configuring a sync for an iPhone. An iPod touch is very similar; for ease of reference, the steps cover just iPhone. The other iPod models require different details, but the overall process is similar.

**①** Connect the iPhone to the MacBook using its USB cable.

The iPhone appears on the Source list.

**②** Select the iPhone.

**③** Click the **Music** tab.

**④** Check the **Sync Music** check box.

**⑤** Select the **Selected playlists, artists, and genres** radio button.

**⑥** Check the **Include music videos** check box to move music videos onto the iPhone.

**⑦** Check the check box for playlists you want to move to the iPhone.

**⑧** Check the check boxes for artists and genres you want to move.

**Note:** You can click the triangle next to folders to expand their contents. Scroll within the expanded areas to see all available content.

**⑨** Click the **Movies** tab.

**⑩** To move a rented movie onto the iPhone, click its **Move** button.

**⑪** Check the **Sync Movies** check box.

**⑫** Check the check boxes for movies you want to move onto the iPhone.

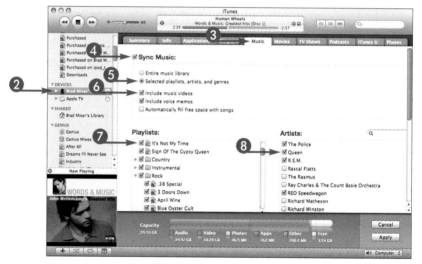

⓭ Click the **TV Shows** tab.

⓮ Check the **Sync TV Shows** check box.

⓯ Check the **Automatically include** check box and configure the pop-up menus to determine how many episodes and which shows are moved onto the iPhone.

⓰ If you chose selected shows in Step **14**, check the check box next to a series to move all the episodes it contains meeting the criteria onto the iPhone.

⓱ To move selected episodes, select the series and check the check box for each episode you want to move.

⓲ Click the **Podcasts** tab.

⓳ Check the **Sync Podcasts** check box.

⓴ Check the **Automatically include** check box and configure the pop-up menus.

㉑ Select a podcast and check the check boxes next to episodes to move those onto the iPhone.

㉒ Check the check box for podcasts for which you want to move all episodes meeting the criteria onto the iPhone.

㉓ Click **Apply**.

The content you selected is moved onto the iPhone.

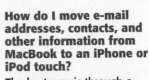

**TIPS**

**Can I move content from more than one computer onto the same iPhone?**

Yes, but you can only sync one type of content from a computer onto an iPhone. For example, you can sync movies on one computer and podcasts on a second, but you cannot sync movies and podcasts from both computers.

**How do I move e-mail addresses, contacts, and other information from MacBook to an iPhone or iPod touch?**

The best way is through a MobileMe account, which you can configure on an iPhone so that this information is synced wirelessly. You can also use the tools on the Info tab to sync this information when the iPhone is connected to MacBook using a USB cable.

# Explore iPhoto

iPhoto is an amazing, powerful, and easy-to-use application that enables you to do a lot of cool things. From storing and organizing photos to publishing your photos to the Web to creating professional-quality photo books, iPhoto does it all for you.

**You might think that iPhoto looks and works a lot like iTunes. If you think that, you are right. The two applications use similar interfaces and concepts, and so once you learn how to use one of them, using the other one comes quickly and easily.**

## Standard View

### Source list

The various sources in which your photos are stored and organized.

### Photos

When you select a source, the photos it contains appear in the right pane of the iPhoto window.

### Library

All the photos you add to iPhoto organized by various categories.

### Albums

Collections of photos you have created.

### Projects

Projects you created using your photos, such as photo pages posted on your MobileMe Gallery Web site.

### Add

Enables you to add albums, smart albums, photo books, and other items.

**Info**
Opens the Information pane.

**Full Screen**
Puts iPhoto in Full Screen mode.

**Play**
Plays the photos in the selected source in a slideshow.

**Search tool**
Enables you to search for photos.

**Size slider**
Changes the displayed size of photos' thumbnails (does not actually change the size of the photos themselves).

## Edit View

### Selected source

Select a source of photos to work with them.

### Photos in selected source

Thumbnails of the photos in the selected source.

### iPhoto in Edit mode

Edit photos to fix problems or make improvements.

**Photo being edited**

Changes you make to photos are shown immediately.

**Editing tools**

Tools you can use to improve your photos.

**Size slider**

Increase the size at which the photo you are editing is shown.

## Photo Book View

### Photo book

A book you design containing a collection of photos that you select.

### Page thumbnails

Represent each page in the book.

### Page view

Where you work on individual pages.

### Layout tools

Tools you use to design pages and the book.

**Buy Book**

Order professionally printed photo books from Apple.

**Next page/Previous page**

Move through the book's pages.

# Import Photos from a Digital Camera

To work with photos, you need to add them to the iPhoto Library. The most common way to do this is to import them from a digital camera. By default, when you connect a camera to MacBook, iPhoto opens and prepares to import the pictures stored in the camera's memory.

**Once imported, photos are added to your iPhoto Library, at which point you can edit them, create photo books, and do all the other amazing things iPhoto empowers you to do.**

**1** Connect the digital camera to a MacBook USB port.

**2** Turn the camera on and put it in playback or computer mode.

iPhoto launches and mounts the camera.

● The camera is selected as the import source in the Devices section of the iPhoto Source list.

**3** Type a name in the Event Name field for the collection of photos you are importing.

When you import photos, they are automatically organized into events based on their time stamps.

**4** Type a description of the photos in the Description field.

**5** To have iPhoto automatically create events based on the dates of the photos, select the **Autosplit events after importing** check box.

When you select this option, photos you import are placed into events based on when the photos were taken.

**6** If you have already imported some of the photos on the camera, select the **Hide photos already imported** check box.

**7** Click **Import All**.

iPhoto begins to transfer photos from the camera to the computer.

● As each photo is imported, you see a preview of some of the photos in the iPhoto window.

● The progress of the import process and the number of photos remaining are shown at the bottom of the window.

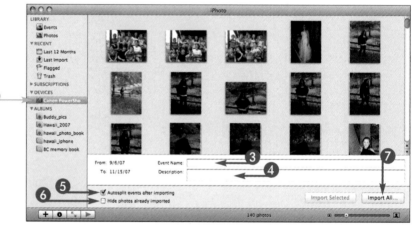

**8** When the import is complete, click **Delete Originals** to delete the photos from the camera, or click **Keep Originals** to leave the photos on the camera.

iPhoto completes the import process.

● The Last Import source is selected automatically and you see the photos you imported.

*Note: The Last Import source always contains the group of photos you imported most recently.*

**9** Disconnect the camera.

If you selected the Autosplit events after importing option in Step **5**, each group of photos is placed into a separate event. You can rename each event to make getting back to groups of photos easy.

**10** Select the title of an event.

The event name becomes editable.

**11** Type the event name.

**12** Press **Return**.

The event name you typed is saved and you can always return to that group of photos by selecting the event.

---

**TIPS**

### How do I import photos taken on an iPhone?

When you connect an iPhone on which you captured photos to MacBook, it opens in iPhoto just like a digital camera does. The same steps you followed to import photos from a camera are used to import photos from an iPhone.

### How can I import photos from other sources?

Open the **File** menu and choose **Import to Library**. Use the resulting dialog to navigate to and select the images you want to import, and then click **Import**. The image files are imported into the iPhoto Library where they can be used just like photos you import from a camera.

# Browse and Search the iPhoto Library

One of the first steps for most of the projects you do in iPhoto is to find and select the photos you want to work with. There are a couple of ways to do this: You can browse for photos, and you can search for photos by using information associated with those photos. After you find some photos, you can select them to work with them.

**Finding photos through either method is easier when photos are properly labeled, which you learn about in the next section, "Label Photos."**

## Browse for Photos

① To browse photos grouped by the events they are associated with, click **Events** in the Source list.

**Note:** To browse the photos in an event, double-click the event. The photos within the event appear.

② To browse photos individually, click **Photos**.

③ To browse by one of the recent collections, such as **Last 12 Months**, click the collection you want to browse.

**Note:** You can click **Last Import** to browse the photos you most recently imported.

④ Drag the **Display Size** slider to make the thumbnails of the photos larger or smaller.

⑤ Drag the vertical scroll bar down to see more of the photos you are browsing.

● As you drag, the date and event associated with the photos currently shown in the window appear.

**Search for Photos**

1 Click the source you want to search, such as **Last 12 Months**.

● The photos in the selected source appear.

2 On the pop-up menu in the Search tool (🔍), choose the kind of information you want to search by.

*Note: In this example, **Keyword** is selected. You can choose **Date** to search by date, **Rating** to search by your ratings, or **All** to search by all information.*

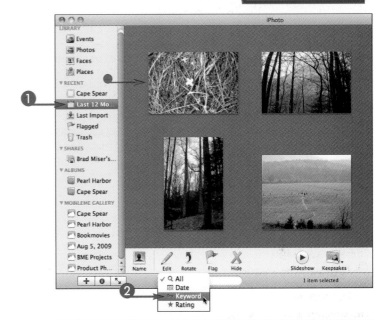

The search tool appropriate to the kind of information you select appears.

3 Select the values in the Search tool you want to search for.

*Note: If you click **All** on the **Search** pop-up menu in Step 2, type the text or numbers you want to search for in the Search field.*

● Only photos that meet your search criteria are shown in the window, and the found photos are highlighted in a box. For example, only photos associated with the keywords you clicked are shown.

**TIPS**

**What is an event?**

iPhoto uses the concept of an event to group photos together based on time. The application assumes that any photos captured within a specific amount of time (within one week, one day, the same 8-hour period, or the same 2-hour period, depending on the preference set on the Events tab of the iPhoto Preferences dialog) are part of the same event. By default, iPhoto automatically organizes photos into events based on the timeframe selected when you import them from a digital camera or other source.

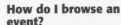

**How do I browse an event?**

When you browse events, you see a thumbnail for each event, which can include multiple photos. When you point to an event, the number of photos it contains and the associated date are shown. Drag within an event's thumbnail to browse the other photos it contains. Double-click an event to browse all of its photos in the iPhoto window.

# Label Photos

As you accumulate large numbers of photos in iPhoto, it is important to label those photos so that you can more easily find and identify them.

**There are two primary ways to label photos. First, you can associate combinations of keywords with images so that you can easily find images by searching for keywords. iPhoto includes a number of default keywords that you can use, and you can create your own keywords. A second way to label photos is by adding a title, description, and rating.**

## Label Photos

### Configure Keywords

1. Select the Photos source, and on the **Window** menu, choose **Show Keywords**.

● The Keywords window appears, showing all the keywords currently available.

2. Click **Edit Keywords**.

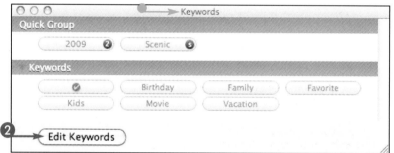

The Edit Keywords dialog appears.

3. Click the **Add** button (⊞).

A new, blank keyword appears.

4. Type the keyword you want to create.

5. Press `Tab` to navigate to the Shortcut column.

6. Press the key that you want to use for the new keyword's shortcut.

*Note: By default, this is the first letter of the keyword if that letter is not already being used for another keyword.*

7. Press `Return`.

8. Repeat Steps **3** to **7** until you have configured the keywords you want to use.

9. Click **OK**.

## Associate Keywords with Photos

**1** Browse or search for the photos you want to associate with keywords.

**2** Select the photos you want to associate with keywords. Photos you select are highlighted with a yellow box.

**3** Press ⌘+K to open the Keywords window.

Keywords that shortcuts are assigned to appear at the top of the window; remaining keywords appear at the bottom.

**4** Press the shortcut key for the keywords, or click the keywords that you want to associate with the selected photos; you can apply multiple keywords to photos.

The keywords are applied to the selected photos and become highlighted.

● The keywords you apply appear underneath each photo.

● The check mark keyword (☑) is a generic marker that you can use to temporarily mark photos for a specific project.

You can search for photos by their keywords and you can create smart photo albums using the keywords you have applied to photos.

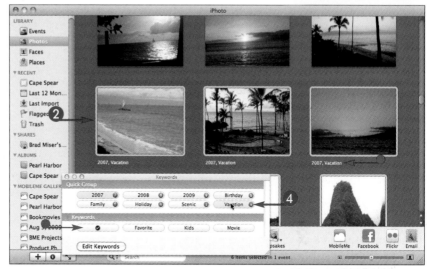

## Rate and Describe Photos

**1** Select a photo.

**Note:** *To apply labels to a group of photos at the same time, press and hold ⌘ and select each photo you want to label.*

**2** Click the **Info** button (☐) in the photo's thumbnail.

● The Information dialog appears; the photo is shown in the upper-left corner of the dialog.

**3** Type a title for the photo.

**Note:** *If you have selected more than one photo, check the check box next to the information that you want to apply to all the selected photos.*

**4** Rate the photo by clicking the dot corresponding to the number of stars you want to give the photo.

**5** Type the location of the photo and choose from the locations that iPhoto suggests to you.

● A map showing the location is shown.

**6** Type notes about the photo.

**7** Click **Done**.

**TIP**

### What labels does iPhoto assign to photos automatically?

iPhoto enters a title for each photo you import, which is the filename for the photo file; you can change this to be any text you want. iPhoto also adds the date and time on which the photo was captured; you should usually leave this information alone unless there was a problem with the camera's date function when you took the photo. iPhoto also captures information about the kind of image, its resolution, and file size. If you capture photos with a GPS-equipped device, the location information is captured automatically too.

One of the great things about working with digital photos is that you can easily edit photos to make them better. Before you jump into a project, such as creating a photo book, take some time to edit the photos you are going to use to make them the best they can be. This makes the end project much better.

**Using the Edit tools in iPhoto, you can rotate, crop, straighten, enhance, remove red-eye, and retouch. You can also apply effects and adjust specific aspects of photos. Each of these tools has specific functions that you can use to make improvements in your photos. The more common editing tasks of rotating and cropping and removing red-eye are covered here.**

## Edit Photos

### Rotate and Crop Photos

1 Select the photos you want to edit.

*Note: This example shows photos grouped as Event collections.*

2 Click **Edit** (✏️).

iPhoto switches to Edit mode.

● Thumbnails of each photo you selected in Step **1** appear at the top of the window.

● The thumbnail of the currently selected photo is highlighted, and the photo appears in the editing pane.

● The Edit tools appear at the bottom.

3 Select the photo you want to edit.

4 To rotate the photo in the counterclockwise direction, click the **Rotate** button (↺).

*Note: To rotate the photo clockwise, press and hold* Option *and click* ↺.

5 To crop the photo, click the **Crop** button (▢).

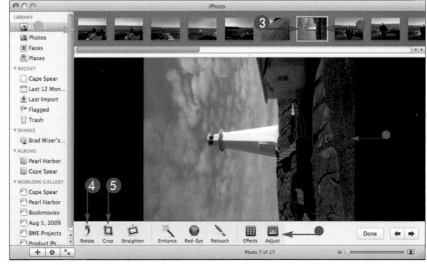

The Crop tools appear.

**6** Select the **Constrain** check box.

*Note: If you do not want to limit how you crop the photo, leave the check box unchecked and skip to Step **8**.*

**7** Choose the proportion you want to maintain. For example, to keep the photo proportioned as for a 4-x-6-inch photo, choose **4 x 6**.

**8** Drag the edges of the selection box until just the part of the photo you want to keep is in the box.

*Note: Once you have sized the selection box, you can drag it to change the cropped part of the photo.*

**9** Click **Apply**.

The photo is cropped and the Crop tools close.

**10** Click **Done** to save your changes.

*Note: Editing changes are also saved when you select another photo by clicking its thumbnail or clicking the left- or right-arrow buttons ( ◄ and ► ) next to Done.*

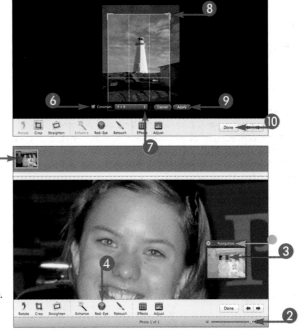

### Remove Red-Eye

**1** Click the thumbnail of the image you want to edit.

**2** Drag the **Display Size** slider to the right to zoom in on the photo.

● When you can no longer see the entire photo, the Navigation box appears so you can see your relative position (within the location box).

**3** Drag the location box so the eyes that have red-eye are in the center of the screen.

**4** Click the **Red-Eye** button ( ☺ ).

● The Red-Eye tool appears.

**5** Click the **Auto** button.

iPhoto removes the red from the eyes. If the eyes look the way you want, skip the rest of these steps. If not, manually remove red-eye using the rest of these steps.

**6** Drag the **Size** slider until the cursor is about the same size as the red area of the eye.

**7** Move the cursor so it covers the red-eye and click.

● Red is replaced by black.

**8** Click **Done** to save your changes or select another image to edit.

TIPS

### What do the other editing tools do?

The Straighten tool ( ▱ ) aligns the subject of a photo with a grid; this is typically used to improve a distorted photo. The Enhance tool ( ◥ ) improves the color balance and other characteristics of a photo. The Retouch tool ( ◥ ) enables you to remove scratches and other imperfections. The Effects tool ( ▦ ) opens a palette of effects that you can apply to photos. The Adjust tool ( ▣ ) opens a palette of tools that enable you to make very detailed changes, such as tint and sharpness.

### Should I really edit photos before I collect them for a project?

In some cases, it makes sense to organize the photos you plan to use for a project before editing them, in which case you perform the steps in "Organize the Photo Book's Photos in an Album" before you do these. This way, you do not spend time editing photos you are not going to use. Sometimes the project in which you are going to use photos impacts how you edit them.

# Organize the Photo Book's Photos in an Album

You use photo albums to gather and organize photos for various purposes, such as to make it easy to view the photos for a specific event, like a vacation. Creating a photo album is also a good first step in most projects, such as creating a photo book.

**There are two kinds of photo albums. For a standard photo album, you manually place photos into the album. For a smart album, you define criteria for the photos to be included, and iPhoto automatically finds the photos that match and places them in the album.**

## Organize the Photo Book's Photos in an Album

### Create a Standard Photo Album

1. Select the photos you want to include in an album.

2. Click the **Add** button (⊞).

   The New Album sheet appears.

3. Click the **Album** tab.

4. Type a name for the album you are creating.

5. Select the **Use selected items in new album** check box.

6. Click **Create**.

The album is created and is selected on the Source list.

7. Drag photos from the Browse pane onto the photo album you created.

   The photos are placed into the album.

**8** Select the album on the Source list.

All the photos in the album appear in the Browse pane.

**9** Drag the photos around the album until they are in the order you want them to be.

Photos are ordered from left to right and top to bottom.

**10** To remove a photo from the album, select it and press Delete.

The deleted photo is removed from the album but remains in the Library.

*Note: Most projects go much easier and faster if you take the time to organize the photos in an album in the order that you want them to appear in a project, starting at the top left and moving to the right and down.*

**Create a Smart Photo Album**

**1** Open the **File** menu and select **New Smart Album**.

The New Smart Album sheet appears.

**2** Enter a name for the smart album.

**3** Configure the first condition for the smart album.

**4** Click **Add Condition** (⊕).

**5** Configure the next condition.

**6** Repeat Steps **4** and **5** until you have added all the conditions for the smart album.

**7** On the **Match** pop-up menu, choose **all** if all the conditions must be met for a photo to be included, or **any** if only one of them must be met.

**8** Click **OK**.

The album is created and all the photos in the iPhoto Library that meet the conditions are placed in it automatically.

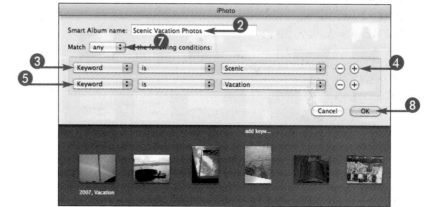

**TIPS**

**What happens when I edit a photo in an album?**

When you add a photo to an album, you are actually just adding a pointer to that photo instead of making a copy of it. Any changes you make to a photo in an album, such as cropping or rotating, are made on the photo everywhere it appears, including the Library and other albums. So, be careful if you use the same photos in multiple projects because changing a photo in one location changes it in every location.

**What if I want to have multiple versions of the same photo?**

To use different versions of the same photo in different projects, make a copy of it. Select the photo in the Library, open the **Photos** menu, and select **Duplicate**. The copies are independent, and so you can make different changes to each version and use them in multiple projects.

# Create a Photo Book

A photo book is a great way to display a collection of photos. You can use the photo book on your computer, print it yourself, or for best results, send it to Apple where it is printed on acid-free paper and bound with a cover for a truly professional-looking result.

**Once you have created a photo album in iPhoto, you can create a photo book of it. When you select the photo album, the photos it contains are placed in the new book. From there, you can choose from a variety of layouts, with each having a different printing price.**

## Create a Photo Book

① Select an album.

② Open the **Keepsakes** menu and choose **Book**.

*Note: In some cases, the Book button (🖺) may appear on the toolbar. If so, click it.*

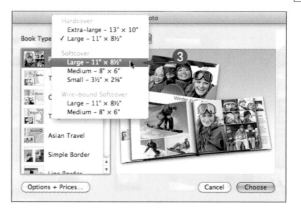

The Book sheet appears.

③ Click the **Book Type** pop-up menu and choose the type of book you want to create.

For example, to create an 11-x-8 1/2-inch book with a soft cover, select **Large – 11" x 8 1/2"** in the Softcover section.

④ Select a layout from the list shown on the left pane of the sheet.

● A preview of the layout you select appears in the right pane.

*Note: To see how much the type of book you want costs to print, click the Options + Prices button to open a Web page that shows current pricing.*

⑤ Click **Choose**.

● The photo book is created in the Keepsakes section.

● The photo book window appears.

● At the top of the window, you see previews of the photos in the photo album you selected.

● In the center of the window, you see the page preview that you use to build each page; the first time you view a book, it shows the cover.

● At the bottom of the window, you see the book tools.

You are ready to lay out the book's pages (see the next section).

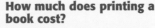

**TIPS**

**Do I have to have a book printed by Apple?**

No, you can print photo books yourself, and I recommend that you print a draft version that you check carefully before you order a copy from Apple. Except for resolution problems, Apple does not check a book when it is printed; what you send to be printed is what you get back. Print a draft copy or create a PDF to check the book before you print it. You can also take the PDF version to a local printing store to have it printed.

**How much does printing a book cost?**

At press time, 8 1/2-x-11-inch hardcover books were $29.99 for 20 pages (double-sided) or 10 pages (single-sided). Additional pages cost $.99 for a double-sided page (100 pages maximum) or $1.49 for a single-sided page (50 pages maximum). Check the Apple Web site for current prices for these options.

# Lay Out a Photo Book

Laying out a photo book is definitely the most time-consuming part of the process. It is also the most important one. For each page in the book, you choose the photos that appear on the page, the page's theme, and other aspects of its design.

**Fortunately, you can use the Autoflow tool to get started and then make manual adjustments from there as needed.**

## Lay Out a Photo Book

### Use Autoflow to Lay Out Pages

**①** Select the book on the Source list.

● You see the book's cover with a title.

**②** Click the **Autoflow** button (⊜).

iPhoto places the photos in the book on various pages, starting with the first photo in the photo album being placed on the book's cover.

**③** Click the **Show Pages** button (▣) to show thumbnails of the pages in the book instead of the photos.

You can manually adjust the Autoflow layout as needed.

**Note:** *When a photo is marked with an exclamation point (⚠), it means that the photo's resolution is too low to print properly at its current size. You need to fix resolution problems before you send the book to Apple for printing or you probably will not be pleased with the results.*

### Adjust Each Page's Layout Manually

**①** Select the cover thumbnail.

The cover, along with its text, appears in the center pane of the window.

**②** Click the cover page photo.

The size and placement tools appear.

**③** Drag the slider to increase or decrease the size of the photo relative to the cover.

**④** Click the **Hand** button (✋).

**⑤** Drag the photo to position the part that is visible in the frame.

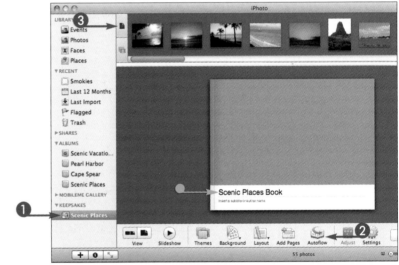

6 Click the book's title and change it to what you want to appear on the printed cover.

7 Click other text on the cover and edit it.

8 Click the thumbnail of the next page.

● The page appears in the editing area.

9 Drag the **Size** slider to zoom in or out so that you can work with the page effectively.

**Note:** *The Size slider only changes the size at which the page is being displayed.*

10 Use the scroll bars to change the part of the page you see.

11 Edit the page's title if it has one.

12 Edit any other text on the page.

**Note:** *You can write text in any application, such as a word processor, and then copy and paste it into a text block on a book page.*

13 Click the **Next** button (➡).

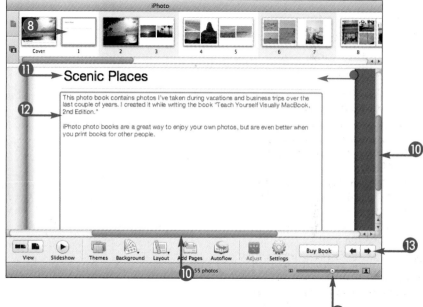

## TIPS

**How do I fix photos marked with an exclamation point icon?**

When a photo's resolution is too low to print with the best quality at its current size, it is flagged with an exclamation point icon (🔳). This means that the photo is sized too large for its resolution. If you have cropped the photo, uncrop it to restore more of the original photo so that its resolution is sufficient at its current size. You can also place the photo in a smaller frame on the same page or on a different page, or change the page's layout so that there are more photos on the page (which makes all the photos smaller). If you have zoomed in on the photo, zoom out again to include more of the photo in the frame. If none of this solves the problem, remove the photo from the book or print it as is, realizing that its quality might not be very good.

**Can I add more pages to a book after I have created it?**

Yes. You can add more pages to a book by clicking the **Add Pages** button (🔳). When you do, two empty pages are added to the book (the number of pages in a book must be even). You can then add photos and design the layouts of the new pages. Realize that each page you add to a book above its original number also adds to the cost of the book, and so you want to make sure you do not add too many pages.

continued

One of the reasons why laying out a book is time consuming is that changes you make to pages in the book can impact the layout of other pages. For example, when you change the number of photos on a page, and the photos reflow, you might end up with blank spots on pages later in the book.

**Laying out a book is an iterative process and usually requires several passes through the book, examining and working on each page as you go. You usually get to a better result quickly if you always work from the front of the book toward the back on each pass.**

## Lay Out a Photo Book *(continued)*

The next page of the book appears.

⑭ Select the next page.

● The page you selected appears in the layout pane.

⑮ To change the layout of the page, open the **Layout** (  ) pop-up menu.

⑯ Choose the page's layout.

**Note:** *The current layout of the page is marked with a check mark.*

Placeholders appear for each photo on the page.

⑰ To add a photo to the page, click the **Show Photos** button (  ).

● The photos in the book are shown. Photos marked with a check mark are included on at least one page in the book.

⑱ Scroll through the photos to find one you want to add to the page.

⑲ Drag the photo onto the open position.

The photo is added to the page in the frame where you placed it.

⑳ To change the location of a photo on the same page, drag it on top of an existing photo.

The photos swap locations.

㉑ Move photos between pages by dragging them from one page to another.

**Note:** *If a photo exists in the new location, the photos swap places.*

㉒ Edit any text on the page.

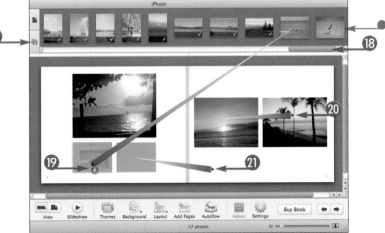

23 Remove a photo from a page by dragging it from the page back onto the photo browser, or select it and press Delete.

***Note:** When you delete a photo from a book, it is only removed from the book and remains in the Library.*

24 When you finish with the page being displayed, click the **Next** button (➡).

25 Continue moving through the pages in the book until you lay out all of them.

The book is now ready for an editing pass.

TIPS

Can I add photos to the book that are not in the photo album that I started with?

Yes. To add photos to the book that were not in the album you started with, find the photos you want to add in the Library or other sources, and drag the photos onto the book icon on the Source list. The photos are added to the book, and appear at the far-right end of the photo browser pane. You can then place them in the book.

What if I need to edit a photo in a book?

Double-click a photo on a book page; it opens in the Edit mode. After you edit the photo, click **Done**. You return to the photo in the book and the changes you made are reflected in the photo, whether you have already placed it on a page or not. (Remember that when you edit a photo, it changes wherever it is used.)

# Edit a Photo Book

Once you have finished laying out a book, you should edit it to make sure that what you send to be printed is going to please you.

**Editing passes are necessary to find those problems that you may have missed when you laid out the book, or you may decide that you want to improve some aspect of the layout that you might not have discovered while you were laying out the book. It is much better to discover problems when you can fix them easily and for free, rather than after you spend money on printing a book.**

## Edit a Photo Book

① Select the photo book.

② Set the preview size so that you can see all of the pages in the window.

③ Look for photo problems or layout issues.

④ Click the **Next** button (➡).

The next set of pages appears.

⑤ Use the **Zoom** slider and scroll bars to navigate the pages containing text so that you can read the text easily.

⑥ If you find a text problem, fix it.

*Note: iPhoto has a spell checker that underlines misspellings and suggests corrections. Make sure you check the text on each page carefully because text problems are not as obvious as image problems.*

7 To apply a background to a page, click the **Background** button (⬚).

8 Select a background from the pop-up menu.

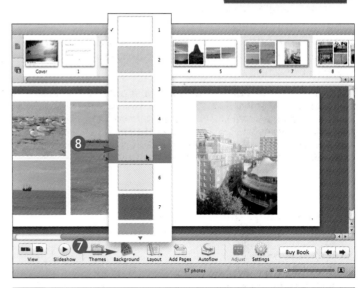

The background is applied to the page.

9 When you get to the end of the book, note how many pages there are to determine how much the book costs.

10 If you want to remove pages, select the page you want to remove, open the **Edit** menu, and select **Remove Page**.

The page is removed from the book.

11 Check whether deleting the page has affected the rest of the layout, and fix any problems you find.

*Note: If you are using a book with double-sided pages, you must add and delete pages two at a time.*

---

**TIPS**

**Can I change a book's design after I lay it out?**

Using the Themes menu, you can choose a different design for a book you have laid out. When you choose a new design, the pages are redone according to the new design. This can cause problems with some of the pages, especially if the pages have text on them or the number of photos per page changes. Make sure you do some additional editing passes with the new design to make sure the results are acceptable.

**What does the Adjust button do?**

When you select a photo and click the **Adjust** button (⬚), the Adjust palette appears. The Adjust palette has tools that enable you to apply effects and adjust many aspects of the photo, such as brightness and color temperature. These are the same tools available in the Editing toolset.

ADJUST PALETTE

# Configure a Photo Book's Settings

Each book has a set of configuration options that you can adjust. These include fonts and whether you want the Apple logo included on the book.

**Before you are really done with a book, you need to configure these settings.**

Configure a Photo Book's Settings

① Select the photo book.

② Click **Settings** ([icon]).

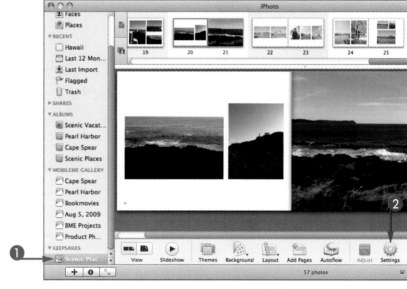

The Settings sheet appears.

③ Use the **Font** pop-up menus to set the fonts.

*Note: If you change the fonts significantly, review the book again to ensure that changes you make do not mess up the book's layout.*

④ If you do not want an Apple logo included on the book when it is printed, uncheck the **Include Apple logo** check box.

⑤ Check the **Automatically enter photo information** check box to have photo information such as titles added automatically.

⑥ Select the **Show page numbers** check box to include numbers on pages.

*Note: Like font changes, if you add photo information, review the impact of those changes on the book before you print it.*

⑦ Click **OK**.

Any changes you make are reflected in the book.

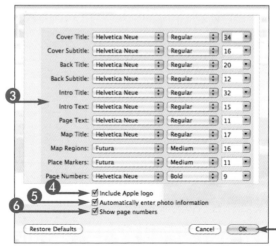

# Print a Photo Book

You can print photo books yourself or have Apple print them for you.

Apple prints photo books using high-quality printers, binds the books for you, and even ships them to the locations of your choice. However, you should know how to print books yourself, so that you can proof a book before you send it to Apple for printing.

## Print a Photo Book

### Print Photo Books Yourself

1. Select the photo book you want to print.
2. Open the **File** menu and select **Print**.

   The Print dialog appears.
3. Click the **Preview** button.
 • A preview of your book appears in the Preview application.
4. Review the book in Preview.
5. If you want to make changes, go back into iPhoto and make the changes.
6. If you made changes, repeat Steps **2** to **4** to generate and review a new preview.
7. When you are ready to print the book, click **Print**.

   iPhoto prints the book using your selected printer.
8. Check the printed version and fix any problems you notice, especially if you are going to have Apple print it.

### Have Apple Print Photo Books

1. Select the photo book you want to print.
2. Click **Buy Book**.
 • The Order Book dialog appears.

**Note:** You need to have and sign in with an Apple ID to order books. This is the same account you use to order from the online Apple Store and the iTunes Store. The first time you buy something in iPhoto, log into your account from the Order Book dialog.

3. Configure any options for the book. For example, if the book is hard copy, select the color of the cover on the **Cover Color** pop-up menu.
4. Select how many copies of the book you want in the Quantity field.
5. Select where and how to ship your book.
6. Click **Buy Now**.
7. Follow any on-screen instructions to complete the process.

   Your book is printed and shipped to the address you selected.

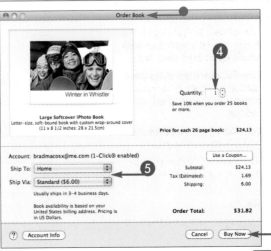

# Explore iMovie

As iPhoto is to photos, iMovie is to video. You can create amazing movie projects using video clips, photos, sounds, music, and other content you have created with or that is stored in the other iLife applications.

**In addition to your movie's content, you can use iMovie's tools to add titles, special effects, and transitions between clips to create a movie that flows. Once your movie is complete, you can share and enjoy it in many ways, such as viewing it in iTunes or on an iPhone.**

## iMovie Window

### Project Editor

This is where you build a movie using video clips, transitions, music, titles, sound effects, and more.

### Toolbar

Contains different tools you use to build movies.

### Event Library

Video content you import from a camcorder or other source to use in your movies.

### Selected Event

To work with content, you select an event.

### Video Clips

Clips in the selected source that can be added to the movie by dragging them onto the Project Editor.

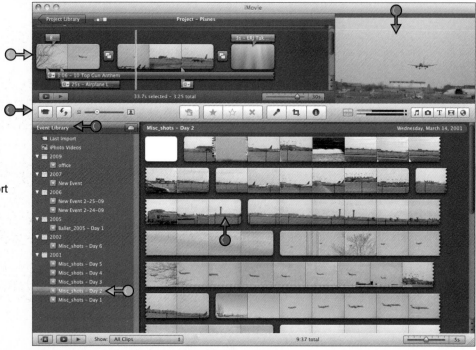

### Preview Pane
Where you can preview clips or a project.

## Project Editor

### Project
An iMovie is a project.

### Video Clips
Clips that have been added to the project.

### Soundtrack
A movie's soundtrack can include music, sound effects, and narration.

### Transition
An effect that smoothes the flow between video clips.

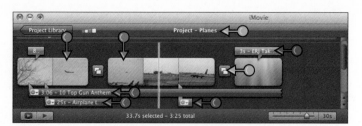

### Title
A clip showing text for titles, captions, and credits.

## Project Library

### Projects
You can create many projects in iMovie.

### Selected Project
You can select a project to preview it or click the **Edit Project** button to work on it.

## Event Library

### Events
Events are collections of video clips that have been imported from a camcorder or other source.

### Event Clips
The clips in an event are available for movie projects; you can preview a clip by selecting it and pressing Spacebar .

## Browser

### Audio Browser
Enables you to add content in your iTunes Library and sound effects to movies.

### Photo Browser button
Use your photos in movies.

### Titles Browser button
Add titles to movies.

### Transitions Browser button
Add transitions to movies.

# Add Video to the Event Library

You store the video clips you use in your movie projects in the iMovie Event Library. In many of the movies you create, you will probably use video you have captured with a camcorder. You can import video content from a camcorder into the iMovie Event Library where it is available for as many projects as you want to use it in.

**If you want to add all of the video on a tape or other media to the Event Library, use the Automatic Import tool to capture that content easily. Once you have added content to your library, you can use that content to build movie projects.**

## Add Video to the Event Library

### Import Video from a Camcorder

1. Connect the camcorder to MacBook.

2. Launch iMovie by clicking its icon on the Dock.

3. Click the **Import** button (🎬).

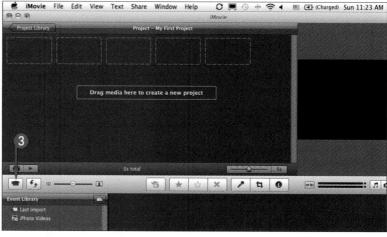

The Import dialog appears.

4. Select your camcorder on the **Camera** pop-up menu.

5. Place the switch in the **Automatic** position.

6. Click **Import**.

   The Save sheet appears.

7. Select the disk on which you want to save the video you are importing.

8. To create a new event, select the **Create new Event** radio button and enter a name for the event.

9. Click **Import**.

   iPhoto rewinds the media, starts playback, and begins importing the content.

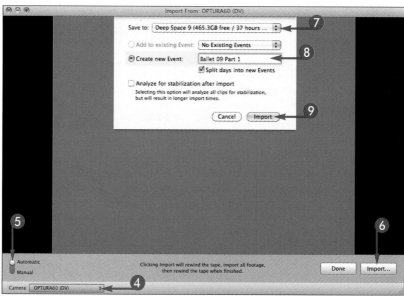

● As content is imported, you see a preview in the Import dialog. The process continues until all of the video has been imported or you click the **Stop** button.

**Work with the Event Library**

❶ Expand the content collections (by default, video is collected by year) to see what video they contain.

❷ Select content you want to preview.

● The clips in that collection appear.

❸ Drag over a clip until the red line is where you want to start watching the clip.

❹ Press the Spacebar.

● The clip plays in the Preview window.

### How do I keep from filling up my hard disk with video?

Importing video takes a while, and you probably do not want to have to do it more than once. But, video takes up a large amount of disk space. If you work with video regularly, consider obtaining a very large external hard drive for the purpose of storing your video media on it so you can use the MacBook hard drive for the files you use more frequently. You can store video clips on as many hard drives as you need and access them all at the same time in iMovie.

### What is Manual import?

If you have a camcorder that stores video on a tape and want to import only selected parts of a video, place the import process in **Manual** mode. Use the camcorder to move to the start of the clip you want to import, start the clip playing, and click **Import**. When you reach the end of the segment you want to import, click **Stop**.

# View and Create Projects

When you create a movie, you do so using a project. A project is a container for all the content that makes up the movie, which can include video clips, photos, titles, transitions, music, sound effects, and so on.

**You can have many projects in iMovie at the same time; you view and select projects to work with using the Project Library. To start a new movie, create a new project.**

## View and Create Projects

### View Projects

① Expand a disk on which projects are stored.

● You see each of the projects stored on that disk. You see the length of each project along with the date on which it was last saved.

*Note: If you have never used iMovie before, your Project Library is empty and you see the Project Editor instead. After you create your first project, the Project Library becomes active.*

② Use the scroll bars to view all of the projects in the library.

*Note: If you want to view the Project Library in a larger window, click the Swap button ( ). The Event Library and Project Library trade places.*

③ To view a project, select it.

④ Click **Play** ( ).

● The project plays in the Preview pane.

### Create a New Project

① Select the disk on which you want to store the project.

② Click the **Add** button ( ).

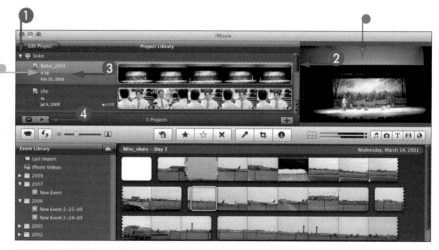

The New Project sheet appears.

③ Enter a name for the project.

④ Choose the project's aspect ratio, such as **Widescreen (16:9)**.

*Note: For best results, the project's aspect ratio should be the same as the video content you are using in it.*

⑤ Click the theme you want to apply to the movie.

*Note: To preview a theme, drag the pointer across its thumbnail.*

⑥ If the theme includes automatic titles and transitions, but you do not want them included, uncheck the **Automatically add transitions and titles** check box.

*Note: If you select **None** as the theme, check the **Automatically add** check box and choose the transition you want to be automatically added between clips on the pop-up menu.*

⑦ Click **Create**.

● The project is created and opens in the Project Editor.

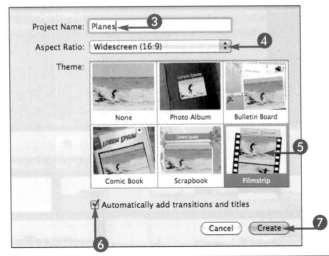

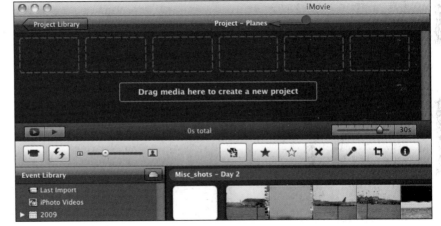

**Is there a limit to the number of projects I can create?**

No. The only limit is the amount of storage space available to you for the elements you use in your projects, especially video clips. As mentioned previously, if you create many projects, consider adding a large external hard drive for your iMovie work.

**Can I use the same content in more than one project?**

Yes, when you add content to a project from the Event Library, that content remains in the library. Adding content to a project does not change the content in the Event Library in any way.

# Add Video to a Movie Project

It might be a bit obvious, but video content is an important part of most movies. You can add any video stored in your Event Library to a project. You can add as much or as little of a video clip to the project as you want. You can even add the same clip to a project more than once, such as when you want to show a clip rewinding.

**You select the event containing the video you want to add to a project in the Event Library. Then select the part of the clip you want to add and drag it from the Event Library onto the project.**

## Add Video to a Movie Project

① In the Project Library, select the project you want to work on.

*Note: If you have not created a project before, you can skip Steps 1 and 2 because iMovie automatically opens the Project Editor.*

② Click **Edit Project**.

The project opens in the Project Editor. You see boxes representing clips you can add to the project.

③ Select the event containing the video you want to add to a project.

④ Preview the event until you identify a clip you want to add to the project.

⑤ Move the pointer so that the playhead line (the red line) is at the start of the clip you want to add to the project.

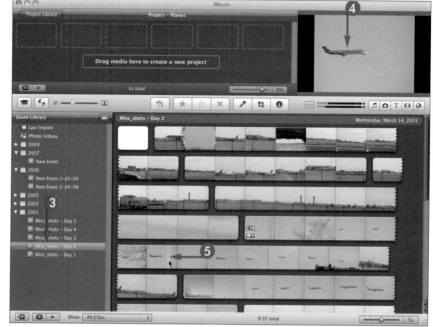

6 Drag across the clip until you reach the end of the segment you want to add to the project.

● The section of the clip you have captured is marked by the yellow box.

● The duration of the clip you have selected is indicated just to the right of the right edge of the selection box.

7 To adjust the start of the clip, drag the left edge of the selection box.

8 To adjust the end of the clip, drag the right edge of the selection box.

9 To change the content of the clip, but keep the same duration, click in the center of the selection box and move it to the left or right.

10 When you are ready to add the clip to the project, click in the center of the segment you have selected and drag it onto the project at the location where you want it to play.

When you release the trackpad, the clip is added to the project.

● If the theme you selected includes titles, a title clip is added automatically.

11 Repeat Steps **3** to **10** to add more clips to the project.

*Note: When you add a clip to a project that already has clips in it, you can place the new clip before, after, or between existing clips. When you drag a clip between existing clips, they slide apart to make room for the new clip.*

● If the theme includes transitions, they are added automatically too.

*Note: To remove a clip from a project, select it and press the* **Delete** *key. The clip is removed from the project, but the source remains in the Event Library.*

## TIPS

**What are some clip selection tricks?**

Click a clip to select a 4-second segment, and then drag the selection box to enclose the 4 seconds you want to capture. To quickly select an entire clip, click just before it starts and drag until just after it ends; the entire clip is selected. Do not be too concerned about being precise when you select clips in the Event Library; you can always edit them once they are in a project.

**What if a clip is shaky?**

iMovie has a stabilization filter that can make shaky clips look less shaky. To apply it to a clip in the Event Viewer, point to the beginning of the clip so that the **Action** menu (⚙) appears. Open the menu and choose **Clip Adjustments**. Click **Analyze Entire Clip**. This process takes a while, so doing it while you are not actively working on a project is usually best.

# Add Soundtracks to a Movie Project

Sound is an important part of any movie, and your iMovie projects can have complete soundtracks that include music, sound effects, and other audio. You can incorporate the audio that was part of the video clips into your movie, or you can exclude that audio content.

**In this section, you learn how to add music from your iTunes Library to a movie, and how to add sound effects to enliven your movie.**

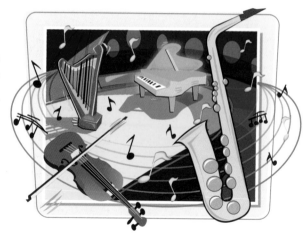

## Add Soundtracks to a Movie Project

### Add iTunes Music to a Movie

1 Click the **Music and Sound Effects** button (🎵).

   The Music and Sound Effects pane opens.

2 On the pop-up menu, choose **iTunes**.

● The contents of your iTunes Library are shown in the lower part of the window.

3 To preview a song, select it and click the **Play** button (▶).

4 Search for the song you want to add to the project.

5 Drag the song from the Music and Sound Effects pane onto the project where you want the music to start.

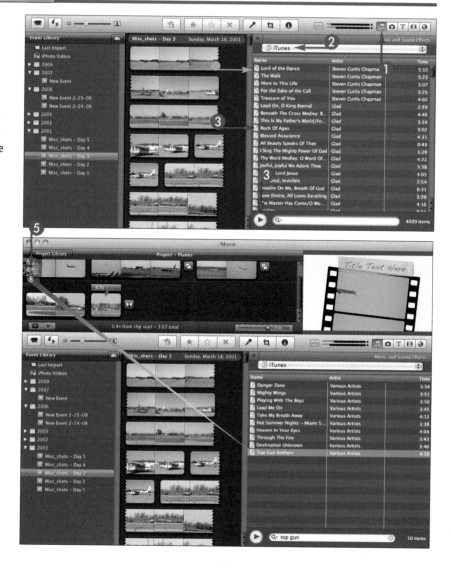

● The song is added to the project; you see the name of the song in its bar.

⑥ Preview the project by clicking the **Play** button (▶).

You see the video and hear the music.

## Add Sound Effects to a Movie

① On the pop-up menu in the Music and Sound Effects pane, choose **iLife Sound Effects**.

② Browse the available sound effects.

③ Select a sound effect and click **Play** (▶) to hear it.

④ Drag the sound effect from the Music and Sound Effects pane onto the project where you want it to play.

You see the sound effect bar in the project.

⑤ Preview the project to hear the movie with the sound effect added.

*Note: You can overlap sounds in a project, including music, sound effects, and other sounds.*

### TIPS

**How do I make the music end at the end of the project?**

If the music is too short, you can add the same song or a different one until the music lasts as long as the video. If the music is too long, iMovie automatically fades it. To change how it fades, select the audio clip and open the **Action** menu (⚙). Choose **Audio Adjustments**. On the Audio tab, click the **Manual** button for Fade Out and drag the slider to change the fade.

**How can I mute audio that I recorded with my camcorder?**

Select the video clip that contains the audio you want to mute. Open the **Action** menu (⚙) and choose **Audio Adjustments**. On the Audio tab, drag the **Volume** slider all the way to the left. The audio is muted.

# Add Transitions to a Movie Project

Transitions can help the flow of a movie because instead of one clip ending abruptly when another starts, a transition clip makes the movie flow more smoothly. iMovie supports many different types of transitions; you add transition clips between video clips to add them to a project. You can also configure transitions by changing their durations or configuring their effects.

**Some themes add transitions to a project automatically. You can select and configure those transitions just like the ones that you add.**

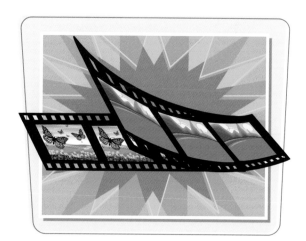

## Add Transitions to a Movie Project

### Add a Transition

**1** Click the **Transitions** button (🔲).

The Transitions pane appears.

● At the top of the pane, you see the transitions associated with the project's theme.

● In the lower part of the pane, you see all available transitions.

**2** To preview a transition, point to it.

The transition plays within its thumbnail.

**3** To add a transition to the project, drag it from the Transitions pane and drop it between two clips.

**Note:** *If you are using a theme with automatic transitions, you must disable automatic transitions when you add a transition manually. The transitions that were added automatically remain in the project.*

● The transition clip is added to the project.

**4** Move the playhead to the left of the transition clip and press the Spacebar to preview the transition.

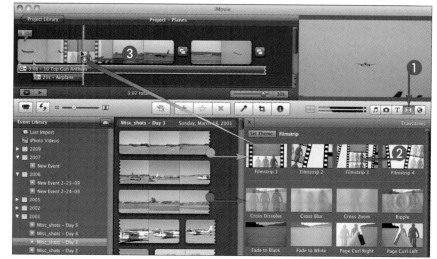

## Configure a Transition

1. Select the transition effect.

2. Open the **Action** menu (⚙).

3. Choose **Transition Adjustments**.

4. Enter the duration of the transition.

5. If you want the duration to apply only to the selected transition, uncheck the **Applies to all transitions** check box.

6. Click **Done**.

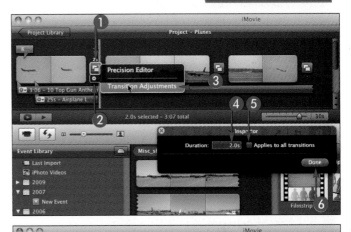

7. Open the **Action** menu (⚙) and choose **Precision Editor**.

   The Precision Editor replaces the Event Library.

8. Drag the transition bar to the left or right to change when it starts and finishes.

9. Click **Done**.

---

**TIPS**

### How can I use the Precision Editor on other types of clips?

Select the clip you want to edit, such as a video clip. Open the **Action** menu (⚙) and choose **Precision Editor**. The Precision Editor replaces the Event Library. The tools you see in the Precision Editor depend upon the type of content you selected.

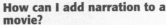

### How can I add narration to a movie?

Click the **Voiceover** button (🎤). Choose the input source, such as the **Built-in Microphone**. Place the playhead where you want to start recording. After the countdown, iMovie starts playing the project. Speak the narration while the movie plays. When you are done recording, press the Spacebar . The narration appears as a purple track in the project.

# Add Titles to a Movie Project

Titles are text effects you can use in movies as titles, credits, captions, and other areas where text will make the movie more what you want it to be. Titles can appear as distinct clips, or you can place text over a video clip. Like transitions, some themes add title clips automatically. You can also add your own title clips.

**Whether iMovie adds a title clip or you do, you determine the text that appears and the configuration of the title clip.**

## Add Titles to a Movie Project

### Add a Title

1 Click the **Titles** button (T).

The Titles pane appears.

● At the top of the pane, you see the titles associated with the project's theme.

● At the bottom, you see all available titles.

2 To preview a title, point to it.

The title plays within its thumbnail.

3 Drag the title clip to the project and drop it where you want it to play; to have it play between clips, drop it between two clips, or to have it play over a video clip, drag it onto the video clip (the video clip turns blue to show you that the title clip will play over it).

4 If the title has a background, click the background you want to apply.

The title is added to the project. If the title has a background, you see the background in the title's thumbnail.

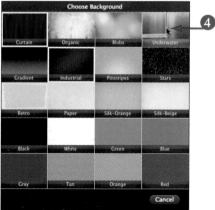

## Configure a Title

**1** Select the bar over the title clip you want to configure.

● The title clip appears in the Preview pane.

**2** Select the title's text.

It becomes highlighted.

**3** Type the title's text.

*Note: iMovie uses Mac OS X's spell checker to check your spelling as you type.*

**4** Click the **Preview** button ( ).

**5** Click **Done**.

**6** Double-click the title's bar.

The Inspector appears.

**7** Enter the title's duration.

**8** Click **Done**.

TIPS

### How do I save my project?

You do not need to save a project because iMovie automatically saves it as you work with it.

### Can I change the font used in a title?

Yes, when the title is not one created automatically based on the project's theme. In that case, select the title. In the Preview pane, click the **Show Fonts** button. Use the Choose Font dialog to configure the font type, color, size, and other parameters.

# Add Images to a Project

You can add images from your iPhoto Library to movies. You can apply effects to images, and set the time an image appears on the screen.

**1** Click the **Photos** button (🖼️).

The Photos Browser appears.

**2** Select the source of photos you want to add, such as iPhoto to see all the photos in your iPhoto Library.

**3** Browse or search until you see the photo you want to add.

**4** Drag the photo onto the project where you want it to appear.

**5** Select the image clip.

**6** Open the **Action** menu (⚙️) and choose **Cropping, Ken Burns & Rotation**.

**7** To crop the image, clip **Crop** and drag the crop box so it encloses the part of the photo you want to appear in the movie.

**8** To rotate the image, click the **Rotate** buttons (↩️ and ↪️).

**9** To apply Ken Burns motion effects, click **Ken Burns** and use the resulting tools to set the starting point, ending point, and other aspects of the effect.

**10** Click **Preview** (▶️).

**11** Click **Done**.

# Share a Movie Project

When your project is ready for prime time, you can share it in many ways. (The term "share" is a bit misleading. It really means saving your movie outside of iMovie in a variety of formats.) Some sharing options are designed for online delivery, whereas others are designed for computers and mobile devices.

**Two of the most useful ways to share a movie are to save it to your iTunes Library and to post a movie to your MobileMe Gallery.**

## Share a Movie Project

### Save a Movie in iTunes

1 Open the **Share** menu and choose **iTunes**.

The iTunes sheet appears.

2 Select the sizes of the movie you want to create.

The grid shows the devices on which the various sizes can play. You can publish to multiple sizes at the same time.

3 Click **Publish**.

The movie project is published and added to your iTunes Library.

4 Go to iTunes and find and watch the movie you created.

5 Use iTunes to copy the movie onto an iPhone or iPod.

### Publish a Movie to Your MobileMe Gallery

1 Open the **Share** menu and choose **MobileMe Gallery**.

2 Enter a title and description.

3 Choose the sizes you want to publish.

4 Configure the other Gallery options.

5 Click **Publish**.

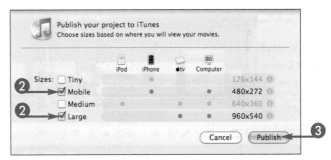

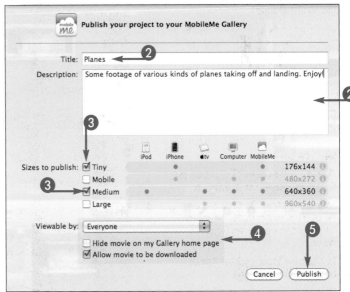

● When the process is complete, you see the movie's URL.

6 Click **OK**.

# Index

# Index

# Index

# Index

# Index